QUESTIONING BORDERS

Global Chinese Culture

GLOBAL CHINESE CULTURE

David Der-wei Wang, Editor

Cheow Thia Chan, *Malaysian Crossings: Place and Language in the Worlding of Modern Chinese Literature*
Michael Berry, ed., *The Musha Incident: A Reader on the Indigenous Uprising in Colonial Taiwan*
A-Chin Hsiau, *Politics and Cultural Nativism in 1970s Taiwan: Youth, Narrative, Nationalism*
Calvin Hui, *The Art of Useless: Fashion, Media, and Consumer Culture in Contemporary China*
Shengqing Wu, *Photo Poetics: Chinese Lyricism and Modern Media*
Sebastian Veg, *Minjian: The Rise of China's Grassroots Intellectuals*
Lily Wong, *Transpacific Attachments: Sex Work, Media Networks, and Affective Histories of Chineseness*
Michel Hockx, *Internet Literature in China*
Jie Li, *Shanghai Homes: Palimpsests of Private Life*
Andrea Bachner, *Beyond Sinology: Chinese Writing and the Scripts of Culture*
Shu-mei Shih, Chien-hsin Tsai, and Brian Bernards, editors, *Sinophone Studies: A Critical Reader*
Alexa Huang, *Chinese Shakespeares: A Century of Cultural Exchange*
Michael Berry, *A History of Pain: Literary and Cinematic Mappings of Violence in Modern China*
Sylvia Li-chun Lin, *Representing Atrocity in Taiwan: The 2/28 Incident and White Terror in Fiction and Film*
Michael Berry, *Speaking in Images: Interviews with Contemporary Chinese Filmmakers*

Questioning Borders

Ecoliteratures of China and Taiwan

Robin Visser

Columbia University Press   New York

Columbia University Press wishes to express its appreciation for assistance given by the Chiang Ching-kuo Foundation for International Scholarly Exchange and the Council for Cultural Affairs in the publication of this series.

Columbia University Press
Publishers Since 1893
New York   Chichester, West Sussex
cup.columbia.edu
Copyright © 2023 Columbia University Press
All rights reserved

Library of Congress Cataloging-in-Publication Data
Names: Visser, Robin, 1962– author.
Title: Questioning borders : Ecoliteratures of China and Taiwan / Robin Visser.
Description: New York : Columbia University Press, [2023] | Series: Global Chinese culture | Includes bibliographical references and index.
Identifiers: LCCN 2023000877 (print) | LCCN 2023000878 (ebook) | ISBN 9780231199803 (hardback) | ISBN 9780231199810 (trade paperback) | ISBN 9780231553292 (ebook)
Subjects: LCSH: Ecoliterature, Chinese—History and criticism. | Chinese literature—20th century—History and criticism. | Chinese literature—21st century—History and criticism. | Boundaries in literature. | Ecocriticism in literature. | Human ecology in literature. | Indigenous authors—China. | LCGFT: Literary criticism.
Classification: LCC PL2275.E35 V57 2023 (print) | LCC PL2275.E35 (ebook) | DDC 895.109/3553—dc23/eng/20230411
LC record available at https://lccn.loc.gov/2023000877
LC ebook record available at https://lccn.loc.gov/2023000878

Cover design: Milenda Nan Ok Lee
Cover image: Robin Visser

To Katherine

Contents

Introduction: Ecoliteratures Inhabiting Borders — 1

CHAPTER ONE
Beijing Westerns and Hanspace Elixirs in Southwest China — 34

CHAPTER TWO
Grassland Logic and Desert Carbon Imaginaries
in Inner Mongolia — 69

CHAPTER THREE
Sacred Routes and Dark Humor in Grounded Xinjiang — 100

CHAPTER FOUR
Cosmic Ecologies and Transcendent Tricksters
on the Tibetan Plateau — 147

CHAPTER FIVE
Island Excursions and Indigenous Waterways
in Activist Taiwan — 189

Epilogue: Indigenous Entanglements in Techno
Hypersubjectivity   231

Acknowledgments   237
Notes   239
Bibliography   287
Index   313

QUESTIONING BORDERS

Introduction

Ecoliteratures Inhabiting Borders

> This-here is the weave, and it weaves no boundaries. Let us say this again, opaquely: the idea of totality alone is an obstacle to totality. We see it as radiant—replacing the absorbing concept of unity; it is the opacity of the diverse animating the imagined transparency of Relation.
> —ÉDOUARD GLISSANT, *POETICS OF RELATION*

> The Dao that can be stated cannot be the eternal Dao.
> 道可道非常道.
> —LAOZI, *DAODEJING*

How are we to achieve planetary consciousness in this present climate emergency? Given that all known civilizations have been founded on the universality of their cosmologies, and the pluriverse comprises multiple cosmologies connected in power differentials, how, in practice, can we decolonize our minds and practices? After all, the material histories of cultures are now so entangled, through deeply violent and traumatic histories, that they are mutually implicated. One approach, suggested by Walter Mignolo, is to respond from the embodied position of inhabiting the border: "I sensed [the border], and sensing is something that invades your emotions, and your body responds to it, dictating to the mind what the mind must start thinking, changing its direction, shifting the geography of reasoning."[1]

Questioning Borders inhabits borders as a method for comparing and theorizing distinct literary imaginations of relational dynamics between humans, nonhuman animals, regional ecosystems, and the cosmos. This

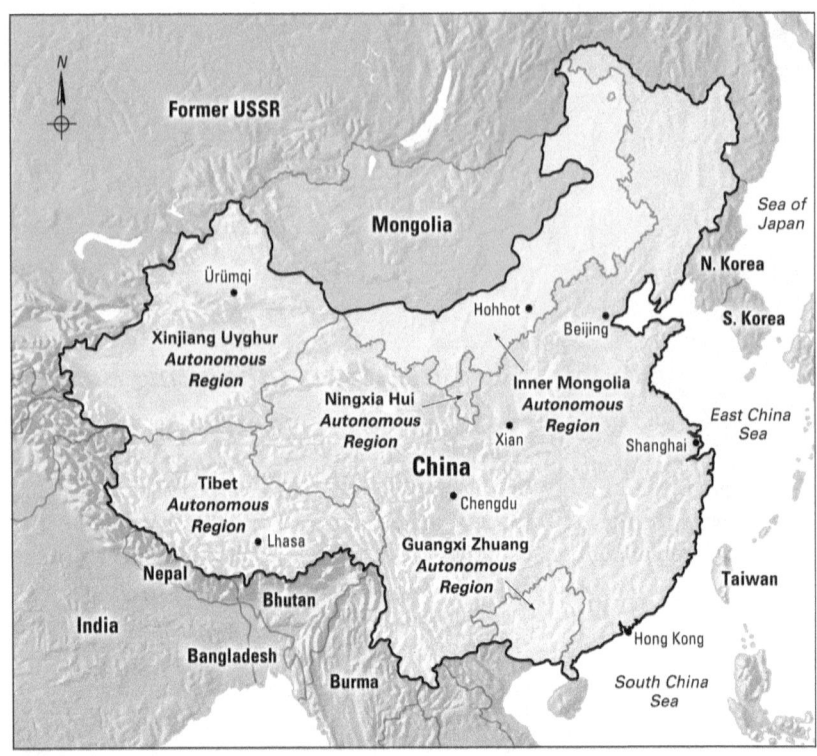

FIGURE 0.1 Map of Taiwan and Autonomous Regions in the People's Republic of China.

regional case study focuses on four decades of ecoliterature by Han Chinese and non-Han writers in global contexts of climate crisis, interimperiality, and neoliberalism. It features works by Mongol, Tibetan, Taiwanese, Tao, Bunun, Yi, Bai, Kazakh, Uyghur, and Han writers set in rapidly transforming ecologies in Xinjiang, the Tibetan Plateau, Inner Mongolia, Southwest China, and Taiwan (see figure 0.1). It argues that while Beijing promotes its ecological civilization globally, and Taipei celebrates its trans-Indigenous maritime ties, they also strategically appropriate Indigenous perspectives in ecoliterature for geopolitical ends, even as these works raise awareness of environmental devastation. By comparing cosmologies from various Asian ecoliteratures, the study aims to relativize Han ecological paradigms, while also diversifying Chinese, Asian, and global ecocriticism.[2] While geopolitical borders enact realpolitik, this book does not use the term "borderlands." In fact, questioning borders is a process of deconstructing and decentering "borderlands" paradigms that reinforce imperial cosmologies of center and periphery. The Indigenous civilizations discussed in this book are not peripheral, remote, or located in frontiers. They are themselves central.

This book understands inter-imperial dynamics to dominate global geopolitics and ecological thought. Many scholars attest to the challenges of delinking one's thought from the Western universal, given that the universalization of Western universality was part of its imperial project. To quote Édouard Glissant, "The West is not in the West. It is not a place; it is a project."[3] While most contemporary instantiations of the Han Chinese civilizational universal of *tianxia* ("all under Heaven") disavow its own status as a universal, this is because power differentials in global geopolitics derive from the logic of coloniality covered up by the rhetorical narrative of modernity. Precivilizational Indigenous cosmologies have not rationalized imperialism; thus stories from animist Indigenous cultures warrant special attention in attempts to achieve planetary consciousness. Such consciousness aims at what decolonial thinkers call a "pluriverse," where many different conceptions of "worlds" exist on a single planet. Mignolo claims pluriversality as a universal project is aimed at changing the understanding of the world to change praxis in the world.[4] While experiential learning of shared sensing and sensibilities from the border can shift the geography of reasoning and behavior, the stories most effective in decolonizing our worldview are not those that merely react to the universals claimed by colonial power but those that respond from highly specific, localized, centralized, historicized, embodied positions. These responses cannot become a universal project with clearly defined tactics. Instead, Édouard Glissant's animating idea of opacity as a politics of ecology in *Poetics of Relation* illuminates literary strategies adopted by many of the Indigenous writers featured in this book. As Glissant explains, "that which protects the Diverse, we call opacity."[5]

Far from romanticizing indigeneity or lapsing into nostalgia for tradition, the book identifies unacknowledged assumptions governing dominant cosmologies, attempting to reconcile our global technological condition with the reality of the Anthropocene. In the spirit of Yuk Hui's call for a cosmotechnics, it acknowledges technological development as innate to humans as a species.[6] Thus, the central question of the book is how to reconcile the human drive to create and develop with the possibility of its extinction. What Indigenous cosmologies reveal is that humans need not be alienated from technology, as globally dominant cosmologies rooted in naturalism (which separates nature from culture) would have us believe. Might perspectives from Indigenes embedded within empire(s) provide alternate perspectives on human creativity that fosters sustainable flourishing in the globally technological era of the Anthropocene?

This project raises multiple questions about civilization, territoriality, the nation-state, indigeneity, and empire. What does it mean to theorize indigeneity in contexts when neocolonial nation-states have also been victims of imperiality? How do we address inter-imperiality when longstanding civilizations vie for power in a globalized world? Is Taiwan part of the Global South, or a first-world power vying with China for resources in the South China Sea and Southeast Asia? What do People's Republic of China (PRC) literary projects such as Grassland Literary Culture Series mean in relation to its "Go West" policies and its Belt and Road Initiative (BRI) infrastructure projects in Central Asia? Can we divorce literary studies from realpolitik? Do shamanistic cosmologies provide hope for ecological flourishing in a climate emergency? How do we decolonize our thinking when imperialist paradigms from Newtonian physics have conditioned us to conceptualize matter as substance (atoms) + void (potential)? When the land, cultural practices, and bodies of Indigenous Others such as Kazakhs and Uyghurs are conceptualized as empty of life and historical meaning? When the historical military success of the Mongols is attributed to an infusion of "wolflike" genes? When Nuosu Yi or Gyalrong Tibetan foraging is exoticized and stigmatized as a means of governing difference? When sustainable nomadic livelihoods are decimated by "green governance" practices of "ecological civilization?" Can civilization even *be* ecological?

A key argument of the book is that nation-state discourses of eco-exceptionalism derive from imperialist cosmologies that replicate those of other empires. For example, ideologies of biological determinism and social Darwinism inform discourse on both Chinese ecological civilization and the U.S. conservation movement.[7] Such similarities are unsurprising: the rise of civilizational consciousness in pre-Qin China (600–400 BCE) anticipates linguistic and epistemological developments that emerged in early modern Europe.[8] Current practices of green governance support bioprospecting on unprecedented scales, with Indigenous ecological knowledge absorbed into nation-states as postcolonial governments rationalize that they must guard against biopiracy and bioprospecting from imperialist outsiders. The right to protect diversity in a decolonial sense is, on the other hand, a "politics of ecology that has implications for populations that are decimated or threatened with disappearance as a people. For, far from consenting to sacred intolerance, it is a driving force for the relational interdependence of all lands, of the whole Earth. It is this very interdependence that forms the basis for entitlement."[9] Willingness to decolonize our cosmologies has potentially life-altering ramifications.

ECOLOGICAL CIVILIZATION AND THE BRI

Settler colonial practices inform both the American exceptionalism justified by Manifest Destiny and the Chinese exceptionalism promoted in the PRC as Ecological Civilization (*shengtai wenming*). Since the 1980s, the Chinese Communist Party (CCP) has promoted the idea of a China-led global transition from "Western industrial civilization" to "socialist ecological civilization."[10] First introduced in 1984 by Chinese agricultural economist Ye Qianji (1909–2017) to promote sustainable agriculture in place of industrial civilization, ecological civilization was highlighted as one of the key political guidelines of the CCP in its 17th National Congress held in 2007, and it was written into the constitution of China in 2018 as the ideological framework for the country's environmental policies, laws, and education.[11] In China's pastoral regions, for example, ecological civilization policies dictate state-led rehabilitation projects that exclude Indigenes as stakeholders in grassland resource management (which ironically requires more human intervention and diminishes local resilience). Yet the state presents such green governance as an affective politics of care for the land and the people to reinforce its political legitimacy.[12] Ecological migration (*shengtai yimin*) policies are seen to both conserve the ecology and improve the living standards of people who relocate.[13] Ecological civilization is not only to maintain economic growth and consumption while solving China's environmental issues via science and technology; it is also presented as a vision for our global future.[14]

It is important to note that the *ideals* of ecological civilization, rooted in early Chinese philosophical understandings of symbiosis between human life and natural ecosystems, greatly differ from a reductionist materialism that instrumentalizes nature for human purposes. Yet while Chinese ecological philosophy is often characterized as "harmony between humanity and nature," historically *tianren heyi* was "a cultural reaction to ecophobia and was not a spontaneous expression of innate Chinese biophilia."[15] An idea originally articulated within ecocentric Daoism to counter ecophobia, it was soon adapted to more anthropocentric Confucian thought. The Daoist Zhuangzi (ca. 369–286 BCE) did not view nature as benign, yet believed that "Heaven and earth were born at the same time I was, and the ten thousand things are one with me."[16] His Confucian contemporary, Mencius (372–289 BCE), alters Zhuangzi's emphasis on "going with the flow" (humans adapting naturally to change) by centering the "human" in his virtue ethics. Adopting agrarian metaphors, Mencius argues that humanity's "four sprouts" (*siduan*) of virtue, if properly cultivated, extend to harmonious relations with the nonhuman world. Dong Zhongshu (179–104 BCE), a Confucian scholar in the Han dynasty, goes further by seeing nature as caring: "nature is the paragon of benevolence that nourishes everything infinitely and unceasingly."[17] As ecocritics Guo and Zhuang put it, "Dong's vision of mutually benevolent human and nonhuman natures apparently leaves no room for ecophobic conflict." They elaborate:

> This development of "Tianren Heyi" emphasizes the essential goodness of nature and humanity, and establishes a reciprocal relationship that differs greatly from the polarized antagonism of early Chinese ecophobia. After Mencius and Dong, Chinese people came to believe that human beings were no longer dominated by fear of and antagonism toward nature. As long as humans act according to their own nature, nonhuman nature will appreciate and protect them. Unfortunately, the Confucian refinement of "Tianren Heyi" is a mere linguistic imposition of benevolence, not a real achievement of ecological harmony.[18]

As many environmental historians have documented, sustainability ideals inherent in classical Chinese aesthetics are at odds with the environmental harm caused by Chinese imperial and modern governance practices.[19] This may undermine President Xi Jinping's claim that ecological civilization, as a global endeavor, will benefit generations to come through the implementation of a "new model of modernization with humans developing in harmony with nature."[20]

China's ecological civilization policies include its flagship national carbon market and the BRI, the largest infrastructure and development project in human history. While the national carbon market exemplifies China's changing approach to domestic environmental policy, the BRI extends the Chinese model of ecological civilization overseas. Formerly known as One Belt One Road (*yidai yilu*), the BRI was officially launched in 2013 as the Twenty-First Century Economic Belt and Maritime Silk Road by President Xi Jinping, replicating routes that had for centuries facilitated trade and cultural exchanges across Eurasia and oceans. Initially intended to increase trade and connectivity among China, Central and South Asia, the Middle East, Europe, and Africa, global expansion of the BRI is now underway. Its five main components are policy coordination, transport connectivity, trade facilitation (i.e., more efficient border crossings), currency convertibility, and people-to-people exchanges.[21] As of 2022, 146 of the world's 195 countries, contributing over 40 percent of the world's GDP, were signatories to the BRI.[22]

While the premise of China's ecological civilization concept is that China is uniquely positioned to simultaneously guide economic growth and protect environments, studies to date show mixed results. On the one hand, an environmental study of BRI coal plants in Asia finds that plants owned, managed, or built by Chinese companies tend to have lower emissions rates and higher efficiency than those associated with non-Chinese companies.[23] Of course, carbon emissions from coal plants are unsustainable at any level of efficiency. Further, an interdisciplinary team of social and natural scientists conducted a BRI horizon scan that identified eleven key "environmental or social" frontier issues. The issues most relevant to themes in the literary works examined in this study include:

1. Groundwater pumping threatening the viability of freshwater ecosystems;
2. Invisible invasives (the incidental spread of fungi, bacteria, and viruses);

3. Cementing extinction (sand mining is a known biodiversity threat, but the impact of cement production on limestone ecosystems is often overlooked—about 20 percent of terrestrial ecosystems are irreplaceable limestone-based karsts);
4. "Polar/Arctic Silk Road" (the thawing Arctic ice cap is enabling marine traffic and extraction pressures for natural gas, oil, fish, and minerals along a "Polar/Arctic Silk Road");
5. Threat to coastal ecosystems (the East Asian–Australasian Flyway, a bird migratory route, spans much of East and Southeast Asia's coastlines, but coastal reclamation and pollution, especially in key breeding grounds, have already driven the loss of over 70 percent of some species populations for the estimated 50 million migratory birds that annually use this route);
6. BRI and traditional Chinese medicine support and stimulate markets in wildlife trade;
7. Regreening the never green (attempts at "anti-desertification" and "restoration" of natural ecosystems across Central Asia through large-scale planting of drought-resistant and deep-rooted species, while converting native deserts and savannas into more economically productive systems, as recently executed in a third of the Kubuqi Desert in Inner Mongolia).[24]

It is in this context of the globally influential governance regime of ecological civilization that writers became sensitized to the impact of its related policies on local ecosystems.

RELATIONALITY, BORDERING, INDIGENEITY

Methodologically, *Questioning Borders* substitutes the relational thinking prominent in Indigenous and East Asian thought for the substantialist thinking that has dominated Anglo-European philosophy and global modernity.[25] It adopts ideas from Indigenous scholars such as Linda Hogan's animal studies, Zoe Todd's kinship studies, Hau'ofa Epeli's and Syaman Rapongan's ocean studies, and Édouard Glissant's poetics of relation, which have influenced Taiwanese ecocritics such as Hsinya Huang and Peter I-min Huang. It also characterizes ontologies via Phillipe

Descola's ecology of relations and Alfred North Whitehead's constructive postmodernism (as modeled by Isabelle Stenger's *Thinking with Whitehead*), ecocritical approaches that inspire prominent ecocritics such as Zeng Fanren, Cheng Xiangzhan, and Wei Qingqi. Put simply, these approaches elide stark distinctions between entities (e.g., human/animal, male/female, domestic/foreign, urban/ rural) but instead delineate processes. They conceive of "nature," "gender," "human," or "nation" temporally, rather than statically. Most ecoliterature conveys one of the relational, process-based ontologies (understandings of reality) characterized by Descola in *Beyond Nature and Culture*. Descola theorizes three ontologies—animism, totemism, and analogism—in contrast to a fourth ("Western") ontology of naturalism. Each ontology, he argues, has a different conception of personhood, the mind or soul (interiority), and the body (physicality). Animism is characterized by beings' similar souls and different bodies, totemism by similar souls and bodies, analogism by different souls and bodies, and naturalism by different souls and similar bodies. What the three non-Western cosmologies share is that they "draw no clear ontological distinctions between, on the one hand, humans, and on the other numerous animal and plant species."[26]

This study finds that ontologies expressed by contemporary Han Chinese ecowriters most often manifest as analogist, while non-Han writers often express animist or totemist ontologies. Yet the study also seeks to complicate such simplistic contrasts. For example, perspectivism is a particular type of animism, an ontology that resonates with the early Daoist thought articulated by Zhuangzi.[27] Additionally, both Western influences on Chinese modernity (such as Marxism) and other modes of early Chinese thought (such as legalism) are based in naturalism. Further, it is well known that ethnic designations are constructions. Sun Zhongshan (Sun Yat-sen) invented "Han" as an ethnic category in the early years of the twentieth century for the purpose of rallying Chinese nationalism to unify the broadest possible support against the Manchus, who then ruled China. Yet "Han" disguises a plethora of other identities, such as Hakka, Minnan, Cantonese, and so forth, that are not identified as one of the fifty-six nationalities in China. Complex historical interactions between ethnicities with different languages, religions, and philosophical worldviews complicates straightforward identification of ontologies. In general, scholars have noted overlap among ontological approaches and acknowledge the importance of morality in them. For example, Santos-Granero suggests rather than being conflicting theoretical models, constructivism may be an artifact of focusing on the local sphere of human relations and perspectivism of focusing on the outside sphere of interspecific communication.[28]

While various Asian ontologies overlap, the distinction between Han and non-Han retains relevance because it informs the term "Chinese." The fact that both the People's Republic of China (*Zhonghua renmin gonghe guo*) and the Republic of China (Taiwan; *Zhonghua Mingguo*) both call themselves Zhonghua speaks to the inseparability of Han or Hua from "China," which makes minority identity ambivalent. Uradyn E. Bulag claims that "the notion of Chinese Nation (*Zhonghua Minzu*) as an inclusive concept presumes the 'Han' as its core and is deeply inflected by racism."[29] It is important to understand that China and Taiwan are multinational rather than polyethnic (e.g., due to immigration) or multiracial (e.g., due to slavery) states. They are comprised of "national minorities" as opposed to "ethnic" or "racial" groups. They are culturally diverse because they have incorporated previously self-governing, territorially concentrated peoples into a larger state. Thus, one can refer to many non-Han minority writers as Indigenes.

Unsurprisingly, diverse geopolitics in the Sinophone world complicate understandings of indigeneity in Chinese-language literatures. Taiwan refers to Indigenous Austronesian tribal groups as *yuanzhumin* (lit., "native inhabitants"), while the PRC term for indigenous is *tuzhu*, meaning native or local, in contrast to outsider or foreigner (especially "imperialists"). The PRC term *shaoshu minzu* is used to identify Indigenous groups, classified as fifty-five "minority nationalities" (or "ethnic minorities," a more recent translation of *minzu* that weakens the term's territorial connotations). Concerned with unifying the nation-state, the PRC sets ideals of national unity (*minzu tuanjie*) against national splitism or secessionism (*minzu fenlie*), a norm that sustains the majority and delegitimizes minority difference (see figure 0.2).[30] This logic also undermines the legal regime providing the basis for global understandings of Indigenous rights. The influential 1981 UN Report on Indigenous Populations (Cobo Report) defines Indigenous Peoples as those that (1) have a historical continuity with lands subsequently confiscated,

FIGURE 0.2 Uyghur: "The Unity of the Nation Is the Soul of the Nation." Chinese: "Unity Is the Lifeline of All Nationalities." Kashgar Middle School, Xinjiang. Photo by author, July 2012.

(2) consider themselves distinct from dominant societies, and (3) wish to continue existing in accord with their own distinct cultures and customs.[31]

While current PRC policy on ethnic minorities is largely in agreement with the Cobo Report, it rejects the claim that Indigenous lands were confiscated, and many believe Beijing's aim is cultural Sinification and the elimination of ethnic differences altogether.[32] The Cobo Report also explicitly contrasts non-Indigenous approaches to "the development of land and its effective use" from Indigenous approaches that are, "in ecological terms, more rational and sound."[33] This strategic linking of indigeneity to ecological knowledge begins in the 1970s, first by associating Indigenous communities with their lands, then expanding in the 1980s to incorporate religious practice to mark transnational Indigenous identity by endowing specific rights for "Indigenous Peoples." In the wake of global neoliberalism, however, by the 2000s the original aims of self-determination had transformed into claims for autonomy *within* states. This is one reason that Indigenous cosmology became crucial to legal arguments claiming rights to ancestral territories and resources when fighting against eminent domain or corporate interests.[34]

In the PRC, however, the indigenist-environmentalist alliance does not hold sway, partially due to secular rejection of Indigenous cosmologies as sacred, but also to different understandings of indigeneity itself. The nation-state of Mongolia notwithstanding, for example, the PRC does not recognize a historic continuity of ethnic Mongols in Inner Mongolia Autonomous Region (IMAR) to confiscated lands and ways of life. On the other hand, Indigenous writers in Taiwan and the PRC increasingly identify with global indigeneity. For example, Indigenous writers often imagine animist ontologies based in shamanistic religions that predate the development of Buddhist or Islamic civilizational cultures in, for example, Tibetan, Mongolian, Kazakh, or Uyghur ecoliteratures. And many Taiwanese writers promote a southward-oriented ocean imagination in order to decolonize ecocriticism and reterritorialize trans-indigeneity from a South Seas perspective.

Like "Han" and "indigeneity," "border" is also a fraught term. While many of the works examined in this book are set in locales near the borders of Taiwan and the PRC, they challenge attempts to "stretch the short, tight skin of the nation over the gigantic body of empire," to quote Benedict Anderson.[35] The vectors evoked in ecoliterature from IMAR extend northeast and west to the Manges and Gobi Deserts, north to Mongolia, up toward Tengger ("Sky") and downward into sand; occasionally they point southwest to Qinghai and Tibet, and south toward Beijing. The multiple "centers" imagined in Xinjiang ecoliterature are Kashgar, Altay, Istanbul, Tashkent, Ürümchi, single-family farms, summer and winter nomadic camps, and pilgrim shrine cycles. Beijing is conspicuously absent, excepting occasional ironic references to government policy or alienating student experiences. Ecoliterature set on the Tibetan Plateau is simultaneously hyperlocal and ultraglobal, imagining vast ecosystems of water, mountains, plants, animals, and people extending to India, Britain, Hunan, Nanjing, Hong Kong. Taiwanese ecoliterature actively counters the looming boundaries of the PRC nation-state to its west by connecting with the south Pacific roots of its Austronesian Indigenes. By "moving southward" (*nanxiang*), Taiwanese ecoliterature imagines its transnational Indigenous maritime connections to the Way of the Ocean, as theorized by Tongan and Fijian scholar Epeli Hau'ofa (1939–2009).

Questioning borders in ecoliteratures of China and Taiwan resists the nationalist boundary-producing project of *minzu tuanjie* (unification of national minorities). It questions attempts to interpret diverse regional literatures according to a Sinocentric (Han-dominant, center-periphery) discourse of ecological civilization. To the contrary, it is an attempt to allow multicentered worlds of regional ecoliteratures, inspired by diverse ecologies, languages, and historical dynamics, become visible to fields of Chinese, Sinophone, and global ecoliterature. *Questioning Borders* views cosmologies expressed in literature as a dynamic, generative process. In comparing ontologies produced within historically formed civilizations, it views each as contingent and constructed rather than timeless or inevitable. It problematizes highly anthropocentric understandings of the cosmos, seeking to radically decenter Europe as paradigmatic and prescriptive. The book also seeks to avoid the trap of Cold War knowledge categories, whereby works produced by "first-world" ("imperialist") thinkers seemingly transcend both national and disciplinary boundaries, while those produced by the Global South ("Indigenes") merely reflect the essence of their societies of origin. Moving beyond East-West paradigms, the book recognizes "China" and "Taiwan" as multinational and aims to further the incomplete project of deimperialization in Asia, as Chen Kuan-hsing advocates in *Asia as Method*.[36] It undermines ontologies informing bio-orientalist necropower rationalized by cosmological imaginations of unchanged cultures and outdated modes of thought.

Thus, the book's methodology extends beyond that of relativism, or even that of "relational ontologies," to the scale of "relational cosmologies" (how cosmologies based on naturalism relate to those based in animism, analogism, totemism, perspectivism, shamanism). Unlike methodologies that strictly operate within imperial ontologies informed by naturalism, or within relational ontologies that equalize the organic and inorganic entities comprising the cosmos, this book attempts to characterize their dynamics as a whole. In this sense, it is inspired by Karen Barad's theorization of matter as inherently relational and finds that Indigenous cosmologies are always already embedded within imperial ones though they operate within different logic streams.[37] In general, the book identifies and destabilizes ontological categories derived from cosmologies that rationalize empire. It historicizes regional ecologies to illuminate global dynamics. And it acknowledges radical deterritorialization, following Ursula Heise, viewing exponential rates of climate migration, species extinction, and environmental racism as systematically and territorially tied to the planet rather than delimited by localities.[38]

Literary accounts of anthropogenic impact on the environment are a global phenomenon, yet ecocriticism remains dominated by Anglo/European concepts of humans and environments. Despite an explosion of scholarship in Chinese ecocriticism,[39] there are few English monographs on the topic, and fewer on Indigenous ecowriters in China and Taiwan. Karen Thornber's monumental *Ecoambiguity: Environmental Crises and East Asian Literatures*, and *East Asian Ecocriticisms: A Critical Reader*, are highly significant yet do not center Indigenous writers.[40] Four edited volumes—*Ecocriticism and Chinese Literature*, *Embodied Memories, Embedded Healing*, *Chinese Environmental Humanities*, and *Ecocriticism in Taiwan*—each include, respectively, an essay on Zhang Chengzhi (Hui), Guo Xuebo (Mongol), Chen Danling (Tujia) and Mao Mei (Hui), and Neqou Soqluman (Bunun).[41] This book differs methodologically and theoretically from existing scholarship by systematically engaging Indigenous studies within Asian ecoliterature. It challenges homogenous constructions of national identity by centering discourses and processes constructing non-Han identities, civilizations, and literatures within their respective regional and global histories. As such, questioning borders can productively relocate a Han "center-periphery" metaphysics as one among many political and ecological imaginations in the region. In this sense, the study builds upon Mark Bender's introduction to *The Borderlands of Asia*, which foregrounds cross-border regional ecological knowledge in poetry from Northeast India, Myanmar, Southwest China, Inner Mongolia, and Mongolia.[42] It also considers trans-indigeneity, such as that modeled by Peter I-min Huang's *Linda Hogan and Contemporary Taiwanese Writers*.[43]

INTER-ASIAN REGIONAL KNOWLEDGE IN ECOLITERATURES FROM CHINA AND TAIWAN

Questioning Borders comprises an introduction, epilogue, and five body chapters informed in part by summer field research conducted in Southwest China, Inner Mongolia, Xinjiang, the Tibetan Plateau, and Taiwan from 2007 to 2019. Such visits provided opportunities to meet with local ecocritics, writers, and environmental experts who directed this scholarship. It also allowed me to immerse myself within a wide variety of local ecosystems and cultures (by, for example, living among Amis Indigenes in Taiwan, artist communes on the Inner Mongolian grasslands, and archaeologists on the Tibetan Plateau). While I rarely directly reference these experiences in this book, they inform my understanding of the texts under analysis. Because my language of research was limited to Mandarin Chinese, English, and (occasionally) French or Japanese, I also consulted with experts in the Tibetan, Mongolian, Yi, Uyghur, and Kazakh languages. I do not exclusively focus on works originally written in Chinese, but I do rely upon translations into Chinese or English from Indigenous languages. For example, Perhat Tursun's *The Backstreets* is translated (to English) from Uyghur; Mandumai's stories are translated (to Chinese) from Mongolian; Nurila Qizihan's *Hunter Stories* are translated (to English) from Kazakh; Ju Kalsang's poems (to Chinese), and Tsering Döndrup's and Takbum Gyel's stories (to English) are translated from Tibetan. I recognize the limitations of translation and encourage future ecocritical scholarship in Indigenous languages.

The second half of this introduction historicizes *tianxia* and the naturalizing of civility to explain the dominant Han Chinese cosmology of center and periphery that informs what I refer to as "Beijing westerns." It also details the influence of global eugenics on contemporary Chinese exceptionalism with its ostensible qualities of harmony, transformation, tolerance, and peace. Chapter 1, "Beijing Westerns and Hanspace Elixirs in Southwest China," defines "the west" and contrasts fictional works set in China's "exotic" southwestern provinces written by Beijing-based writers such as Ah Cheng and Gao Xingjian to those by local Indigenes such as Zhang Chang (Bai), Burao Yilu (Wa), Bamo Qubumo (Nuosu Yi) and Aku Wuwu (Nuosu Yi). In general, Beijing westerns appropriate indigenous ecological perspectives to critique Maoist destruction of the environment and the concomitant undermining of Han neo-Confucian values, while Indigenous tales of the Anthropocene radically center the border as a place of home, heritage, and everyday humanity, though under great duress from climate change. Chapter 2, "Grassland Logic and Desert Carbon Imaginaries in Inner Mongolia," is a case study of ecoliterature written by three male writers born around 1949, set in the grasslands and deserts of Inner Mongolia. It contrasts the imperial cosmology conveyed in a Beijing western by Jiang Rong with hybrid cosmologies in works by Guo Xuebo and Mandumai, Mongol writers who express cosmologies of a post-extinction world in regimes governed by geontopower.

In contrast to the highly abstracted landscapes in Beijing westerns, stories that symbolically rehabilitate a neo-Confucian metaphysics of the cosmos, chapter 3, "Dark Humor in Grounded Xinjiang," focuses on a diverse Xinjiang literary culture particularly sensitive to the earth, nonhuman animals, and experiences of the sentient body. Relations between humans and their environments are frequently characterized by dark humor, with poignant contrasts between urban and rural ecologies. Chapter 3 analyzes lyrical essays by Shen Wei (Han), Yerkesh Hulmanbek (Kazakh), Nurila Qizihan (Kazakh), Liu Liangcheng (Han), and Li Juan (Han) and fiction by Memtimin Hoshur (Uyghur) and Perhat Tursun (Uyghur). The intimate, local, intercultural, and multilingual exchanges and dynamics featured in Xinjiang stories differ significantly from the stories featured in chapter 4, "Transcendent Tricksters on the Tibetan Plateau." In Tibetan literature tensions between alternate ecological worldviews are conveyed through metafictional forms that embed local practices within grand discourses of imperialist and Sinoglobalization. Despite a variety of literary styles and genres, each work prominently centers Tibetan cosmologies in ways that disrupt Hanspace assumptions. Poetry by Jangbu (Dorje Tsering Chenaktsang), Ju Kelzang, and Dekyi Drolma critiques rampant environmental devastation on the Tibetan Plateau. Fiction by Alai and Tsering Döndrup reincarnates trickster characters to foreground empires of resource extraction, and Takbum Gyel's humorous dog tales suggest environmental racism. While these writers come from religiously and ecologically diverse Tibetan subcultures, they inherit a shared literary culture where profane tricksters and social outcasts illuminate hypocrisies among clerics and local leaders in a hierarchical society.

Chapter 5, "Island Excursions and Indigenous Waterways in Activist Taiwan," recounts activist dynamics in the influential four-decade Taiwanese ecoliterature and environmental educational movement on the island of Taiwan, long recognized as one of the epicenters of international ecocriticism. The chapter analyzes the urban ecology of Liu

Ka-shiang and Bunun Indigene Topas Tomapima, and Indigenous waterways in the historical fantasies of Wang Chia-hsiang, in ocean tales by Tao Indigene Syaman Rapongan, and in climate change–related fiction (cli-fi) by Wu Ming-yi. It especially focuses on how ocean imaginaries decolonize ecocriticism and reterritorialize trans-indigeneity from a South Seas perspective. In comparing Southern, maritime trajectories of development to Western, continental ones, theorizing South Seas dreamscapes as expressions of Hanspace cosmology that differ from Beijing westerns. The epilogue, "Indigenous Entanglements in Techno Hypersubjectivity," relates dynamics from this regional study of inter-Asian ecoliterature to global trends.

TIANXIA AND THE NATURALIZING OF AGRARIAN CIVILIZATIONAL EMPIRE

To understand contemporary instantiations of ecological civilization and the dominant cosmology informing Han Chinese ecoliterature, it is helpful to historicize *tianxia* ("all under Heaven") and Han cosmologies of center and periphery. Two millennia before the European concept of "civilization" emerged, and Anglophone Europeans applied the English word *barbarian* to groups they considered civilizationally inferior, a similar process occurred in today's China (see the following boxed text). Zhou civilizational consciousness, signified by a shift to normative linguistic markers of what seemed aesthetically "natural" to farmers, altered earlier understandings of neighboring forager-gatherer or nomadic people groups. According to linguist and cultural historian Uffe Bergeton, at the beginning of the Warring States period (481–221 BCE) moral philosophers "coined the term 'civility/civilization' (*wen*) and began distinguishing between the 'Great ones' (*Xia*) and the 'civilizationally inferior others' (*yi*)."[44] The resulting *Xia/yi* dichotomy became a central element of the Zhou elite's civilizational consciousness, where "the Zhōu versus non-Zhōu dichotomy was defined largely in terms of differences in conventionalized behavior, such as, for example, differences in clothing, food, dwellings, burial customs, language, moral decorum, normative values, and so forth."[45] The Zhou adopted the earlier Shang dynasty (c. 1600–c. 1046 BCE) mythological geography, conceived of as a large square with the Shang center surrounded by a peripheral domain divided into four regions, with ethonyms of *man, yi, rong,* and *di* systematically associated with the four respective cardinal directions of south, east, west, and north. The civilized world of the central states of the Zhou elite, signified by the term *tianxia,* comes to mean a regime of value defined by "civilization/civility" and "rites" (*li*), similar to the universal ideas of refinement and police in the civilizational discourse of early modern Europe (see the following text box). The paternalistic *tianxia* notion of universality, a construct frequently updated throughout Chinese history, meant barbarian people could become civilized through accepting the culture of the realm under heaven. This idea extends the hierarchical, commonsense speciesism of the Mencian principle of "love with distinctions," which eventually dominated ideas in competing schools of thought, such as the "universal love" of Mohists. Differentiation in love implies caring for other nonhuman animals and benevolence toward nonfamily members, but not devotion.[46]

COMPARING THE MODERN EUROPEAN AND PRE-QIN UNIVERSAL CONCEPTS OF "CIVILIZATION"

English/French "civilization"	Pre-Qin "*wén*"
1. Progress	A notion of "change for the better" is implicit in narratives of the ancient sages "civilizing" humankind
2. Civility	"'Moral refinement"/"civility" (*wén*), "rites" (*lǐ*)
3. Police	"Laws"/"promulgated models" (*fǎ*), "rites" (*lǐ*)
4. Distinctions	
a. Barbarians vs. the civilized	"The barbarians" (*yí*) vs. "The Great ones" (*Xià*) "(Local) customs" (*sú*) vs. "(Universal) rites" (*lǐ*)
b. Primitive past vs. civilized present	"Living in nature" (*yě chǔ*) vs. Golden Age Western Zhōu
5. Universality	"All under Heaven" (*tiānxià*) = "civilized world"

Adapted from Uffe Bergeton, *The Emergence of Civilizational Consciousness,* figure 3.2.

18 *Introduction: Ecoliteratures Inhabiting Borders*

Differentiation between imperial subjects became institutionalized during the expansionist Eastern Han (25–225 CE), when the emperor was the focal point for the farmers who paid taxes and for the steppe peoples who provided the military. The Han dynastic formulation of what later became axiomatic as "using barbarians to control barbarians" meant that internally resettled steppe peoples, guided by their own rulers and loosely directed by Han military officers, remained separate from the standard administrative hierarchy. Employing separate hierarchies of control to draw diverse peoples into a single political order under the emperor, in whom the two hierarchies converged, reappeared in diverse forms throughout the history of imperial China.[47] Depending on their degree of cultural Sinicization, barbarians became categorized as "raw barbarians" (*shengfan*, since some were thought to eat uncooked food) and "cooked barbarians (*shoufan*)," yet this status was fluid. Inner Mongol cultural historian Nasan Bayar points out that even people groups that ruled China would be reclassified as "people beyond culture" if, after later overthrown, they returned to their native land and resumed their previous non-Chinese way of life.[48] This was the status of Jurchens, rulers of the Five Dynasties (907–979) and Jin dynasty (1115–1234), and the Mongols, rulers of the Yuan dynasty (1271–1368).

The assimilationist racism of culturalist *tianxia* perspectives is based on civilizational hierarchies of human worth.[49] Segregationist racist perspectives based on protogenetic differences also date to the pre-Qin period.[50] For example, the *Zuozhuan* (4th century BCE) includes the line, "if he is not of our race, he is sure to have a different mind," while the *Chunqiu* (722–481 BCE) includes several passages, later cited in the *Shiji* (ca. 94 BCE), which compare foreigners to animals and present them as subhuman.[51] There are many later instances of ethnospatial determinism in Chinese imperial history. For example, during the Southern Song, the neo-Confucian scholar Chen Liang's (1143–94) conception of psychophysical energy (*qi*) separated different people groups by environment. He argued that the Central Plain of North China possessed the most central and proper spatial energy in the cosmos, which allowed the Chinese to construct a superior culture. In contrast, the nomadic domains of the barbarians had a perverse and inferior energy, which contaminated the spatial energy of the Central Plain due to the Jurchen conquest of North China.[52] Another prominent example is the influential Ming-Qing philosopher Wang Fuzhi (1619–1692), whose discourse on *qi* resonates with that of Chen Liang: "Barbarians [Yidi] and Han [Huaxia] were born in different lands; the difference in these lands is a difference in *qi*. When *qi* is different, customs are different; when customs differ, then knowledge and actions differ. Hence, each has intrinsic differences between noble and base. Each land is distinct, with set boundaries and unique atmospheres that cannot mix. Mixing will yield destruction; the Han will be devoured and languish."[53] Like Chen, Wang perceives of geographic location defining ethnicity in an explicit hierarchy, where mutually conditioning place and "race" is determined by *qi*, which he understands as oscillating natural matter-energy, a (meta)physical substance comprised of the two complementary, but also hierarchical, components of *yin* and *yang*.[54] Wang believes the agrarian environment and the peoples it produces is so unique that ethical relations with barbarians are unnecessary, since they are a "different species." In the wake of the Manchu Qing conquest of the Ming dynasty, Wang declared:

> The difference between Chinese and Manchus is like that between jade and snow: though both are white, their qualities are utterly diverse. Or to put it in more offensive words, the distinction between them is like that between human and horse of the same color. . . . As for the *Yi-Di*, to annihilate them is not unmerciful. To plunder them is not injustice. To cheat them is not dishonesty. Why? Because fidelity and righteousness, or relational modes between men, do not apply to a different species.[55]

As a Ming loyalist, Wang Fuzhi's racist discourse, rationalized by an idealized, naturalized cosmology, was expedient, intended to motivate political agitation to restore the civilized realm. Centuries later, in an era when eugenics theories circulated globally, Mao Zedong joined a Wang Fuzhi study society in Hunan, their home province.[56]

Such idealized cosmologies masked the realpolitik advantages of ruling over farmers, who were taxed and worked to the bone and thus were easier to govern. This was clear to the imperial Chinese state from its inception, which praised farmers as "diligent" as opposed to hunters, fishers, or foragers, deemed "lazy." For example, the "Orders to Clear

Wilderness for Cultivation" chapter of the legalist *Book of Lord Shang* (ca. 3rd century BCE), tells the state to take control of mountains and moors, cultivating wastelands so that "people who hate agriculture, the tardy, the lazy, and the greedy," will need to rely on agriculture for subsistence.[57] According to David Bello, legalist agrarian theory's main product was not simply produce, but people, who would be made "guileless" (*pu*) and thus easy to rule, through farming.[58] And yet, farming cereals in temperate-zone conditions initially seemed "unnatural" to its inhabitants. Mark Elvin points out that "the Chinese ruling class had to exert itself in early times to prevent its farmers from moving back to hunting, fishing, and gathering—the original occupations of humanity." He elaborates: "The work was backbreakingly hard. Those who did it were exposed to the extraction of rents and taxes, conscription for wars and public works, and raids of human predators from outside, and a less varied and healthy diet. Increased density of population caused 'crowd diseases' and domesticating animals allowed zoonoses to transfer themselves to human beings."[59] While humans could have flourished in more ecologically sustainable ways, such occupations did not sustain the coffers of empire, so those who failed to devote themselves to agriculture were deemed inferior, and rhetoric denouncing nonfarmers as "lazy" has prevailed for millennia.[60] Although Inner Asians, such as the Jurchens or Mongols, had learned agriculture from Han and Korean captives in earlier centuries, most did not devote themselves wholeheartedly to farming because of more intimate connections to foraging, herding, and regional ecology. Similarly, the Dutch imperialist agrarians that colonized Taiwan (Formosa) declared Indigenous Sirayan fishers and foragers, who flourished in marshlands, to be "lazy."[61]

Thus farming came to dominate a Han metaphysics of empire, replicating what environmental philosopher Timothy Morton argues is the "western" expansion of most agrarian-based "civilization" is born of ecological crisis and desperation, activating a long-term collaboration between humans and wheat, rock, and soil: "we turned the region into a desert and had to turn west."[62] Civilization, according to Morton, is a form of agrilogistic retreat, and that agrilogistics (logistics governing agrarian, versus nomadic or hunter-gatherer, forms of settlement, civilization, and technology) is responsible for the Anthropocene, because it conceptualizes nature as separate from humans.[63] Morton's thesis in

Dark Ecology is that agrilogistics arose 12,500 years ago at the end of the Ice Age, when a climate shift experienced by hunter-gatherers as a catastrophe pushed humans to find a solution to their fear about where their next meal would come from. Other ecofeminist philosophies underscore how patriarchy structures many agrarian societies, with relations to women, children, animals, trees, and soil often characterized by systemic violence.

Environmental historian Charles Sanft confirms that agrilogistics dictated early Chinese imperial expansion westward. Agriculture and logging expanded greatly throughout China in Qin (221–206 BCE) and Western Han (206 BCE–24 CE), causing substantial environmental damage, including in modern-day Xinjiang in the northwest. Although plants had once been plentiful in the region, which is currently arid, deforestation intensified in the Western Han to meet demands for coffins and building.[64] Mark Elvin's environmental history of China traces the deforestation of Han lands for farming back to the Zhou (1046–221 BCE), which destroyed elephant habitats as far north as modern-day Beijing. Elephants eventually retreated to the far south, where they had a less confrontational relationship with non-Han foragers. The war against wild animals, a defining characteristic of early Zhou-dynasty agrarian culture, was later canonized in Confucian classics such as the *Classic of Poetry* (Shijing, ca. 11th–7th c BCE) and the *Mencius* (Mengzi, ca. 4th century BCE).[65] The Zhou waged war on elephants, for example, by destroying their forest habitat, defending crops against their plundering, hunting them for their ivory (the trade was established by the 7th century BCE) or trunks (considered a delicacy), or training them for war, transport, or ceremonial purposes. The "war on animals" informing Han agrarian-based civilizational identity has influenced Chinese relations with animals, and with subhuman "barbarians," to the present.

In theory, many precepts in both Confucian and Daoist classics, and laws in the Qin legal code, aimed at sustainable resource management. For example, the Confucian philosopher, Mencius, considered it the duty of the ruler to care for the land so it would provide an environment to nurture native human goodness. He suggested sustained-yield forestry, advising careful balancing of timber harvesting with the planting of trees, and opposing the waste of cut logs. He restricted overfishing and generally advocated sustainability via moderation: "If you do not interfere with the busy seasons in the fields, then there will be more grain than the people can eat; if you do not allow nets with too fine a mesh to be used in large ponds, then there will be more fish and turtles than they can eat; if hatchets and axes are permitted in the forests on the hills only in the proper seasons, then there will be more timber than they can use."[66] The early modern Chinese state also had innovative forest management, with individuals planting trees to profit from timber sales and the Southern Song (1127–1179) taxing reforested lands like agriculture.[67] Reforestation continued during the Ming (1368–1644) and Qing (1644–1911), with tree planting replacing logging from natural habitats as the major source of timber supply, particularly as virgin forest disappeared in the more accessible Hunan and Guizhou regions.[68]

Yet even market-based reforestation practices are a form of agrilogistics, naturalized as universal civilizational values deemed necessary to sustain empire. In his theory of governance, Mencius derived a supernatural political order from equating the way the ruler relates to his subjects to how Heaven (*tian*) relates to the myriad things (*wanwu*). By the late 4th century BCE, *tian* had come to mean something more like "natural," but it retained its normative force in the culture.[69] The moral and political philosophy in the *Mencius* presents, as ethically prescriptive, metaphors from plant and mammalian biology and from water and land management for farming. As linguist Edward Slingerland notes, in early Chinese agrarian thought "that which is 'natural' is, by definition, 'good.' The image of a root growing naturally into a full-grown plant or offspring going into adults was ... attached to a powerfully positive somatic marker, in that survival and economic success are dependent upon the process of natural fruition."[70] Such "commonsense" agrarian metaphors, in turn, rationalize violence against land, animals, and ethnic others. By the late Qing dynasty, statesmen such as Zuo Zongtang attempted to resolve multiple crises by studying "how to squeeze more 'profits' from the earth through the meticulous management of soils, waters, plants, and animals, seeing increases as productivity as key" and "by suggesting that untapped resources on the frontiers were essential to solving China's problems."[71]

In other words, Chinese ecological civilization naturalizes extraction from peripheries to serve the core. But historical examples expose the contradictions of agrilogistics idealized in Confucian metaphysics.

For example, environmental historian Ling Zhang points out that various Confucian states over the past two millennia regularly dealt with floods—especially of the Yellow River—by discharging water beyond their borders, "treating the neighboring state like a gully."[72] During the Northern Song Dynasty (960–1127) this meant that the flood-prone peripheral region of modern-day Hebei Province, then a frontier with the nomadic enemy to the north, trapped the imperial state and its empire in a "hydraulic mode of consumption ... that extracted political capital, labor, and other resources and channeled them toward the bottomless black hole of the Yellow River–Hebei environmental complex." As a result, "the disaster-ridden land of Hebei failed to serve the empire as a self-sufficient, stable, and obedient periphery that the state endeavored to make it. Instead, it became a de facto center of the empire, the 'root of All-Under-Heaven' (*tianxia zhi genben*), where resources flowed in to be consumed, rather than the reverse" resulting in "an inverse core-periphery structure."[73]

In the "core-periphery" cosmology of Hanspace,[74] environmental relations are naturalized by a patriarchal, agrarian imperial worldview based in *yin-yang* complementarity comprising dynamic yet hierarchal opposites. Southern shamanistic beliefs and Daoism, considered exotic and anticivilizational, constituted the initial *periphery* to a Hanspace cosmology that informed subsequent imperial expansion. In early China the Confucian school evolved from ancestor worship in the northern kingdoms around the Yellow River, focusing on *ren* (love of kinship) and *li* (rituals externalizing *ren*, or love of ancestors). Shamanism, or *wu*, the worship of natural and supernatural deities, emerged contemporaneously in the south, evolving into Daoism and other Indigenous religions. Thus, "ancestor worship (*ren/li*) and worship of natural deities (*wu*) became two most important poles in Chinese cosmology," with the canon of Confucianism forming the *core* of Chinese exceptionalism in dynastic times.[75]

Grain is an anthropological example of Hanspace core-periphery metaphysics. As the core of a Chinese meal or funeral, it is seen to extend land and lineage back and forward in time, guaranteeing the success of the family on its land and the state in its territory. Robert Weller explains that, in this worldview, "each of us is embedded in the hierarchical and environmental relations that result, with fathers anchoring families as emperors anchored the state and rice or wheat anchored a meal. Fathers and emperors are ultimately responsible for the welfare of their people by maintaining nature/heaven in its proper course, as shown by the abundance of grain they produce."[76] Meanwhile, the role of the peripheries is seen in the more varied and medicinally powerful energies that come from side dishes. Weller explains, further, that just as rice needs *yin* qualities of earth and rain to be fertile, lineages must have women from outside the clan. Likewise, the most powerful dishes come from the peripheries, from "physically distant and inaccessible places" that "confound standard categories of thought and experience."[77]

In Hanspace metaphysics, peripheries are intended to strengthen the core, infusing energy via exoticism. In Chinese medicine the most tonic dishes come from areas associated with non-Han ethnic minorities or foreign lands. Roots and herbs include caterpillar fungi (*Cordyceps*) and "winter-insect summer-grass" harvested from Tibetan nomads on the Qinghai Plateau.[78] As a caterpillar parasitized by a fungus, it dissolves conceptual distinctions between insect and plant, and comes from a location "remote" from China proper; it is seen to fortify the core/body. Other exotic dishes considered highly nutritious include mountain pangolins from Southwest China, bear and camel paws from the northwest, bird nests and civet cats from Southeast Asia, rhinoceros horns from Africa, and shark fins from the ocean's depths. When the core becomes enervated, the intended role of the peripheries is to fortify the core with reproductive potency. "Rebellious" peripheries like flood-prone eleventh-century Hebei that drain imperial coffers by failing to produce requisite tax revenues invert the "natural" core-periphery relationship and need disciplining. Such Hanspace cosmologies and racially infused ideas of *tianxia* continued to inform governmentality of border cultures into the modern period, just as European racist constructions of "civilization" informed late colonial governance practices of peripheries.[79]

GLOBAL EUGENICS AND CHINESE EXCEPTIONALISM

In the twenty-first century, the Chinese Communist Party has explicitly denounced the universalism claimed by Western civilizational values and its legacy of colonialism, instead promoting the universalism of Chinese exceptionalism (variously labeled *tianxia*, Chinese Ecological Civilization, and the Chinese Dream, among others) with its ostensible qualities of harmony, transformation, tolerance, and peace. For example, Yan Xuetong claims that pre-Qin political philosophy is based on principles of "humane authority," which can curtail the violence of contemporary geopolitical conflicts by combining a moral *tianxia* with strategic alliances.[80] Yan builds upon Zhao Tingyang's hugely influential *The Tianxia System* (2005), which resurrected the notion of *tianxia* as an alternative to the modern nation-state and has shaped Chinese public opinion and state policy. In Zhao's conception, the Zhou defeated the Shang because they achieved buy-in by "appealing to the hearts and minds of the population" (*de minxin*). Sustained by affective ties rather than coercion, *tianxia* distinguishes inside from outside less by geography and ethnicity than by cultural competence: "the outsider can move in based on merit."[81] Similar to the U.S. aphorism of "pulling oneself up from one's own bootstraps," both China and the United States have historically inculcated assimilationist paradigms based on hierarchical civilizational values. In Ge Zhaoguang's words, "from ancient times on, no matter how the concept of *tianxia* changed, it always contained three fundamental distinctions, between 'inside' and 'outside,' Hua Chinese and non-Chinese Yi or 'barbarians,' and societal 'superiors' and 'inferiors.'"[82]

Notions of *tianxia* also absorbed the social-evolutionary scientism that dominated late nineteenth-century intellectual currents in Japan, Europe, and the United States. With the introduction of "Western learning" curriculums, eugenics thought was introduced, primarily through Japan, in a context of social reforms aimed at "preserving the race" and "preserving the nation" amid fears of racial degeneration. Yan Fu's hugely influential, loose translation of Thomas Huxley's *Evolution and Ethics* (1898) popularized such phrases as "the science of selection for a superior race" or "the betterment of the race." His essay "Toward Race Preservation" insists that human beings cannot escape the competition for survival and natural selection, citing the "remarkable progress" of whites in the previous two centuries, accompanied by the "enslavement" and annihilation of "red, black, and yellow races."[83] Yan stressed that "if the white people themselves are beginning to practice [eugenics], then it is even more important in China! There is no cause under the heavens more important than 'evolving the race.' It is a most difficult task. There can only be evolution or regression, there is no neutral position."[84]

According to Hiroko Sakamoto, eugenics discourse disseminated via Japanese intellectuals directly influenced the new political movement in Hunan, in turn influencing Mao. Tan Sitong (1865–98), in his major work, *Exposition of Benevolence,* uses the term "the study of the advancement of the race." Yi Nai's 1898 articles in *Xiangbao* argue for "mixing races" (*hezhong*), particularly "intermarriage of yellow and white races" as a "plan for the preservation of the race" (*liu zhong zhiji*), arguing that marrying Westerners with superior intelligence and physique will produce a superior child. Tang Caichang's 1898 articles "He zhong" ("Racial Mixing") and "Tong zhong shuo" ("Thesis on Mixing the Races") replicate ideas in Yan Fu's *Tianyan lun*. Based on theories of improving plant species, Tang explicitly connects eugenic thought to Confucianism, concluding that, "the intermingling of races is the beginning of the advancement of the race, and the advancement of the race is the profound and subtle will of both Confucius and Mencius."[85]

In his influential utopian treatise *Datong shu* (various translated as "One World" or "Book of the Great Community"), Kang Youwei also introduces the notion of racial evolution. For Kang, "the 'One World' of the races in fact means the 'evolution' from black to brown, then to yellow, and finally to white, and thus it is clearly based on a view of the races as ranked according to a social-evolutionary model."[86] Ban Wang's analysis of *Datong shu* interprets it as a theory of cosmopolitanism, where "a world where the hierarchical distance between peoples and their rulers and between different individuals in their social relations would be markedly diminished."[87] What Wang fails to point out is that Kang's supremacist views, informed by eugenics theories, mean that "he argues for 'relocation' and 'selection' as a means of achieving 'oneness,' as well as calling for the sterilization of diseased or inferior blacks."[88]

Such late Qing racialized notions of biological determinism, in turn, informed the New Culture movement of 1915–1925, where the discourse on eugenics was prevalent, dominating May Fourth ideas of love, marriage, the home, women's liberation, sexuality, mental and physical health, population growth, and the development of a national identity. As Andrew Jones points out, "evolutionary thinking" relied upon "developmental narratives in which human history is figured in terms of natural history, and individuals as much as nations are assumed to move along a continuum from the 'savage' to the 'civilized.'"[89] The "Humane

Literature" touted by Zhou Zuoren (1885–1967) was strongly influenced by socialist Fabian Society member Havelock Ellis's ideas, including in the fields of sexology and eugenics, which he proposed as required subjects in school curriculums.⁹⁰ In fact, as Lydia Liu argues, "Zhou's much-touted notion of humanism takes evolutionary theory as the foundation of a new literature whose defining feature consists of the writer's ability to transcribe and study human life in realistic detail," and claims that Zhou's grafting of the Confucian *ren* onto the biological taxonomy of *human* is "as radical as the making of modern Chinese literature itself and signals the beginning of a new biomimetic technology that seeks to ground the truth of life in literary realism."⁹¹

Lu Xun (Zhou Shuren, 1881–1936), was also fascinated by biogenetics. Lydia Liu perceptively notes his translation of the term "life-germ" as *renya* 人芽 (human seedling) in a 1905 science fiction story on human cloning titled "Technique for Creating Humans" (造人術), where "the characters 'human' and '[vegetarian] seedling' figure a reproductive process that brings humans and plants together in a unified cellular conception of the roots of life."⁹² Lu's metaphorical figuring of animals and plants sharing the same embryonic development process was largely influenced by biologist and eugenicist Earnest Haeckel's fraudulent theory of unified cellular development represented in his drawings of vertebrate embryonic development. On the one hand, Lu Xun appeared to support eugenics, such as his 1919 article in *New Youth* arguing that since venereal disease and mental and physical deficiencies are hereditary, measures proposed by eugenicists would be unavoidable and that eugenics would save future generations.⁹³ On the other hand, he also challenged notions of literary realism as biomimetic mastery of life as form, according to Lydia Liu's interpretation of Lu's 1923 story "New Year's Sacrifice" as a challenge to the contemporary science and metaphysics debate.

Nonetheless, Lu Xun guided his youngest brother, Zhou Jianren (1888–1984), into the study of biology and evolution, which in turn led him to focus explicitly on eugenics. From 1919 to 1923 Zhou Jianren published a wide variety of articles on eugenics in *Eastern Miscellany*. For example, in "Eugenics and Its Founders" (1920), he locates historical antecedents for contemporary eugenics in the notion of "improving the race" in Plato's *Republic* and Aristotle's works, as well as in Tommaso

Campanella's *The City of the Sun* (*La Città del Sole*, 1602), a utopian treatise featuring astrological knowledge and "a community of wives" for breeding purposes. In "What Must Be Said Before Giving Birth" (1922), Zhou Jianren argues the population should be limited, but China should "increase the number of superior and limit the reproduction of the inferior."[94] In "Love, Marriage, and the Future of our Race" (1922), he says, "Love marriage is the best form of marriage for improving the race. . . . When the two sexes come together, there is a principle of selection at work; moreover, the basis for selection is primarily one of advancement."[95] Here, he draws upon the work of Leonard Darwin, son of Charles and then head of the British Eugenics Education Society.

The foundation of Zhou Jianren's thought was biometrics, and he actively promoted Karl Pearson's work on criminology and Francis Galton's work on physiognomy, adapted to mathematical indexing of fingerprints, phrenology, and facial characteristics.[96] By the 1920s biometric techniques were widely known and were reflected in Zhou Zuoren's biomimetic theories of literary realism and Lu Xun's sublimation of posthuman notions of "life as form" in his fiction. Of the three brothers, perhaps only Lu Xun began to question the ethical dilemmas posed by biometrics. In fact, most Chinese intellectuals embraced eugenics uncritically. Lydia Liu asks rhetorically what happens the idea of mimesis is pushed beyond the analogical realms, answering that the power of mimesis is seized to replicate life's own reproductive process.[97]

While many May Fourth elites promoted eugenics, American-trained eugenicist Pan Guangdan (1898–1967) ultimately popularized it. An evolutionary biologist, sociologist, and mentor of anthropologist Fei Xiaotong (1910–2005), Pan first learned of eugenics at Tsinghua University, but U.S. institutions directly indoctrinated him in eugenics theories. Before his graduate work at Columbia University in 1924, while still at student at Dartmouth, Pan took the course "Basic Human Heredity," taught by Charles Davenport, founder of the Cold Spring Harbor Station for Experimental Evolution, funded by the Carnegie Institute. This was a summer eugenics course taught from 1911 to 1924, mainly to students of prestigious women's colleges, with donations from Mrs. E. H. Harriman and the Rockefeller Foundation.[98] At the Cold Spring Eugenics Record Office, Pan composed a number of state-of-the-field reports on eugenics including "The Eugenics Problem in China" (1924), "The Eugenics

Movement Around the World in the Last Twenty Years" (1925), and "An Overview of Eugenics" (1927).[99]

Upon his return to China, Pan spread eugenics ideas in the 1920s and 1930s through his affiliation and publications with the Crescent Society, eventually helping the Nationalist government draft guidelines for the National Population Policy, passed on May 5, 1945. According to Taiwanese historian Yuehtsen Juliette Chung, Pan's guidelines encouraged interracial and interethnic marriage "to strengthen national unity and provide human resources for military conscription," in hopes that "Han Chinese and the frontier minorities could supplement and strengthen each other in order to produce better Chinese offspring."[100] In general, Pan viewed eugenics as a science aimed at increasing the overall racial stock by regulating marriage and childbirth. Like Mendel and Galton, whose genetic hereditary theories he embraced, his views of the environment were contradictory: environment was irrelevant to inherent and inherited physical strength and intelligence, yet it could function as an agent of natural selection in that famines and diseases could eliminate those with inferior genes. Pan insisted that China's geopolitical troubles arose because it had deviated from the natural path laid out by Confucius, whom he characterized as a sociobiologist and eugenicist entirely vindicated by the most cutting-edge racial and population science.[101]

Although Pan was criticized during the Anti-Rightest Movement in 1956, his thought was rehabilitated after Mao's death. In 1987 he was praised as China's "pioneer" in the field of eugenics, and in 1993 one of his daughters, sociologist Pan Naimu, edited *The Collected Works of Pan Guangdan*.[102] In 2012, Beijing University Press published a new edition of Pan's collected essays, *An Overview of Eugenics*, in what Sakamoto calls "the somewhat perplexing and highly positive reevaluation" of Pan in the postsocialist era.[103] Indeed, since the 1980s "eugenics science" in China has evolved into a "gigantic interdisciplinary system" comprising basic, social, clinical, and environmental eugenics—all aimed at "reproducing better Chinese."[104] While international media has exposed China's forced abortions and sterilizations of rural women, sterilization of the mentally disabled, forced displacements of ethnic minority populations to enhance racial mixing, and, most recently, sterilizations in Xinjiang of "separatist" ethnic minorities, decades-long propaganda campaigns have normalized the idea of improving population "quality" (*suzhi*).

The Maoist approach to *minzu* (nationality/ethnicity) deserves special attention, as socialist developmentalism remained grounded in earlier teleological imperatives of biopower. The term *minzu*, introduced into Chinese in the late Qing via the Japanese neologism *minzoku*, served as a useful tool for anti-Qing (anti-Manchu) activists influenced by Social Darwinist concepts. Zhang Binglin (1868–1936) distinguished Hanzu from Manzu, essentializing racial categories as mutually exclusive, hierarchically ordered by what Kai-wing Chow calls "Han racism."[105] While Marxist theory views nationalities as parts of the superstructure, manifestations of underlying relationships and process that will wither away once the inherent contradictions within the economic structure resolve dialectically, the CCP insisted on categorically recognizing ethnic minority groups, in part to maintain the territorial integrity of a highly diverse empire with extensive resources in the west. As Mao Zedong put it, "We say China is a country vast in territory, rich in resources and large in population; as a matter of fact, it is the Han nationality whose population is large and the minority nationalities whose territory is vast and whose resources are rich."[106]

Although the CCP promised proportional representation for non-Han communities in the first National People's Congress, more than four hundred self-categorized ethnonyms emerged from their inaugural census. According to Thomas Mullaney's study of the process by which the CCP eventually settled upon fifty-six *minzu* for its 1954 ethnic classification project, British colonial officer Henry Rodolph Davies looms large. Davies's method, heavily influenced by Darwin, reconstructed linguistic genealogies by comparing grammars and word lists to infer a common ancestry between seemingly disparate groups. Language became a biometric marker to identify the racial structure of humanity.[107] The CCP also strategically altered the taxonomy model formalized in Stalin's *Marxism and the National Colonial Question* (1913), influenced by evolutionary theories of Lewis Henry Morgan and Friedrich Engels. This model includes two key elements. First, it labels a group a nationality if it shares a common language, territory, mode of economic production, and psychology (culture). Second, it ranks groups according to a five-stage evolutionary scale from primitive communism, slavery, feudalism, capitalism, to socialism, where precapitalist communities are clans, tribes, or tribal federations rather than nationalities.[108] The Stalinist model posed a problem to the Chinese ethnographers because the ethnic groups were precapitalist; strict adherence would proliferate more categories and complicate attempts at simplification. Chinese ethnographers thus circumvented the second tenet of the Stalinist model by proposing the notion of *minzu jituan* ("ethnonational blocs"), identified according to their "ethnic potential."[109] This allowed the CCP to actualize the potential of the proposed *minzu* categories. The classification team of ethnographers and cadres produced these categories understanding that the state would intervene to close the gap between their forecasted categories and on-the-ground realities, following an imperative for socialist realism codified by Chairman Mao in his 1942 Talks in Yan'an. Rather than naturally evolving through natural selection, this ethnogenetic taxonomic enterprise was one in which biometric markers of potentiality were developed through voluntarist human intervention.

Beyond campaigns to develop the potential of ethnic minority groups, one of the most memorable slogans of Maoist voluntarism was "Man's Determination Conquers Nature" (*ren ding sheng tian*). Mao resurrected this slogan, which dates to the Warring States era (4th–3rd centuries BCE), to encourage the transformation of the landscape and society via mass mobilization efforts. During "Mao's War against Nature," as Judith Shapiro puts it, "Nature was to be 'conquered.' Wheat sown by 'shock attack.' 'Shock troops' reclaimed the grasslands. 'Victories' were won against flood and drought. Insects, rodents, and sparrows were 'wiped out.'"[110] Shapiro identifies four war fronts: political repression of (environmental) scientists; development models based on dogmatic uniformity ("one knife cuts all," *yi dao qie*) that ignored indigenous knowledge of local ecosystems; utopian urgency of the Great Leap Forward (remolding landscapes to achieve socialism); and state-ordered relocations (sending Han Chinese to western "wasteland" areas to create farmland, enhance military defense, and "bolster national security"). Yet from 1957 to 1980, the net loss of cultivated land averaged nearly 1.35 million acres per year.[111] Environmental and cultural decimation due to Maoist activism also continued in the post-Mao era. Take, for example, the "three great cuttings" (*san da fa*) during the Great

Leap Forward, the Cultural Revolution, and the early 1980s. The latter occurred because after rural families rented state-owned farmland and forests from 1980 to 1982, they quickly cut the trees, fearing they would soon lose their rights to the land. By the mid-1980s, the environmental and psychological trauma resulting from extreme Maoist campaigns activated desires to reconnect to earlier environmental philosophies within the Chinese tradition, those that promoted more moderate, sustainable relations to the people and land while still advocating development.

In sum, while the core-periphery Hanspace cosmology remains intact, an interventionist development model aimed at strengthening the "quality" of the population and environment has dominated Chinese policy making since the late nineteenth century, with consequences for non-Han peoples, resources, and lands. As subsequent chapters will detail, in recent decades ethnic minority writers from throughout the PRC have expressed, with both gratitude and dismay, the ways the state strategically "developed" their culture and environment. For example, a popular 2007 memoir written in the local nomadic dialect of Amdo Tibetan by Naktsang Nuden Lobsang or Naktsang Nulo (*nags tshang nus ldan blo bzang*), was published by Qinghai Nationalities Press but quickly banned, though translations were published in Taiwan in 2011 and by Duke University Press in 2014. The first PRC publication to critically cover the CCP's "Peaceful Liberation" and "democratic reforms" launched in Tibetan areas of Gansu, Qinghai, and Sichuan in the 1950s, *My Tibetan Childhood* details scenes of extreme violence and kindness by both Tibetans and Chinese. One of many memorable scenes detailing ethnic genocide is when hundreds of Tibetans are packed into putrid "ant holes" (underground pits), in conditions not unlike the Holocaust cattle cars or transatlantic slave ships, where many died from suffocation, injury, or starvation.[112] Again in 2013 Naktsang Nulo, then a retired cadre, published an online essay expressing empathy for the more than 150 Tibetans who had set themselves on fire to protest their repression while also calling on the Dalai Lama to beg them to stop killing themselves.[113]

CHAPTER ONE

Beijing Westerns and Hanspace Elixirs in Southwest China

> We say China is a country vast in territory, rich in resources and large in population; as a matter of fact, it is the Han nationality whose population is large and the minority nationalities whose territory is vast and whose resources are rich.
>
> —MAO ZEDONG, *ON THE TEN MAJOR RELATIONSHIPS*

> References to non-Han peoples living in the upland regions of the south and southwest have appeared in histories of China for over two thousand years. . . . For centuries they were viewed as incomplete and imperfect human forms with strange tongues, customs, and social practices. Seen for the most part to inhabit the dangerous worlds of beasts and goblins, these peoples were at once marginal figures in the Chinese imperial imagination and yet at the same time central to it. They provided a cultural and political other against which the center of power in Imperial China defined its identity.
>
> —RALPH LITZINGER, *OTHER CHINAS*

On March 6, 1984, film theorist Zhong Dianfei gave the keynote address at a conference held at Xi'an Film Studios entitled, "Face the Great Northwest, Develop a New Type of 'Western.'" In this influential speech, Zhong inaugurated a new genre of Chinese western for post-Mao cinema, literature, and arts. In accordance with "the Central Government's mandate to develop the Northwest," he encouraged writers, directors, and actors to start by developing the "spirit of the westerner" on the silver screen. This new aesthetics was to take as its object the northwest as opposed to Shanghai, Beijing, or Guangzhou, places already "aestheticized" thousands of times. Zhong insists "America has its 'Westerns' so why can't we have 'Westerns' with our own special characteristics?"¹ Indeed, just weeks prior to the address, Chinese theaters had begun to screen the 1981 film *The Legend of the Lone Ranger* at a time when only a few Hollywood films were being screened in the country each year.² Zhong concludes his address with an agrarian metaphor of conquest: "If you use the plows of cinema to cultivate the virgin land in the northwest, just waiting to be developed, you will definitely yield a two-fold harvest."³

Zhong Dianfei's speech had an immediate impact, and the term "Chinese western" gained traction in cultural circles. There was a national conference on western film and fiction in 1985, and the journal that printed his address, *New Film Age*, changed its name to *Western Films*, while the province-specific literary journal *Xinjiang Literature* was renamed to *Chinese Western Literature* to emphasize the new genre. Xie Jin and other prominent directors recruited Zhong Dianfei's son, Ah Cheng, to write screenplays of the emerging Chinese western.

But first, what is *the west*?

Historical understandings of Hanspace ecological metaphysics (see the introduction) updated with settler colonial notions of the American West, inform modern Chinese ideas of the west. The notion of "western regions" (*xiyu*) dates to Han dynasty (202 BCE–220 CE) conquests against the Xiongnu. In modern China, "the west" (*xibu*) is inscribed by the Hu Line, a farming-pastoral ecotone marking the transition between eastern agricultural to western animal husbandry zones (see figure 1.1).⁴ Identified by demographer Hu Huanyong in a 1935 research paper, nearly 94 percent of the population (over 1.2 billion people) live east of the line, on just over one-third of the land. The rest, including much of the ethnic minority population, share the vast and varied terrain some still think of as the "wild west." Importantly, the term "west" in twenty-first-century western development projects (*xibu da kaifa*) does not literally mean the geographic region in the west of China. As Inner Mongol scholar Shinjilt points out, "it refers to regions that are not politically centralized, have economies that are not agricultural, with cultures that do not use Chinese writing or language (*hanwen* or *hanyu*), or with inhabitants whose ethnicity is not Han ... the east is considered the center of China and the 'west' is regarded as 'remote' and 'heterogeneous.'"⁵ Further, researchers formulating such policies, who consider

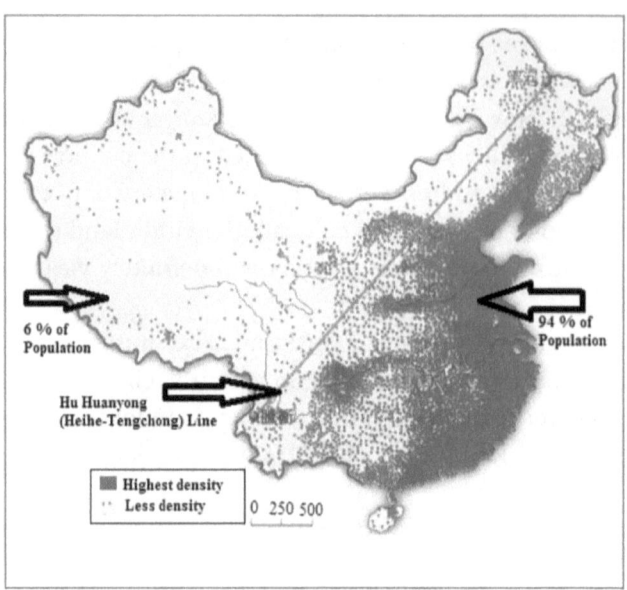

FIGURE 1.1 China's low-density population west of the Hu Huanyong Line. Terefe Hanchiso Sodango et al., "Review of the Spatial Distribution, Source, and Extent of Heavy Metal Pollution of Soil in China: Impacts and Mitigation Approaches," *Journal of Health and Pollution* 8, no. 17 (2018): 54, figure 1.

ethnic minorities heterogeneous and "backward" and Han Chinese as "universal" and "advanced," share a common belief in social evolutionism: "This philosophy would claim that in regard to subsistence patterns, agriculture is more advanced than raising livestock; in living patterns, a fixed residence is more advanced than a mobile tent; and in living environments, urban is more advanced that rural. It assumes that less developed areas (west) inevitably evolve towards becoming more advanced (east)."[6]

Ah Cheng's *The King of Trees* is an exemplar of the reemergence of the "western" in modern Chinese literature, a genre that symbolically abstracts the vast landscapes of western China while subtly rationalizing developmental policies. In accordance with Party mandates to develop the west, many writers produced ecologically conscious stories set in "remote" western provinces. In these westerns, predominantly by Beijing-based urban youth sent to the countryside during the Cultural Revolution, "narration of temporally defined trauma was reclassified as geographically defined regional character."[7] There are marked contrasts between fictional works set in ethnically diverse southwestern provinces written by Beijing-based Han Chinese writers and works by local Indigenes, including Zhang Chang (Bai), Burao Yilu (Wa), Bamo Qubumo (Nuosu Yi), and Aku Wuwu (Nuosu Yi). In general, Beijing westerns appropriate Indigenous ecological perspectives to critique Maoist destruction of the environment and the concomitant undermining of more moderate ecocivilizational values. Indigenous tales of the Anthropocene, on the other hand, resist such objectification by radically *centering* border locales as embodied places of home, civilizational heritage, and everyday humanity, though under great duress from climate change. The abstracted landscapes in Beijing westerns, stories that symbolically rehabilitate a neo-Confucian metaphysics of the cosmos, contrast sharply with representations of Indigenous knowledge of local ecosystems grounded in intimate practices.

During the Cultural Revolution (1966–1976) the "educated youth" (*zhiqing*) were sent "up to the mountains and down to the villages" (*shangshan xiaxiang*), allegedly for reeducation by the peasants, though their work teams espoused Maoist ideologies of mastery over nature, or what Morton would call a form of imperialist agrilogistics. The state sent many to locales west of the Hu Line, introducing urban Han youth to diverse ecologies, ethnic groups, dietary customs, languages, and religions. While they carry within themselves the strong indoctrination to "struggle against heaven" (*yu tian dou*), as Mao Zedong once put it, they simultaneously are deeply impressed by nature's unyieldingness and the sense of futility of their own actions in respect to vast nature. Mobilized as soldiers to battle Heaven, Earth, and class enemies, the youth soon recognized that Maoist voluntarism, which encouraged intensive deforestation and extensive water diversion projects, ran counter to the wisdom of the locals and other ecological experts.[8] The students not only encountered Daoist, Buddhist, and animist cultural practices that challenged the Maoist mandate to control nature, they were also estranged from the land. In contrast to earlier writers of the rural, such as Shen Congwen (1902–1988), Zhao Shuli (1906–1970), Zhou Libo (1908–1979), and Xiao Hong (1911–1942), or contemporary environmental writers such as Jia Pingwa (b. 1952), Liu Liangcheng (b. 1962), and Li Juan (b. 1979), the sent-down youth grew up in cities. Their 1980s nature narration is dubbed "seeking for roots" (*xungen wenxue*) in part because, as Gang Yue puts it, "they believe that the past can be rediscovered as reality, not simply remembered in writing."[9] Despite *zhiqing* claims to novelty, Yue's point underscores the continuity of agrarian, developmentalist biological paradigms informing the "root-seeking" aesthetics of the 1980s. Like the earlier socialist realism of the 1940s–70s, and May Fourth critical realism, biometric notions of life as form grounded all three literary movements.

Philosophical ideas in 1980s Beijing westerns, while espousing Daoist, animist, and Buddhist perspectives on the natural environment, primarily convey a syncretic humanist philosophy of neo-Confucian idealism. These literary works explicate environmental ideas from less anthropocentric perspectives than Maoism, yet the underlying assumptions remain strongly humanist. Although these stories are preoccupied with anthropogenic damage to the environment, they are optimistic about the potential to minimize human impacts via enlightened participation in the cosmos (which includes both the natural and built environment). Post-Mao ecoliterature shares a worldview in which, as Roger Ames puts it when describing twentieth-century neo-Confucianism, "human beings as the most complex and sophisticated force in the world, must take responsibility as an active and creative partner in the productive unfolding of the epoch in which they are located."[10] The underlying sensibility is one in which the human being and the cosmos are mutually determining.

To make my points I examine three influential works of 1980s environmental literature, each of which launches an explicit assault against Maoist voluntarism, and, by implication, critique contemporary Dengist developmentalism. Ah Cheng's 阿城 1985 *zhiqing* novella *The King of Trees* (*Shuwang* 树王) is an early example of ecological consciousness in the post-Mao era.[11] Xu Gang's 徐刚 1986 book of ecological reportage, *Woodcutter, Wake Up!* (*Famuzhe, xinglai!* 伐木者，醒来!), uses moral suasion from the margins to alert the center to the problem of deforestation on the Wuyi mountain range in Fujian. Gao Xingjian's 高行健 1989 novel *Soul Mountain* (*Lingshan* 灵山) details a search for self via a primeval forest on a fabled mountain. Each work shares thematic concerns with preserving mountain forests, which are also imagined as conduits for enlightenment.[12]

These literary themes are consistent with broader post-Mao philosophical trends attempting to reconstruct subjectivity within a Marxist framework, such as philosopher Li Zehou's appropriation of idealist German philosophy and historical materialism, and literary critic Liu Zaifu's reinvention of humanist and Marxist aesthetics. Familial and societal betrayals suffered under Maoism left many with unanswered questions about personhood, and understandings of human nature become a shared cultural quest in the 1980s, compelling many intellectuals to explore answers in a realm between "earth" and "Heaven" that synthesized scientific rationalism with idealist cosmology.

Post-Mao ecoliterature was initially motivated more by a search for personal and cultural identity than a solution to ecological crisis, yet the two concerns became mutually informing. At the diegetic level each of these narratives privilege Daoism, in particular, as a means of cultivating awareness of more ecologically sustainable human/environment relations. Daoist philosophy, especially as articulated in the *Zhuangzi* (ca. 3rd–1st centuries BCE), posited itself as a corrective to the narrowly anthropocentric assumptions of the Ru (Confucian) school of thought. Nonetheless, the narrative structures and metaphors within post-Mao ecoliterature are permeated with ancient Ru notions of anthropocosmic resonance (*ganying*),[13] in evidence in the *Book of Songs* (ca. 10th–6th centuries BCE), and agrarian metaphors canonized in the Confucian classic, the *Mencius* (ca. 4th century BCE). Ultimately, the dehumanizing and desacralizing effects of the Maoist will to power prompted an ecoliterature that identified the traumatized human soul with that of its ravaged environment.

THE TRIUMPH OF NEO-CONFUCIAN CIVILIZATION IN *THE KING OF TREES*

Zhong Ah Cheng (b. 1949) had a privileged upbringing and education in Beijing before being "sent down" to the countryside in 1968 during the Cultural Revolution. First sent to Shanxi Province, he was transferred to Inner Mongolia to paint the grasslands, then settled in Yunnan Province in southwestern China before returning to Beijing in 1979 to write about his experiences. In Yunnan, Ah Cheng was one of approximately 200,000 educated youth sent to Xishuangbanna, whose rain forests contained species thought to date back millions of years, and where educated youths felled more than 600,000 acres, changing even the region's climate.¹⁴

The publication of his popular trilogy *The King of Chess* (1984), *The King of Trees* (1985), and *The King of Children* (1985) established him as a leading "root-seeking" author. While *The King of Trees* is a prominent example of ecological literature, in his desire to graft disparate branches of philosophy onto a unifying cultural root, Ah Cheng reduces the natural environment to largely symbolic metaphors. Set in a nameless southwestern province, the novella features a generic tree, a generic mountain, and a generic "King of Trees" who, in keeping with the prediscursive Daoist hermit he at times invokes, rarely speaks.¹⁵ The story begins with the animated youth encountering passive farmers. The urban youth are enthusiastic: "already in raptures over the rugged scenery along the way, when we learned we had arrived at our destination our excitement reached its peak, and we hopped off eagerly" (109; 3). By contrast, the rural dwellers are dull: "in front of the huts stood a row of people: big, little, young and old, they gazed at us open-mouthed, hardly moving" (109; 3).¹⁶

This *yin-yang* complementarity of energy, which reinforces an urban-rural and core-periphery dualism, is immediately disrupted by local villager Knotty Xiao, whose electrifying handshake leaves the narrator feeling "I had caught my hand in a doorjamb" and the urban youth "silent, trying to work our fingers loose" (109; 3). Here Knotty Xiao embodies the role of the Zen master, who jolts his pupils into a sudden state of enlightenment, allowing them to view the cosmos as a synthesis of opposites where rational judgments become irrelevant. Knotty continues, at various junctures throughout the story, to leave the students speechless, and to render them passive in their confusion. The mere presence of this largely wordless master makes model Maoist youth Li Li's crate of Marxist-Leninist-Maoist texts appear ludicrous. After Knotty easily hoists the heavy wooden crate off the trailer, his Daoist manifestation of "effortless action" (*wuwei*) leaves the students speechless once again. They merely gather around the crate "as if it were a monster," gazing at its decorative Maoist painting of a sun, yellow rays fanning out, and a semicircle with the words: "a vast land for mighty deeds" (111; 5).

Later in the story, Knotty Xiao exemplifies a paternalistic Confucian ethic of moderation. While the youth burn wood for a bonfire, singing songs while rowing a boat "just for fun" rather than to fish,

Knotty asks the protagonist if the youth have been sent to their village to clear trees. The narrator demurs, but his answer reveals their confused mission, "We're here to be re-educated by the poor and lower-middle peasants, to build up and defend our country, and to eliminate poverty and ignorance" (115–16; 11). When Knotty persists, the narrator acknowledges the youth will cut down useless trees. At this Knotty says, protectively, "Trees can't run away" (116; 11). Eventually the youth deforest the mountain in order to plant "useful trees." Beyond the obvious allusion to the "usefulness of being useless" (*wuyong zhiyong*) in the *Zhuangzi*, the story evokes the Mencian story of the Farmer of Song who pulled at his roots to make them grow, a foolhardy belief in mastery over nature. The story implies that the Maoist "will to power" relies upon two forces, an internal tendency harnessed by an external teaching, ways of relating to the environment that have long been understood to be both morally and biologically "unnatural" in the Chinese tradition.[17] The metaphor of "natural" behavior arising from some internal essence and "unnatural" or "forced" behavior coming from the "outside" was already an entrenched worldview by at least the fourth century BCE in ancient China, and it informed the successful Mencian argument against the Mohists that their moral philosophy is based on "two roots" (*Mencius* 3A5).

It becomes clear, as the story progresses, that Knotty Xiao simultaneously symbolizes a Buddhist master of unified consciousness, a Daoist perspectivalist on the usefulness of uselessness, and a Mencian protector of the environment. The character's syncretism evokes the idea of *sanjiao heyi*, literally, "the fusion of the three teachings of Confucianism, Daoism, and Buddhism as one," a conventional expression frequently invoked to describe the composite nature of Chinese philosophy. When the youth attempt to fell the oldest, largest, and most "useless" King of Trees, its spiritual guardian, Knotty Xiao, wordlessly obstructs their way. The Party Secretary intervenes, allowing the deforestation to continue. As the giant tree falls, and the mountain is set ablaze, Knotty eventually loses his will to live and is buried near the fallen tree. In his final days what Knotty embodies is neither Buddhist detachment nor Daoist acceptance of what is, but a hapless victim of Maoists conquering nature.

Yet the story does not end with Knotty's death. Instead, the mountain "would not have" the Tree's spiritual protector, who embodied the three strands of traditional Chinese thought: "Knotty's grave had burst open: the white coffin was raised high above the grave, gleaming in the sunshine" (55; 160). While Maoism decimated the core, the spirituality of the southwestern periphery (local Yi animist beliefs in mountain and tree spirits) resurrected it. Taken as a whole, the dynamic manifests *yin-yang* complementary of anthropocosmic resonance. This final image in the novella, one of potential rejuvenation, is presaged by a penultimate scene where an entire mountain is engulfed in flames as students attempt to deforest the mountain:

> The rumble of the fire shook the ground and rustled the thatch on our huts. Each loud bang was followed by a shrill hiss as the fire twisted into a ball and violently broke apart. A log leaped up and flew through the air, trailing a million sparks, somersaulting then falling down again, scattering countless flaming torches. The bigger logs dropped; the smaller ones continued to soar thousands of feet up, tossing and turning for ages before they drifted down. The fire by now had approached the mountaintop, illuminating an arc around the summit so that it was as bright as day. (156; 51)

This passage in the novella calls to mind a classic passage on the four sprouts of virtue (*siduan*) that are so central to Mencian thought: "If anyone having the four sprouts within himself knows how to develop them to the full, it is like fire catching alight, or a spring as it first bursts through. If able to develop them, he is able to protect the entire world; if unable, he is unable to serve even his parents" (*Mencius* 2A6). Not only did the raging fire and scorched earth refuse to devour Knotty Xiao's corpse, the metaphor of a magnificent "fire catching alight" symbolizes that the sprouts of virtue, if cultivated, were powerful enough to "protect the whole world."

The novella suggests the anthropocosmic revival of the Confucian *tianxia* system, seen to be a system of moral governance that transcends racial and geographical boundaries. Although the Maoist youth uprooted the King of Trees, its great Root began to extend new roots into the very soil that had rejected the coffin of a civilization's philosophical exemplar. The story's final line depicts resilient "sprouts" (of virtue): "a tangled mass of shoots were growing vigorously from the earth in which the coffin had been laid" (160; 56). The metaphor is clear:

the root system of the felled tree was putting forth new roots in the soil of the would-be grave of a virtuous civilization. The mandated drive to overcultivate the countryside thus stands in contradistinction to the newly forming interiority of sent-down youth such as Ah Cheng, who imbues the ravaged rural landscape of his story with the self-generating power or virtue (*de* 德) that informs neo-Confucian thought.[18] Through cultural transformation and instruction (*jiaohua* 教化) in Beijing westerns such as *The King of Trees*, the moral center holds sway over the (imperial) realm and knows no bounds; those on the periphery join via attraction and consensus.

IMPERIAL GOVERNANCE AND THE MASS LINE: ECOLOGICAL REPORTAGE LITERATURE

In *The King of Trees*, the Maoist "war against nature" is utterly discredited in favor of an environmental ethic derived from syncretistic Chinese moral philosophy. The novella also intimates a need to return to the conservationist environmental governance instituted by the People's Republic of China, practices adapted from Republican institutions that applied contemporary scientific knowledge to long-standing imperial practices established as early as the Qin and Han dynasties. It is important to note that Chinese law, from at least the late third century BCE, if not earlier, contained extensive provisions regulating the harvest of natural resources. For example, legal documents excavated in the late twentieth century include both Qin and Han law sections entitled "Statutes on Fields" (*tianlü* 田律), which contained provisions regulating agriculture and the harvest of various natural and agricultural resources. The Qin version from the Shuihudi archaeological site reads, in part: "From the second month, spring, do not cut wood in mountain forests or dam rivers. If it is not [yet] a summer month, do not burn grass for ash; pick new irises; or take fawns, eggs, or hatchlings. Do not ... take fish or turtles by poison, or set pitfalls or snares. When the seventh month arrives these are permitted. It is only in case of a death, when cutting wood for the coffins, that the [law for the] season is not adhered to.[19] Charles Sanft, an expert in early China legal history, indicates that the Han version recovered at Zhangjiashan is very similar to the Qin legal code, and even includes matching phrases: "In spring and summer do not cut wood in mountain forests; dam rivers or springs; burn grass for ash; or take newborn fawns, eggs, or hatchlings. Do not kill heavily pregnant animals. Do not take fish by poison."[20] The point I am making here is that the ecoliterature of the 1980s portrays the Maoist war on nature as an excessive aberration from historical understandings of environmental protection, while rampant Dengist developmentalism is seen to flout conservation policies already instituted in contemporary PRC environmental law.

As environmental degradation intensified in the Reform Era, the generic, metaphorical depictions of the environment in post-Mao root-seeking literature such as Ah Cheng's *The King of Trees* soon gave way to more localized, historical accounts of the land with the rise of "ecological reportage literature" (*shengtai baogao wenxue*). Bai Indigene Zhang Chang's 张长 1980 short story "Green Leaves of Hope" ("Xiwang de lüye" 希望的绿叶), which won the inaugural national prize for ethnic minority fiction, addresses the challenges of doing ecological reportage on deforestation and is the earliest example of post-Mao ecological fiction, though it is not always identified as such.[21] In the story, a forest management bureaucrat in a southern Yunnan tropical rainforest considers writing a report to his superiors, exhorting them to enforce the newly issued Forestry Law (*Senlin fa*). The story is full of scientific details about subtropical plants, wildlife, and the percentage of the forest decimated by earlier Maoist campaigns. The narrator's wife, a forestry PhD who is utterly disillusioned with politics in the aftermath of the Cultural Revolution, discourages him from "sticking his neck out," asking repeatedly, "do you *have* to be so conscientious?" In the end he wins her over, and they clink wine glasses, toasting "the green leaves of hope," as he starts writing another draft report.[22] Despite this fictional depiction, mainstream chronologies attribute Sha Qing's "Beijing Loses Its Balance" (1986) as the earliest piece of eco-reportage in the PRC.[23] Its literary success, combined with the nationwide attention it generated, initiated a wide variety of works in the genre, which tends to focus on specific environmental issues such as water pollution, desertification, or deforestation.

One of the most influential early examples of eco-reportage in the category of deforestation is Xu Gang's (b. 1945) *Woodcutter, Wake Up!* (1986). The story recounts his trip to Wuyishan, a mountainous region in Fujian Province famous for an aesthetic ideal often emulated in Chinese traditional landscape painting. As the author arrives, he finds the forests have almost completely fallen prey to extensive logging. King's Peak, the main mountain peak of Wuyishan, used to be covered with "old trees that reach up to heaven" (*gumu cantian*) and impenetrable brush that provided a haven for bird life:

> In 1984, farmers from Ji'an county kept felling and felling trees until Jade Maiden's Peak (Yunü feng)—yes, that very same Jade Maiden's Peak that appears on the television screens every evening as the symbol of Fujian province—until even this maiden's skirt had been pulled down!... I would kindly like to warn the reader: If this continues for any longer, will not the whole of *Wuyi* Mountains then become "the mountains without clothes."[24]

The problem, as presented in the story, is threefold. First of all, the local villagers, trapped in bitter poverty, embrace the new slogan by Deng Xiaoping's "To get rich is glorious!" and the *Zeitgeist* of the economic reform era has unleashed the local population's entrepreneurial spirit ("Want to make a buck?—Cut a tree!" *yaofu kanshu*!). Second, due to corruption, the local cadres fail to enforce the national Forestry Law. The cadres not only do nothing to prevent illegal logging, but often they themselves are the first ones to actively lead the way in this illegal activity. As Xu Gang wanders through endangered forests, he meets a villager who has returned from cutting trees up in the mountains:

XU GANG: "Are there no forest rangers in your village?"
VILLAGER: "Those are the first ones to cut trees! Whether it's the forest officers, or party cadres, they're all the cousin of some village head, or the nephew of some party secretary: They pocket 40 Yuan a month for 'forest protection' and continue logging as before. Why should we common folk not also cut some trees ourselves then?"
XU GANG: "But what about the higher-ranking cadres?"
VILLAGER: "Oh, they all do it. But for them, it doesn't matter, because they can have [the timber] delivered right to their doorstep, isn't that even better?"[25]

The central problem in Xu Gang's story is presented as misinformation remedied through writing to awaken the consciousness of the center. Just as the root-seeking writers appealed to ancient moral virtue, so, too, the eco-reportage of the 1980s was motivated by the ancient imperial idea of opening communication lines between the localities and the center. Sources as early as the *Book of Changes* (ca. 10th century BCE) refer to inspection tours by the first kings. Such imperial tours, which included elaborate rituals and the communication of imperial edicts erected on steles in auspicious sites such as sacred mountains, were long understood to be a way of gathering information from, and exercising central authority in, the peripheries.[26]

The Maoist "mass line" was, of course, inspired by traditional rituals for strengthening central power through soliciting detailed accounts of local conditions. Xu Gang's reportage is based on a 1980s social imagination that remains strongly informed by imperial and socialist communication rituals and institutions. Such literature assumes the efficacy of a long-standing Confucian hermeneutic of exerting moral pressure on the central authorities to enforce existing laws, including those that protect the environment. *Woodcutter* encourages a cooperative approach towards environmental governance, which invokes selective alignments between activists and central government actors against local corruption.

HANSPACE SYNTHESIS OF THE HEGELIAN DIALECTIC OF *SOUL MOUNTAIN*

By the late 1980s a third type of environmental literature emerges in the PRC, one that strengthens the historical specificity of eco-reportage and incorporates far more detailed scientific accounts of environmental conditions. Unlike the abstracted representations in *The King of Trees* where "the trees are not of any specific particular species, and the animals are placed on the landscape as images rather than written into it with detail," Gao Xingjian's 1980s ecoliterature "borrows from the contemporary discourse of environmentalism, and incorporate the language of science, with an emphasis on taxonomy."[27] The unusual exactness with which nature is described in *Soul Mountain* sets it apart from most 1980s works of environmental literature from the PRC, though it shares similarities with the Taiwanese nature writing and eco-documentary movement that emerged in the early 1980s.[28]

Soul Mountain is a fictionalized account of the travels that Gao Xingjian (b. 1940) made to Qiang, Tibetan, Miao, Tujia and Yi indigenous areas and nature reserves "at the borders of Han civilization in western China, and a description of his encounters during a return to Han civilization on the east coast."[29] Written from 1982 to 1989, the conceit for this monumental novel of wandering by the Nobel Prize–winning novelist, playwright, and artist is a need to rediscover the soul (of China, of the self) after Gao received a false cancer diagnosis, and to escape a repressive Beijing environment due to the 1983 Spiritual Pollution Campaign.[30] A 1962 graduate of Beijing Foreign Studies University with a degree in French, Gao was persecuted during the Cultural Revolution and sent down to Anhui Province for six years of hard labor before returning to Beijing, and he considers *Soul Mountain* a collection of root-seeking tales. Yet, as Jeffrey Kinkley puts it, "for Gao Xingjian ... the frontier where one seeks one's true self is an internal, Chinese cultural frontier, not one defined by an international boundary."[31] The novel is, in this sense, a high modernist Beijing western predicated upon Hanspace practices of defining the Chinese Self through the Other.

Gao Xingjian, like other 1980s root-seeking writers "of outlandish and primitive practices," satisfies "a hunger among intellectuals, both in China and in the West, for representations of an 'other China' in which 'the masses' were not heroic characters who followed the Communist Party to ever greater victories, but were deformed, cruel or sexually depraved."[32] In addition to magical realism, the 1980s root-seeking school, including Gao, were inspired by the ancient *Chuci* (Songs of the South), local gazetteers, and records and tales of the strange found in unofficial writings of the past millennia. As discussed in the introduction, the two poles of Chinese cosmology oppose northern ancestor worship (*ren/li*), manifest in a deified Chairman Mao and Party dogma (strict adherence to which was exhibited by Li Li in *The King of Trees*), to southern *wu*, nature deities manifest in southern shamanistic beliefs and Daoism, considered anticivilizational. As in *The King of Trees*, *Soul Mountain* engages resonance theory, revitalizing the center or "soul" of the empire with an infusion of exoticism from the peripheries.

Soul Mountain chronicles widespread environmental destruction in the regions traversed by the narrator. These include the Shennongjia National Nature Reserve, a forestry district in Hubei, listed as a UNESCO's World Network of Biosphere Reserves in 1990); Guizhou's Caohai, an important habitat for migratory birds that was designated a provincial level nature reserve in 1985; and the Wolong Nature Reserve in Sichuan's Aba Prefecture, listed as a UNESCO Biosphere Reserve in 1979. For example, in chapter 59, at Shennongjia, the narrator hears about researchers that study golden pheasants and giant salamanders. In chapter 18 the narrator meets with the chief ranger of Caohai Nature Reserve, who is breeding red-headed cranes, black neck cranes, and gray cranes, waterfowl that had been hunted to near-extinction. The ranger has research notebooks from his predecessor, a biologist with a foreign PhD who traveled from Shanghai to Caohai in the 1950s to launch a breeding program to reestablish populations of coyhu, ermine, and speckle-headed geese until poachers beat him to death.

It may seem ironic that the example of 1980s environmental literature that describes environmental conditions with the most scientific precision also imbues it with qualities most reminiscent of philosophical Daoism. However, this calls to mind earlier precedents for Chinese environmental writing. For example, Tang essayist Liu Zongyuan's (773–819) empirical observations of his environment during his exile to the south presaged the scientific rationalism of Zhu Xi's (1130–1200) neo-Confucian "investigation of things" (*gewu*), even as he metaphorically imbued Liuzhou's landscape with shamanistic virtues. Whereas Gao's earlier work, *Wild Man* (*Yeren* 野人, 1985), conveyed the message that ecologists must assume responsibility for connecting humankind to nature because the shamans are dead, in *Soul Mountain* science and Daoism inform each other. In fact, synthesizing these two modes of thought—the empirical thinking of scientific observation, and the aesthetic thinking of sensual intuition—is the primary motif of the novel.

Soul Mountain comprises eighty-one chapters (like the *Zhuangzi*) and features a split protagonist, starting with stories of "You" in odd chapters and "I" in even chapters. "You" and "I" tour remote parts of China, as did the novel's author. "I" is intent on distinguishing mental constructs from haptic experience and conceptualizes knowledge through a temporal episteme. He (the split protagonist is clearly a Han male) is fascinated with scientific and historical data, the customs of non-Han peoples, and archaeological artifacts. "You" longs to experience an atemporal, prelinguistic state of being. He searches for the fabled soul mountain by attempting to "lose himself" in primeval forests, a feminine other (a third character, "She"), and mythical tales.

Some scholars identify a narrative tension in *Soul Mountain* said to derive from the fact that, at both the diegetic and structural level of the novel, it appears that "I" cannot be reconciled with "You." Because the "I" chapters inextricably link the power of interpretation to perspectival distance, this appears to reinforce his gap between "You" and his "Others." "You" seeks to experience the authenticity and immediacy to be found in so-called primitive cultures, the primeval feminine and pristine Nature, yet the shadow of "I" causes "You" to fear absolute immanence in a fixed system of beliefs. As a result, many studies interpret the novel as a failed attempt to reconcile the dichotomies of modernity. For example, Andrea Bachner concludes that the novel presents "the dichotomizing analysis of culture versus nature ... as an unachievable ideal," while Thomas Moran argues that the narrator is frustrated in his attempts to comprehend nature, and hence, self, thus remains "lost in the woods."[33] Karen Thornber does not analyze the split narrator but concludes that Gao's narrator views himself as struggling alone against humanity, leading "not to determined resistance to ecological abuses but instead to further contemplation and then despair that nothing he does will make a difference."[34]

To my mind, the foregoing scholarly interpretations close off the creative potentialities inherent in the narrative. My alternative reading suggests that the novel achieves an idealist synthesis of disparate subjectivities (or ontologies), not in the sense that a unified subject emerges by novel's end, but as a generative process of transformation. To illustrate my point, I will examine the protagonist's repeated excursions into forests. In chapter 6, "I" arrives at the giant panda observation compound at Haiba in Sichuan Province, and in chapter 8, a botanist shows him a giant metasequoia (dawn redwood) he discovered in the camp's maple and linden secondary growth forest. "I" initially maintains a strong sense of perspectival distance, interpreting his experience temporally via geological and botanical developments: "It is a living fern fossil more than forty metres high, a solitary remnant of the ice age a million years ago, but if I look right up to the tips of the gleaming branches some tiny new leaves can be seen" (50; 47).[35]

This scientific description is what philosopher David Hall characterizes as a "rational order" episteme, an ordering that instantiates or realizes a presupposed structure or pattern.[36] Yet when "I" climbs inside a cavernous hole within the trunk of the tree, his description begins to combine empirical descriptions with metaphorical ones: "The walls are covered in moss. The inside and outside of this huge tree has a green fuzz growing on it and the gnarled roots are like dragons and snakes crawling everywhere over a large area of shrubs and bushes" (50; 47). "I" begins to order his world aesthetically in a style reminiscent of that of the Tang dynasty essayist Liu Zongyuan. Again in chapter 10, when the botanist leads him to a primary growth forest to collect signals on giant panda activity, "I" relates to his environment even more intimately, describing his bodily experience. Gao writes: "Big bright, transparent drops of water, drop after drop, slowly drip onto [my] face, down [my] neck, icy cold. [I] tread on thick, soft, downy moss, layer upon layer of it . . . [my] singlet is soaked in sweat and clings [to me]. Only [my] belly feels slightly warm." (62; 58). There is no personal pronoun in the original Chinese. The agent of the dripping water is not named. In this passage Gao's language begins to approach that of the Buddhist nature poet, Wang Wei (699–759):

WANG WEI, "IN THE MOUNTAINS"	山中　王維
In Ching Brook white stones jut out,	荊溪白石出
The sky is cold, red leaves thinning.	天寒紅葉稀
On the mountain path there had been no rain.	山路元無雨
The cloudless blue, clothes are dampened.[37]	空翠濕人衣

In Wang Wei's poem, the agent of the dampened clothes (humidity? sweat?) is not named. "Cloudless" (lit. "empty" *kong* 空) may be a descriptor, connoting an "empty" sky, or a Buddhist term for enlightenment.

In other words, as "I" moves further into the forest, his episteme transforms from anthropocentric rational ordering to aesthetic ordering, which Hall characterizes as "an alternative method of knowing in which the ordering elements are insistently unique particulars which

50　*Beijing Westerns and Hanspace Elixirs*

cannot be discussed in terms of pattern concepts defining regularities or uniformities."[38] Aesthetic ordering approaches a form of non-anthropocentrism in that it denies any privileged perspective, whether the Divine, the human, the material, or the Ideal. These literary descriptions of the environment express what Alfred North Whitehead has referred to in *The Concept of Nature* as "the ingression of scientific objects," where he defined nature as "what we are aware of in perception."[39] Furthermore, aesthetic ordering accounts for the fallacy of the "individual" or "separate element" (as in Aristotelian substance philosophy). As Whitehead puts it in *Science and the Modern World*, "it is important to ask what Wordsworth found in nature that failed to receive expression in science. I ask this question in the interest of science itself... his theme is nature in *solido*, that is to say, he dwells on that mysterious presence of surrounding things, which imposes itself on any separate element that we set up as an individual for its own sake."[40]

As the journey into the primeval forest progresses, the distinctions between "I" and "Nature" collapse to the point of temporarily losing both his guide and his sense of self. He experiences immanence first as ecstasy ("The air penetrates to the soles of my feet, and my body and mind seem to enter nature's grand cycle") and then as terror ("I shout out again but hear my own muffled trembling voice immediately vanish without even echoing... terror ascends from my feet and my blood freezes" (65; 61). He associates his terror with the loss of a recognizable sign, a cognitive signifier to orient him existentially. He has his scientific bearings but remains "lost in the three thousand meters of ancient forest in the 12-meter band of the aviation chart" (63; 68). Eventually he attaches self to a sign, a strangely shaped tree that looks like a giant harpoon, and concludes that it is "futile to struggle while impaled upon the fish-spear" (68; 64). He moves from a sense of "being" distinct from nature to a sense of "being with" nature (albeit he is still in an uncomfortable state of "being with" the tree). Clearly, he is coming to terms with the possibility of the death of self. While "I" never returns from the journey into the primeval forest in chapter 10, the story in chapter 12 recalls the cancer diagnosis that motivated the long journey in the first place, and in chapter 66, "You" emerges from a deathlike state after encountering the fish-spear tree in the primeval forest and continues to transmute in subsequent chapters.

Beijing Westerns and Hanspace Elixirs 51

A continually regenerative process that synthesizes "I" and "You" occurs both structurally and diegetically as the narrative progresses. The rigid logic of the structural dichotomy is reversed in chapter 33: after two consecutive chapters on "You" the odd-numbered chapters begin to narrate "I." Similarly, previously fixed thematic dichotomies start to permute as "She" enters the temporal realm of "I" in chapter 45. Chapter 52 is a metadiscourse on all three characters: "In this lengthy soliloquy you are the object of what I relate... as I listen to myself and you, I let you create a she... so you talk with her, just like I talk with you. She was born of you, yet is an affirmation of myself" (341; 312). In chapter 66 it is now "You" that is lost in a primeval forest, but with a renewed sense of agency: "You refuse to be skewered to death on a fishbone like a fish out of water" (465; 418). He arrives at the edge of the forest and, attracted by the churning foam of a valley river, instinctively takes an ecstatic plunge into Nature:

> You seem to glide into the air, disintegrate, disperse, lose physical form, and then serenely drift into the deep gloomy valley, like a thread of drifting gossamer. This thread of gossamer is you, in an unnamed space. All around is the stench of death, your lungs and bowels are chilled, your body icy cold.... The drowned, sighing women drift by but you do not think to rescue them, do not even think to rescue yourself. (466–67; 419–20)

The "You" that was "I" experiences immanence in the dissolution of distinctions between self and other, life and death, mind and body, culture and nature, civilization and barbarism, man and woman, time and eternity. In chapter 72 "I" and "You" dissolve into the character "He," and in chapter 78 "I" narrates the story of "You" and "Her." In the penultimate chapter the "You" that is "I" spirals upward from a state of immanence into one with conceptual distinctions of time and space, as "the physical body you failed to abandon recovers its sensitivity" (561; 504). In the final chapter "I" asks a small green frog, asks God, what else to seek. Snow is falling. Though "I" cannot stop thinking, he ends: "I understand nothing. This is how it is" (563; 506).

The question of whether or not the epistemological tensions within *Soul Mountain* are infinitely self-perpetuating or genuinely transformative is debatable. If we read the novel as a construction of identity with and through its Other(s) in order to individuate, as do scholars such as Andrea Bachner or Thomas Moran, it is logical to understand the novel as presenting an impasse between rationality and immanence. Indeed, it becomes impossible to imagine distinct ontological categories of being (including "human beings") in the natural environment without becoming absorbed in it without remainder. What *Soul Mountain* narrates, however, is less a teleological individuation of "self" than an ongoing process of becoming. The dichotomous categories and structures in the novel are not static. Rather, the perpetual transmutation of the protagonist recalls precepts within Whitehead's process philosophy that resonate with neo-Confucian cosmology. In *Process and Reality*, rather than assuming substance as the basic metaphysical category, Whitehead introduces a new metaphysically primitive notion that he calls an "actual occasion," which is not an enduring substance of being but a relational process of becoming. Donald Sherburne explains, "It is as though one were to take Aristotle's system of categories and ask what would result if the category of substance were displaced from its preeminence by the category of relation."[41] As Whitehead puts it, "For Kant, the world emerges from the subject; for the philosophy of organism, the subject emerges from the world."[42]

While *Soul Mountain* unquestionably expresses a relational process of becoming, it can also be characterized by the reverse Hegelian synthesis first proposed by Liang Shuming (1893–1988), the founding father of modern neo-Confucianism. Liang Shuming theorizes a clear teleology of phasal developments that move from a "Western phase" in which the human will is able to satisfy the basic needs of the human experience by disciplining the environment to a "Chinese phase" in which this human will is harmonized within its natural environment, and then to a final phase of Daoist or Chan Buddhist philosophy that provides an intuitive negation of the self/other dichotomy. Just as Liang Shuming's theories extend Wang Yangming's (1472–1529) "philosophy of heart-and-mind" (*xinxue*), so, too, Gao Xingjian's Daoist rationalism is in part a syncretic attempt to synthesize the modern Hegelian dialectic. As such, Gao's narrative appears to share Liang Shuming's "existential and aspirational quest for Confucian enlightenment rather than an attempt to establish an expository, systematic account of reality."[43] While the processes within Gao Xingjian's narrative are not as clearly demarcated as Liang Shuming's schema proposes, the protagonist does appear to move from a more scientifically rationalist way of relating to nature, to an acceptance of his relationship to nature, to an intuitive negation of the self/other dichotomy.

Furthermore, the bifurcated subject that forms the original premise of the "self" replicates assumptions in the metaphysical ethics of modern neo-Confucian philosophers such as Tang Junyi, who claims: "With whom can we identify if we are to transcend our actual selves? Nature or essence makes our 'ethical self,' or spiritual self or transcendental self, be what it is. In contrast, the 'actual self' is 'the self that is trapped in present space and time.' The ethical self, which is not limited by space and time and is permanent and true, represents one's genuine self."[44] While Gao Xingjian adopts Tang Junyi's constructs of an "actual self" (time- and space-bound) and an "ethical self" (immanent in nature), his narrative rejects the privileging of the latter. In this sense Gao appears to be most heavily influenced by the post-Marxist philosopher Li Zehou, whose discourses on *zhutixing* 主体性, dominated cultural discussions in the 1980s. In 1999, Li wrote:

> Sometimes there is a kind of misunderstanding regarding my so-called *zhutixing*. It does not have the Western sense of "subjectivity" (*zhuguan*). I feel we should rather use a new term "subjectentity"— even though there is no such word in the English dictionary—that means that a human person is the capacity of an active entity. *Zhutixing* is not a concept of epistemology; instead it implies that a human being is considered as a form of material, biological, and objective existence and as an active capability in relationship to the environment.[45]

Li's formulation of "subjectentity" illuminates Whitehead's notion of the "organism" in *Process and Reality* and vice versa, in that both conceive of personal, social, political, and cosmic order as historicist, particularist, and emergent. In this sense, we can understand Gao Xingjian's narrative as proceeding according to a transformative dialectic that synthesizes non-anthropocentric aesthetic ordering, as one element among many, into an emergent cultural ecology. It ultimately rejects the unified theory of cosmological perspectivism that underlies Daoist philosophy. Like other examples of 1980s environmental literature, *Soul Mountain* expresses a correlative sensibility in which the human being and the cosmos are mutually determining, albeit with far more linguistic, philosophical, and scientific sophistication.

Despite the philosophical brilliance of the novel's construction and narrative development, a Han male heteronormative experience of the world predicates the entire search for "subjectentity." As such, it remains a historical product of Hanspace cosmologies based in hierarchical assumptions. Kam Louie points out that in *Soul Mountain* "the subject (whether it be "I" or "you") is unambiguously male and the object being talked about or talked to is female. The narrator's 'truth of women' is one where the female object is 'stalked, hunted, torn apart, devoured.'" Further, while the narrator ultimately incorporates "she" into his psyche, it is a synthesis motivated by the male narrator's need to "triumph over women, or at least the feminine part of his psyche."[46] Indeed, the narrative repeatedly undermines displays of feminine power and autonomy, whether through voyeuristic descriptions of misogynist violence, expression of narrative revulsion, or interpretations of female vulnerability as weakness, immaturity, and abjection. In short, women are a subsidiary part of the male order where it is a cardinal sin to refuse or overpower men. For example, after sharing a meal with a lesbian, the narrator finds her so disgusting that "in the middle of the night I have an attack of vomiting and diarrhoea" (515; 463). In chapter 33, a ranger of the Fanjingshan Nature Reserve at Heiwan River in Guizhou Province recounts a particularly gruesome tale to the narrator about his experience during the Cultural Revolution. "Women are troublesome" he says, then tells of a nineteen-year-old girl who became a top-ranking shooter in the province, but after running out of ammunition during an armed battle in the mountains "she was caught, stripped and a soldier fired a magazine of bullets from his submachine gun into her vagina" (201; 187).

The novel is full of similarly lurid and sensationalist tales of orgies, rape, and murder of young women which are minimized and normalized in the narrative. "You" narrates many of these stories to "She," who mostly listens passively, or asks for reassurance when afraid. Portraying women as sexually voracious, the novel cautions against them having their carnal appetites unleashed, because "once the floodgates had opened there was no stopping" (472; 425). Instead, the novel valorizes the voice of the frightened and beleaguered young woman in search of paternalistic comfort. If, as Louie argues, "the 'she' in these dialogues is meant to represent the feminine part of the narrator's ego, this immature and insecure self, like the history of the masses, must be transcended for individual growth and fulfillment to take place."[47] At the midpoint of the novel, three chapters examine how to leave a "troublesome woman," insisting a man must "refuse to submit to a woman, to be a woman's slave" though he struggles not to succumb to her "seduction" (298; 274). It is precisely this type of violence that rationalizes eugenics thought.

Far from embracing philosophical Daoism and its valorizations of the feminine principle as one of power, Gao's novel reinforces its abject positionality within an imperial Hanspace cosmology. Simultaneously a passive reinforcement of the patriarchal status quo and an overwhelming threat to its coherence, "She" cannot but be aligned with the ethnic other; "I" and "You" must discipline the dark barbarism that threatens the coherent subject by rescuing "Her" from her own abjection. That "she" signifies abjection is explicit throughout the novel and is inherent in the narrator's interpretation of the foundational Han creation myth: "When Nüwa created humans she also created their sufferings. Humans are created from the entrails of Nüwa and born in the bloody fluids of women and so they can never be washed clean" (350; 381). Such a slippage between the metaphysics of a feminine principle in all subjectivity and embodied sex occurs throughout the novel, a slippery form of narrative double-speak that implicates the text in normalizing misogyny against women. Women stand in for the mindless masses, which, in raging against the violent ravages of the Cultural Revolution, "I" calls "a race of people who have lost their souls!" (395; 361). The "soul" of the race must be retrieved through the individual journey of the Han male ethnographer in search of primeval power to purify the "people today [who] are greedier than the ancients [which] casts doubt on Thomas Huxley's theory of evolution" (400; 366). As such, "I/You" gender the ethnic minority myths, epics, shamans, and rituals encountered along the route as feminine supplements, which he consumes to nourish the core. The sophisticated narrative ostensibly rejects a thoroughgoing exoticization of the periphery: "she" once insists on telling stories to "you" (174; 186) and a Yi intellectual convinces "I" to concede that Han civilization is as barbaric as Yi aristocratic society (133; 123). Yet although "she" and Indigenous spokespeople at times push back against psychic objectification, such instances are minimal, red herrings drowning in a narrative sea of patriarchal racial supremacy.

In Beijing westerns, the exotic southwestern periphery is ultimately deemed the property of the Han, viewed as an ancient vestige of a pan-ethnic, gender-fluid culture. The embodied reality of the non-Han or woman as modern citizen is symbolically eradicated. In the twentieth century, when ethnic identity had become conscious and schematized, for root-seeking writers such as Gao Xingjian, Han Shaogong, Jiang Rong, Ma Yuan, and Shen Congwen, "this means prizing 'primitive' and primeval non-Han customs and rituals not as an ancient ethos of Miao, Yi, or Tibetans, but as 'original Chinese culture,' as 'roots' that were sloughed off by the Han in their long history."[48] This coopting of the periphery by the core is what Jeffrey Kinkley deems a long-standing practice of creating new mythologies of "the Chinese cultural myth" from old ones, which Ge Zhaoguang calls the metamorphosis of an "imaginary utopia of 'all under Heaven.'"[49]

THE BORDER AS HOME IN INDIGENOUS POETRY FROM SOUTHWEST CHINA

In his study of the Yao of Southwest China, Ralph Litzinger asks if Indigenous self-representations are driven by the same postsocialist nostalgia that drives the Han intellectual appropriation of the ethnic margins.[50] I would argue that, to the contrary, Indigenous ecoliterature from Southwest China counters the prevalent exoticization of the ethnic other by adopting postcolonial strategies of opacity, mimicry, exaggeration, or evasion. Many incorporate motifs from traditional epics, then undermine them in what I call the "anti-epic of the Anthropocene."[51] Above all, Indigenous literature from Southwest China *centers* the "border" as a place of home, heritage, and everyday humanity (see figure 1.2).

For example, journalist and poet Burao Yilu (Ilu Buraug, b. 1955), of the Mon-Khmer speaking Wa (Va) ethnic group of Yunnan Province, recenters creation myths while demystifying ritual practices in her writing. The Wa peoples number nearly a million and reside across the border in Myanmar in addition to Yunnan. They have historically

FIGURE 1.2 The Wa region spans multiple national borders. Magnus Fiskesjö, *Stories from an Ancient Land: Perspectives on Wa History and Culture* (Oxford: Berghahn Books, 2021), figure 0.1 by Nij Tontisirin Anantsuksomsri.

inhabited the Wa States, a territory they claim as their ancestral land, a rugged mountainous area located between the Mekong and the Salween River, with the Nam Hka flowing across it. Most Wa are animists, though a small number practice Buddhism or Christianity. In the 1950s, the Wa received the Marxist designation of "primitive society" because of its economic base in swidden agriculture, perceived matriarchal elements in the society, and the practice of headhunting, outlawed in 1958.[52]

Burao Yilu began writing in 1986 and has since published numerous Sinophone poems and personal essays on environmental and Indigenous themes, some translated into French and English. These include her prize-winning "Four Generations of Wa Women" ("Wazu sidai nüren" 佤族四代女人, 1995), written while studying at the Chinese Academy of Social Sciences in Beijing, and the prose collection, *Pledge to the Sacred Tree: Songs from the Heart of a Wa Woman* (*Shenshu de yueding: Wazu nüren xinzhong de ge* 神树的约定：佤族女人心中的歌, 2010). Her poem "Language of Bauhinia Flower" ("Zijing hua wuyu" 紫荆花悟语, 2018) received a Silver Award for the World Chinese Poetry Contest. Her daughter, Burao Yiling, is an accomplished painter. In her 2002 poem, "Moon Mountain" ("Yueliang shan" 月亮山), Burao Yilu starts with stanzas that immediately highlight Hanspace notions of sexual exoticism in "isolated" (*fengbi*), "remote" (*youyuan*), and "desolate" (*huangliang*) mountains, Mandarin terms typically associated with landscapes inhabited by barbarian others. She also foregrounds headhunting, the most exotic Wa practice (frequently referenced in *Soul Mountain*):

Dancing drunkenly, encircling the edge of moonlight,	围着月亮的边缘醉舞
natural and unrestrained.	一定浑然又自在
Generations of Awa peoples	阿佤人一辈子一辈子
harvesting in isolation and desolation sanguine and remote	收获封闭又荒凉 豁达与悠远
The elders achieved the pinnacle of perfection.	登峰造极的老祖先
The sacrificial object of belief they created was	开创祭祀的信奉物是
a majestic human skull.	一架威严的人头骨
This totem	这图腾
was for the youths who run the night trails,	为奔走夜路的小伙子
enabling them to traverse mountains and hills	翻山越岭不怕蛇毒兽猛
unafraid of deadly serpents or savage beasts.[53]	

In the subsequent passages, Burao Yilu shifts from the exoticizing tone of the opening passages to the prosaic present, claiming the Awa people *enjoy* living in the cool of the Moon Mountain, "chewing betel nut to fend off the sultry monsoons, the frenzied winds." They relish their communal way of life; "the fierce Awa blade used to cut off heads" divides meat between villagers. By embedding Awa rituals in scenes of everyday life, such as the "unconstrained wooden drum dance" and the *moba* divining the future with chicken bones, she normalizes them. The poem ends by focusing on an elderly couple, the woman's "white hair flying / as she washes red grains for beer," the man "bending his bare back / smoking a pipe as he sets a trap." The poet recollects that decades earlier the old woman's betrothed had bit his finger, letting drops of blood fall on her white hemp cloth to "seal their Wa love, the color to never fade." These are long-standing customs that sanctify the ordinary life of normal humans. The poet ends with the line, "Who can say that these people, so in tune with nature, can lack human feeling?"[54]

In his incisive cultural analysis and translation of the poem, Mark Bender notes the contrast between Burao's initial depiction of the Wa as marginal, and later references to the Wa origin myth, *Si Gang Lih*. The myth claims the Wa emerged from the aperture of a cave (see figure 1.3) and "places the Wa at the center of the world, and as the first people on the land."[55] For example, a major drum ritual is held for the *moik krok* ("life force") residing in the drum, thought to represent female genitalia and fertility.[56] Burao refers to the cutting of vines, which recalls, in the primal flood myth, how the culture hero wields a large knife to open a giant gourd, which releases the people and creatures inside: "The Awa, roasting and eating by the bonfires, / eating with such gusto / Each cut slicing the green vines / of their nest / within their mountain lair." "Moon Mountain" ultimately displays the centrality and power of Wa myths, rituals, and folk customs, restoring dignity to a people long denigrated and exoticized.[57]

Burao Yilu is particularly sensitive to the accomplishments of Wa women, as she recounts in "Four Generations of Wa Women," a biographical synopsis of her grandmother, mother, herself, and her daughter. The account makes clear that far from living in a "matriarchal" society, her grandmother and mother had to navigate both patriarchal Wa and Han social norms. Her mountain-dwelling grandmother, daughter of a Wa chief, was not allowed to attend school. Widowed at a young age, she

FIGURE 1.3 Burao Yilu stands near mythical Si Gang Lih cave from which the Wa emerged after the Great Flood, and in front of bamboo aqueducts that irrigate upland fields. Burao Yilu via Mark Bender, "Echoes from *Si Gang Lih:* Burao Yilu's 'Moon Mountain,'" *Asian Highlands Perspectives* 10 (2011): 99–128.

never remarried and raised their children alone, struggling to make a living, farming millet and digging sweet potatoes and taro on mountain slopes. When Burao's mother fell ill, her grandmother sent for her brother to divine the future, and a chicken was killed. In this account, as in many contexts, religion was used to rationalize misogyny: "My great uncle put some Va medicine in a wooden bowl, which he then filled with water. Standing in the center of the grass hut like a shaman, he stirred the water with two fingers and mumbled incantations. Then he said: 'All of this is because the widowed woman has offended the spirits, and she cannot stay.' He wanted my grandmother to take her children and leave. She would have to make a living elsewhere."[58] Her grandmother survived by opening an inn on the main street of a nearby town. In the 1980s, her great-uncle visited her grave and repeatedly kowtowed, expressing regret for uttering the words that harmed his beleaguered sister.

Like her grandmother, Burao's mother was a pioneer in that she broke with Wa tradition by marrying a "Wu" man (a man of Han descent from a nearby mountain village, whose clan was "Wa-icized" by marriage). Several years later, using money she had saved from weaving cloth and embroidering flowers, Burao's mother and young children traveled weeks from the Burma border along mountains and rivers by donkey and bus to join her husband in the provincial capital of Kunming, where he worked as a technocrat. Several years later, when Burao's father was sent to a labor reeducation camp during the Great Leap Forward and her mother was publicly accused of being a counterrevolutionary, her mother responded forcefully:

> As if struck by a stick, Mother suddenly lost her "ethnic minority" temper and stormed into the factory director's office. "Even if my husband comes from a family of counter-revolutionaries," she argued, "I come from a solid, modest family, several of my brothers are military commanders. If a man has violated the law, he alone should bear the consequences. Why should his wife and children take the blame? Is this a Communist Party policy?" What she said was so clear and logical that it won the factory director over.[59]

Burao attributes her mother's successful defense to her clear logic even as she lost her "'ethnic minority' temper," highlighting the prevalent stereotyping of southern ethnic minorities as hot-headed or irascible. Like the "angry Black woman" stereotype in the United States, or what Litzinger calls "the minority . . . as an object of cultural excess,"[60] such labels also delegitimize valid reasons for female anger, reinforcing the status quo. In fact, Burao's mother's rage-fueled action stands out in her biography as an exception to her stoic norm. To defend herself and her children she had to overcome the stigma of being perceived as irrational and impetuous, simply by virtue of being an "ethnic minority."

Burao Yilu wrote "Four Generations of Wa Women" at age forty while engaging in advanced literary studies at the Chinese Academy of Social Sciences. She claimed she had an "anemic knowledge of literature" after a decade of work in a steel plant, and despite her literary accomplishments and acceptance into the Yunnan Chinese Writers Association in 1989, she characterizes her writer life as "itinerant." Many faced such difficulties due to lack of schooling during the Cultural Revolution, though her self-deprecation may also be related to suffering discrimination due to skin color or ethnicity. She recounts that her daughter, Burao Yiling (later a recognized Wa artist) wrote in an elementary school essay that "since I was born with a dark complexion, my classmates have taunted me, calling me 'little Africa! little Africa!'"[61]

Thus, Burao Yilu's 2016 poem, "Mengdong River," while proudly referencing Wa rituals and epics, remains patently realistic about present-day challenges. It opens with "The Mengdong River / flows from the home place, / Carrying with it quietude / And laughter and joy / But not carrying away / Poverty." It references the ancient petroglyphs on the Wa cliffs, "each a world-class masterpiece," and yet, as they gather by the river to celebrate the festival of the Si Gang Lih, "Wa people beat the wooden drum / to address the sky god / Crying out, beseeching the mountains / But evoking no response from them." Despite the fact the Wa receive no divine assistance, they continue their traditions without shame. Countering Han stigmatizing of the Wa as a superstitious people, she continues: "The Wa people play instruments of joy—the calabash reed-pipes—/ And dance before the river, / Invoking no irreverence from their people."

In general, the poem expresses the fortitude of the Wa people: "The river has known tears; / but also strength." It ends by indicating that intimate relations with the river and mountains nurture and strengthen the Wa, even as anthropogenic pressures on the environment intensify:

The worn-out Mengdong River
Churning the storm-battered water wheels;
Making those difficult climbs through
Whatever obstacles in the Wa mountains.
With only simple desires:
Generation by generation they engage with the mountains,
Generation by generation they are within the mountains free

Mengdong River, ah,
Flowing through childhood memories,
And flowing through the Wa mountains, inch by inch,
Utilizing the pure integrity of those mountains
To relieve the Wa people's hunger,
And water the Wa people's hustle,

Witnessing the greening of each and every life,
Growing stronger within the reaches of
The home place's river.[62]

The mountains and rivers of the Wa ethnicity, far from being the remote and harsh wasteland characterized by Hanspace imaginations, are central to the Wa cosmology and sense of home.

The cosmographic sense of place in Burao Yilu's poems resonates with themes within Nuosu Yi poet Bamo Qubumo's "The Origin of Patterns." A poet and folklore scholar born in Liangshan, Sichuan, Bamo Qubumo (b. 1964) obtained her PhD in folklore at Beijing Normal University in 2003. A researcher at the Institute of Ethnic Literature of Chinese Academy of Social Sciences (CASS), she directs the Oral Traditions Research Center there. She has published numerous books, articles and poems and is the co-author of *Mountain Patterns: The Survival of Nuosu Culture in China* (2000). Bamo's strategic centering of the historical prominence, civilizational heritage, and diversity of the Yi Peoples, a population of over eight million with dozens of local subcultures, is one adopted by Tibetan poets as well (see chapter 4). The poem reads, in its entirety:

THE MEANING OF PATTERNS:

1) Sun and the rays of sunlight
2) The twelve terms: the twelve-animal calendar
3) The ten terms: the ten-month solar calendar
4) The eight terms: the eight cardinal directions
5) The four terms: east, south, west, north

SOLILOQUY:

Walking barefoot in the baking son
Do you remember Zhyge Alu—
Seven days calling to the sun, day and night in chaos
Not a leaf on the beach trees
We hear only the sound of melancholy falling

Small, cold hands restlessly
Touch the clear and turgid pneumas

CHORUS:

The twelve animals dancing, sacrificing
Twelve ritual sites established
    Rhythms barely audible
Twelve sacred strips of bamboo like a forest
Ritual bell wagging, quickened tone resounding
    The sacrifices like white silk
We gather like ripples amassing in a wave
Twelve flags of the Nuosu people
Drawing the sun with sacrificial blood
Descendants all of the black tiger

SOLILOQUY:

The murk not yet divided the murk not yet divided
The black tiger cut apart, changing into the myriad beings
of heaven and earth:
    The left eye became the sun,
    The right eye became the moon,
    The whiskers became sunlight
    The white teeth became stars,
    The backbone became highlands.

CHORUS:

The highlands undulate like a baha serpent
Charging forward through the misty swirling Heishui River
The sun a mirror streaming toward the wild lands
    Our tears streaming down like waterfalls
These deep beliefs in the dark of night
Transforming each perilla seed into a glimmering star
Shining upon our ceaseless flourishing

CHORUS:

> Treading barefoot upon thorns
> You must remember those long, hard paths trodden
> By your ancestors[63]

In his interpretation of her poem, Mark Bender states that Bamo utilizes imagery from *Meige*, an epic, major myth in the oral tradition of northern Yunnan "to highlight links that create an eco-mythic genealogy connecting more than eighty subgroups of the Yi separated by migration and history to a common creation event, despite their varied places of inhabitation, folk ways, dialects, differences in foundational myths, and names for themselves."[64] We read of the culture hero Zhige'alu, who shot down six of the seven suns in Yi mythology and was accompanied by the *baha* serpent, a snakelike creature. In the epic, a giant black tiger (black, a positive color in many Southwest Chinese ethnonyms, here symbolizes the Nuosu Yi) is dismembered to become elements of sky and earth. The perilla plant, common throughout Asia, has abundant black seeds used for food and fodder. The poet calls on Yi readers to recall their glorious ancestry as they toil barefoot under the scorching sun.

In the opening stanza of a simpler poem, "Water Lines," Bamo Qubumo elicits an idyllic scene: "Mists rise from the warm springs that bathe the mountain / The riverbed, with glittering gravel / Fans out into the deep valley, cold but serene / Buckwheat grows, minnows hide beneath stones." But later stanzas denote climate duress: "From wild gusts and pelting monsoons / Most all of the men have returned home / Their experiences mostly bleak, distressing. / Muddy, carrying smells of sweat and tobacco. / ... / Though having taken neither prey, nor harvest, nor salt / In exhaustion they return home." This poem, like Tibetan writer Takbum Gyel's "The Illusion of a Day" (see chapter 4), describes events over the course of one day, yet this cycle can stand in for a life span, or generations, or geological eras. The people mourn the survival pressures they face from deforestation, extreme weather events, and dwindling water supplies in the final stanza: "The women welcome them / Beneath the vast and empty skies / Gently soothing them, / With countless silent tears flowing / As if a river flowing."[65]

Like "Water Lines," the poem "Spring Water" (2015) by Nuosu Yi poet and scholar Aku Wuwu (Apkup Vytvy, b. 1964),[66] describes effects of climate change through dwindling resources, although he does so more cynically with lines such as "Spring waters flow into lakes and seas, thanking the world / but the world does not believe it." He writes "Tears are close relatives of mountain springs / Tears that teach are many; / yet tears that cheat people are also many." He continues:

> Have you seen the tears of sacrificed pigs at New Year's?
> Have you seen the tears of sacrificed cows at Torch Festival?
> Have you seen the tears of sacrificed cocks at enemy-cursing rituals?
> Have you seen the tears of rams sacrificed at funeral rites?
> Have you seen the tears of game killed in the hunt?
> —
>
> Have you seen the sweat of work?
> Have you seen the sweat of war?
> Have you seen the sweaty waters of reproduction?
> Have you ever seen the sweat on the brows of dreamers of the age?
> It seems that the bones of spring water are human sweat.
> —
>
> The lifeforce, *gep*, that fell from the sky is spring water;
> The raging fires on earth are also spring water;
> The human lifeforce, *gepfi*, is also spring water.
> The world is a water world.
> The world is a fire world.
>
> In the world of endlessly reproducing beings,
> The mountain god oversees the mountains,
> The house god sits there overseeing the household,
> The god of fortune stands there overseeing the fates of mankind.
> The world's spring water is forever flowing.[67]

Far from romanticizing his own tradition, Aku Wuwu draws attention to the suffering of all sentient beings, including animals sacrificed for Yi rituals such as the August Torch Festival or "enemy-cursing" rituals. At the same time, he implies that humanity's secular distance from the sacred keeps it from caring for the earth as it should ("spring waters ... thank the world ... but the world does not believe it"). In one stanza the poet refers to colored snow, alluding to an episode in the Nuosu Yi epic *Book of Origins* when red snow falls from the sky to reseed life on earth after a period of conflagration caused by too many suns in the sky.[68] According to Yi cosmology, that era of new life was destroyed once more by a great flood, followed by our age. Ultimately the poem conveys the Yi worldview that the cosmic lifeforce or *gep*, represented by spring waters, will never cease. Nonetheless, great destruction may ensue to reestablish balance and humanity's fate is indeterminate.

In his 2016 poem, "Black Bear," Aku Wuwu is even more dire: "History is like a black bear, / for thousands of years, secluded in the mountain ravines, / regardless of day or night, licking, *"shyr, shyr"* its paws." He evokes the *Book of Origins*: "Bears, too, are the offspring of snow." Yet the poem ends abruptly: "Humans capture bear cubs to make profits on the streets; / this era has no bones, there being no dignity."[69] Epic time in the Anthropocene is short: the era is spineless, nature exploited, humanity cheapened. Power ultimately accrues to no one. While Indigenous poetry of the Anthropocene is powerful, it offers no guarantees of human survival.

CHAPTER TWO

Grassland Logic and Desert Carbon Imaginaries in Inner Mongolia

Beijing westerns set in Southwest China's mountains, rivers, and forests, symbolically rehabilitate a neo-Confucian metaphysics of the cosmos by reinvigorating the core with energy from the periphery. By contrast, Indigenous ecopoets such as Aku Wuwu and Burao Yilu center the border as home, conveying understandings of power from animist cosmological perspectives. Inner Mongolian ecofiction illuminates Indigenous knowledge of the grassland and desert ecosystem on the steppes. This occurs at national, global, and cosmological scales, given the proximity of Inner Mongolia Autonomous Region (IMAR) to Beijing, the existence of an independent Mongolian nation, which complicates understandings of the indigenous-environmentalist alliance,[1] and the radical nonattachment inherent in shamanism and Tibetan/Mongolian Buddhism.

Unlike conceptualizations privileging agrarian-based empire in which center and periphery relations remain hierarchical, if dynamic, the "grassland logic" intrinsic to Indigenous Mongol ecoliterature radically equalizes the organic and inorganic entities comprising the cosmos, seeing each as vital to its existence. One way to examine these differences is to compare diverse cosmologies of similar ecosystems. Fiction set in IMAR by three male writers born just prior to the founding of the PRC in 1949 demonstrates complex dynamics between Indigenous and non-Indigenous knowledge and practices, describing environmental practices and perspectives of nomadic pastoralism, hunting, and agrarianism, variously informed by Han, Mongolian, and hybrid cosmologies.

Mongol Indigene and Party member Mandumai 滿都麦 (b. 1947) publishes in Mongolian and Mandarin translation. While his ecofiction is constrained by certain Party norms, it also highlights environmental racism and evokes Buddhist taboos against practices that ravage ecosystems. Philosophically eclectic ecofiction by Mongol-Han Sinophone writer Guo Xuebo 郭雪波 (b. 1948) reveals fault lines in rights discourses that abstract "nature," "Indigeneity," and "ethnicity." Instead, he highlights the violence inherent in agrilogistics. Finally, Beijing political science professor Jiang Rong 姜戎 (b. 1946) combines Han scientific rationalism with Mongolian ecocentrism in his best-selling 2004 novel *Wolf Totem*.

Beijing westerns by former sent-down youth, such as Jiang Rong, often appropriate Indigenous ecological perspectives to energize the center.[2] While *Wolf Totem* is an intriguing novel that transmits scientific knowledge of grassland ecosystems and admiration of nomadic culture, it exoticizes the ethnic other to legitimate extracting its ecological knowledge, just as Beijing's Go West policies instrumentally commodify the lands, resources, and customs of border societies. Ecofiction by Indigenous writers, on the other hand, radically complicates dynamics between Han and non-Han ecological knowledge and practices and the borders created by Hanspace. Guo Xuebo's desert fiction in particular unleashes the possibilities of what Timothy Morton calls "dark ecology" by radically contextualizing the carbon imaginary of the Anthropocene as mere figure.

It is helpful to provide a brief overview of the environmental history of IMAR to contextualize the literary works. IMAR, China's third largest province, is 70 percent grassland. Temperate steppes lie across a plateau confluence of dry alpine rain shadows to the west, and moist ocean winds to the east, with extreme sensitivity to interannual variation in climate and land-usage change.[3] Despite temperate average temperatures, the steppes experience temperature fluctuations of as much as 30 degrees Celsius in a day, combined with harsh winters and punishing summers. For example, in 2001 a steppe winter event caused the worst natural disaster in IMAR recorded history, during which 30 percent of the total herd population died because the forage was impenetrably frozen.[4]

Migration of farmers to the region accelerated in the eighteenth century when the Qing lifted Han migration limits to present-day Inner

Mongolia to mitigate starvation. Although Mongol nomads in the southeast of the region had long practiced "casual cultivation" to supplement their livelihood from foraging and hunting, "Han-style cultivation," as official Manchu documents refer to it, restricted mobility vital to herding populations, creating seriously and potentially irreversible environmental damage to herd areas.[5] Because of recent government policies designed to tackle desertification, which Beijing blames on overgrazing, many herders have been required to relocate to cities and encouraged to seek alternative lifestyles.[6] Today the few pastoralists who remain on the grasslands find their livelihood challenged by stocking limits, mining concerns, infrastructure projects, and land-enclosure fences.[7] Pastoralists are usually non-Han; thus tensions over land use implicate the "nationalities question" (*minzu wenti*). According to environmental historian Ling Zhang, Beijing has historically viewed the northern grasslands as a "green barrier" protecting the capital: its function within an ecological system is to conserve water, act as a wind barrier, and inhibit shifting sand.[8] Pastoralists, however, view their ecosystem more holistically: rather than merely shield the nation's capital against sandstorms, grasslands should sustain multispecies life. Because the PRC does not recognize a historic continuity of ethnic Mongols to confiscated lands and ways of life, many Chinese still refer to the previous Qing territory by its former name of "Outer Mongolia" (Wai Menggu) despite its independence, conceiving it as politically contiguous with "Inner Mongolia" (Nei Menggu).

Historically, Chinese rarely romanticized nomads, instead considering them a barrier to the expansion of civilization; the Great Wall is a symbol of defense against northern barbarian invasion. Yet in the twenty-first century, the PRC has adopted neoliberal strategies similar to those of Brazil and South Africa, safeguarding "indigenous" knowledge from foreigners ("imperialists") by converting it into intellectual property of the indigenous nation-state. Han Chinese that previously viewed Mongols as peripheral to the state now celebrate them as key partners in narratives of the Chinese nation. In the early 2000s, China churned out numerous books and movies celebrating Mongols, especially Genghis Khan, as "The Only Chinese to Defeat the Europeans."[9] In the early 1900s, China also celebrated Mongols in a context of pan-Asian racism, inciting iconoclastic writer Lu Xun's sarcasm: "When I was a kid, I knew that after 'Pangu created the world' China had the Song dynasty, Yuan dynasty, Ming dynasty, and 'Our Great Qing.' At the age of twenty, I then heard that 'our' Genghis Khan conquered Europe, and it was 'our' most glorious era. Only when I reached twenty-five did I learn that 'our' most glorious era was nothing but when the Mongols conquered China and we were slaves."[10] Lu Xun satirizes Chinese selective historiography, and specifically its claims that central Asian Mongols and Manchus ("Our Great Qing") become "Chinese" when it is strategic to incorporate them into the empire. Still, there is no compound nomenclature of "Mongolian Chinese," unlike U.S. designations of Asian American or African American. Although Mongols have full citizenry rights in the PRC (unlike, for example, the *zainichi*, the ethnic Koreans who are permanent residents of Japan), the ethnic Mongolian marker retains an ambiguous status in the Chinese nation-state.

Outer Mongolia declared independence four days prior to the founding of the Republic of China in 1912. Sun Yat-sen, as provisional president, adopted the five-color flag to represent the unity of the "republic of five nationalities" (*wuzu gonghe*): Han, Manchus, Mongolians, Tibetans, and Muslims. He advocated equal relations while stressing assimilation into Han (Hua) culture, inherent in the name *Zhonghua* of the Republic of China (*Zhonghua minguo*). Later, although many Mongols were farmers, the Chinese Communist Party classified them as nomadic pastoralists, using a lower economic designation legitimating class-based paternalism by Han agrarians. Post-Mao Chinese ethnopolitics shifted from evolutionary Marxism to cultural commodification as the entire economy privatized. Twenty-first-century Mongolian culture is interpreted via the pseudo-anthropological notion of "grassland culture," a part of Chinese civilization. In 1998 Mongolia established the International Institute for the Study of Nomadic Civilizations (IISNC) with support from UNESCO. After Chinese academics participated in IISNC projects from 2000 to 2002, Inner Mongolia Academy of Social Sciences launched a Grassland Culture Research Project (GCRP). According to Nasan Bayar, dean of the School of Ethnology and Sociology at Inner Mongolia University:

> One can see this action as a response to international academic projects focusing on nomadic peoples, including those on Mongolian

history and culture. It is a sensitive field for China, because China's Mongolian population is greater than that of Mongolia proper, and China claims that the cultural centre of Mongolia is in China, arguing that the traditional Mongolian writing system, Chinggis Khan's mausoleum, and other forms of Mongolian culture are preserved in China alone.[11]

The first dozen GCRP volumes, published in 2007 and mostly written by ethnic Mongols, provides evidence of culture on lands depicted in ancient Chinese literature as wild, desolate, and barren. Importantly, the authors almost exclusively compare "Grassland Culture" to "Yellow River Culture" and "Central Plain Culture," despite other scholarship associating nomadic culture with Central Asian or Eurasian cultures. Nicola Di Cosmo, for example, concludes that a nomadic steppe culture emerges in the Mongolian Plateau from the sixth through the fourth century BCE with "the appearance of the Scythian-triad assemblage: weapons, horse gear, and objects decorated in animal style."[12]

Not only does GCRP scholarship subtly reinforce Hanspace cosmologies based in narratives of civilizational superiority dating back to the Warring States period, but it also rationalizes contemporary "go West" policies by associating the spirit of grassland culture with that of neoliberal development. As Bayar summarizes, GCRP characterizes grassland culture as exhibiting four qualities: "the spirit of pioneering and forging ahead (*kaita jinqu*), the spirit of freedom and openness (*ziyou kaifang*), the spirit of heroism and optimism (*yingxiong leguaan*), and the spirit of esteeming integrity and justice (*chongxin zhongyi*)."[13] By linking grassland culture with Chinese civilizational values (such as core Confucian values of integrity and justice), researchers imply that grasslanders have the potential to be modernized within the framework of Chinese civilization. Unlike hierarchical cosmologies that blatantly assign lower status to minority cultures via center-periphery, civilized-barbarian, or progressive-backward dichotomies, the GCRP celebrates grassland culture yet views it as static. According to Nasan Bayar, the GCRP

> emphasized the geo-body of the Chinese nation state in order to retain the culture within the bounds of China. *The aim is thus to*

prevent the culture of Inner Mongols from being connected with a nomadic civilization that exceeds the bounds of the Chinese nation. Otherwise, the culture of the Inner Mongols risks being considered as a part of culture or civilization of Mongolia, a part of Buddhist civilization in Huntington's perspective, and thus potentially leading to a "clash of civilizations" between Chinese and Buddhists.[14]

Thus, the GCRP reifies culture to contain Indigenes within the nation state. It defines grassland culture as encompassing the Mongolian Plateau to Xinjiang to the Tibetan Plateau, thus blurring diverse historical, ecological, religious, and linguistic differences among nationalities who were historically hunter-gatherers, slash-and-burn agriculturists, mountain farmers, or pastoralists.

Understanding Indigenous ecologies as ways to acknowledge the impact of the Anthropocene on conceptual frameworks of governance is of great importance, for through this these sorts of examples may be viewed as instances of strategic appropriation of Indigenous ecological knowledge by reifying Indigenous culture in the service of the nation-state. Recognizing that Foucauldian biopolitics inadequately reveal contemporary mechanisms of power, Elizabeth Povinelli suggests that settler late liberalism is governed by geontopower, a mode of power that operates through the regulation of the distinction between life and nonlife and the figures of the desert, the animist, and the virus.[15] Povinelli argues that prior to the era of the Anthropocene the distinction between life and nonlife was thought to matter, but today we are faced with a posthuman conundrum: "It is certainly the case that the statement 'clearly, x humans are more important than y rocks' continues to be made, persuade, stop political discourse. But what interests me . . . is the slight hesitation, the pause, the intake of breath that now can interrupt an immediate assent."[16] The "slight hesitation" comes from both environmentalists and capitalists: environmentalists prioritize the integrity of a mountain ecosystem over locals dependent on the mining economy; operators prioritize mineral extraction over miner safety if cost-benefit analyses favor compensation payouts. Although biopolitics has always been subtended by geology, critical awareness of the Anthropocene makes this transparent.

Indigenous cosmologies illustrate ecology as method because they elude the posthuman crisis posed by geontology. Indigenous writers do not tend to "hesitate" because they readily attribute agency to inorganic mountains, minerals, and sand, informed by belief systems governed by radically non-anthropocentric detachment from human life. While some consider shamanistic beliefs scientifically irrational and even suicidal, critical theory increasingly questions ontological distinctions among biological, geological, and meteorological entities.[17] Given the extreme duress to life in IMAR, it is not surprising that much of IMAR ecofiction, particularly by Indigenous writers, explores Anthropocene themes of nonlife.

MANDUMAI: FROM POLITICALLY CORRECT TO COSMOLOGICALLY BUDDHIST ECOCRITICISM

The Mongolian-language ecoliterature of Indigene Mandumai is a case in point. His stories not only level critiques against Han chauvinism despite constraints of political correctness, but they ultimately convey the radical nonattachment to life that undergirds Buddhist and Shamanistic philosophies. Born in Chifeng in eastern Inner Mongolia, where he herded sheep until publishing his first story in 1971, Mandumai graduated from the Literary Studies Department of Inner Mongolia University in 1983, and currently lives in south-central Inner Mongolia in Ulaanchab. His posts in the Chinese Communist Party and Chinese Writer's Association include vice director of Ulaanchab History and Literature Committee, chair of the Ulaanchab Literary and Art Association, and former chief editor of the now-defunct Mongolian-language journal *Spacious Steppe* (敕勒格尔塔拉杂志 *cheleger tala zazhi*).

The CCP's promotion of grassland culture as an attempt to contain Indigenous culture within Chinese civilization gave rise to the Key Works in Grassland Literature Project. In 2015, the Chinese Writers Association published *Horse, Wolf, Home* (*Junma, Canglang, Guxiang* 骏马·苍狼·故乡), a two-volume collection of fifteen of Mandumai's Mongolian ecostories published in Mandarin translation between 1981 to 2007. In her foreword, Wu Lan, chief editor of the Grassland Literature Project, and then propaganda minister of the IMAR Party Standing Committee, wrote, "more than a creative undertaking for Inner Mongolian literature, the project is a contribution of the grassland to literature."[18] Chinese civilization offers its imprimatur to (previously denigrated) grassland culture, deeming it a worthy contributor to literature. This, notwithstanding the fact that Mandumai had already won multiple Mongolian literary awards throughout his career and that literacy in Inner Mongolia has historically been higher among Mongols than Chinese.

Yet reifying the grasslands in cultural arts to promote national aims is not new. For example, in 1964 IMAR Party Secretary Ulanhu promoted the hugely popular story "Heroic Little Sisters of the Grassland" ("Caoyuan yingxiong xiao jiemei" 草原英雄小姐妹), based on a true event but with strategically altered facts (see figure 2.1). He published it prominently in the leading IMAR Party newspaper, and two weeks later staged it as a Peking Opera by the Inner Mongolia Art Theater. Highly praised by Zhou Enlai, the opera may have inspired the subsequent creation of model operas during the Cultural Revolution.[19] What is new about the twenty-first-century grassland culture initiative is that it does not merely represent nomads as willing participants in the civilizing mission of "the Great ones" (whether a kingdom, an empire, or a nation-state), but it incorporates nomadic culture into the very fabric of agrarian civilization. This calls to mind the grafting metaphor used by Chen Zhen, protagonist of *Wolf Totem*, who states, "There'd be hope for China if our national character could be rebuilt by cutting away the decaying parts of Confucianism and grafting a wolf totem sapling onto it."[20] Similar logics prevailed among nineteenth-century North American eugenicist conservationists: "Not only could Indians provide white Americans with cultural values that were free of civilization's corrupting influence, so this argument ran, but they could also offer an infusion of untainted, primitive blood."[21]

Mandumai's stories, however, introduce cosmological complexities into so-called grassland literature that defy evolutionary or civilizational paradigms, even when they hew closely to Party norms. His 1981 story "Source of Fortune" ("Ruizhao zhiyuan" 瑞兆之源), anthologized in Chinese and Mongolian textbooks, features politically correct themes including the ravages of the Cultural Revolution, kind Mongolian "mothers," and interethnic marital unity between a Mongolian woman and a Han man. Aidebu searches for his lost horses and is aided by long-suffering, widowed Mongolian women from a neighboring village. The

(72) 玉荣支撑起疲劳的身体,靠着山石站住脚,羊群围拢到她的身边来了。她细心地查点羊群的数目。

FIGURE 2.1 Cover and page from a 1970 version of "Heroic Little Sisters of the Grassland." The Mongol sisters are portrayed as selfless shepherds protecting state assets.

story's dramatized message is that all grassland mothers embody the hard-working, honest, compassionate Mongol national character.[22]

Mandumai types Mongols as compassionate Mothers partly out of political exigency: in the post-Mao era, Han male anxiety regarding "masculine" Inner Asians still manifested in culture and realpolitik. For example, Cao Yu's 1978 play *Wang Zhaojun*, awarded China's highest national literary award, emasculates the non-Han male (unlike in ancient versions of the tale). Han consort Wang Zhaojun marries Xiongnu prince Huhanye, who swears to be "a good horse" for the Chinese Emperor, one that "isn't unruly in eating and moving, and [when] on its back, it does not bolt or run amok."[23] Cao Yu may have been influenced by Wang Fuzhi's notorious claim that the difference between Chinese and Manchus is like that between a horse and a man whose natures are distinct even if both are white.[24] Mandumai thus astutely promotes politically correct gender types. Aidebu is easily cowed by Mother Eji. The elderly widow first encounters the young man kneeling to drink from a pond, orders him back on his horse, then demands he follow her, threatening to attack him. He follows meekly, but when she confirms he is not a thief she laughs at him, and he feels mortified. Such comic relief at the expense of the male Mongol likely eases Han anxiety.

Despite capitulating to gender stereotypes, Mandumai still undermines dominant narratives of the "unscientific" or "lazy" nomad destroying the grasslands through overgrazing. The Mongol widows, standing in for the nationality as a whole, protect the grasslands through their Indigenous knowledge. They know lost livestock destroy newly recovered grass, so they rescue livestock at their own expense and lead them to graze elsewhere since the survival of all living beings depends on the health and abundance of grass. The ecological Mother nurturing a female-gendered Nature is a long-standing trope in many societies. Yet as ecofeminist Carolyn Merchant points out, "The image of the earth as a living organism and nurturing mother had served as a cultural constraint restricting the actions of human beings. One does not readily slay a mother, dig into her entrails for gold or mutilate her body."[25] Even in the twenty-first century, nomadic communities in Mongolia continue to promote such ideas. Morton Pedersen's anthropological study of a northern Mongolian pastoral community includes a humorous anecdote of a Mongolian woman, bored with the tired metaphors, who insists on singing something other than "those songs about Mother and Nature that we always sing."[26]

While Mandumai sometimes anthropomorphizes animals similar to Han Chinese ecoliterature such as the *Book of Poetry* (*Shijing*, ca. 1000–600 BCE),[27] Tang dynasty prose parables by Han Yu (768–824) and Liu Zongyuan (773–819), or Xiao Hong's (1911–1942) ecofeminist fiction, he also uses zoomorphism to criticize environmental racism. For example, in "Deep in the Wilds" ("Biye shenchu" 碧野深处, 1985), a hungry mother wolf and cub stalk wounded Najide and a wounded gazelle. Najide equates the plight of the gazelle with that of Mongols. When the (Han-like?) wolf cub lunges, Najide lets out a blood-curdling scream and kills it with his knife. Najide screams again, and the "cowardly" mother wolf runs away. Then, in an almost comic embrace of Deng era neoliberalism, Najide vows to make it home to install his girlfriend's TV antennae, inspired by the wounded gazelle forging ahead for a better life (1:35).

Han cosmologies and didactic literary traditions in Confucianism and Socialism influence the anthropocosmic resonance between humans and animals in Mandumai's fiction.[28] Indeed, most Chinese literary critics interpret his ecofiction via such paradigms.[29] Yet it also criticizes secularism by evoking Lamaist taboos against overhunting gazelles (and metaphorically, Mongols). Party membership notwithstanding, Mandumai incorporates legends and motifs from both Buddhism and shamanism in his fiction. In Mongolian cosmology, the sky (*Tengger*) is father, earth is mother, and each natural element had its own *lus* (spirit master). The devout make offerings and follow rules to coexist with these entities, promoting ecologically sound practices such as limited digging of earth, defiling of rivers, cutting of trees, destroying the roots of grasses, disturbing the nests of birds, or killing of animals. Mongolian Buddhists believe breaking these taboos results in great misfortune to person, family, and community.

The fascinating story "The Four-Eared Wolf and the Hunter" ("Si'er lang yu lieren" 四耳狼与猎人, 1997) cautions against flouting such taboos. Crooked Hand Baladan, who tumbles into a deep ravine when his rifle backfires while shooting a fox, reflects on his life. He and his hunter friends have all incurred disabilities in the process of greedily killing wolves for their pelts and medicinal innards. When his sixth wife (the previous five died in childbirth) releases the wolf cubs he was raising to sell, he viciously beats her. She curses him as a "beast" and leaves with their son (1:203).

The closing scene is ominous. A vulture hovers above the helpless man; it sweeps down to eat the fox he had shot. A pack of male wolves circle menacingly at the top of the ravine. Strangely, a "four-eared" female wolf in heat prohibits the pack from attacking. Baladan recalls how, when one of the wolf cubs had fallen ill, he had rashly grabbed his wife's sewing scissors and sliced through its ears, anxious about losing the 300 yuan. Chunks of blood fell off as the cub's ears healed. Could this be that same wolf his wife had released into the wild? The female wolf tortures the male wolves, and Baladan, with agonized waiting. He knows they restrain their attack only because she is in heat.

Awaiting sure death by famished wolves and vultures circling the ravine, Baladan agonizes over hunters using wolf pelts and hearts for warmth, medicine, vitality. He also repents of his violence against women. His ruminations call to mind the Buddhist doctrine of the dual nature of reality (Sanskrit: *satya*) as he eventually unites "provisional" (*saṁvṛti*) truth with "ultimate" (*paramārtha*) truth. His meditations situate humans in interspecies relationships where death is not a simple ending, but central to the ongoing life of multispecies communities. In his seminal book, *Flight Ways*, Thom Van Dooren describes vultures as liminal creatures, inhabiting a strange space between life and death. Similarly, "The Four-Eared Wolf and the Hunter" conveys how the real and metaphorically dead—through the active presence of decaying bodies (the fox, Baladan's friends, his deceased wives) or the absence of their living participation (his ex-wife)—help to shape the world in which all creatures make their lives.

Mandumai's 1987 story "Old White-Hair" ("Lao Cangtou" 老苍头) also criticizes hunting with unequivocal recourse to Buddhist philosophy. Written in the magical realist style popular with Chinese writers in the 1980s, the parable opens by introducing a venerable old man who ritualistically honors nature by scattering his day's first bowl of milk tea to the "Rich Samsara" (*bayan sangsar*). In their youth, Old White-Hair and his Buddhist teacher had been avid hunters for sport, but one day a long-bearded old man appeared as they were about to shoot a deer drinking at a pond. He warned that continued cruelty toward heavenly beings would end their own lives, but if they would protect the Rich Samsara, the grassland's birds and beasts, then Heaven will not only forgive them, but will also grant blessing and long life. He then disappeared. The Buddhist monk built a temple in the mountains, where he meditated for life. Old White-Hair farmed quietly, proselytizing against hunting, and bringing alms to the monk every few days. One day Old White-Hair goes missing and the villagers find him on the mountain, mutely fasting, but the monk is gone. When the I-narrator returns to feed Old White-Hair, he and the temple have disappeared without a trace. The reader is left to ponder the significance of the story's disappearing characters, reminiscent of Tsagaan Uvgun (T: Tsering Nam Tuk; Ch: *Shoulao* 寿老), Lord of Nature and Bodhisattva of Longevity in Buddhist mythology.

Framed by disappearances at the beginning (a bearded old man) and end (Old White-Hair, the recluse, the temple), the story again evokes the Buddhist doctrine of the dual nature of reality, where "provisional" (*saṁvṛti*) and "ultimate" (*paramārtha*) truth are meant to unite. As Śāntarakṣita (705–762) explains, "If one trains for a long time in the union of the two truths, the stage of acceptance (on the path of joining), which is attuned to primordial wisdom, will arise."[30] "Old White-Hair" illustrates this practice, implying the bodhisattvas (the story's disappearing characters) enact ecological harmony and attain enlightenment by unifying dual truths. Mongolian Buddhism emphasizes the interconnectedness of all elements of nature, in both the visible and invisible worlds. Da Lama Bayambajav of Gandan Monastery in Ulaanbaatar explains this by contrasting organic and internal worlds: "environmental issues and problems in the organic world are due to impurities in the internal or non-organic world. Human greed is unlimited—but the environment is limited—and Buddhist teachings try to regulate this."[31]

Constrained within the narrower confines of political correctness, Mandumai's fiction both censures and enacts anthropocentrism and environmental racism (self-orientalism). Yet such contradictions are precisely those sublimated in his stories by the eventual Buddhist unity of provisional and ultimate truth. His moralistic vignettes aim at enlightening readers to regain ecological balance by cultivating virtues of moderation and inner purity, including compassion toward animals and women. At the same time, they contradict their formal (Party) objectives in their bleak portrayal of irreversible extinction and merciless cruelty.

GUO XUEBO'S ANTI-AGRARIAN ECOCRITICISM

In general, Mandumai's ecoliterature engages the reality of nonlife as karmic retribution for nonorganic impurities within humans. In fact, Baladan predicts that his grandson will have no game to hunt, because his generation had flaunted the ancestral taboos on overhunting. Species extinction is a given. In other instances, such as when Baladan calmly awaits his death, or when Old White Hair actively fasts to hasten his transmutation, it also conveys a radical acceptance of nonlife as inevitable or even desirable. Guo Xuebo's ecofiction includes these themes but extends them far beyond individuals embracing death, or repenting for species extinction, to the eradication of all life, particularly by the figure of the Desert. Both Indigenous writers anticipate, as early as the 1980s, the recent evolution in critical inquiry from posthuman to post-life queries of a post-extinction world.

Guo Xuebo's Shandong ancestors intermarried with Mongos in the Horchin Sandy Lands, stabilized sand dunes spreading from eastern IMAR to western Jilin and Liaoning provinces.[32] He was born in Hure Banner (Kulun Banner 昆仑旗), where he lived alongside Koreans, Manchus, and Hui. In an interview included in *Desert Wolf*, a translation of his fiction, Guo attributes his intimacy with the desert to indelible childhood experience:

> The first thing I saw when I came into this world was sand. The women in my hometown would spread a layer of dry, comfortable sand on the *kang* when they gave birth. That's probably why I have an affinity with sand. I know the desert all too well. When I was a child, I would run naked after hares on the dunes, dig out edible roots and break off thin branches of willow to make a horse whip; I'd cover myself all over with yellow sand and splash in small pools in the low-lying land—childhood is unforgettable.[33]

His Mongolian father, a painter and balladeer, inspired Guo to write, and his ecological knowledge of desert sand, vegetation, and animals pervades his stories. After working as editor in a county broadcasting station, and scriptwriter for a song and dance ensemble, he graduated from the Beijing Central Institute of Drama in 1980 and did research in the Literary Research Institute of Chinese Academy of Social Sciences, specializing in Mongolian history, culture, and literature. Unlike Mandumai, Guo Xuebo chose to write stories in Mandarin to reach a broader audience. After achieving acclaim for his 1980s series of desert ecological works he joined the Chinese Writers Association and to date has published more than thirty works, many of which have been translated into Japanese, French, and English. While it is difficult to summarize such a large corpus of ecological writing, his powerful fiction is poignant, penetrating, even haunting (see figure 2.2).[34]

Guo's earliest stories are particularly noteworthy for their attention to the figure of the desert, and their critique of the carbon imaginary of agrilogistics. As a whole, his literary corpus conveys ambivalence toward agrarianism in terms resonant with Timothy Morton's claim that agrilogistics (logistics governing agrarian, versus nomadic or hunter-gatherer, forms of settlement, civilization, and technology) is responsible for the Anthropocene, because it conceptualizes nature as separate from humans.[35] Morton sees civilization as a desperate long-term collaboration between humans and wheat, rock, and soil: "we turned the region into a desert, and had to move west."[36] This calls to mind the opening paragraph of "The Sand Fox" ("Shahu" 沙狐, 1985), the first story in Guo's desert fiction series. It starts by noting the evolution of the Horchin from grasslands to sandy lands, starting in the Sui and accelerating in the Qing due to agrarian practices.[37] The story then describes the "blind enthusiasm" of Han migrant farmers during the Great Leap Forward (1957–1959), when an army of laborers arrived carrying a banner inscribed "Wrest grain from the desert!" (85; 87). Although settlers from the interior had to immediately relocate after a sandstorm buries them in their tents, they retained their enthusiasm for opening up and cultivating the desert, rationalizing desperation with civilizational willpower.

The story focuses on Sandy, an ex-convict from the interior, and his teen daughter, Willow, who apply for abandoned sand dunes under the new household contract system in 1980. The story's climax comes when two visitors, Old Beardy, forestry center head, and Little Yang, forestry center secretary, insist on visiting his dunes with their rifles. Ostensibly tasked with sand control and afforestation, Sandy knows Old Beardy is

FIGURE 2.2 Mongol author Guo Xuebo. Photo by author, July 2019.

known primarily for drinking and hunting, despite having drawn a paycheck for twenty years. Thus, Sandy fears they will shoot a sand fox with which he has a mutually beneficial relationship. The plants he cultivated on the dunes had initially withered because rats ate the roots. Sandy had set traps and poison, which instead killed his hens. One day the rats disappeared, and Sandy discovered that a sand fox eats three thousand rats per year. Ironically, although Sandy raises Willow to respect all living beings, telling her not to hurt a single blade of grass or insect because "life depends on other life" (86–87; 89), he aggressively poisons rats and "happily slaughters" chickens to treat the visitors. Guo elaborates in gruesome detail: "He did it in a strange way, breaking the chicken's spine first, twisting its head round to tuck under a wing, then dashing it to the ground so that its legs stretched and went stiff" (93; 95).

When the visitors first shoot in the dunes, Sandy does not respond, because he assumes they are shooting his chickens, which he devalues, but when he heard more shots, he jumped as if scalded (like his chickens) (93; 96). Sandy knows the exact number of hares and pheasants in the dunes; after planting the dunes with vegetation, they attracted animals and birds. Willow also feels proprietary, protesting that Beardy and Yang are shooting *our* hares and pheasants (94; 97).

Sandy and Willow's hierarchical ecologic notwithstanding, they see the dunes as an interconnected ecosystem. Beardy and Yang, on the other hand, dualistically bifurcate nature and culture. Yang tells Willow that the hares and pheasants are *wild* (unlike Sandy's chickens). By abstracting some animals as wild, Yang rationalizes their rights to hunt them. Father and daughter have more holistic ecological knowledge than the visitors, yet Sandy, a migrant farmer who treats domesticated animals and agricultural pests with cruelty, also imports agrarian biases into the grasslands, regularly referring to the desert as a demon with which he must wage battle.

In fact, most desertification science written by settlers treats dune sand almost exclusively in the context of environmental hazard. As ethnographer Dee Mack Williams puts it, "at the more sensational extremes, dune sand is even indiscriminately *demonized* as the sure sign of natural (even moral) disorder."[38] Yet based on fieldwork in the Horchin Sandylands, he found that Mongols see dune sand as a necessary and welcome component of the desert-steppe environment. Rather than view sand as a wasteland (*huang* 荒) as Han scientists do, Mongols speak of *huang* as yellow-tinted "living sand," rife with potential, in contrast to white "dead sand," which nonetheless also had utility.[39] In general, he found that Mongol herders appreciated landscape diversity and saw sand as aesthetic pleasing, resilient, and economically useful.

Guo Xuebo frequently uses ecofeminist tropes to critique ignorant ravaging of natural environments. For example, Sandy was willing to partner with a woman that had been "deserted by her husband because he and his mother had condemned her for being barren." However, "this 'barren' woman bore him a daughter and died giving birth to a second child" (86; 88). The daughter, Willow, also faced the effects of sexism. When Sandy feared that Beardy and Yang would shoot some of the wild animals that had made their way to the dunes, Sandy asked his daughter to accompany the men, both on horseback, but she rides a donkey. Soon, the men catch sight of the fox, and run after her. Willow explains to her frustrated father that her donkey couldn't keep up so she was unable to restrain the hunters (95; 98). Here Guo portrays women as being expected to fulfill their duties with fewer resources than are allocated to men. Willow's heartbreak is palpable, as she knows that she has failed to protect the sand fox, also female and vulnerable as she nurses her three cubs. When the hunters approach the fox "instead of running away, she looked with pleading, pitiful eyes at the humans who were the masters of the world" (103; 106). Beardy shoots the fox but immediately becomes bewildered, feeling "insignificant" in the desert, as blood seeps into the sand, a cub still clinging to its mother's teat. Beardy's loneliness and helplessness stems from a lack of connection to other living beings. Guo is clearly denouncing anthropocentric and androcentric views, suggesting that with more humility, Beardy may learn to accept his place in the cosmos by connecting with the desert ecosystem and his fellows.

Guo Xuebo again illustrates how fear is rationalized as civilizational willpower in his award-winning 1996 novella *Sand Rites* (*Da Mohun* 大漠魂, lit. Desert Soul), where two shamans and lovers survive the 1940s to 1980s, only to experience yet another devastating drought. Because high socialism prohibited shamanism, Old Shuangyang had learned to farm. Early in the story he is portrayed as a highly motivated shaman turned settler seeking to survive, against all odds, a harsh environment hardly amenable to farming:

> Awaiting him was a great combat, a great clashing of wills, a knock-down drag-out fight, and he would wrench his livelihood and his reward from her with his blood and sweat. It had always been like this for the peoples of sandy precincts, ever since ancient times. No matter how stingy Heaven and the sandland proved, generation after generation, they had carried on indomitably, ploughing and planting and harvesting, harvesting and ploughing and planting, building up a life for themselves imbued with a distinctively regional purpose and meaning. (29; 139)

Yet his tendency to "organically" link a landscape to the "spirit of a people" can also veer into the type of geographical determinism inherent in Hanspace cosmologies or, at an extreme, can even justify the Nazi doctrine of *Lebensraum*.

In his stories, Guo repeatedly highlights his characters' ahistorical, "naturalized" understandings of their lives by contextualizing their lives within a broader environmental history. By the end of the novella, the female shaman retains her spirituality, while the male shaman is portrayed as brutally misogynistic and cruel to animals, children, and the land. When Old Shuangyang takes an orphan to plant millet in the desert, he kills their dog, which drinks the water; brutally whips their starving bullock; and forces the orphan to walk the plough in place of the bullock. Only after promising to adopt him does the child agree to shoulder the yoke, declaring that he hates his adoptive father as the ploughshare stabs into the sandy soil (49; 171). The story implies violence inheres in fear-based agrarian exploits.

Guo Xuebo also masterfully executes an ecofeminist critique of agrilogistics in the 1996 novella *Sand Burial* (*Shazang* 沙葬), a complex story that features perspectives of sand, nonhuman animals, plant species, Mongols, and Han Chinese as multispecies components of a desert ecosystem. An exiled Han scientist attempts to remediate the ravages of Han agrarian practices adopted by Mongolian pastoralists by creating a green biosphere around a Buddhist temple in the desert. The scientist's viridity model was to plant xibag artemisia and sand willows, yet sand buries him alive while he is trying to draw the root of a Chinese pea shrub. Whether the story conveys anthropocosmic resonance where the cosmos responds to human actions in kind or the perspectivalism of Daoist or shamanistic cosmologies (where one accepts death as "natural"), a similar fate befalls his friend, the lama. During a deadly sandstorm the lama saves a menagerie of desert birds and animals along with humans, ignoring his nephew's pleas to give water and oxygen only to the humans. His Sinicized nephew, a Party officer, believes in Confucian love with distinctions (prioritizing humans), and Mao's mandate that humans must overcome nature, but the Buddhist lama insists on protecting all living creatures. He refuses to exit his sand-battered shelter, allowing the sand to bury him alive.

The title of the novella does not refer only to the sand burial of the "politically incorrect" Han desert plant researcher, forced into labor reeducation, which requires pulling the harrow to gather vegetation for the profligate burning by village Party elites. Nor does it refer only to the suffocation of the "politically incorrect" Mongolian lama, forced to pull the harrow, painfully kneel during public criticism sessions, and give up his beloved wolfdog, all because he was said to be hiding golden religious statues. Nor does it refer to the imminent sandstorm burial of the scientist's "politically correct" but guilt-stricken ex-wife, and the lama's loyal wolfdog. Instead, the Anthropocene suggests human existence is so malignant that life itself faces planetary extinction. This changes the topical foci. The political camps of the Cultural Revolution, the ecological differences between Lamaism and Han rationalism, the distinctions between human and nonhuman animals, pale in comparison to this stark fact. As Povinelli puts it, "increasingly not only can critical theorists not demonstrate the superiority of the human to other forms of life—thus the rise of posthumanist politics and theory—but they also struggle to maintain a difference that makes a difference between all forms of Life and the category of Nonlife."[40]

The indeterminate ending of *Sand Burial* means the birds, humans and nonhuman animals that escape the lama's oxygen-deprived structure during the sandstorm may or may not survive the elements. Yet its message is bleak. Povinelli claims the figure of the desert maintains the distinction between life and nonlife by dramatizing life at threat from the creeping, desiccating sands of nonlife: "The Desert is the space where life was, is not now, but could be if knowledges, techniques, and resources were properly managed . . . the Carbon Imaginary lies at the heart of this figure."[41] Yet *Sand Burial* calls the figure of the desert into question. Admittedly, it indulges the dream of the Carbon Imaginary—the final scene features hard-won expertise contained in hard-won documents transported by the desert researcher's ex-wife, supported by the wolfdog through the sandstorm—the desert refusing to definitively kill her off as a third sand burial. Yet, as in Guo's other works, such figures call attention to themselves *as* figures. The desert ecosystem is described in such utopian ways that it resembles Tao Qian's 陶潜 "Peach Blossom Spring" ("Taohuayuan ji" 桃花源记), an agrarian fantasy that persists in the Han Chinese cultural imagination.[42]

ECOLOGICAL IMPERIALISM AND EUGENICS THOUGHT IN *WOLF TOTEM*

If Mandumai's fiction critiques environmental racism and Guo Xuebo's fiction sublimates dynamics between Indigenous and exogenous knowledge of ecosystems, Jiang Rong's *Wolf Totem* coopts Indigenous knowledge to strengthen the center. The semiautobiographical, best-selling novel won the 2007 Man Asia Literary Prize, has been translated into more than thirty languages (including Cyrillic Mongolian) and has been adapted to film. Set during the Cultural Revolution, it ostensibly criticizes Han insensitivity to ecological, religious, and cultural diversity, implying that ignorance of the fragile ecosystem of the steppe destroys it. Yet detractors have denounced the work as didactic and even fascist. Like his novel, Jiang Rong's past is mysterious and controversial. His father, a doctor of Chinese medicine, was denounced as a "black gang capitalist-roader" and beaten to near-death during the Cultural Revolution. His mother worked with the Communist Party underground. Jiang was a Red Guard at Beijing Art Academy middle school before shepherding in IMAR. Imprisoned in 1970 for criticizing Lin Biao, his death sentence was commuted. He was active in the 1978 Beijing Spring, was imprisoned after the 1989 Tiananmen Square protests, and then taught political science in Beijing.[43]

The novel follows the exploits of Chen Zhen and Yang Ke, two sent-down youth from Beijing who develop a deep appreciation of Mongolian culture during their decade-long stay with the nomads. Old Bilgee, his daughter-in-law, and grandson embody qualities they most admire: experiential knowledge of the grassland ecosystem, courage, and resilience. The major themes center on ethnic difference between Han agrarian and Mongolian grassland philosophy: Han Chinese are "sheep-like" while Mongols are "wolf-like;" Han are secular materialists while Mongolian Lamaists revere Tengger; Han are scientific materialists while Mongols are holistic, if superstitious.[44]

The novel has been critiqued for its eugenicist views, reinforced by chapter epigraphs (in the Chinese version) offering historical "evidence" of the Mongolian racial character.[45] To be a Mongol, Chen Zhen tells Yang Ke, "All you need is an infusion of wolf blood. Hybrids are always superior creatures."[46] The Han are said to "meekly submit" to a "Dragon King" (versus a Wolf Totem) (23; 33) and greedily kill wolves, dogs, gazelles, marmots, and swans. *Wolf Totem* seemingly criticizes the Han as weak, narrow-minded, cruel, and ignorant. Yet it also attributes the historical agency of Genghis Khan and the Mongols to their wolf mentors (36; 57).

Many Mongol scholars are outraged at the novel's primary trope, the wolf totem, saying that nomads are more likely to shoot wolves than worship them. In contrast, Mandumai pointedly identifies the ovoo (Mn. *oboo*; Ch. *aobao* 敖包) as the Mongolian totem in a 2013 book of essays on Mongol ecological civilization (see figure 2.3).[47] Guo Xuebo criticized *Wolf Totem* after its 2015 adaptation to film (see figure 2.4):

> Wolves have never been a Mongolian totem, the Mongolian nationality has absolutely no historical records of this! This is a false Mongolian cultural framing by a Han sent-down youth who only lived on the grasslands for three years. Mongols initially believed in Shamanism and later in Buddhism. Wolves were considered the natural enemies of Mongols. Wolves don't exhibit "team spirit." They are selfish, greedy, ruthless, and cruel. To preach "wolf spirit" is anti-human, Fascist thought. We reserve the right to resort to the law to defend our ancestors and national culture.[48]

FIGURE 2.3 A sacred ovoo on the Inner Mongolian Grasslands. Photo by author, July 2019.

FIGURE 2.4 Mongol author Guo Xuebo's Weibo post critiquing the 2015 film *Wolf Totem*.

Guo's critique is valid. Jiang juxtaposes accepted Han cultural tropes against fabricated ones, notably Yellow River aphorisms by "the Chinese race" and reverence for the wolf totem by "grasslanders":

> After thousands of years, during which unknown numbers of minor races had died out or were violently displaced, the grasslanders would never question their predatory totem, which would remain their sole icon even after killing seventy or eighty fine horses. Chen was reminded of the sayings "The Yellow River causes a hundred calamities but enriches all it touches;" "When the Yellow River overflows its banks, the people become fish and turtles;" "The Yellow River—cradle of the Chinese race." The Chinese would never deny that the Yellow River was the cradle of the Chinese race or that it was crucial to the survival and development of their race even if it sometimes overflows its banks and swallows up acres of cropland and thousands of lives. The grasslanders' wolf totem deserved to be revered in the same manner. (57; 90–91)

This false equivalency is problematic on several counts. First, a majority writer manipulates historical fact about a minority nationality while the narrative voice presents it as factual: the power differential makes false narratives difficult to contest once propagated in the popular imagination. Second, it both praises and denigrates minority culture as other-than-human hybrid. Finally, the "wolf totem" rationalizes the suffering of Indigenes in IMAR due to state development, just as the state has long evoked the "Yellow River totem" to normalize the suffering of Chinese peasants. Such evolutionary musings rationalize the annihilation of Mongolian culture in much the same way that white Americans adopted eugenics ideas to romanticize the diminishing populations of Native Americans.[49]

The novel attributes desertification to Han agrarian logic, but the grasslands and Mongolian customs become decimated nonetheless, and Old Bilgee's folk wisdom is nostalgically conveyed as inadequate to a scientific era. Indigenous knowledge is instead coopted by Han rationality. Chen Zhen coins the term "grassland logic" (which "intrigues" his Mongol friend) as a hybrid between Mongol ecocentrism and Han science.[50] In fact, the novel's central question is how to save the Han

Empire. Halfway through the novel Chen Zhen asks what will happen to Beijing if desertification occurs north of the Great Wall (164; 258). The apocalyptic epilogue, set in 2002, declares that 80 percent of the Olonbulag pastureland is desert and that China's imperial city is a hazy city of yellow sand (408; 524).

In a Confucian metaphysical cosmology, the solution to a weak center is to energize it from the periphery.[51] As IMAR scholar Nasan Bayar quips, "one Inner Mongolian told me once after reading *Wolf Totem* he realized that the Mongolians had become Viagra for the Chinese!"[52] This raises the question of whether *Wolf Totem*, as Sinologist Wolfgang Kubin has argued, is a fascist novel.[53] In 2017, I conducted a series of interviews with five Inner Mongolian academics who each received their doctorates at prestigious universities in England, Japan, and Taiwan and who specialize in Mongolian sociology, religion, and literature. I asked them about their understanding of the novel, and specifically its nationalist implications. A sociologist said that *Wolf Totem* promotes Chinese nationalism by encouraging more "wolf-like" Mongol aggressiveness. He compared the novel to the 1980s TV drama *River Elegy* (*Heshang* 河殇), which he said claims that Chinese civilization is too modest and insular but should instead expand outward, like colonizing Westerners.[54] A Taiwanese postdoctoral student commented on the novel's gender politics, claiming only the elder, Bilgee, and his daughter-in-law, Gasmai, as heroic, while the young Mongolian men were less impressive.[55] A social work professor liked the novel, seeing it as cathartic for a traumatized author witnessing desertification of the cherished landscape of his youth, even if his understanding of Mongol culture was inauthentic.[56] Another social work professor claimed it was an Orientalist exaggeration of Mongol ecoconsciousness: "Why was *Wolf Totem* so famous? It was a Han writer writing about Mongolian culture for a Han audience ... It emphasized the need for the Han race to strengthen itself and expand outward, to use wolf spirit to overcome domestic and international relations. I felt both proud and very embarrassed."[57] While individual opinions of the novel differed, the consensus was that although the novel raises awareness of ecologically responsible Mongolian practices, it ultimately denigrates the culture as inadequate to facing the challenges of the twenty-first century. The Han Chinese, with their scientific rationalism, must adapt Mongolian "grassland logic" to effective ecological solutions and

FIGURE 2.5 Red tourism: Bingtuan construction corps set for the 2015 film *Wolf Totem*. "Celebrate the 70th Anniversary of the Founding of Inner Mongolia Autonomous Region." "Garrison to Construct, Cultivate, and Protect the Border." Photo by author, July 2017.

infuse Mongolian "wolf-like spirit" into developmental agendas informed by eugenics thought (see figure 2.5).

THE LOGIC OF RESOURCE EXTRACTION IN *MONGOLIYA*

Mongolian nomads may be celebrated in films and narratives of the Chinese nation, but their sacred sites are not honored, and their land rights are minimal. Indigenes are elevated to accomplish other aims, such as energizing state nationalism by incorporating peripheral areas into the Chinese nation. In this sense, Jiang Rong's econovel is a Beijing western that maps Hanspace cosmologies onto exotic peripheries to rationalize development and inspire Han nationalism based on so-called ecological civilization (*shengtai wenming* 生态文明). One of twelve provinces slated in 2000 for western development (*xibu dakaifa* 西部大开发), IMAR has become a site of bioprospecting and mining on unprecedented scales. Chinese researchers understood the severity of IMAR desertification but insisted on implementing "environmentally friendly production" (*huanbao shengchan* 环保生产) throughout the province.[58]

Such absorption of the "Indigenous-environmentalist" alliance into the nation-state is occurring on a global scale. Geontopower manifests as governments worldwide safeguard what they deem to be *their* indigenous knowledge by guarding against biopiracy and bioprospecting from outsiders. Whereas previously Brazil's nationalists viewed Amazonia's Indigenous populations as suspicious outsiders, now they are increasingly included in the Brazilian nation and identified as strategic partners in efforts to regulate bioprospecting in the national interest.[59] In 2009, Bolivia approved a constitution that extends rights not only to Indigenes but also to the Earth, and "in seeking to reappropriate control of the nation's resources from foreign corporations, has itself come into conflict with the communities it originally empowered."[60]

The calculus of "humans versus rocks" is increasingly indeterminate. For example, in 2011 a truck ran over a herding activist, Mergen, while he attempted to block a coal transport caravan trespassing on IMAR pastureland. Infuriated, cyberactivists called for May 10 to be declared "Herders Rights Day."[61] The government publicly denounces such atrocities but fails to act. Instead, intensified censorship since Xi Jinping's appointment as president and general secretary of the CCP in 2012 has significantly curbed protests. Zhao Liang 赵亮 only managed to produce his apocalyptic environmental film *Behemoth* (*Beixi moshou* 悲兮魔兽, 2015) in IMAR through what he calls guerrilla filmmaking. The film depicts once thriving grasslands ravaged due to intensive coal mining, with miners dying of black lung disease, the most prevalent occupational disease in China. Zhao claims he had to film surreptitiously: "These coal mine owners are so rich you can't bribe them to solve your problems."[62] *Behemoth* cannot be screened in the PRC (see figure 2.6).

While agrilogistics prevails at present, writers such as Guo Xuebo powerfully unleash the possibilities of dark ecology by conveying indigenous knowledge that acknowledges the carbon imaginary of the desert *as* mere figure. Guo's desert fiction exposes fault lines in the Indigene-environmental alliance based on "rights" discourses that abstract "nature" or "indigeneity" or "ethnicity." Instead, he foregrounded violence inherent in agrilogistics. Like *Behemoth*, Guo Xuebo's most recent novel, *Mongoliya* (*Menggu liya* 蒙古里亚, 2014), attempts to broach taboo

FIGURE 2.6 A displaced Mongol family passes a coal mine in Inner Mongolia. Still from the 2015 film *Behemoth*. Courtesy INA.

subjects such as the exploitation of pasturelands by ruthless coal mining firms, and self-immolation among ethnic minorities to protest policies aimed at acculturation. Bruce Humes suggests it is only because of its carnivalesque tone that the novel avoided censorship.[63]

Moŋgoliya comprises three distinct but intertwined narratives. The first is a semiautobiographical spiritual journey in which the narrator seeks his shamanic roots, long obscured in post-1949, officially atheist China. The second are stories of the Danish adventurer Henning Haslund-Christensen (1896–1948), based on vignettes recounted in his real-life anthropological masterpiece, *Men and Gods in Mongolia*. The third recounts the struggles of Teelee ("Idiot") Yesu, a Mongol herdsman battling desertification and the machinations of a coal mining company seeking to occupy his pasturelands. The three strands of this elaborate historical novel converge, quite literally, on the body of the "idiot," a savant with savior-like qualities.

Framed by the I-narrator's spiritual quest for shamanic spirits, the novel opens with "Guo," a renowned Beijing author, visiting an ancient cairn said to be a shaman's altar, at the summit of Mount Gahai near his home village in Inner Mongolia.[64] There his diseased great-uncle, an acclaimed balladeer and shamanic healer whose life spanned the late Qing dynasty to Manchukuo,[65] appears to Guo in a dream and tasks him with the mission of protecting Yesu, a herdsman. The novel later reveals that Yesu is the balladeer's grandson, and that Haslund, who

96 *Grassland Logic and Desert Carbon Imaginaries*

strongly identified with Mongol culture and was an avid musicologist, was instrumental in rescuing the balladeer from the dungeon of a ballad-loving Mongol prince. The novel implies that because Guo has inherited his family's shamanic powers, transmitted by his grandmother and mother, he must bear witness to his cousin's plight.[66] In this way, the narrative recounts the fate of the Mongols at various periods, evoking the thirteenth-century epic *The Secret History of the Mongols* and Haslund's encounters with shamans and "living Buddhas" as threads weaving the numinous soul of the great Genghis Khan to that of his humble Mongol descendent, Yesu.

The twenty-first-century enemy of Mongol culture and land is a coal mining company, which enriches local officials while destroying the water, air, and land quality vital to local herdsmen and farmers. Yesu lives with an amnesiac pregnant and widowed Han woman, whom he had rescued in his pasture. The kind-hearted herdsman attempts to support her yet battles huge coal transport trucks that bypass tolls on paved highways by barreling through his fenced-in pastureland, uprooting sparse vegetation, and killing his livestock. Midway through the novel a dramatic scene unfolds where Yesu drops carcasses of dead sheep, hit by yet another coal truck, in the office of the mining company executives. When they refuse to compensate him, he climbs a tall building, threatening to douse himself with gasoline and set himself on fire. When nervous mine owners grudgingly produce the cash, Yesu climbs down, only to be hauled away to the Banner detention center. Although Yesu admitted he was bluffing and that his bucket contained only water, by the time the narrator visits his incarcerated cousin, Yesu is a reluctant celebrity. Journalists rush to interview him, which in turn attracts officials aimed at spin control, and successive nights of sleep deprivation exhaust him.

The novel satirizes self-serving media hype over Yesu's plight, and caricatures government spin in successive nightly "investigation and clarification" interrogation sessions. The darkest comic scene features an intelligence officer's foiled attempt to determine which western cleric (Tibetan Buddhist "separatist" or Uyghur Muslim "terrorist") influenced Yesu.[67] Yet it is not as religious devotee but prophetic savior that the simple-minded village idiot emerges as a larger-than-life character in the novel. While it initially seems comic that the pregnant Han woman calls him "Brother Jesus,"[68] mispronouncing his Mongolian name as "Yuesu" (Jesus) in Mandarin Chinese, he comes to exemplify a sacrificial lamb, savior, and eternal life, his life cut short just as he comes into his own.

In the penultimate scene of the novel, Yesu, one of the few villagers who had not abandoned pastoralism for farming, recovers a rudimentary understanding of his cultural roots by replacing his mud hut with a Mongolian yurt to house his new family. After the birth of the Han woman's child, the thirty-year-old virgin (Yesu) finally consummated his relationship with her, and she is now pregnant with his son. Guo (an expert on Mongol culture) is napping in the yurt, having educated his cousin on its ecologically sustainable design. Suddenly a coal truck breaks through the steel fencing, again barreling toward Yesu's sheep. Refusing to cower, he bolts directly into the path of the oncoming truck, waving his hands and shouting at it to stop. Instead, the driver accelerates and decimates Yesu, arms and legs akimbo, "like Jesus" on the cross (357). The annihilation of the antihero in the farcically titled *Moŋgoliya* (a misspelled homonym for *Mongolia* in Chinese) is witnessed by his cousin-shaman, awakened by screams of "Brother Jesus!"[69] The narrator lyrically aestheticizes the gruesome scene of Yesu's body torn into bits and pieces, spit out by the tenaciously turning tires, splattering blood, flesh, and bone shards in a fifty-meter path that stains the grassland. Shocked out of her amnesia, the Han woman screams the name of the driver, recognizing one of the men who had gang-raped her after she refused the out-of-court settlement to compensate for her migrant husband's asphyxiation in the mines.

The apocalyptic ending of *Moŋgoliya* is abrupt and senseless, implying that no form of life will escape the catastrophic logic of resource-extraction capitalism that eradicates humanity. The ravaged land and bodies in the novel accurately depict real-life events. Even prior to such callous violence, scholars have attributed violations of land and limb in IMAR to poverty-inducing enclosure policies that "graze the body."[70] Yet the chilling epilogue to the novel is titled "Please Drink Tea," a euphemism for being treated to a "little talk" by Chinese security officers. A phone caller invites Guo to tea, warning him that a viral photo depicting protestors of Yesu's death was traced to his computer. Still, the postscript begins and ends with Guo sensing the live presence of Yesu's spirit. Despite its Kafkaesque ending, the novel repeatedly expresses the shamanistic belief that an entire people can reincarnate, that their souls cannot be destroyed.

Guo's ecofiction over four decades consistently conveys the philosophical sense that in the era of the Anthropocene, organized religion and scientific positivism are impotent. While his fiction suggests human existence may result in planetary extinction, he also conveys shamanistic ontologies that link *geos* and *bios*. In his anthropological study of shamanism in northern Mongolia, Pedersen explains that shamanic spirits "exist as actual things in the landscape, as virtual hypersurfaces made visible by the design of certain sacred artifacts, and on the transcendental plane of *tengger*" (sky, heaven).[71] As an "ontology of transition,"[72] shamanism differs from the naturalism that dominates imperial cosmologies, destabilizing the ontology and hero-worship that rationalizes empire.

Indigenous writers from Inner Mongolia tend to acknowledge the fact that, in a post-extinction world, distinctions between life and nonlife no longer matter in regimes governed by geontopower. Mandumai's dialectical Buddhism purifies humanity by transmuting it in the face of impending annihilation for ecological sins. Guo Xuebo's radical ecocritique favors no one, but his dark ecology suggests a possible upside: the Anthropocene has a way of leveling distinctions. Jiang Rong's agrarian ontology of biopower, on the other hand, maintains the civilizational illusion that if farmers enervated China into the sick man of Asia, grafting the wolf-nomad onto the national body can revitalize it by bordering, bioprospecting, and consuming its diverse nationalities, lands, resources, and customs.

CHAPTER THREE

Sacred Routes and Dark Humor in Grounded Xinjiang

> We have forgotten something that was originally in our bodies. We have forgotten that fragrant smell of mud, the kind that makes you close your eyes to relish it, that emanates after a rain, from grass, fields, and the mud walls in front of one's home.
>
> —YERKESH HULMANBEK, *ETERNAL LAMB*

Xinjiang Uyghur Autonomous Region (XUAR), in northwestern China, comprises one-sixth of the PRC, is approximately the size of Iran, and is home to thirteen official minorities. I first visited Xinjiang in 2012 for a conference on regional literature in Shihezi, a city of 333,000, known to the Han Chinese as "a shining pearl in the Gobi Desert."[1] Built by the Xinjiang Production and Construction Corp (*bingtuan*) in 1954 and said to have more trees per acre than any other city in China, Shihezi is located in the northern foothills of the Tianshan Mountains in the southern edge of the Junggar Basin (Dzungarian Basin). The Tianshan divide Xinjiang into two geographically, historically, and ethnically distinct regions: Dzungaria to the north and the Tarim Basin (Altishahr) to the south, prior to its unification as Xinjiang Province in 1884 (see figure 3.1). At the time of the Qing conquest in 1759, steppe-dwelling, nomadic Tibetan Buddhist Dzungar peoples inhabited Dzungaria, while sedentary, oasis-dwelling, Turkic-speaking Muslim farmers, now known as Uyghurs, inhabited the Tarim Basin, home to the Taklamakan Desert. Today the dominant pastoralists in Xinjiang are Kazakhs and Kyrgyz, while most farmers are Han, Uyghur, and Hui. After the conference I traveled south to interview writers and visit sacred shrines, local markets, ecological

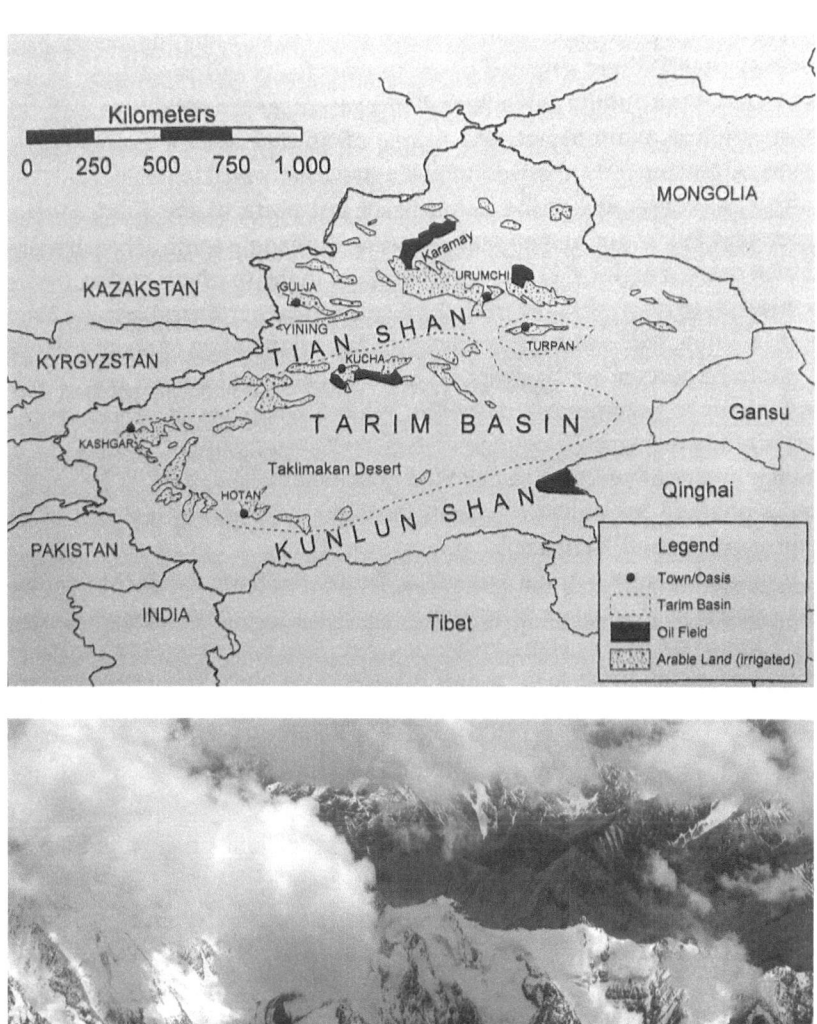

FIGURE 3.1 The Tianshan range divides Xinjiang into north (Dzungaria) and south (Altishahr) (top) S. Frederick Starr, ed., *Xinjiang: China's Muslim Borderland* (London: Routledge, 2004), 265; (bottom) photo by author, July 2012.

sites, and bookstores in Ürümchi and Kashgar. I also traveled the Karakoram Highway to the Pakistani border, where herders still lived in yurts along the mountain passes. By 2017, however, such access to local intellectuals and sacred sites was highly restricted. Even doctoral students from Inner Mongolia who had done years of field research among ethnic minorities in Xinjiang found their projects sharply curtailed, partially because they would endanger their research subjects.[2]

In contrast to the highly abstracted landscapes in Beijing westerns, stories that symbolically rehabilitate a neo-Confucian metaphysics of the cosmos, Xinjiang literary culture is particularly sensitive to the earth, nonhuman animals, and experiences of the sentient body. Relations between humans and their environments are frequently characterized by dark humor, with poignant contrasts between urban and rural ecologies. While deeply connected to the land, a dominant motif in much of Xinjiang ecoliterature is *mobility*. In the south, Altishahr peoples moved for centuries along routes of sacred pilgrimage through desert landscapes, inculcating intimate regional knowledge. Similarly, mobile Kazakh and Kirghiz pastoralists in the northern grasslands of Xinjiang regularly traverse mountains, rivers, lakes, and rock formations that mark their seasonal moves between winter and summer encampments. Thus, much of Xinjiang ecoliterature manifests tensions between an embodied heritage of mobility in conflict with settler colonial policies of state-planned urbanization or farming settlements. Like Mongol and Tibetan writers, Indigenous Kazakh and Uyghur writers employ absurdist comedy to address identity-eradicating transformations. Humor expressed by Han ecowriters in Xinjiang (whether long-term sojourners or lifelong residents) is somewhat lighter, expressing a fatalistic acceptance of ecological civilization state policies as inevitable.

The essays and fiction of two female Kazakh writers, Nurila Qizihan and Yerkesh Hulmanbek, express Indigenous knowledge of the northern grasslands in Altay, while two male Uyghur writers, Memtimin Hoshur and Perhat Tursun, examine urban ecology in their absurdist fiction. Indigenous prose from Xinjiang details local ecologies and expresses parity between humans and animals, while Indigenous fiction presents humans as either fully merging with, or utterly dissociated from, their ecosystems. Three Han writers deliver lyrical prose to readers: there are Shen Wei's taxonomy of southern Xinjiang's history, geography, plants, animals, landscapes, products, and arts; Li Juan's humorous accounts of her mother's and grandmother's attempts to survive as settlers among Kazakhs in northern Xinjiang; and Liu Liangcheng's musings on his home village in eastern Xinjiang. These writers represent but a small subset of the rich literary and linguistic culture of the region. Some Indigenous writers (Qizihan, Tursun, Hoshur) write in their native languages, which I read in English or Mandarin translation, while others (Hulmanbek) write primarily in Chinese. Han sojourners in Xinjiang (Li Juan, Shen Wei) both express appreciation of their adopted culture, yet express varying degrees of awareness of their positionality as outsiders. While Li Juan actively works to disrupt settler colonial assumptions of the "other," all three Han writers naturalize the disappearance of rural life and Indigenous cultural practices as evolutionarily determined.

INDIGENOUS KAZAKH KNOWLEDGE OF NORTHERN XINJIANG'S ALTAY GRASSLANDS

Human/Animal Relations in Nurila Qizihan's Hunter's Stories

Mobile pastoralists and their political organizations have long managed and shaped the steppe ecology that extends from Inner Mongolia to northwest Xinjiang and into the Tibetan Plateau in ways that have enhanced biodiversity. Those systems are currently under duress, as highlighted in the Inner Mongolia Autonomous Region (IMAR) novels *Wolf Totem* and *Moŋgoliya*, although herders and hunters have historically sustained resilient environments based on low density, mobility, and flexibility. They let the grassland lie fallow by taking customary seasonal migration routes, enabling diverse types of grass to spread through animal consumption and waste. According to Guldana Salimjan, a Kazakh scholar from Xinjiang, over the past seven decades the Communist Party has radically altered the ecology of northwest Xinjiang: "the state's programmatic modernization of the pastoral economy intervened heavily in the region's ecology and lifeways by introducing cattle breeds that were more suitable for fenced animal husbandry or ranching, killing-off of masses of predatory animals, and widescale monocropping on grasslands."[3]

Nurila Qizihan (b. 1951) is a Kazakh essayist, poet, and folklorist from a small village in northwest XUAR, where she serves as vice president of the Writer's Federation in Altay District of Ili Kazakh Autonomous Prefecture. She has worked as a government clerk, hospital accountant, and has published many anthologies since 1979, including *Mother's Songs* (Ana jiri), *The Light of the Northern Star* (Soltustik uyek jarqili), *The Sound of Awil* (Awil awenderi), *The Fragments of Aspiration* (Qyal qyindilar), and *The Fragrance of Happiness* (Baqitting ysi). Her 2014 anthology *Kazakh Hunting Cultures* (Qazaqting sayashiliq madenyeti) is based on field research among former hunters. Set during the collectivization era under Maoism (1953–1980), Qizihan's essays recall a period when "state power infiltrated Kazakh social space and appeared in institutions like 'pastoral production cooperation communes,' marginalizing local chieftains and clan leaders, disrupting Indigenous mobile pastoral social administration on the steppe."[4]

Qizihan published *Hunter's Stories* (Angshiliq Hykayalari) in 2009 to commemorate her hunter father, Qizihan Ahman (b. 1921), whom she accompanied herding and hunting as a girl. Her grandfather, Ahman, and great-grandfather, Ozenbayev, were also hunters. When her father was born, the Qizihan family pasture spanned the Republic of China and the Soviet Union, but when the border was demarcated, they lost their winter pasture on the Soviet side. Qizihan Ahman worked for his commune as a designated hunter from 1959 until hunting was banned under the Wild Animal Protection Law of China in 1988.[5]

Qizihan's "A Houseful of Birds" recollects her return home in 1967 at age sixteen to the winter encampment after working for a year in the Women's Federation in the city of Altay. She was shocked to find two eagles, one falcon, one peregrine, a white-headed vulture, and two crows, alongside two wounded hunting dogs, sharing the tiny residence of their two-room mud-brick house, a typical lodging for a herder. Although these were temporary houses assigned annually by local cadres, her family maintained a tidy lodging, even when shared with animals. During this visit home, having been acculturated to her "hygienic" urban life, Nurila wrinkled her nose and questioned the family on their living arrangements. Her father responded quietly, "What else could this be? My child, are you new to this now? These Altay eagles are called *aq-yiq*."[6] Here her father conveys his knowledge of local mountain eagles and ecosystems. In Kazakh there are more than forty names for eagles, based on their physical characteristics and place of origin. For example, Altay mountain eagles are called *aq-yiq* ("white shoulders") because of the white feathers on their wings, Ural mountain eagles *zor-tabin* ("huge talons"), Khovd regional eagles *qarager* ("dark brown feathers"), Ili regional eagles *quwzghinmurti* for the whiskers alongside their beaks, and Sawur mountain eagles *sarabaq salasi* for their longer leg feathers.[7]

In her account, Qizihan subtly conveys the tension she experienced between her newly forming identity as a radicalized, newly urbanized Maoist youth, and her family's pride in retaining the legacy of their hunter Kazakh heritage. In contrast to the "sent-down youth" narrator of *The King of Trees* (see chapter 1), who also expresses ambivalence about the tension between Maoist will to power and Indigenous ecological wisdom, Qizihan's account is far less abstract, metaphysical, and impersonal. She directly transmits personal knowledge about each creature, including the two hunting dogs, named Tuyghin and Ushar, which had been badly injured during a hunt. The story ends with her recounting her father's deep understanding of Kazakh relations with animals: "The vulture is wounded in its shoulder and cannot fly now. I will free it when it gets better. I was commissioned by some people to capture the peregrine and falcon. Dungan people love falcons, they train them to catch rabbits. Hunting with peregrines is a great pleasure too, when it's trained, we can hunt geese and ducks with it."[8]

In this account, rural Kazakhs dwell in the same abode as birds and animals, nurturing them, befriending them, training them, hunting them. They are habituated to smells that assault the now sedentary urban author's senses. Unlike Beijing westerns, where neo-Confucian synthesis metaphysically mediates the relation between humans and (ethnic, animal) others, Kazakh writers tend to focus on the lack of physical and epistemological distance between *Homo sapiens* and other species. Kazakh understandings of relations with animals also differ from the Mongolian Buddhist relations expressed in Guo Xuebo's novella *Sand Burial*, where a Lama protects a menagerie of birds and animals in his shelter during a sandstorm (see chapter 2). The Lama expresses equanimity toward all beings because of his belief in reincarnation and karma, while the Central Asian shamanism informing Kazakh rural culture does not advocate vegetarianism nor prohibit the killing of sentient creatures. Human/animal relations are further interpolated among Kazakhs via Islamic ecological theory, which views humans as responsible to other animals in the sense that humans are more *accountable* as recipients of Allah's revelation.[9] Qizihan's father takes responsibility for nursing the vulture back to health before releasing it to freedom while having no qualms about training the peregrine and falcon to help hunt for geese, ducks, and rabbits. Since the vulture cannot be trained, the human should nurture its freedom given that birds can do that which is difficult for humans, worship Allah naturally, *sunan*: "Have you not seen that Allah is glorified by whatever is in the heavens and the earth, and by the birds in flight. He knows the prayer of each and its glorification. Allah knows well what they do" (Q 24:41). Humans, however, in Islamic civilizational understandings, must worship ritually, *tasbih*.

Further, just as *Desert Burial* features hybrid cosmologies in post-Mao Inner Mongolia, Kazakh ecoliterature illustrates the intersecting cosmologies in northwest Xinjiang, where Han Chinese have migrated from the interior and nomadic Kazakhs were urbanized or made sedentary herders for nation-building purposes. In Qizihan's "We have Surpassed the Bears," based on a true story from 2005, Sinocentric perspectives on animal/human relations influence both the urban author and the urban Kazakh team leaders in the story. During Xinjiang's collectivization period, Maoist officials viewed bears and wolves as pests, and a national program from 1956 to 1967 mandated their elimination in order to enhance agricultural production.[10] As in *Wolf Totem* (see chapter 2), Indigenous peoples were politically mobilized to eradicate predator animals to protect livestock, acting counter to their ecological knowledge in order to achieve the production quotas required by the Communist Party cadres; otherwise they would be denounced as "counterrevolutionary" and severely persecuted. Then, in a decisive reversal, in 1988 China enacted the Wildlife Protection Law, prohibiting the hunting and killing of wildlife.[11] Because of this, the bear population rose, and many pastoral villages and livestock areas were threatened. "We Have Surpassed the Bears" is a tongue-in-cheek rebuttal of the folly of environmental laws that go against Indigenous knowledge while also affirming speciesism.

In Qizihan's account, in 2005 after four brown bears killed sheep in multiple corals, terrifying villagers, high-level urban cadres permitted the hunting of one bear. The cadres from the local pastoral office warmly welcomed an eight-person bear-hunting team from the city, greeting them by sacrificing a sheep for the banquet and reciting Muslim blessings, *"Allahu akbar"* (God is great). After three days and two more sacrificed sheep, the hunting team had tripled in size, yet despite their best efforts, they returned empty-handed. Though the hunting team was to return after five days, they found it difficult to decline their hosts' invitation to linger. The rural hosts served their guests "nectar-like mutton in fragrant broth," "fermented horse milk poured straight from the churn," "alcohol in small shot glasses" and "flattering compliments." Finally, when all were tipsy, the team leader expressed sincere gratitude to the herders, asking, "How many sheep have the bears around here eaten recently?" When a herder answered "four," the leader's smile froze on his face: "then we have surpassed the bears. Since we got here, we have eaten five sheep. Dear brothers, please don't make us stay any longer. You see what we have done? We came here as humans, let's stop eating like the bears."[12] By employing both Confucian and Islamic civilizational logics in which humans are to be more *humane* and *accountable* than beasts,[13] the urban Kazakhs could save face in declining the hospitality of their rural compatriots and adhere to their superiors' dictates to return to the city.

Ecofeminist Folklore in Yerkesh Hulmanbek's Eternal Lamb

If Nurila Qizihan engages hybrid cosmologies in recounting human/animal relations, Yerkesh Hulmanbek's essays highlight feminist ideas from Kazakh folklore that foreground human connections to the earth, returning to pre-Islamic myths from Central Asia. Hulmanbek (b. 1961) is a prominent Kazakh writer born in the pastures of the Beita Mountains (Baytak Bogd) at the foot of the Altai Mountains, shared by Russia, Kazakhstan, and Mongolia (see figure 3.2).[14] After graduating from the Chinese Literature Department of the Central University of National Minorities in 1983, she was appointed editor of the journal *Xinjiang Nationalities Literature.* Hulmanbek gained national recognition with her 2003 publication of *Eternal Lamb* (*Yongsheng yang* 永生羊), a collection of philosophical essays which won the inaugural Tianshan Literary Prize.[15] She joined the Chinese Writers Association in 2005. In 2006, she published a story collection entitled *Fire Mother of the Grasslands*

FIGURE 3.2 Kazakh author Yerkesh Hulmanbek in Ürümchi. Photo by author, July 2012.

(*Caoyuan huomu* 草原火母), which offer a fascinating reflection on Kazakh history and traditions, mostly in the form of semiautobiographical stories. Hulmanbek is also an acclaimed translator, most recently *Selected Poems from Kazakhstan* (*Hasakesitan shixuan* 哈萨克斯坦诗选, 2019) as part of a literary translation series dubbed "The Classic Poetry Library of Countries Along the Belt and Road."[16] Historian James Millward explains the BRI moniker: "with official PRC claims for the primordial 'Chinese' identity of the Xinjiang region increasing in shrillness and ahistoricality, it is only in the context of the Silk Road [a.k.a. "the Belt and Road"], that the region's cultural diversity and multidirectional linkages may be safely discussed in China."[17]

Eternal Lamb is a collection of thirty philosophical essays that recount Hulmanbek's childhood growing up on a state-run pasture from 1961 to 1974 when the government transferred her parents, both teachers in Ürümchi, to work on the collective. Owing to the impact of Asiatic anticyclones in a high-pressure region, the regional climate is severely continental. The winter is long and bitterly cold, while summers are short but usually temperate. Hulmanbek's essays examine human relations to the environment and, like Qizihan's essays, also pay tribute to her father. In the final essay of the collection, "Memories of Baitag Bogd Mountain," she reflects on how her father, one of the first college-educated Kazakhs in the PRC, established the first school for Kazakh nomad children in the Baitag Bogd Mountain region (also known as Baytikshan), still operative when Yerkesh returned with her son on a visit to her childhood home in 2002.[18]

Hulmanbek's essays express a Kazakh cosmology of mud based in a visceral imperative to connect to the earth. She opens "Grandmother Mud" ("Zumu ni" 祖母泥) with the thought that all of us search for our roots, and even get DNA tests attempting to pinpoint our precise ancestry. Yet unlike *zhiqing* root-seeking narratives which are highly metaphysical, she reflects that perhaps this is because "we have forgotten something that was originally in our bodies," namely, "we have forgotten that fragrant smell of mud, the kind that makes you close your eyes to relish it, that emanates after a rain, from grass, fields, and the mud walls in front of one's home" (186). She praises the "earthy smell of mud" for connecting humanity to the ancient truth that we need not fear because we come from the earth and ultimately return to her embrace, becoming "a speck of dust in the vast universe, where our fate is the earth's fate" (186).

"Grandmother Mud" recounts three creation stories prominent in Kazakh culture that emphasize grounded (vs. colonialist), peaceful (vs. invasive), and feminist (vs. patriarchal) values. The first tells of a flood engulfing all the earth, and when it recedes, a black and a red mountain emerge. Two small clumps of mud fall from the mountain cliffs, and after nine months they form gender identities and mate; their descendants call them Moon Father and Moon Mother. The most noteworthy aspect of the story, claims Hulmanbek, is that it is inspired by "soil" rather than the notion of "god" or "original sin": "Before religion, gods, and sin, our ancestors' perception of life, their sense of past lives, and their divination of future lives, all came from the soil under their feet" (188). She suggests that such a cosmology does not support imperial expansion. As her Beijing-based Kazakh compatriot Aydos Amantay writes elsewhere, "Kazakhs aren't known for producing great heroes."[19] Hulmanbek also foregrounds the innocence of Moon Mother, particularly compared to Eve of the Hebrew scriptures who was blamed for the sin of mankind, a story that "caused untold pain for women" (189). In contrast, she imagines Moon Mother to be free and unselfconscious:

"She was just as natural as the earth, sunshine, and air from which she was made: her life, urges, feelings, love, and descendants came from nature" (189). She points out that in this story there is no serpent tempting the woman to do evil, no "original sin," and not even the notion of "gods" or "spirits" as in Daoist creation stories which emphasize uncanny craftsmanship (*guijiang shengong* 鬼斧神工). She attributes gods to fear (*kongju chuangzao shen* 恐惧创造神), underscoring, by contrast, the lack of fear and pain in this Kazakh creation story.

A second origin story in Kazakh lore centers on a woman, kok apa (*kukerapa* 库克阿帕), living in a yurt on the grasslands with a dairy cow as her sole companion and source of nourishment, who forms two dolls of mud. Nine months later when they ask "Grandmother" for food, kok apa feeds them the excess milk she had previously thrown out every day, and they grow into humanity's ancestors. This story made a huge impression on Hulmanbek in her childhood, when she would feed milk to mud figurines. She developed great respect for cows, feeling in them a kindred spirit to humans. She asks her readers to note how her Kazakh ancestors place kok apa on the same level as the natural elements which clearly preceded her existence (191). She concludes that folktales that connect maternal love with nurture, the grassland, and milk, have had a profound cultural influence on the modes of thought, actions, and relational attitudes of the Kazakh people, despite later belief systems such as Islam.

A third story from Kazakh folklore claims that the mud boy formed by kok apa grew up and became a brave and wise hunter. The mud girl became a wise and capable weaving woman. They married and cared for kok apa in her old age, honoring her in her death. Because the hunter's body was made of mud, the scorching heat and brutal cold posed a huge challenge, yet he provided his offspring with nourishment and clothing from forest and wilderness animals. Humans gradually grew stronger and named him "Naked Father." When he became too old to hunt he retired to a mountain cave, and people consulted with him in times of trouble. One day, when a tremendous rainstorm threatened flooding, he rushed to help his people, but "he only had a mud body; he wasn't a god" (193), so his body melted into the mud, and he transformed into a swan. Today when Kazakhs experience natural disasters, they pray to Naked Father (Kz. *atam*) to help them survive and recover from natural calamities.

Understanding "mud" as constitutional to humankind, says Hulmanbek, directly influences how Kazakhs relate to the land, make lifestyle choices, relate to humans and animals, and their value systems.

The entire Kazakh steppe is landlocked. Current-day Kazakhstan, which neighbors Xinjiang, is the largest landlocked country in the world. Thus, Hulmanbek contrasts Kazakh beliefs with Greek myth, where humans are born of water, and cultures (such as Hebrew) with earth-related origin stories that consider God (or gods) to be creators. Hulmanbek claims Kazakh culture is unique in its assignment of creation to the natural elements rather than a god: they see nature as the collective mother, and the "Moon Mother" and "kok apa" as an incarnation of Mother Nature. Further, Kazakhs lack the notion of repentance for sin; the sense of debtor guilt, or the idea of animal sacrifice to appease ancestors or gods, is completely lacking in the culture. She claims that the Central Asian (now Muslim) practice of mourners throwing a handful of dirt on the grave of those who have passed away symbolizes collective trust that the earth welcomes the body's return to the elements (195). We have the sense, she adds, that we must personally toss dirt on the grave of those we care for in a timely manner, otherwise we feel shame.

In *Eternal Lamb*, centuries of nomadic migrations inform the narrator's spatial and temporal cosmology. The title essay conveys a sense of perspectivism, as does Takbum Gyel's "The Illusion of a Day," on the cyclical life experiences of Tibetan shepherds (see chapter 4). Hulmanbek opens "Eternal Lamb" with a poignant description of the millions of cattle and sheep that migrated twice a year from their summer pasture on the west side of her native Baytikshan in the Altai Mountains, to the east side sand dunes, and back again: "Like the herds, the memories of the mountain itself spill from a point in the distant past and flow toward an unforeseeable future" (146; 19).[20] Nomadic time is indeterminate, seemingly infinite, indelibly marked by organic indicators. The life span of a sparrow is shorter than the time it takes for the livestock to migrate; the fall of a dying sparrow coincides with the death of a herd animal en route. In Takbum Gyel's story, an eagle kills a newborn lamb as the boy narrator herds his flock to pasture; cries of devoured baby lambs and his grief punctuate the story as he ages. Hulmanbek's story focuses not on the human lifespan but the life of one lamb. A shepherd passing by their mountain home asks her father to care for the runt of the litter. He gives the lamb to Yerkesh, calling both fledglings *saribas* (*huangmao* 黃毛). Yerkesh believes she was destined to nurture the lamb. The lamb stares at her and she stares back, expressing mutual recognition: "Centuries before, Saribas had been the fully-grown sheep and I was the lamb. We had walked a long, long way together, up and down many mountains, had drunk from the same streams and breathed the same mountain air. We had arranged to meet centuries later on Baytikshan, and this encounter would prove to people that what the world was really about was not love, but life and time" (147–48; 20).

Hulmanbek emphasizes a rural Kazakh sense of meaning being rooted in one's current life, nurtured by reincarnated transspecies lives, as opposed to investment in modern notions of love.

After successfully raising Saribas through the harsh winter, the climax occurs after a calamitous flash flood on the summer solstice holiday in 1972. While much of the story focuses on the girl's futile attempts to become more sheep-like (150; 21), on this day, "she spoke unmistakably to me: 'Come on! We'll go take shelter in a cave. A flash flood is coming'" (151; 22). They fled to a cave, which saved their lives. Lightning scorched a cow, floodwaters rose rapidly, yet they were safe. As they made their way home along swampy ground under a cliff, an overhead rock dislodged, hitting Saribas on the hock, causing excruciating pain. Yerkesh realizes, "we had reared her for one reason only—to eat her" (152; 23). As her father sharpens the knife, she recalls a Kazakh saying before slaughter: "You were not born for sin, and I was not born to go hungry. Forgive me!" (152; 24). The story ends starkly:

> Saribas seemed to understand this better than I. She and her kin were not crops; they did not grow only if humans planted them. When a sheep was slaughtered, another would come along to take its place. Their lives recycled ceaselessly. Being slaughtered and eaten by humans was just a way of coming back to life again, nothing more significant than that. It was like a flash flood: it was just water, it explained nothing. So Saribas seemed quite unconcerned and did not even bleat as Dad laid the knife against her neck. (152; 24)

Her father tells her it is unlucky to weep for a sheep; many will give up their lives for her. Sheep are not born for sin and humans are not born to go hungry: "It's as simple as that" (153; 24). The detachment inherent in the pre-Islamic shamanistic practices that still inform popular folklore and everyday life practices in Central Asian cultures shape rural Kazakh sensibilities about humans slaughtering sheep for food. These practices encourage a respect for all beings while accepting death as a natural, inevitable process devoid of moral culpability.

Hulmanbek's interpretation of the sheep's willingness to be slaughtered differs from Shen Wei's 沈苇 (b. 1965) depiction in his acclaimed *A Dictionary of Xinjiang* (*Xinjiang cidian* 新疆词典, 2005), a lyrical prose taxonomy of the Xinjiang in 111 entries. In "Lamb" ("Yang" 羊) he writes:

> A baby that will never grow up, an eternal infant. Its eyes are two limpid springs from which flow purity, innocence, meekness, and blamelessness, purging the world of filth. The world isn't good enough to serve as its home, so its home is temporary, ended by a knife. It ruminates on death as though chewing fresh, tender grass, accepting death as its other half. When it sees a knife, it lowers its head, submitting to the inevitable without alarm. It is peaceful and willing, because it knows nothing of brutality or blood. It faces Mecca, eyes closed to the world; it passes on into the distance in the form of a nursery rhyme. It returns the weight of its body to the earth, its blood flows into the mud, its flesh boils in the pot, leaving its flavor in people's mouths.[21]

Unlike the ageless wisdom conveyed by the perspectivism of the "eternal lamb" in Hulmanbek's story, Shen Wei's sheep is an "eternal infant," naïve and innocent. It faces Mecca, "eyes closed to the world," embracing death as one who "knows nothing of brutality or blood," a particularly revealing instance of anthropomorphism. Like simplistic Muslim practitioners, its existence is no more substantial than that of a "nursery rhyme," its teleological aim is to leave "flavor in people's mouths." This is a dark take on the Kazakh notion of "you were not born for sin."[22] The final line of Shen's essay evokes Abrahamic practices of animal sacrifice, and the lamb's body floats up to "sit beside its beloved Lord's body," but (mis)quotes the Christian New Testament book of Revelations: "It is the true light of God... They need not the light of lamps or of the sun...

for they have the light of lambs" (*Tamen yi shanyang wei deng* 他们以山羊为灯).²³ Shen Wei detaches the lamb's body (which "returns the weight of its body to the earth, its blood flows into the mud") from its innocent mind (and by analogy, the naivete of religious devotees), portraying lambs and devotees as delusional. Hulmanbek's portrayal of Saribas, in contrast, is one of wisdom incarnate. This lamb is sentient and conscious of environmental cues, taking action to preserve life when that is possible, yet radically accepting fate when death is imminent and ends its suffering.

The Kafkaesque portrayal of dissociation in Yerkesh Hulmanbek's short story "Painless" (Wutong 无痛, 2005) serves as a counterpoint to the simplistic disembodiment conveyed in Shen Wei's *Dictionary*. A surreal tale of a family whose fellow villagers eventually notice that their daughter had chewed off her fingers, the story matter-of-factly presents absurdist details:

> Nobody in the village noticed that my brother's six-year-old daughter had chewed off all her fingers. Only her little palms were left, like two tiny shovels. But more mobile and fleshier, with a child's warmth. She took bowls of food using her palms like pincers. The sight stopped her mother's heart for an instant; the right ventricle blocked and wouldn't let the blood through so the breath caught in her throat. It was a bit like when their pasta-maker choked on a lump of dough, or the neighbour's tractor spluttered to a halt outside.²⁴

Though her sister-in-law's heart stops periodically, the narrator's brother knows how to "restart it." The narrative thread jumps abruptly from keeping the "family secret" to circumstances surrounding the child's birth: "They kept it quiet, right up until the little girl was on the fourth finger. It was an easy labour, compared to most. She almost gave birth in the cow pen."

Reminiscent of the ecofeminist Kazakh folklore recounted in "Grandmother Mud," the narrator insists the baby girl was lavished with nutrients and lacked for nothing: "She gave birth at the ideal time: bright sunshine, fresh air, the cows and even the mares giving milk . . . and she gave plenty, so much it dripped down her dress . . . she was well-fed." Pure milk overflows, fruits of the land are abundant, the mother dotes on her child. Since there is no environmental or cultural explanation, the cause of the girl's self-cannibalism is unclear. The family first recognizes the child feels no pain during an accident with a knife, but only when her daughter wails at the sight of a "broken" waning moon, does the mother discover one of her fingers is a stump. Once villagers learn the family's secret, they endlessly debate its cause. Despite the rampant theorizing about the source of the child's malady—ranging from psychological neglect, undiagnosed disease, toxic medicines, and environmental pollution to humanity's decline—the story implies the true source of the problem, like the girl's horrifying stumps, is in plain sight.

The child's extreme dissociation from bodily pain appears to symbolize the cumulative effects of generations of trauma inflicted on Xinjiang ethnic minorities, visibly manifest, yet taboo to discuss in an era of socially engineered labor transfers, long-term detentions, child separation, and forced assimilation.[25] Significantly, the only time the child expresses pain is when she perceives the moon to be "broken," its "mere thumbnail clipping" signifying her cosmic existential terror of annihilation. This illuminates a cryptic passage in the story:

> I think someone once told me that for a baby, being in the womb is like being a boat in the harbor, moored by the umbilical cord. When the mother is moving, they clutch on to that rope for fear of drifting away. When she is still, they let go and suck on their thumbs so they won't feel hungry.
>
> People have such lovely imaginations. They make it something beautiful.
>
> But that daughter of theirs showed us how ugly it could be.[26]

Clearly, the penchant to romanticize biological, maternal attachments to the baby, the body, the homeland, becomes grotesque in the face of the reality of the horrors of traumatized offspring. The child sucks on her hand, chews off her fingers, in a futile attempt to reconnect to an ethnic and national body traumatically severed from land, children, and cultural practices. Because the true cause of her trauma remains disavowed, her attempts to "ground" are ineffective. The story invokes "object relations theory," which understands the need for attachment as the bedrock for the healthy development of the self and the psychic organization that creates the sense of identity, where the first "object" in someone is usually an internalized image of one's mother. Rather than deriving from the local biological community, the story locates the failed maternal attachments in the larger abstract state.[27] The dissociated girl identifies with the waning moon, but she has become severed from rapidly disappearing Moon Mother.

URBAN ECOLOGIES IN UYGHUR FICTION OF SOUTHERN XINJIANG

Merging of (Psychotic) Mind and (Polluted) Matter in Perhat Tursun's The Backstreets

One reason Xinjiang ecoliterature is "grounded" derives from visceral, psychological imperatives to connect to the land, orient to a sense of time and place, and attend to the body under conditions of extreme dissociation and disorientation. A comprehensive enumeration of Chinese spatial reengineering policies is beyond the scope of this study, but a few examples will demonstrate the scale of state efforts to eradicate built environments and uproot geographically embedded expressions of Uyghur culture. According to numerous studies, the spatial desecration of Xinjiang in the twenty-first century has been extreme, systematic, and intentional (see Figure 3.3). Of 349 shrines and sacred sites that existed in 2004, 30 percent were demolished by 2021, with another 27.8 percent damaged in some way. Between 2017 and 2020 alone, 8,000 mosques were demolished and another 7,500 damaged, with domes, minarets, and crescents removed.[28] Uyghur anthropologist Rahile Dawut notes: "If one were to remove these material artifacts and shrines, *the Uyghur people would lose contact with the earth*. They would no longer have a personal, cultural, and spiritual history. After a few years we would not have a memory of why we live here, or where we belong."[29] Ecological features of Xinjiang are even being removed from children's textbooks. A 2018 revision of Uyghur textbooks completely erased geographical elements native to the region: oases, snows, sands, desert, and indigenous fruits such as pomegranate, sweet melons, grapes, walnuts. Instead, textbooks about animals and nature depict elements of inner and coastal China physical geography and ecology. Uyghur literature and folklore

FIGURE 3.3 Soon-to-be demolished ancient Uyghur town of Kashgar. Photo by author, July 2012.

were largely absent, replaced by Chinese folk stories and poems translated into Uyghur. References to Turkic, Middle Eastern, and Islamic literatures were eliminated.[30]

Perhat Tursun's (b. 1969) 2013 novella, *The Backstreets* (*Chong Sheher*, lit. Big City), is a powerful literary representation of psychic dissociations from the body amid such environmental degradation and cultural estrangement.[31] An acclaimed Uyghur poet and novelist who has been described as China's Salman Rushdie over the controversy sparked by his 1999 novel *The Art of Suicide*, Tursun is a native of Altishahr in southern Xinjiang, where centuries of movement through routes of pilgrimage to *mazars* (holy shrines) creates identity, as Rian Thum argues in *The Sacred Routes of Uyghur History*.[32] In a 2015 interview, Tursun told translator Darren Byler that he based the novella on his experiences in Beijing as a college student and in Ürümchi as a bureaucrat. In Beijing, five of his Uyghur classmates had mental breakdowns because of the pressures that confronted them there; seeing this happen to his classmates had a major impact on him, since he himself had not been mentally stable at times. Byler says, "It made him want to explain the way displacement is related to mental illness."[33] Strongly influenced by

Camus's *The Plague*, which Tursun read multiple times, *The Backstreets* is a first-person account of a day in the life of an anonymous white-collar worker in an unnamed metropolis. Such modernist Uyghur literature is rare: most modern Uyghur literature is satirical tales influenced by socialist realist moralism or historical fiction influenced by Indigenous traditions of epic storytelling that privilege didactic and heroic Uyghur moral instruction.[34]

In the novella, the "fog" (a euphemism for the industrial pollution that made Ürümchi one of the most polluted cities in the world in the early 2000s) acts as an ambient character, along with city sights, sounds, smells, tastes, and temperature. As the novel opens, the narrator steps out of his office into the pervasive fog. The sun has not yet set, but this is irrelevant because "in this city the sun never really rises" (1). The silhouettes of white-clad people standing a few feet away flicker like reflections in dirty water, while those of black-clad people are invisible. The sounds of incessant traffic that permeates the fog is "more frightening than no sound at all because it was an unbreakable silence" (3). A constant mechanical hum permeates the senses and invades the body, the "silent" noise pollution creating a perpetual sense of terror: "Every time I *stood in the noise* I felt as if I faintly heard a woman screaming with a strangled voice" (3, italics mine).

Unlike metaphysically mediated econarratives by Beijing writers, the narrator's bodily immersion in his environment in *The Backstreets* is visceral and pervasive. Punctuated with cryptic one-line paragraphs, such as "The fog spread through my shivering body like a feeling of fright" (61), the novella collapses subject/object distinctions. The narrator equates "the cloudy condition" of the city in the fog with the mental condition of his brain and his identity in the land, claiming this results in "the constant threat of choking from the inside, being smothered or drowning" (49). This overdetermined blending with the environment, on the other hand, results in dissociative alienation from the self. While attempting to identify an unsettling noise, the narrator reflects, "the more I focused the more it seemed to be dividing and mixing into different sounds, transmuting and then vanishing. This might have been because I wasn't hiding what that sound was from others, but rather from myself" (62–63). At some level, he is aware that denial foils his attempts to identify the lost object (which turns out to be his mother's voice).

The urban ecology of Tursun's novella expresses far more existential alienation from the immersive environment than the bucolic musings by fellow Xinjiang native, Liu Liangcheng. In *One Man's Village* (1998), Liu also evokes the simile of the woman in distress to signify psychic anxiety and sensory powerlessness: "The wind blew hard one night. Howled me awake halfway to dawn, crying something terrible over my hut and over the stacks of wheat like an unhappy woman."[35] While isolation leads to bouts of paranoia for both narrators, in *The Backstreets* it intensifies, while in *One Man's Village* it dissipates, and the environment ultimately presents as benign. The *Village* narrator, left to finish harvesting his wheat by himself, notices a menacing shape in the distance that seems to be growing larger, moving closer to him, only to learn it is a tree grown leafier. In *The Backstreets*, the narrator lapses into neurotic superstitions to manage his feelings of unease in the city. He believes the woman's voice causes automobile accidents, distracting people when they cross the street. He leaves buildings right foot first to ward off bad luck. Instead of calming him, the environment permeates the narrator's body and estranges him to greater degrees. After failing to note the license plate of a car flashing past him, he says "I was suddenly lacking something inside.... The empty space that remained from the number of that car also vanished in the fog" (4). His dark spirit merges with that of the smog. Like the "missing" license plate, the empty space inside him vanishes, negating him twice over.

The Backstreets is rife with such double negations, recalling the dissociative self-annihilation of the suicidal first-person narrator in Chen Ran's 1995 Beijing novel *Private Life*, who dubs herself "Little Miss Zero." Both works feature traumatized first-person narrators where the alienating metropolis threatens the integrity of marginalized individuals, exhibiting symptoms detailed in the opening line of Georg Simmel's classic essay, "The Metropolis and Mental Life" (1905): "the deepest problems of modern life derive from the claim of the individual to preserve the autonomy and individuality of his existence."[36] A man in *The Backstreets* recites: "Chop the people from Six Cities, chop, chop, chop, chop, chop, chop, chop ["chop" repeats 215 times]" (9). Because the Six Cities, or Altishahr, refers to the six oases that form the ancestral homeland of the Uyghurs (Turpan, Korla, Aksu, Kashgar, Yarkand, and Hotan), the psychic threat is clearly to the integrity of the ethnic body (see figure 3.4).

FIGURE 3.4 A Uyghur couple in modernizing Kashgar. Photo by author, July 2012.

Dissociated Uyghur urbanites in *The Backstreets* engage in simulated mental cutting to counter threats to bodily and psychic integrity. Like Hulmanbek's "Painless," where a girl cuts off her fingers to psychologically ground her dissociation from maternal origins, the narrative of *The Backstreets* devolves into absurdity as a man imagines chopping down 4.5 million Uyghurs: "If he rushed in his passion and didn't land the cleaver on the right place on their necks they might not be killed. So, he would need to measure properly and make sure the cleaver wouldn't get stuck in the neck bones. He would need to calculate the additional minute it would take to get the cleaver unstuck from each person's neck; for four and a half million people it could be as long as seventy-five thousand hours" (10–11). In general, the characters in *The Backstreets* suffer from the intense "intellectualization" (dissociation from the body) that, according to Simmel, characterizes metropolitan life.

The Backstreets presents an urban ecology where pollutants permeate and constitute the body. The toxic physical environment directly informs subjectivity: "Now the fog was slowly flowing like filthy water in a waste ditch along the narrow street. The shapes of people were floating like debris in the water, with a slow but shivering force. The lights of cars were like red tissues floating in the water or decomposing rags moving lightly. I felt like I would choke in the sewage of this road" (13–14). There are olfactory assaults from discarded hygienic pads, excrement, and perfume. The smell of dirty socks, which "would fill their inner organs and cause them to look at each other with anger and resentment," (40) permeates dorm life. Fog seeps through sleeves and mingles with bodily microbes, which, transformed, excrete back into the fog. Fog ages bodies, skin loosening, bones becoming brittle and eyes cloudy. The fog becomes "trapped" in a narrow alleyway, its dilapidated windows a murdered man's body, where "the light floated away like gradually-clearing yellowish pus from those gashes" (26). A sewage-filled alley evokes cosmological musings: "This street seemed to be at the limit of an earlier time when nothing existed, and the universe was just being created. I felt myself seeking a sign of truth about creation from the murky fog. My little body was very weakly trembling as if being choked in the amniotic fluid of a womb. Every gash seemed like an open door to me, but I didn't have the courage to walk through" (26). As in "Painless," characters in *The Backstreets* attempt to ground in nurturing visions of amniotic fluid yet find it nightmarish, remaining disconnected.

The radically immersive sensibility of *The Backstreets* differs from the ecological biopolitics in Yan Lianke's *Dream of Ding Village* and the existential blending with "Nature" in Gao Xingjian's *Soul Mountain* in that the dominant paradigm explored by these Beijing-based writers is epistemological. After winning the prestigious Franz Kafka award, Chinese writer Yan Lianke said in an interview: "We all know what happens to Gregor *after* his metamorphosis.... What I need instead is a meticulous description *of* his metamorphosis, the process of his metamorphosis. Kafka did not give me this.[37] Yan Lianke describes his own fictional style as *shenshizhuyi* (神识主义 "mythorealism"): "the connection between reality and *shenshizhuyi* does not lie in direct cause-and-effect links, but rather relies on human souls (灵魂) and minds (精神).[38] Yan emphasizes humanistic spirituality abstracted from the body, while Gao Xingjian's Nobel Prize–winning novel attempts to synthesize epistemological mind/body splits via sophisticated neo-Confucian metaphysics (see chapter 2). Superficially, all three writers explore similar issues of *bios* 生 and *zoe* 活, yet the synthesis process in *The Backstreets* occurs organically rather than metaphysically: "After I came to this city,

I felt as though the threat of getting lost and the desire to lose myself were strangely becoming one inside me" (38). Perhat Tursun's urban ecology conveys the organic biological process of pollutants from the artificial built environment permeating the narrator's body and consciousness to the point of annihilation.

To "ground" in Xinjiang requires freedom of movement rather than rigid enclosures. The narrators of Soul Mountain and The Backstreets both express strong urges to merge with their environments, tempered by existential terror at being lost, and epistemological dread posed by the notion of infinity. The split narrator (I/you) of Soul Mountain gets lost in primeval forest, and only "locates" himself with an oddly shaped tree resembling a fishhook. Similarly, the narrator of The Backstreets gets lost in the desert in his youth. His comfort comes not from a fixed totem, such as the fishhook tree, nor from a familiar constellation, but rather from the falling stars. As an Altishahri who grounds identity in centuries of movement through routes of sacred pilgrimage, stars in a fixed constellation were meaningless to the narrator: movement creates connection. In practice, lonely shrines in the desert are meaningless and almost impossible to locate on a map; instead, "the historical potential of the shrine was activated by pilgrimage."[39]

Unlike the expansive sacred routes in deserts, Uyghur routes in cities radically contract. The narrator of The Backstreets is unable to journey to the outer reaches of empire (the *west*) to "find" himself in the ethnic "other."[40] After returning from Beijing to Ürümchi to work, the narrator's boss "often asked why I didn't speak his language perfectly since I had gone to college in Inner China" (64). They spent their life in college, he explains, traversing between the dormitory, class, cafeteria, and the library (64). And again, "We never had any way of practicing the language of the city while we were there. For us, the strange people from the city weren't much different than the trees by the road. The only difference was that unlike the trees, they moved around" (64). Uyghur assimilation, like movement or self-expression, is restricted. Clearly, Uyghur alienation in the Han-dominated cities of Beijing and Ürümchi is partially due to discrimination and Han Chinese perceptions of linguistic and ethnic supremacy.[41] Byler also attributes the protagonist's disorientation to the material and digital enclosure of the city: "in Ürümchi every company, every school, every mosque, every police station, every park, every residential area was surrounded by walls and gates. There was no way to enter these spaces without the tacit consent of the police contractors who, along with automated camera systems, watched who came and went."[42] He explains, further, that geographical features that orient rural Uyghurs are scrambled in Ürümchi: mountains to the north are now in the southwest; abodes facing Mecca are now high rises aligned with rectilinear street grids.

The disoriented narrator of *The Backstreets* displays extreme object attachments, similar to the traumatized child in "Painless." When "lost" in the city, the narrator "locates" himself via a single desk drawer in an office: "The only thing which gave me a sense of direction was the only thing that belonged to me in this city—the drawer in the office" (45). Other drawers in his office remain "occupied" by a retired bureaucrat's things, which the narrator fears removing lest that person lose himself completely (46). Such extreme manifestation of "object relations" signifies the loss of the original maternal object, according to the psychological theory. The novella ends with the narrator beaten bloody in the streets with the numbers he had been searching for crystalizing in his mind's eye as a street address for the psychiatric hospital. His final thoughts are, "I couldn't see anything; just the sound of shoes and *that* sound, gradually coming closer until it could be heard very clearly. I recognized the sound as the sound of my mother's voice. She was calling my name in a long, drawn-out way" (136). The voice of the woman in distress that perpetually haunts him in the city is the longed-for mother, a mother who had neglected him due to her fixation on her drunken husband who ends up murdering her. Ultimately, *The Backstreets* enacts a double sense of alienation, for the nurture promised by the biological mother and the paternalistic empire is but a myth.

Dark Humor in Memtimin Hoshur's Urban Ecofiction

Memtimin Hoshur (b. 1944) grew up in the town of Ghulja near Kazakhstan, studied at Xinjiang University in Ürümchi, and published his first story in 1965. His 2003 epic *The Sand-Covered City* (*Qum Basqan Sheher*) is regarded as his masterwork, but he is most widely known for the vitality of his biting short stories of social satire. His short story collection *This Is Not a Dream* won the Fourth Junma Literary Prize, and he has won a wide range of awards in Xinjiang. While the tone of Tursun's *The Backstreets* is hardly lighthearted, it is clearly absurd. Similarly, Hoshur's urban ecologies enact agency via multiple modalities of madness and humor. Uyghur sociality particularly values farce, or what anthropologist Nathan Light calls "joking." Drawing on James Scott's research on surreptitious resistance by Malaysian peasants, Light describes how Uyghur public performances conform to systematic political discourses and uphold dominant ideologies, while challenges and debates emerge on the margins, among friends and in asides and jokes.[43] Uyghurs who can seize an opportunity for joking are highly valued at Uyghur social gatherings. A common joking practice among minority groups (as seen, for example, in Keith Basso's analysis of the Western Apaches) is to take on speech patterns and social attitudes of the dominant group. This type of humor is highly valued in Tibetan culture as well.

For example, Memtimin Hoshur's short story, "Mustache Dispute" ("Burut Majrasi," 1991), features a self-described rambling "idiot/comedian/author" character, whose authorship of the title story destabilizes the legitimacy of its content.[44] "Mustache Dispute," like the canonical "A Madman's Diary" (1918), by Lu Xun, is framed as a story within a story. It begins with a dialogue between a publisher and this character, known simply as the author of the story "Idiot" (the title of a story that Hoshur published in the third volume of *Tarim* in 1989). After the author rambles incoherently, comparing himself to a sarcastic comedian (Uy: *chaqchaqchi*) unique to Memtimin Hoshur's hometown of Ghulja, he hands the publisher a new story. Translators Darren Byler and Mutellip Enwer explain that this figure, which reappears in many of Hoshur's stories, "is an eccentric, highly-opinionated, teller of fables and social dramas. Many of the stories written from his perspective can be read as commentaries on changing social conditions in Xinjiang."[45] As such, the eccentric character is uniquely free, as in stories with Tibetan trickster characters, to criticize social conditions from outside the strictures of "rational" discourse.

The story that follows has a chilling undertone, and like "A Madman's Diary," involves a highly subjective I-narrator prone to paranoia due to terror-inducing governance practices. In the story, a tall man with a mustache reportedly brandished knives during a fight in the local bazaar. The narrator, tall with a mustache, becomes suspect. Out of an abundance of caution (given that persecution of Uyghur men with facial hair *had* been rife during the Cultural Revolution), he shaves his mustache, which officials believe proves his guilt. They tell him to write a "résumé" (简历) of his mustache-wearing history, a humorous reference to the serious practice of writing self-criticisms during the Cultural Revolution. He subsequently starts having nightmares. One is that his wife is unknitting and reknitting his body, with each reknitting shrinking him a bit, until he chokes. A second is that he is spinning in a washing machine. Fearful, he self-isolates for two months, only to emerge and find that everything had returned to normal, with the local official reprimanded for overreacting. After the official apologizes to the narrator, he thinks to himself, "Did this dignified town government director also fall into the washing machine and become dizzy? It's time to unknit these cumbersome people, wash them clean, dry them in the sun, then re-knit them more decently."[46] Such dark humor implicates systematic practices to (mind) control ethnic minority groups in Xinjiang.

Another literary modality employed in Uyghur urban ecology is to anthropomorphize animal characters as metaphors for human sociability. While this is a common trope throughout world literature, particularly in children's literature, especially as fables and fairytales, it also informs animal studies. Most tales deem animals to be of a lower caste, despite their manifestly humanlike qualities and the fact that they exhibit qualities such as wisdom or problem-solving skills that outshine those of human characters. At the same time, animals in such stories often can safely express what a human character cannot; they add a degree of emotional distance for the reader, which is important when the story message is personal, painful, or powerful. As Burke and Copenhaver argue, "having animals do the acting and mistake-making allows the face-saving emotional distance often needed to be able to join the conversation."[47] Animals as characters can also introduce novelty and incongruity, making a story more enjoyable. Unlike in many children's tales, much of the humor in Tibetan or Uyghur stories derives from the self-referential way in which the author acknowledges difference, such as the unreality of talking animals, or the implausibility of human/animal romance.[48] These stories invite readings via cultural animal studies, examining how culture shapes individual experiences, everyday life, and social and power relations; animals in literature are thus historically determined and culturally motivated constructions that negotiate conceptions of the human and the animal.[49]

Memtimin Hoshur's short story, "Festival for the Pigs" ("Choshqilargha Bayram," 1999) illustrates some of these characteristics in Uyghur literature.[50] In this story, a human narrator recounts hearing usually well-fed urban pigs complaining when the restaurants providing their food source (leftovers from banquets) close for cleaning. One pig eloquently opines that the filth being "sanitized" are humans themselves: "'Humans never think about the necessity of first cleansing their spirit. It is said that humans are trying to achieve sanitation by exterminating rats, flies, lice, and fleas. But who is actually polluting the whole land today?' This pig delved into such deep discussions that he must have carefully selected food left over by university professors."[51]

The deeper critique leveled by the pig—that humans fail to recognize their dominant role as polluters of the land—is neutralized by the humorous remark that the eloquent pig had imbibed the food of an academic. Another pig is even more daring in his complaints:

> "As if that's not enough," said a second pig, "they consider themselves to be the highest species of all. They always hook us with their eyes, and enclose us in cage-like, narrow cement walls. When they get into fights, they curse each other with the epithet *pig*. They make clothes out of our skins and wear them unashamedly. They make toothbrushes with our bristly hair and put them in their mouths when they brush. They make all kinds of dishes out of our meat, eat whatever they want, and throw us their leftovers. Who knows by now how much of our brothers' meat we have eaten."[52]

Here, the critique leveled at the humans is that of speciesism.[53] One pig recollects the time that pigs were free, eating pure and natural food in the forests. Yet another explains that because of new anticorruption and austerity programs against wasting food, there will be no leftovers for pigs in the future. If one reads the pigs in the story as a metaphor for Uyghurs, it becomes clear that the power dynamic is one where a minority group, subjected to the whims of the majority, appears ungrateful and entitled when largesse is withdrawn from them. Finally, in a scene reminiscent of *Animal Farm*, the narrator hears "the most incendiary content" when a pig shouts out, "'Who destroyed our ancient homelands where our ancestors lived, changed our natural living conditions, and our nutritional diets? Brothers, the time has come to show them who we are.' After hearing this talk, oh my God, I held my collar in clenched teeth."[54]

The exaggerated fear of the narrator is humorous, yet the deeper implications of this passage must surely be clear to Uyghur readers. On the one hand, the threat posed by the pigs is clearly ludicrous: in the story, when the pigs eventually break out of their pens and wreak havoc on the city, it is merely by dancing on the streets and reveling in food. They show who they are—pigs who love to eat and dance and make merry, freely. On the other hand, the pigs' concerns are legitimate: treated as a lower species, the humans encage them, use them as objects, and coerce them into "eating" each other. Analysis in Chinese of Memtimin's fiction is vague, lightly touching on the fact that "humor is the highest form of irony."[55] The story won the *Ethnicities Literature* prize honoring the fiftieth anniversary of the journal's founding in 1949.[56]

One of the main strategies used in anthropomorphized animal characters in literature is to challenge rigid boundaries between human castes. This occurs in "Festival of the Pigs," during the revelry, when an inordinately fat man ends up riding a plump pig through the city: "Soon a rumor spread through the city that a pig was riding on another pig, circling through the streets, commanding the riot. Some people said this commander was originally a pig that had turned into a human after eating human food. Some other people said he was originally a human who had turned into a pig after eating pig food."[57] Ultimately, the greatest fear of the humans is the potential for species confusion, which they guard against at all costs. A top official analyzes the problem as such: "If animals are not fed the food they are supposed to eat, their nature will change, and this will cause chaos. What if human food begins to resemble that of animals? Ah, then, humans who have been derived from animals will return to their animal nature."[58] Despite what Donna Haraway calls the natural "entanglement" of the human and nonhuman worlds, imperial cosmologies based upon speciesism are threatened by such evolving "naturecultures."[59]

Like Kafka, a modern pioneer in using animals as personas for human emotional states and as allegories for suppressed minorities, Memtimin Hoshur's animal stories confront the human/animal philosophical binary inherent in speciesism. In one sense this exemplifies the very appropriation of animals as images for human attributes which nature writers have resisted. In Memtimin Hoshur's allegorical approach, his animal narratives function as mechanisms of estrangement, allowing reflection on Uyghurs, ethnic minorities, and humanity in general. Yet they differ from traditional animal fables and animal writing for children in important respects. First, the animals depicted tend to be ugly and threatening, rather than the cuddly creatures and companion species of children's literature, the familiar ones of fables and folktales, or the charismatic megafauna of environmental writing. One reason they participate in cultural animal studies critiques is that, rather than portraying "animal innocence" in a nostalgic fashion (a literary trend corresponding to their physical reduction to a commodity as a foodstuff), the pigs in this story are morally complicated creatures. Furthermore, Hoshur's stories introduce unstable or circuitous narrative devices (e.g., gossip and hearsay, the narrator's questionable ability to understand the pig language, dream sequences, embedding stories within stories, etc.), which coincides with post-Darwinian eruption of nonhuman chaotic forces within humanism, forging a distinctly modernist formal embodiment of the animal problem. In this sense, Hoshur exhibits many of the qualities exhibited by Kafka, whose literature contributed significantly to animal studies and ecocriticism.[60]

ENGAGING DIFFERENCE IN HAN ESSAYS FROM XINJIANG

Shen Wei's Lament in A Dictionary of Xinjiang

A native of Huzhou, Zhejiang Province, Shen Wei moved to Xinjiang in 1988 as a graduate of the Chinese Department of Zhejiang Normal University to escape a painful conflict with his father. Yerkesh Hulmanbek, in her role as vice chair of the Xinjiang Uygur Autonomous Region Writers Association, claims that Shen is considered by local writers as a real voice of the land, as if "his family has been living in this place for generations."[61] During his thirty years of residence in Xinjiang, Shen served as vice chair of the Xinjiang Writers Association and chief editor of *Western Literature* (*Xibu wenxue* 西部文学). As of 2023, he resides in Hangzhou and is a professor at Communication University of Zhejiang.

An accomplished poet, Shen Wei became nationally known for his lyrical essays in *A Dictionary of Xinjiang* (2005). Despite his intimate knowledge of Xinjiang life, informed by extensive travels in the province and close friendships with Indigenous writers such as Yerkesh Hulmanbek and Perhat Tursun, Shen Wei's depiction of Xinjiang ecology maps a Hanspace cosmology on the region from the perspective of a sojourner. His prose essays are beautifully crafted, evocative, and emphasize the earthy attachments so prevalent in Xinjiang writing, yet they also convey philosophical ideas metaphysically rather than through immediate sentient experience. In this sense, *Dictionary* is an anatomical taxonomy of place where subject/object boundaries remain intact. The writer is a clinician who provides a detailed description of the subject in compartmentalized fragments that never quite encapsulate the holistic body of Xinjiang. Instead, the near-death of the feminized subject is nostalgically memorialized.

For example, in the entry "Turpan" ("Tulufan" 吐鲁番) Shen Wei divides the desert into "dead Turpan" and "living Turpan," acknowledging that "traveling on this flaming continent means crossing through these two worlds" (129). The former is characterized by ancient city ruins, the Astana Tombs, the Thousand-Buddha Caves, damaged Manichean manuscripts on mulberry bark paper, mummies, rhinoceros fossils: "These are the generous gifts of time, redolent of years and dust. They are a great withering-away yet are well within reach and can be touched by the hand. Dead Turpan is an omnipresent nowhereland" (129). Dead Turpan is masculinized in relation to living Turpan, where "under the grape trellises one finds beautifully dressed girls, lively nazirkom dances, muqam concerts, all-night feasts ... With a stubborn hedonism they resist the forceful violations of another world" (129). This other world is "dead Turpan," which "has a self-satisfied loneliness. It is the other world's mirror, illuminating life's unreality and equivocality. It moves ruins, tombs, and ashes into the sky, pulls death inch by inch toward dizzying heights. The living Turpan, then, is like a solicitous footman, ceaselessly offering the world its enthusiasm, water, soil, nourishment" (129). Dead Turpan wants to be larger than living Turpan, the poet writes, ending his lyrical essay with a rhetorical question, "Can it be that living Turpan is only a stand-in for dead Turpan, a last testament?" (129)

The gendered depiction of Uyghur life in the desert as feminized and embattled, sure to be vanquished, moves beyond depicting anthropogenic desertification to a nostalgic eulogy for minority lifestyles deemed doomed to vanish. The rhetorical linkage of inevitable annihilation with environmental discourse is a common one when written from a neocolonial perspective rationalized by a theory of natural selection which hinges on frequent and continuous extinctions. Miles Powell writes about a similar move by American conservationists writing sympathetically about the demise of Indian ways of life in *Vanishing America*. By writing allegedly genuine last-Indian laments, Powell claims, these authors obtained a form of catharsis. They mourned Native America's passing, even as they reassured themselves that it was inevitable. For example, Powell quotes an 1842 Connecticut newspaper editorial titled "the Last of the Mohegans" that says, "Their decay is the natural, inevitable result of the progress of society, [and] we are not necessarily responsible . . . for the extinction of the Indian race."[62] Insidious, sometimes blatant but often subtle, Social Darwinist thought pervades both the U.S. and Chinese empires to the present day.

The reality is that despite a harsh climate of extreme heat and no rainfall, trade and agriculture in the Turpan Basin have thrived due to an innovative hydrological innovation imported from Persia centuries ago, a system of *karez* (Uy: *kariz*; subterranean aqueducts) that bring water to the oasis from the foothills of the Tian Shan mountains to the north. Architecture professor Don Hanlon explains that these tunnels, dug far beneath the desert surface, are carefully engineered to maintain a constant shallow slope to prevent erosion and have provided the Turpan with clean, cold water year-round for domestic and agricultural use. Yet as early as 1985 Hanlon reported to the UN Development Program that "this ancient architectural tradition was being systematically destroyed as part of a vigorous effort by the Chinese government to eradicate the indigenous culture of the Uighur people . . . who have lived in Turpan continuously for over 1100 years."[63] And by 2019, though Turpan city has a majority Uyghur population of one-quarter million, the Chinese government had demolished all of the Uyghur domestic and religious architecture in Turpan except for a few examples preserved as tourist attractions.

Hanlon details how the *karez* system created a highly sustainable urban ecosystem:

> The karez open into a system of canals in the town that form the boundaries between streets and residences. Tall, straight poplars grow in tight rows directly out of the canals. These ... provide deep shade for the houses and for the street; they create a wind break to control dust; they provide wood readily available for construction and heating; and they create a microclimate in the street by transpiring water through their leaves into the air, producing a natural means of air conditioning that can lower the temperature in the street and adjacent houses by as much as 20 degrees Fahrenheit. After circulating through the town entirely by gravity, water then enters into second system of canals for irrigating agriculture. All of this is accomplished without any mechanical devices or artificial sources of energy—a truly sustainable method.[64]

Hanlon's description of the sustainable environment fostered by the *karez*, a microclimate that allows poplars to flourish, shading the street and creating a windbreak, stands in sharp contrast to Shen Wei's lyrical implication that "dead Turpan" will overtake "living Turpan." Indeed, the notion that the decimation of the rural village in Xinjiang is inevitable is reinforced in Shen Wei's entry "White Poplar Village," which reads, in part:

> From a speck of a dust to a note of birdsong, White Poplar Village shrinks to a button forgotten by the world, a shiver on the tip of a stalk of withered mid-autumn grass. No, it isn't that the village is too small, it's that the wind is too big, the wilderness too wide, bleak and desolate and limitless. It grows in the midst of forgetfulness, and like an almond enclosed in a gray husk, it has no chance to sprout in that secret corner. (127)

The certain extinction of the village, like a dormant almond unable to sprout, is naturalized. It has become lamentably out of date, forgotten by the world. Like the Mongols in *Wolf Totem*, the wholesome ecological wisdom of rural Uyghurs is consigned to the quaint past in an age of scientific civilizational modernization. This, despite the fact that the traditional Uyghur homes and neighborhoods in the Turpan oasis had "entirely rational environmental attributes" according to Hanlon, with "a construction technology based on sun-dried mud brick coupled with simple wood framing using the poplars—materials that were 100% organic, non-toxic, biodegradable, re-usable and required no fossil fuels for processing and transport."[65]

Shen Wei's eulogistic mode of thought continues in an entry entitled "Mérceles" ("Musailaisi" 木賽萊斯).[66] "During the village mérceles festivals—now a lost tradition—each villager would offer a jar of his best wine, which was poured into a big vat with the others, mixing together into a communal mérceles that all the villagers drank from. It was a symbol of unity. Everyone was born from the same roots, like the wine in the vat; the same blood ran in their veins" (133). Such descriptions of local color are benign. They nurture a sense of unity among diversity. The roots of the unity inspired by mérceles wine are said to run deep: the entry claims it was the wine referred to by Tang frontier poet Wang Han (王翰, 687–726), who writes in "A Song of Liangzhou" ("Liangzhou ci" 涼州詞): "Fine grape liquor in a white jade cup / I want drink but the *pipa* sends us to our horses."[67] Liangzhou refers to the Hexi Corridor in present-day Gansu, where the Tang fought the Uyghurs. Unity is emphasized; warfare is downplayed (Shen cites only the first two lines of the poem).[68]

Similarly, in an entry titled "Chickpea Girl" ("Yingzuidou nühai" 鷹嘴豆女孩), the plant/girl "comes into bloom in the dust and hot sun. She's a local girl, a princess of Inner Asia, of old cities, of impoverished villages, a princess for everyone" (137). History is romanticized and strife relegated to its dustbin. She is a princess for everyone to celebrate today, much as Uyghur saints and shrines are coopted as tourist attractions for Han Chinese. Translator Bruce Humes suggests that one reason Chinese state media promotes Shen Wei's *A Dictionary of Xinjiang* so strongly is that it belongs to the politically correct category of Xinjiang "migrant" literature. He adds that unlike Hong Kong, Beijing, or Shanghai, any Chinese citizen can relocate to Xinjiang to live and work there; though the Han comprised only 6 percent of Xinjiang's population in 1949, they are now in the majority.[69]

HAN SETTLERS AMONG KAZAKH NOMADS: LI JUAN'S ALTAY ESSAYS

While Shen Wei laments the death of Uyghur culture and ecology as inevitable, Li Juan humorously details Han settlers' struggles to survive harsh conditions and cultural difference. Li Juan 李娟 (b. 1979) was born in Xinjiang in the *bingtuan* (Production and Construction Corps) of the Ili Kazakh Autonomous Region. She attended school in Sichuan, but after graduation from high school returned to Xinjiang, where she initially worked as a manual laborer in Ürümchi. She literally wrote her way out of this difficult work when her first manuscript was published at age twenty. She later spent much of her young adulthood among migratory Kazakh nomads in Altay Prefecture in northern Xinjiang Province, which borders Kazakhstan to the west and Mongolia to the east, where her mother supported the family with a small convenience store and tailoring business. In 2003 she published *Nine Stories on Snow* (*Jiu pian xue* 九篇雪). Her essay collection *Altay Corner* (*Aleitai de jiaoluo* 阿勒泰的角落, 2010) was awarded the People's Literature Nonfiction Award (2011). *My Altay* (*Wode Aletai* 我的阿勒泰, 2010) is a selection of her best essays written during three periods: "Altay Characters" (2007–2009), "Altay Corner" (2002–2006), and "Nine Stories on Snow" (1998–2001). Li Juan is best known for her 2012 publications: *The Way of Sheep Trilogy* (*Yangdao: Sanbuqu* 羊道三部曲) and *Winter Pasture* (*Dong muchang* 冬牧场), the latter translated in 2021 with the subtitle *One Woman's Journey with China's Kazakh Herders*. Her recent essay collection, *Distant Sunflower Fields* (*Yaoyuan de xiangrikui di* 遥远的向日葵地), also translated in 2021, won the 2017 Lu Xun Award for Nonfiction (see figure 3.5).[70]

As a corpus, Li Juan's essays invite readers to defy conceptual binaries between me and you, insider and outsider, rural and urban, labor and technology, human and animal. Unlike Xinjiang writer Liu Liangcheng's more forthright persona as "village philosopher," Li Juan's conclusions retain a characteristic lack of pretension. They teeter on the brink of profundity. The sensations invigorating mundane struggles to survive are what lingers for the reader. In this sense, Li Juan's writing resembles that of Xiao Hong (1911–1942), who writes of the human need to anthropomorphize animals as solace from the hardships of life. She

FIGURE 3.5 Han author Li Juan in Altay. Courtesy Ou Ning, July 2012.

also acknowledges, as does Liu Liangcheng, that the myriad creatures (*wanwu* 万物) have *ling* (灵 soul; spirit; efficacy), yet unlike Liu she undercuts attempts to instruct us how the minds of these animals think or how their hearts feel. If Liu Liangcheng emphasizes the importance of maintaining the place of the traditional cultural, poetic, spiritual notion of the village (*xiangcun* 乡村) in the Chinese imagination or heart/mind, even as the real countryside (*nongcun* 农村) changes or disappears, Li Juan rejects the idea of imagined landscapes and idealized notions of rural or urban. Her ideas of "labor" in essays such as "The Man Who Watches Me Make Noodles" ("Kanzhe wo lamian de nanren" 看着我拉面的男人) or "Our Tailor Shop" ("Women de caifeng dian" 我们的裁缝店) attend to both laboring and consuming bodies in ways that neither reify them nor deny market economics.[71] In fact, her stories illustrate how attending to the individuality of bodies can be economically profitable. They convey the pragmatism of three generations of Han settler women trying to survive.

Li Juan's essays are set in the 2000s, during a period governed by central policies of regional "urban-rural integration" (*chengxiang tongchou* 城乡统筹).[72] Historically unprecedented in scale and speed, this nationwide urbanization plan aims to industrialize agriculture, enclose pastures, relocate most rural dwellers to cities, and raise the quality of life for all. Resolving the "nationality problem" of a multicultural socialist nation-state via green governance policies enclosing pastures and settling Indigenous nomads is thus embedded in the civilizational logic of urban

Sacred Routes and Dark Humor

FIGURE 3.6 Strip-mined mountains along Karakoram Highway to Pakistan from Kashgar. "Guangxi Hydroelectric Industrial Group Welcomes You to Gezi Hydroelectric Station." Photo by author, July 2012.

modernity. Development of impoverished western regions proceeds via "pair assistance" (*duikou zhihuan* 对口支援) policies, where a wealthier eastern municipality invests 1 percent of its GDP in a developing (western) region (see figure 3.6). Cities are often mechanically reproduced by planning departments in eastern academies, such as Tongji or Tsinghua University, with little regard for local scale, geography, or heritage. Urban gentrification drives poor city residents to relocate, while rural land transfers force massive migrations of agricultural Han workers to the west.

Such policies make subtle appearances in Li Juan's essays and inform her vignettes. She covers a wide variety of both urban and rural experiences: city life in Ürümchi and Altay, moving base camp with the Kazakh nomads on the grasslands, growing sunflowers in the Gobi Desert, life in the rural township of Hongdun. Her essays describe everyday experiences: a walk with her mother at Chinese New Year, feeding pets, her grandmother's daily habits, Kazakh youths calling lovers on the family convenience store phone. For example, during a period when Li Juan has an office job in Altay, her mother calls to offer her a horse for transportation. Her mother's Kazakh customers believe in repaying all

Sacred Routes and Dark Humor

debts before receiving a proper Muslim burial, so her mother rationalizes her daughter's need for a horse to accept debt repayment from an impoverished family in mourning. In "The Horse that Belongs to Me" ("Shuyu wo de ma" 属于我的马), Li Juan reflects:

> Although Altay is the city seat of a farming district, large farm animals are not allowed on the city streets. Animal husbandry teams must always make a large detour around the city. But as for horses, I didn't seem to remember a specific regulation. So, after the odd thought *how could someone ride a horse on the streets*? I quickly had the odd thought *why doesn't anyone ride a horse on the streets*? Fumeng County isn't the same, people ride horses there with their heads held high; it's an everyday scene, especially for Kazakhs. But honestly, how in the world did my mom get that idea: give me a horse to ride to work? Too cool.[73]

Li Juan makes fun of her eccentric mother but more so highlights the artificiality of urban regulations that prohibit animals in a farming district (see figure 3.7). The essay concludes with a story of digging the family well to "construct the new countryside" on a farm in the Gobi Desert:

> We opened a deep hole in the earth until we hit water. It was a magical experience. One person uses a small shovel to dig dirt. Another stands at the side lifting up bucket after bucket of soil. Slow labor makes the windblown earth gradually open its eyes. It sees us, recognizes our faces, and only then truly accepts us.
>
> In the past two years we repaired our house, dug a well, and planted some trees. In time to "construct the new countryside." The village government sent someone to paint our garden courtyard walls. No one considered us "outsiders" anymore.[74]

In the preceding passage, Li Juan uses a transliteration of the Kazakh word for "windblown" (*akehala* 阿克哈拉), well aware that Han are "outsiders" among Indigenous Kazakhs, as well as to the windblown earth, which humans invade and engage in search of water and shelter.

In a 2012 interview, Li Juan states she is uncomfortable with philosophizing on "others," whether they are nonhuman or from other

FIGURE 3.7 A herd takes over the road in Altay. Courtesy Ou Ning, July 2012.

ethnicities. She acknowledges her indebtedness to Yerkesh Hulmanbek: "Her biggest inspiration to me was making me realize that I am Han Chinese, and when I describe the scenes and sights of this faraway, foreign place, no matter how close I myself might be, I'm always in the position of an outsider, standing on the sidelines, looking in, because you're just not the same kind of people."[75] In *My Altay*'s preface she acknowledges the sensitivity of her subject: "Kazakh-related topics, the distant borderlands and so on, these are in the end a tricky topic, you know? Let me write about Sichuan and it should be a lot smoother."[76] Her moving essay "A Snowshoe Hare Merely Twenty Centimeters from Springtime" ("Li chuntian zhiyou ershi gongfen de xuetu" 離春天只有二十公分的雪兔)explores the "other" with considerable subtlety. She starts with complex feelings about her mother's attempts to speak Kazakh with her customers: "In my opinion my mom is overconfident in tackling any type of communication. I guarantee that many aspects of her understanding are faulty. Yet, when she does things according to that flawed understanding, the end result is always correct. So perhaps I'd better not weigh in."[77] This frames a story where the family purchases a wild snowshoe hare, but due to communication issues, thinks it is a gazelle. The narrator is embarrassed by her mother's bargaining techniques (they think they are getting a good deal from a simple Kazakh herdsman), yet in the end it is the Han family that gets taken in. Nonetheless, they look on the bright side and become attached to their new, overpriced pet.

Sacred Routes and Dark Humor

Her grandmother particularly identifies with the rabbit: both feel lonely cold hunger during endless frigid winter days. As spring approaches distantly, the rabbit grows new fur, then disappears. The three women are dumbfounded and grieved by her loss, but eventually busy themselves with spring cleaning. One day the rabbit reappears in her basket within the home, completely disheveled, filthy, and barely alive. The narrator says, "compared to a dead thing, this kind of near-death not-yet-dead thing is even scarier. I always feel that at these moments its spirit is at its most vigorous, at its most vicious" (10). Her grandmother nurses the rabbit back to life, and the narrator eventually discovers the rabbit had burrowed a two-meter long tunnel underneath the house, and was just 20 centimeters from breaking ground, but had turned back in exhaustion and starvation: "that rabbit, so lonely in the pitch black freezing cold underground, braving starvation and the icy cold, bit by bit persisted in repeating the same movement—a movement toward spring... in the quiet of time and in the quiet of the soul, it could feel deep down the coming of spring, drop by drop" (11). Li Juan reflects: "People say rabbits are timid, but in my experience, rabbits are actually very courageous; they do not fear death. Whether entrapped, tied up, fleeing, starving, facing an impasse, even on the brink of death, they maintain that air of calm indifference" (11). She concludes, "The myriad things exist outside of our thoughts. It's impossible to communicate with them. No wonder grandma says 'rabbit, rabbit, you pitiful person'" (11).

For Li Juan, humans do what they do, as rabbits burrow in the earth in response to spring. "Motorcycling Through the Wilderness of Spring" ("Motuoche chuanguo chuntian de huangye" 摩托车穿过春天的荒野) is a humorous take on the fact that most humans love technological advances, speed, and the power associated with their acquisition. She acknowledges she had trouble simply riding a bike, but once she mastered motorcycling:

> I stand on the great earth and point my finger and say, I want to go *there*! Then I go there. And suddenly, when I realize that perhaps nothing is impossible in this world, I feel vaguely uneasy—it seems we've realized, via the motorcycle, that we just can't wait to go *there*; it's so convenient, we're so quickly and absolutely leaving something behind, permanently... at this point, we can't avoid it, we can't deny

reality. Heck, who's to say if it isn't good? Yeah—when I stand on the great earth and point in some direction: I want to go *there*!⁷⁸

In this essay the physical hardships and frustrations of depending upon public transportation to make a living or relocate to a more affordable locale (mentioned in other essays) is nowhere to be seen, replaced by an uneasy embrace of human desires for comfort, speed, convenience, adventure. Rather than separating humans from their technology, Li describes it as an extension of their nature. Humans do what humans do. Humans commune with nature ("feel the wind rushing by") while exalting in technologically enhanced hubris ("[the motorcycle] is essential to making me appear more distinct, more exquisite"). "I" and "we" rationalize what humans do.

Most Chinese ecocriticism on Li Juan's literature replicates the rhetorical logic of the Beijing western in ways that reinforce the supremacy of Han Chinese civilization, emphasizing the "harmony between humans and nature" conveyed in her essays. Chinese literary scholars most often describe Li Juan's writing style is as "purified," "light," "clean," "honest," and "natural." Fudan University professor Liu Zhirong places her writing "between earth and sky" and cultural pundit Xu Zhaoshou describes her work as connected to vital energies of earth and sky (both "grounded" 接地气 and "soaring" 接天气).⁷⁹ In his essay titled "Connect to the Vital Energies of Heaven and Earth: Transcend the Human," Xu goes on to historicize the Chinese civilization as the only ancient civilization that adopted the notion of "breath" (*qi*) at the center of their philosophy, claiming that "only Chinese Confucian and Daoist philosophies depend upon human wisdom to achieve enlightenment."⁸⁰ He cites essays by Xinjiang writers Liu Liangcheng and Li Juan as prime examples of such literary thought. Li Juan acknowledges that her writing was originally influenced by Liu Liangcheng, yet insists it has developed in very different ways. As we see next, Liu Liangcheng tends to write about the routines of everyday rural life in ways that serve as a platform for deeper philosophical reflections. While Li Juan's narrators also attempt to draw meaningful conclusions from everyday interactions and observations, they tend to be more hesitant, open-ended, and even double back on themselves. Li Juan's essays, as a whole, attend to practices and perceptions that confound both Western dualist and neo-Confucian syncretist epistemological categories of urban and rural, including the notions of "nature," "land," "labor," "animal," "machine," and "human" that undergird the dichotomy.

THE VILLAGE AS CHRONOTOPE: LIU LIANGCHENG'S BUCOLIC PHILOSOPHY

Liu Liangcheng 刘亮程 (b. 1962), a Han writer whose family has lived in eastern Xinjiang since the Qing dynasty, first rose to national prominence as "bucolic philosopher" (*xiangcun zhexuejia* 乡村哲学家) with his acclaimed collection of essays, *One Man's Village* (*Yigeren de cunzhuang* 一个人的村庄, 1999), which sparked a "Liu Liangcheng" fad in literary circles. In 2001 the work was adapted for a television docudrama by China Central Television, and scholarly work on ecological literature or literary depictions of the countryside continues to mention it.[81] After his first writing job at the *Worker's Daily* newspaper, he later turned to poetry, essays, and eventually fiction with the novels *Loose Earth* (*Xutu* 虚土, 2006) and *Zaokong* (凿空, 2009). He received the 2014 Lu Xun Literature Prize for his essay anthology *In Xinjiang* (*Zai Xinjiang* 在新疆). The "village" in Liu's essays is an embodied time-space entity that defines "Chineseness." He strives to maintain the place of the traditional cultural, poetic, spiritual notion of the village (*xiangcun* 乡村) in the Chinese imagination or heart/mind, even as the real countryside (*nongcun* 农村) changes or disappears.[82]

Most Chinese scholars read Liu's essays as a symptom of the separation of self from tradition due to rapid urbanization, marking a severing of the harmonious connection between human and nonhuman nature presumed to have existed before modernity, revolution, and capitalism. Characterized as "nature's son" (*ziran zhi zi* 自然之子), a "catcher in the rye" (*maitian de shouwangzhe* 麦田的守望者) and a "gleaner in the wilds" (*xiangyeli de shisuizhe* 乡野里的拾穗者), his work is seen as the product of a several-thousand-year-old agricultural civilization where nature writers explore the landscape to find a way back to the self.[83] However, one reason the self is alienated in the first place is that the foundations of agrarian empire rest on agrilogistics, or social technologies dependent upon separations between nature and culture.

Liu Liangcheng's essays illuminate gaps between self and other that arise from anthropocentrism. For example, in "The Things I Change" ("Wo gaibian de shiwu" 我改变的事务), Liu discusses anthropogenic impacts on the environment in minute, measurable ways. He moves a mound of dirt, forever altering an ant's destiny. He straightens a tree trunk by tying it to another tree, bending the second tree. He pats a cow on the rear with a shovel, moving it to the head of the pack, which alters that cow's fate, since it is the one chosen when the herd runs into a buyer. He writes:

> I pushed aside a black male goat that was just about to mount a nanny goat and let a white buck goat, what was about to burst with impatience, mount her. This took almost no effort from me, just the smallest of movements, but it changed utterly and completely the future of the goats. The nanny would have given birth to a black kid but now it was going to be white. That black buck hated me for sure, but I didn't care. Sooner or later all goats end up as food in our bellies, the meat of the black goat that hated me and the meant of the white goat that loved me would taste the same. In a goat's bone marrow, you can't taste the things we call love and hate, there's just fat, just nutrition.[84]

Liu's tongue-in-cheek entries call attention to the fact that human manipulation of the "myriad things" (*wanwu*) is often capricious, unconscious, or ineffective (from the human perspective). While the essays suggest that the myriad creatures have *ling* (soul; spirit; efficacy), they also convey the idea that each of us is the subjective, selfish center of our perception of the world "and that we eat animals and wear their flesh is *just the way it is* and will be."[85] Liu's agrarian acceptance of "the way things are" differs from nomadic understandings of relations with nonhuman animals. For example, the Kazakh saying recited before slaughter, "You were not born for sin, and I was not born to go hungry"[86] establishes an equivalency between humans and animals, while Liu rationalizes humans eating animal meat by naturalizing anthropocentrism.

The narrator also repeatedly states his belief that human agency alters time. "The Things I Change" ends, "I helped time, I helped that which needed to change to change. When I grow old, I'll say it is 'in time' that I grow old" (*woshi zai shiguangzhong laode* 我是在时光中老的). The dominant cosmology of the essays is clearly not Daoist, as many critics have claimed. Rather, Liu's neo-Confucian philosophy incorporates notions of general relativity and resonates with those of philosopher Alfred North Whitehead, trained as a physicist and mathematician. In *Process and Reality: An Essay in Cosmology,* Whitehead argues that reality is generative rather than a cause-and-effect determination resulting from substances in motion, and its essential character is "becoming" rather than "existence." Viewing the universe as time-developmental, Whitehead sees the fundamental element of reality as "experience," events that do not occur in time, but create time.

The "village" of Liu's anthology title functions as a discrete "timespace" entity that manifests in the flux of spacetime, as understood by quantum physics and first theorized in literature by Bakhtin in his 1937 essay, "Forms of Time and the Chronotope of the Novel."[87] Liu Liangcheng's "village" is a discrete "block" of spacetime in that it, and smaller blocks of spacetime such as "one man" or "I," manifest materially through processes. This can be illustrated in "What I Stopped" ("Wo dangzhule shenme" 我挡住了什么), the penultimate essay in the 2006 edition of *One Man's Village.* Though it harks back to the second essay in the collection, "The Things I Change," its notions of anthropogenic agency have evolved. On a visit back to his native village, the narrator describes multiple forces as a quantum energy field. It opens:

> This expanse of land was stripped clean by the wind long ago. The remnants of soil left on the broken walls were picked off by the wind bit by bit and blown away, a distressing sight. I know I cannot prevent this—many years ago when I moved a tree from the back of my house to the front, herded a flock of sheep surging to the west to a grassy riverbank on the east, I thought I could change many things, that I could stop the dispersal and disappearance of those things. (278)

Though he now realizes his individual force was inconsequential given larger forces, he points to what he *can* change through attention. The village is embodied in his heart/mind: "I actually did stop something. At least I stopped my heart, and let it stay in this village forever. I stopped my gradually fading memory—what I couldn't retain, I cast to the wind.

What this world cannot preserve, I preserve in my heart.... All I have in my heart is a village. Complete with livestock, humans, vegetation, sunlight, rain and footprints, and every single speck of dust in the setting sun" (278).

The conclusion foregrounds the fact that the village is understood to be a space-time entity, a chronotope of the mind that enables the narrator to move through time and space, even as he (on the medium of the written page) moves through a discrete village, Huangshaliang (黄沙梁):[88]

> I slow their harvest down a bit. Though I tread lightly, walking slowly across the village to the field, I still alarm them. They stop hands that are plucking cotton flowers, hands sorting rice, hands mowing grass, and hesitantly turn their gaze toward me—at this moment autumn slows down, like a cart that slowly comes to a stop, while in other places autumn continues as scheduled, the people there busily working for that same bit of food. Only in Huangshaliang this cart full of corn cobs will enter the courtyard a few steps late. A few snow-white cotton flowers will bloom a while longer. The half-carriage of stalks left on the ground will wait a while longer and may stay on the ground overnight.
>
> I, one individual, stood on the side of the road, and caused a small delay in the autumn harvest of a village. (278–79)

Here, the villagers *prehend* the narrator's presence, conveyed in the narrator's mind by depicting the slowing of their hand motions and slow recognition of a former villager as they harvest the fields, where "prehension" (*lingwu* 领悟) refers to the noncognitive "apprehension" of experienced data.[89] The interactions of these entities, in turn, alters time and the fate of individual corn stalks.

The ontology in *One Man's Village* combines evolutionary biology with speculative philosophy. In his evocative article on process-relational evolutionary cosmology, Adam C. Scarfe elucidates James Mark Baldwin's claim that organisms, through their selective activities and behavioral adjustments, play a causal role in directing evolutionary processes, by contextualizing it within Alfred North Whitehead's notion of "prehensive selectivity."[90] In *Science and the Modern World*,

Whitehead conceptualizes organisms as "units of emergent value," constituted by relations to other organisms, thoroughly engaged in their own creative life processes.[91] In *One Man's Village* organisms "prehend" the narrator's arrival (the villagers sense his presence, turn their gaze toward him, slow their hand movements). It conveys experiences of "feeling," "grasping," or "taking account of." Baldwin's theory of organic selectivity understands the organism to "cooperate in the formation of the modifications which are effected."[92] In *One Man's Village*, the narrator does not *intend* to delay the harvest by visiting his former village, but he *does* delay it, resulting in different outcomes for specific cotton plants, corn stalks, cows, and villagers. That the villagers *respond* to him, that they are not completely automated and utilitarian in completing their tasks, means they are open to accommodation. As such, the village is not merely a mechanistic chronotope but an organism.

The narrator's *attention* to the village foregrounds his agency in organic selectivity. His active focus on the village ("What this world cannot preserve, I preserve in my heart. I don't care about anything else. All I have in my heart is a village" [279]) prehends it, incorporating elements of its constitution in the narrator as organism after its physical disappearance. Baldwin insists that the chief characteristic of consciousness is attention, which implies discrimination and selection: "The central fact of consciousness, its prime instrument, its selective agent, its seizing, grasping, relating, assimilating, apperceiving—in short, its accommodating element and process—is attention."[93] By developing new habits of activity, by their own attention and selective activities, the individual organism can indirectly chart the course of the evolution of their species.[94] Baldwin theorizes "organismic evolutionism" versus "materialist evolutionism."

Liu explicitly states his organismic understanding of culture in a 2014 interview with Shu Jinyu. Asked how he feels about the disappearance of the Chinese countryside, Liu answered:

> A traditional culture based on Confucianism dominates the countryside ... generation after generation of peasants moving to the cities carry with them these values from the rural cultural matrix.... Mud-brick walls and tumbledown shacks have nothing to do with culture; people are its true bearers.

> I don't see the need to get overly worked up about these externally imposed changes on the countryside, they're inevitable. I'm more interested in the things inside people that don't change.... As long as a person has the countryside intact in their heart, wherever they go they'll be able to find a place to settle their body and soul.⁹⁵

The organism retains ethnic cultural norms, Liu insists, across vastly differing environments: "People can take rural culture with them to lives in the town. The town cannot give them a fully realized culture. If a Chinese person moves to America, they remain Chinese. They take their culture with them."⁹⁶ He also evokes social Darwinist understandings of racial genetics, concluding, "It doesn't matter if you've read the classics, you have the DNA of traditional Chinese culture in your blood."⁹⁷ By "Chinese" Liu does not necessarily mean exclusively "Han," yet the ethnic diversity of Xinjiang is remarkably invisible in his construction of the countryside (his home region of Shawan County has been populated by Han Chinese since the Han dynasty). Liu insists each of us has "a village," an ideal place of existence and manner of existence, that the idea is universal: "The book has preserved a village that we *all* have in our hearts."⁹⁸ But imperial, hierarchical, and agrarian forms of social organization inform the very notion of universality, manifesting as Confucian sociality in the Han Chinese countryside.

Liu's essay, "A Man Who Understands Donkeys" ("Tong lüxing de ren" 通驴性的人), exemplifies attention, yet ultimately reveals the violent relations comprising Hanspace cosmology. It begins with what Haraway calls an "entangled" understanding of relations between humans and domesticated animals:

> I have never been a donkey, and I can't tell what the heck a donkey is thinking about at any given moment. No donkey has ever been a man. We are two animals at either ends of the rope that connects us. Who can say for sure who is leading whom? Often footprints and hoofprints line up in the same direction only to end up going different ways. My donkey watches me day in and day out as I am busy with the work of being a person, and every day I see him living out the tough life of a donkey. We are each the observer of the other, we each get involved in the affairs of the other. (7)

Liu foregrounds the mutual gaze to emphasize the cataclysmic alienation from "nature" that dominates most societies.[99] Liu counters such separations by embracing "natureculture": the narrator searches for his lost donkey by tracing its tracks and smelling its droppings, concluding "yup, it's him." (6). Scents emanating from his domesticated animals intermingle with those of his simmering stews. Eventually, however, bucolic musings on mutual interdependence expose a dark underside: "I find a bit of myself in every animal's body... From raising them, to using them, to slaughtering them, my entire life is their entire life. I feed them time; they feed me flesh and blood" (7). The exchanges are not commensurate: one offers his time, the other sacrifices her life. Ultimately Liu unmasks the power differentials in intimacies governing village relations. For example, the narrator and other farmers indulge the mating rituals of their donkeys (despite frustration at lost work time) because of the payoff in village status. Men compete by proxy, basing their masculine prowess on their donkey's virility, resembling American slaveowners competing with other whites over slave endowments. Liu's narrator feels emasculated when his donkey views him naked, unlike Derrida in *The Animal That Therefore I Am*, who merely feels chagrined before his cat's gaze as he exits the shower.

As a corpus, Liu's essays expose the violent eugenics thought inherent in an ungrounded "village as chronotope" cosmology. By naturalizing the disappearance of the village as inevitable, while still retained in the heart by former inhabitants, the systematic destruction of Indigenous cultural heritage in Xinjiang is easily rationalized. Like Shen Wei's laments for a lost way of life, such disembodied colonial logics embrace violence. Li Juan's uneasy self-mockery aims to problematize and disrupt these unquestioned assumptions governing settler colonialism.

CHAPTER FOUR

Cosmic Ecologies and Transcendent Tricksters on the Tibetan Plateau

Imperialism . . . is an act of geographical violence.
—EDWARD W. SAID

The strong impetus to ground in Xinjiang stories diverges from cosmic motifs in Tibetan ecoliterature, which embeds local practices within Buddhist or Bön metaphysics and grand discourses of imperial and Sino-globalization. Adopting a variety of literary styles and genres, Tibetan environmental literature prominently centers Tibetan cosmologies that confound Hanspace assumptions. Sinophone novels by Alai and Tibetophone stories by Tsering Döndrup reincarnate trickster characters to foreground empires of resource extraction. Takbum Gyel's humorous dog tales suggest racist human ecologies. Poetry by Jangbu (Dorje Tsering Chenaktsang), Ju Kalsang, and Dekyi Drolma critiques rampant environmental devastation on the Tibetan Plateau. Hailing from religiously and ecologically diverse Tibetan subcultures, these writers inherit a shared literary culture where profane idiocy, devout sincerity, and biting sarcasm illuminate hypocrisies among clerics and leaders within hierarchical social structures.

ALAI'S *AS THE DUST SETTLES*: OPIUM AGENCY, DECIMATED EMPIRES, SHAMANISTIC TRANSCENDENCE

The industrial capitalism of the late nineteenth and early twentieth centuries, to which some attribute the start of the Anthropocene, built upon earlier colonialist drug enterprises rife with gunrunning and human trafficking. The highly acclaimed Sinophone novel *As the Dust Settles* (*Chenai luoding* 尘埃落定, 1998; translated as *Red Poppies*, 2003), by Hui-Tibetan writer Alai (b. 1959), features these themes. Alai was born in Maerkang in Ngawa Tibetan and Qiang Autonomous Prefecture in Sichuan Province. He writes exclusively in Chinese. He served as chief editor of *Science Fiction World* until, after becoming the first Tibetan author to win the Mao Dun Award for *As the Dust Settles* in 2000, he became a full-time writer. He has served as Sichuan Branch Chair of the Chinese Writers Association and Sichuan Ecological and Environmental Protection Ambassador. Alai has published poetry, short story, and essay collections, and his novels include *Empty Mountain* (*Kongshan* 空山, 2009), *The Epic of Gesar* (*Gesa'er Wang* 格萨尔王, 2009), and *In the Clouds* (*Yunzhong ji* 云中记, 2019).

As the Dust Settles is a novel of epic scale, set in the Sino-Tibetan ethnic corridor of Ngawa (Aba) in the decades prior to the communist victory of 1949. It details the Han Chinese introduction of opium into the Gyalrong (Jiarong) Tibetan economy, transforming it from subsistence farming to commodity exchange and ultimately destroying its chieftain system.[1] During the Manchu Qing dynasty (1644–1911), China was semi-colonized (in the form of foreign concessions, extraterritorial legal rights, treaty ports, missionary access, and Hong Kong colonization) by European powers following the Opium Wars of the mid–nineteenth century. Although opium was "banned," networks created by Qing expansion into Xinjiang, Tibet, and Mongolia drove its production deep into the dynasty's multiethnic frontier border regions, including Gyalrong.[2] The three traditionally defined Tibetan regions are northeast Amdo, central Ü-Tsang, and southeast Kham. The Gyalrong region in Ngawa Tibetan and Qiang Autonomous Prefecture in central Sichuan province is located between Amdo-speaking and Kham-speaking Tibetans (see figure 4.1).

Long marginal to both Han China and the rest of Tibet, Gyalrong comprises a contested geographic and cultural region. Some Tibetans suggest that people from Gyalrong are not true Tibetans. Others insist that the Gyalrong language is a very archaic form of Tibetan. After the collapse of the Tibetan Empire (fl. 7th–9th centuries CE) the region broke up into many small principalities. The Mongols briefly conquered the region prior to establishing the Yuan dynasty (1271–1368). While the

FIGURE 4.1 Map of Greater Tibet (Ü-Tsang, Amdo, and Kham) within the PRC. Alai is from Ngawa (Aba); Tsering Döndrup, Dekyi Drolma, Jangbu from Malho (Huangnan); Takbum Gyel from Tsolho (Hainan); Ju Kalsang from Golok (Guoluo).

Chinese loosely governed the region during the Ming Dynasty (1368–1644) by ordaining local chiefs, the Manchu rulers of the Qing dynasty finally tightened control over the region after two protracted wars in the late eighteenth century. Subsequently, many non-Tibetans, mainly Han and Muslim Hui, settled alongside Gyalrong Tibetans and Tibetan-related Qiang Indigenes. Thus, the Ngawa region is ethnically diverse due to migration and intermarriage over many centuries of warfare between rival empires.

Alai's novel largely reflects what happened historically under the rule of Liu Wenhui (1895–1976), a western Sichuanese warlord and the governor of Xikang, in the decade before the 1949 communist victory.[3] It details how the Han Chinese used opium to destroy the Tibetan chieftain system, just as the British undermined Qing sovereignty, by employing a "Capitalocene" logic of criminalizing opium in the center while allowing its quasi-legal circulation in the peripheries.[4] In the novel, the Han Chinese emissary who introduces opium to the region strategically offers to buy back opium from the chieftain if he uses half the proceeds to buy new weapons for his Tibetan compatriots, knowing they will destroy each other more quickly that way. Significantly, the "idiot" son of Tibetan Chief Maichi and his Chinese wife promotes the idea of monocropping opium poppies to the family's local rivals. The other chieftains jettison sustainable crop rotations and end up with depleted soils and no subsistence crops, while the idiot-savant narrator plants grain, monopolizing the food market and outsmarting his elder brother to gain prominence.

Far from a glorious enterprise of epic proportions where the ends justify the means, the novel depicts the opium trade as brutally corrupting and its power as ultimately delusional. Initially it portrays the Han Chinese, including the narrator's opium-addicted mother, as particularly heartless devourers. In one scene, a mouse falls from a roof beam where opium is processed. A worker skins the mouse alive, slicing it open to remove its throbbing lungs and beating heart: "'You're frightening my son,' the chieftain's wife said with a smile. . . . She purred like a cat as she tore at the mouse. 'It's delicious, just delicious. Come, my son, try some.' I felt like throwing up. I ran out the door. I'd never believed all that nonsense about how scary the Han people were."[5] In his youth, the Tibetan-Han narrator displays empathy for the suffering of sentient beings, while the Han infiltrators, despite their affectations of civility, express cannibalistic brutality and strategies rooted in imperial agrilogistics.

Yet, over time the Tibetans replicate such imperialist insensitivity. When a "Living Buddha" of the Geluk school headed by the Dalai Lama (versus the older Nyingma school of Tibetan Buddhism dominant in Ngawa, whose lamas were advising the Maichi family) warns of opium's corrupting influence, the chief orders the lama's execution. His once-sensitive son gazes blankly, "forgetting we were about to kill" the lama, staring as his tongue is cut off: "With a glint of the blade, the tongue sprang out into the space between the prisoner's mouth and the executioner's hand, like a startled mouse" (161). The narrator was once sickened by, not inured to, the skinning of a "startled mouse." Yet once the Maichi family colonizes their compatriots via opium, a drug-addled haze descends on the colonizers themselves: "everything was unreal" yet "the vast territory and never-ending time gave us the feeling the Maichi empire was unshakable and would last forever" (154).

Alai's judicious choice of an "idiot" narrator evokes notions of empire blind to its own idiocy, while simultaneously undermining imperialist characterizations of opium addiction. As Mark Driscoll recounts in his environmental history of European-American imperialism in East Asia, the British associated "idiocy" with Chinese opium smokers and considered the drug less virile than alcohol, the British Empire's drug of choice.[6] Further, Alai's choice of an "idiot" narrator has a double-entendre, as Sichuanese local opera, like Shakespearian drama, famously incorporates the role of the "fool" (*xiaochou jiao* 小丑角) who invariably outsmarts and tricks elite and better-educated characters.[7] Indeed, historically the Sichuanese managed to double opium production and significantly undercut the price of imported British-Indian opium, further hastening imperial decline.

Serialized anti-imperialist novels at the turn of the twentieth century, such as *Lord Jim* (1899–1900) or *Tales of the Moon Colony* (1904–1905), are important generic antecedents to Alai's anti-epic of the Anthropocene. In his seminal work on the global opium trade, historian Carl Trocki argues that Joseph Conrad's *Lord Jim* is a "parable of European imperialism" that associates "idiotic" dreamlike addiction with the imperialist drug pushers rather than the opium addicts.[8] He describes Jim's moral senses as "anesthetized" and his psychic state as "atrophied," "pleasurably languid," and "intoxicated with imaginary success." Conrad, Trocki argues, suggests the British dream of empire was itself a kind of opiate that deluded Britons and made it difficult for them to confront the fundamental evil of imperialism. Similarly, *Tales of the Moon Colony*, one of China's first science fiction novels, also features a "fool" as protagonist and goes to great lengths to delegitimize China as a geographic or moral center. Its looming colonial relationship with the people on the moon suggests a decentering not only of Europe but also of the planet Earth itself, suggesting a narrative trajectory in which the governing metropole shifts to deep space.[9]

As the Dust Settles takes the anti-imperialist theme further by destroying cosmological conditions for an imperial center. In the anti-imperialist novel, the stubborn imperialist fact is merely relocated; in the anti-epic novel, it is annihilated altogether. The idiot-prophet anticipates the apocalyptic decimation of earth's creatures in the penultimate scene of the novel. He dreams that the chieftains' estates have crumbled, leaving behind no life after the dust settles: "I didn't even see the footprints of birds or animals. The earth was covered by dust, as if shrouded in loosely woven silk" (373–74). The Han emissary interprets his dream as a premonition of China's longed-for unification after decades of civil war and warlord governance, but the powerfully aestheticized scene of utter destruction that ends the novel instead evokes the eradication of all living beings, portending global apocalypse in the era of the Anthropocene.

Given its apocalyptic sensibilities, the subject position of Alai's narrator deserves further interrogation. In an interview, Alai claimed his protagonist evokes an epic figure in Tibetan oral folk tales, Aku Tonpa.[10] Stories of Aku Tonpa, which circulate to this day, are said to be based on a twelfth-century practitioner of the Karma Kagyu, a Tibetan Buddhist school which celebrates unconventionality and emphasizes, to the exclusion of other sources of authority, the continuity of oral instructions from the Buddha transmitted from master to disciple.[11] Aku Tonpa, which means "Uncle Teacher," acts both as an advocate for justice, uprooting social oppression and assisting the powerless populace, and as a clever swindler, critical of religious hypocrisy. He also exhibits bawdy sexuality in Tibetan oral tales. The voracious sexual appetites of Alai's idiot narrator signal his continuity with long-standing Tibetan oral tradition as opposed to more recent Chinese communist versions which inculcate political correctness.[12]

While Chinese scholarship often highlights the novel's ironic portrayal of Tibetan Buddhism, it is important to recognize that the Tibetan literary tradition encourages such critique. In his study of oral and literary continuities in Tibetan literature, Lama Jabb emphasizes that prominent clerics and ordinary folk tales regularly denounce corrupting propensities of Buddhist clergy.[13] Instead, Tibetan culture's porous boundaries between sacred and profane means that bawdy "fools" such as Aku Tonpa often transmit profound spiritual insights due to their liminal phenomenological positioning, as Alai's narrator illustrates: "I'd been an idiot all my life, but now I knew I was neither an idiot nor a smart person. I was just a passerby who came to this wondrous land when the chieftain system was nearing its end. Yet heaven had let me see and let me hear, had placed me in the middle of everything while having me remain above it all. It was for this purpose that heaven had made me look like an idiot" (429).

In his analysis of this passage, Gang Yue emphasizes the narrator's spiritual role as a passerby witness to "the end of cyclical history," suggesting a Hegelian-Marxist historiography in which the destruction of the Tibetan chieftain system and triumph of the Communists mark the end of feudal imperial cycles.[14] Indeed, the narrator locates the "speed of time" in "the year when the Maichi family began growing opium" (356–57), seemingly emphasizing the organizing principles of capital, which drive toward what Marx referred to as the annihilation of space by time. Nonetheless, Alai vehemently denies the Marxist notion that the demise of the chieftain system was a "natural" consequence of historical progress.[15] Yue thus suggests that Alai's narrator retains (suicidal) agency: "the passerby must devise his own death along with the demise of the chieftain system upon fulfilling his mission as a witness to—not a martyr of—that history."[16]

Yue's analysis, while compelling, nonetheless fails to account for shamanistic agency in the novel. Ultimately, the entire narrative conveys the mysticism central to Bön, a Tibetan religion influenced by animist and shamanist beliefs still prominent among Gyalrong Tibetans, despite the historical dominance of Buddhism. As Li Jian argues, the novel portrays Bön shamanic practices throughout (exorcisms, rituals, dream-knowledge, prognostication, curses, etc.).[17] In the final scene as the idiot-narrator lies dying, having foreseen and accepted his fated assassination by a Tibetan enemy, the smell of liquor (the Empire's "drug of choice") permeates his room. He describes his body as splitting into two halves and calls on Heaven to reincarnate his soul, which "has finally struggled out of my bleeding body and is flying upward. When the sunlight flickers, the soul will disperse. There will be nothing except a white light" (433). The "idiot" is in fact a "soul" that, by bearing witness to ecological and cultural genocide, ultimately achieves pure awareness, merging with light.[18] Thus the liminal positioning of the idiot savant as a "passerby" conveys not suicidal agency but Bön shamanistic agency of immersion "in the middle of everything" while simultaneously remaining "above it all" (429).

HOLLOWING OUT NGAWA: ALAI'S *EMPTY MOUNTAIN*

In his six-volume novel *Empty Mountain* (*Kongshan* 空山, 2005–2009), Alai depicts four decades of changes under Chinese governance in the fictional Gyalrong Tibetan village of Jicun, presumably located in Ngawa.[19] The first volume, *Scattered in the Wind*, recounts the Party's "Democratic Reform" (1958–1963), where Han cadres supervised infrastructure projects in Ngawa following the violent military crackdown on Tibetan opposition (1956–1958). As the story opens, the monasteries and their artifacts had been destroyed, monks had been defrocked, and villagers who had hunted and foraged were now required to chop down trees to "open up the wasteland" for agriculture. The story subtly denigrates Maoist themes of "conquering nature," which contrast significantly with Tibetan understandings of landscape. As geographer Emily Yeh explains:

> Though Tibetans historically celebrated the "taming" of the landscape through the pinning down of the supine demoness and the conversion to Buddhism, they also praised the quality of being wild and uncultivated in numerous contexts, including the Tibetan origin myth. Tibetan poetry expresses an affinity for open, expansive, unfarmed landscapes, as do continuing cultural practices of hermitage and retreat, and there is no Tibetan equivalent of the "Foolish Old Man who moved the mountain."[20]

Yeh details CCP efforts to transform Tibetans into socialist subjects, which started in 1952 in the Tibet Autonomous Region, including forced labor to "reform" prisoners of war by building a hydroelectric plant, state farms, and ecologically devastating attempts to reclaim "wasteful" wetlands.[21] *Scattered in the Wind* depicts how the Party enacted similar civilizing strategies to discipline landscapes and bodies in a village of hunters and foragers after the 1956 Tibetan uprisings in Ngawa. Although ownership of firearms had been ubiquitous among Tibetan hunters by the 1940s, the People's Liberation Army (PLA) confiscated all arms for "Democratic Reform" without making allowances for game hunters.[22]

Alai's six-volume novel, in its entirety, depicts how Gyalrong Tibetans eventually resigned themselves to the new system of Han domination where land, forest, and watercourses were confiscated. They continued to find refuge in the Bön religion despite the dismantling of Buddhist monasteries, a theme explored in *Celestial Fire*, the second volume of *Empty Mountain*. Set in Jicun during the Cultural Revolution, it features competing ecological paradigms for fire control: shamanistic understandings of the elements, based on hunter-gatherer land management practices, are pitted against Maoist voluntarism of "man overcoming nature" (*ren ding sheng tian* 人定胜天). In the story, officials imprison a Bön shaman, Dorje, for lighting a fire to clear land for Tibetan farmers. Yet when another blaze breaks out, the state's approach is ineffective because people spend as much time in political meetings and struggle sessions as they do in fighting the forest fire. They merely cut down trees and drain a sacred lake, destroying forests and animal habitats. After the fire subsides, the government representatives leave and support is withdrawn, thus the people of the village continue their lives in the aftermath of this "natural" disaster. Contrary to the early promises of liberation and prosperity, by the sixth volume of *Empty Mountain*, set in the 1990s, the valley has become a tourist destination with Jicun villagers engaging in sex trafficking to survive. Recalling the denouement of *As the Dust Settles*, and foreshadowing themes in *In the Clouds*, the series concludes as an anti-epic of the Anthropocene, reducing to "emptiness" the broad sweep of human history. Alai enacts ecocriticism throughout the *Empty Mountain* series by adopting long-standing motifs in Tibetan literature of irony, humor, and the use of trickster characters to challenge prevailing developmentalist ecological understandings and civilizing social norms based on social Darwinist racial hierarchies.

In *Scattered in the Wind*, two central characters are impoverished and socially marginalized: Gela, "bastard" son of a sexually promiscuous woman with mental illness, and Sangdan, whose "idiot smile" Gela shares (6). As in *As the Dust Settles*, "idiots" often conveys profound truths that are politically incorrect. Exijiang is another marginalized protagonist, as the mother of defrocked monk, Enbo, and sister of the former lama, Jiangcun Gongbu. Villagers dismiss her comments as the unwelcome ramblings of an old woman, but she is the sole villager to extend consistent compassion to Gela and Sangdan. At one point, Exijiang says about Gela, "This child is fated to be short-lived. If he lived elsewhere, he would be a Heavenly Gift. But do you know what our Ji Village is? A marshy swamp, have you ever seen a big upright tree grow in a miry bog? No. That's because small trees grow rotten in the mud" (19). Here she implies that Gela's keen sensitivities would be recognized as a Heavenly Gift in an environment that fostered Buddhism and his smaller body would flourish if allowed to hunt and forage like his Tibetan ancestors. However, the village has become a "marshy swamp" environmentally, spiritually, and socially. In Jicun boys from "politically correct" class backgrounds in the "new society" falsely accuse Gela of throwing a firecracker at her grandson, who eventually dies of improperly treated wounds. As an exemplar of Buddhist compassion, Exijiang alone defends Gela's innocence.

Both women, despite their marginalized status in the "new society," deliver scathing critiques of its hypocrisy.[23] Exijiang "interprets" Sangdan's mutterings for the fellow villagers:

> Sangdan continued muttering to herself. "What is Gela's Ma saying?" Rabbit asked his grandma.
> "I know," Exijiang replied. "She's saying that although everyone says the New Society is good, people's lives haven't improved, and there's more work to do than before."
> Sangdan glanced at Exijiang with a knowing twinkle in her eye, as if expressing agreement with the old woman's translation. Then she fell back into her own conversation, her lips moving fast.
> "I think I understand what she's saying," Exijiang nodded. "She's saying that before, the Old Society divided people into upper and lower classes. So how come there are people today who don't do anything but ride in trucks up and down this huge new road, looking more aristocratic than the lords of old?" (99)

Here, the women declare that despite the Party's claims of class-based liberation, elitism and poverty remains: the cadres have merely replaced the Tibetan aristocrats of the Old Society. Further, the cadres have destroyed the natural environment through agrilogistics, deforesting to build roads and farmland and introducing toxins such as chemical fertilizer, the likely cause of widespread eye disease in the village during dust storms.

Through socially marginalized characters such as "idiots," "superstitious clergy," and "insane women," *Scattered in the Wind* conveys

Gyalrong Tibetan cynicism about the Party's developmental messaging. Local cadres urge the villagers to celebrate the first telephone line into the village. They force them into corvee labor to build the first road to the village and cut down trees for a burgeoning timber industry. Despite promises of "trickle down econometrics" or "technology transfer," the villagers begin to note that only the Han cadres use the telephones; they do not have access to them. Further, only the cadres ride in cars. The villagers merely gather around them for entertainment, "not because they wanted to see a car, but because if they didn't there was nothing better to see" (129). The existence of cars is a bitter joke. The Sinicized Tibetan cadre, Suopo, taunts the defrocked monk, Enbo (recently detained for not having "identity papers," a new restriction on Tibetan mobility, when he recently attempted to travel across a county line), saying, "Automobiles are coming! The Communist Party is creating happiness for us Tibetans, aren't you happy?" To diffuse the tension, trickster Gela starts playacting: "Gela walked over, clapping his hands and shouting, 'Bus tickets! Bus tickets! Money, Money, buy bus tickets! Show your identity papers!' After laughing, the people all got quiet, remembering something. That the vehicles would come was certain, but they didn't have money and didn't have identification, this truth was also certain" (59–60). In fact, the workload for Tibetan men doubles, yet they earn only two additional work points for facilitating the timber supply chain out of the village. "The road was paved, but Jicun villagers still had to use their two feet to walk and bear the burden of unprecedented labor due to truck transportation. People were exhausted, but that wasn't so bad, because energy could be replenished, but the leather soles on the men's feet wore out faster than normal, and no one compensated them for that" (97). The social outcasts voice the inconvenient truths that very little in the "new society" has changed.

Thus, the novella describes a society that is much worse than before: animal habitats are destroyed and thousand-year-old primeval forests are razed during the "destroy forests and open wasteland" (*huilin kaihuang* 毁林开荒) campaign. Perhaps the most cynical scene is when Suopo prompts the woodcutters to work harder, with more precision, to contribute to building Mao's "Long Life Palace" (*wansui gong* 万岁宫) located elsewhere in Sichuan Province. The defrocked monk, Enbo, challenges Suopo, saying, "Isn't that a feudal superstition? Don't we say that believing a person's spirit doesn't die, and lives beyond 100 years, is a feudal superstition?" (106–7). While onlookers silence Enbo, an emboldened Suopo commands the work team: "Everyone listen carefully, we are offering our most precious birth wood to the long-life temple. Make sure there is not one single knot or chip in the wood. Chairman Mao likes orderly things!" (107).

> The sound of axes rang out on the eastern mountain slope the very next day, destroying the tranquility of the beautiful forest. The slender birch trees, elegant and straight, spun unwillingly to the ground in quick succession. The woodpeckers, who had ministered to the trees by eating the bugs that lived in them, flew away. The rats and rabbits fled in panic, while foxes, magpies, and the timid musk deer went in search of new homes. One startled bear attacked the axe-wielding men, but it was quickly put down by a few rifle shots. . . .
>
> The trucks kept coming even after the forest had disappeared. The men had long ago given up trying to imagine how massive this Long Life Palace would be. They had cut down more trees than had ever been cut before in the history of Ji village. In the beginning, progressives like Suopo invested a lot of energy dreaming about the palace, yet as the tally of trees rose, even their imaginations faltered. (107)

Ultimately, the socially outcast interlocutors throughout the *Empty Mountain* series convey several important messages. First, they state the obvious: the Tibetans, who, the Chinese claim, were enslaved by feudal masters as serfs, are merely beholden to new masters in the Chinese communist state. Second, they imply that rigid social distinctions (categorizing class status, ethical standards, ideological or religious beliefs, etc.) are arbitrary and easily interchangeable. Finally, they demonstrate that ecological cosmologies determined by empire, or state power, is built upon social hierarchies that discriminate against subalterns. Modern socialist industrialization is merely a new form of serfdom. Mao worship replaces Tibetan superstition.

TIBETOPHONE ECOFICTION FROM AMDO BY TAKBUM GYEL, TSERING DÖNDRUP, AND JANGBU

Tsering Döndrup (b. 1961) was a shepherd from age eight to thirteen in Malho (Henan) Mongolian Autonomous County in Qinghai. He then studied Tibetan and Chinese literature, graduating in 1982 from Huangnan Tibetan Autonomous Prefecture Normal School in Rebkong and publishing Tibetophone stories while serving as deputy head of Tuoyema Township in Malho, director of the Malho County Local History Office, and director of the Malho County Archives Bureau. His literary works have been translated into Chinese, English, French, and Japanese and have won numerous awards. As a corpus, Tsering Döndrup's stories explore double-edged sword of the gift of Chinese development in the twenty-first century. He adapts traditional epic narrative forms to detail statist attacks on nomadic lifestyles, linguistic invasion of the Chinese language, and the threats to Tibet's environment from industrial modernity.[24]

All of his stories take place in the fictional county of Tsezhung, a rural nomad locale along the real Tsechu River in his home region of Malho (or Sogpo, the Tibetan word for Mongol), where residents are ethnically Mongolian but culturally and linguistically Tibetan (see figure 4.1). According to Tibetan literary scholar and translator Heather Stoddard, although the Mongol community had become entirely Tibetanized by the early twentieth century, "they retained something of the bellicose nature of their forefathers, and the boys grew up as proud and unruly fighters. Honor, courage, kindness and hospitality are strong virtues, as well as an independent spirit, playful humor, and delight in conversation, poetry and heroic lore."[25] Just as Gyalrong Tibetans are questioned for their authenticity *as* Tibetans, residents of Malho are sometimes marginalized and stigmatized within elite Tibetan circles.[26] Nonetheless, Malho writers such as Tsering Döndrup, along with Jangbu and Dekyi Drolma, are popular and prominent Tibetophone writers.

The immediate context for his 2012 story, "Black Fox Valley," is a government campaign to "Return the Pastures and Restore the Grasslands," as part of a major "Open up the West" (*xibu kaifa* 西部开发) campaign launched in 1999 to promote economic development.[27] Socially engineered urbanization has incentivized large numbers of nomad communities to resettle to new towns as part of the plan to "retire" grazing pastures. This program is consistent with the twenty-first-century Capitalocene logic of green governmentality, which occurs when "state and non-state actors [seek] to 'improve' conditions of nature and populations by introducing new cultural/scientific logics for interpreting qualities of a state's territory. In doing so, a hegemonic discourse of ecological difference rooted in neoliberal market ideology emerges, defining some 'qualities of territory' as degraded, and others as necessary instruments for the improvement of populations, states, and natures."[28] Yet such green governmentality invokes a scientific logic that interprets these peoples and territories as backward and degraded.[29] Tibetan scholar Huatse Gyal illustrates this point: "Read the opening lines of any Chinese scientific publication or Chinese policy document on the Tibetan Plateau and you will likely see one (or all) of the following descriptors: harsh environment (*huanjing elie* 环境恶劣), cold weather (*qihou hanleng* 气候寒冷), dry land (*handi* 旱地), wasteland (*huangdi* 荒地), and fragile ecology (*shengtai cuiruo* 生态脆弱)."[30]

"Black Fox Valley" adopts narrative conventions similar to those of Alai's *As the Dust Settles* and *Moŋoliya* (analyzed in chapter 2): a farcical title, a "foolish" protagonist, and the aborted temporality that marks the anti-epic of the Anthropocene. Contrasting rich mountain valley ecology to cheap urban commodities and substandard construction, the story details the devolution of Sangyé, father of a family forced to relocate and once respected member of the nomadic community, into a "fool" scorned by Chinese-speaking local officials and alienated from his Sinicized daughter, Lhari Kyi. The opening taxonomy of the diverse botanical species of the mountain valley explicitly evokes the utopian "Thousand Lotus Pasture" described in the *Epic of Gesar* (circa 12th century CE), said to be the longest epic in the world. This idyllic pastoral setting, long romanticized in the Tibetan, Mongolian, and Central Asian cultural imagination, sharply contrasts with the present. It describes how for centuries before the mining devastation, the Malho grasslands in Qinghai were covered with a diversity of blossoming flora: leopard plants, knotweed, lamiophlomis, white snow lotus, black and white gentians, Himalayan aster, Tibetan dandelions, white wormwood, potentilla, and countless other plants and flowers.

In contrast to this "Thousand Lotus Pasture," the title of "Black Fox Valley" signifies a narrative framed by the motif of extracting resources such as the "expensive black rock" out of the valley (196). Although the government presents Sangyé with a fifty-year "pasture usage permit" to the valley, he perceptively asks the resident lama, to no avail, why (usually red) foxes in the valley are black (170). The story's penultimate scene resembles that of *Mongoliya* (chapter 2), portraying a nomad's body and the grassland itself brutally decimated for extraction capital. On a return visit from town to their pastureland, the family compares the excavated land to the ravaged body of Lhari Kyi, crushed in an earthquake due to shoddy school construction.[31]

> They were confronted with a sight even more shocking and incomprehensible than that of Lhari Kyi's crushed little body. The entirety of Black Fox Valley had been dug up and turned into an expense of pitch black. Everywhere you looked there were diggers, loaders, dump trucks, and tractors scurrying like ants from a next, a seething maelstrom of activity. The roar of the machines sounded like a thousand thunderclaps booming at once (196).

Green governmentality enacts biopiracy by extracting Tibetan biological resources and legal land rights. Offspring must learn Chinese, acculturated into Han lifestyles that alienate them from their elders, their very lives considered expendable in the race for more profits (see figure 4.2).

In "Black Fox Valley" the initially hopeful Tibetan family members, though vague about logistics of resettlement, end up impoverished and depressed or dead. Ethnographer Jarmila Ptackova, who did field research on the sedentarization of Tibetan pastoralists from 2005 to 2017, observes that "the smaller the awareness among the pastoral population in Qinghai about the launch of the new development program of the Chinese leadership, the bigger would be its impact on every aspect of their lives."[32] While Ptackova cautions against simplistically viewing sedentarization policies as either forced assimilation or an effective modernization policy of poverty eradication, she acknowledges that by 2017 the Zeku (rTse khog) County Department for Poverty Alleviation in Qinghai had made plans only to construct housing and had not developed plans for helping settlers integrate socially and economically.

FIGURE 4.2 Mining ravages a Tibetan valley. Still from Jangbu's film, *Voices of the Stone* (2018).

The Tibetan stakeholders view these recent government policies as unprecedented. The Chinese state has altered the lives of Tibetan pastoralists since the 1950s through agricultural reforms, people's communes, and granting usage rights over pastures to individual households; yet animal husbandry, their primary occupation had previously been left intact.[33]

Thus, many of the stories and poems of nomadic life that follow either grieve its loss or were written prior to the twenty-first century sedentarization programs. Takbum Gyel (b. 1966) is a prominent Tibetophone writer who grew up on the Sumdo grasslands of Mangra (Ch: Guinan) County, Tsolho (Hainan) Tibetan Autonomous Prefecture in Qinghai. He graduated from Hainan Minzu Normal University in 1986, studied at Northwest Nationalities Institute from 1988 to 1990, and has since been a teacher. A member of the Chinese Writers Association, he has published more than a hundred pieces since 1987, with translations into Chinese, English, French, German, and Japanese. He also wrote the first Tibetophone novel from Qinghai, *The Silent Grassland*.

In "The Illusion of a Day" (1990), Takbum Gyel details nomadic life in a beautifully written account of the life of a Tibetan nomad from Amdo (Qinghai).[34] The illusion in question is time, conflating a day with a lifetime or generations. The story starts with the line "It was getting light," as the little boy, Yangbum, wakes in the tent to the sights, sounds and smells of his widowed mother cooking breakfast. It ends with Yangbum worrying if his grandson will take good care of the sheep: "And like that, like that, it slowly got dark. It got dark." Yangbum's life events and thoughts are seamlessly integrated into the free indirect speech of the limited third-person narrative, gently moving time forward while cyclically accreting actions that emplace his nomadic community in the plateau ecosystem. With the birth and death of Yangbum's precious lamb(s) juxtaposed against his own aging process, Takbum Gyel describes the interdependent relationship between the herder and sheep. References in the story to Tibetan Buddhist beliefs in reincarnation also evoke a cyclic sense of time, where lives are just a single manifestation of a being, and the distinction of past, present, and future can be an illusion. A narrative structure of recurring themes woven into the text reinforces this: the women collecting dung, Yangbum exchanging stories for tips on the best grazing land, and the repeated interjection of "*baa-aa*," signifying the frail bleating of yet another (the same?) newborn lamb.

While beautifully evocative, the story does not romanticize gender inequity in Tibetan nomadic life. It matter-of-factly discloses the community's rigid, unequal gender roles: "Cooking, cleaning, fetching water, milking the animals, gathering dung—that was women's work. Yangbum knew that it was inappropriate for men to do women's work. It just shouldn't be done, he thought, and you'd be inviting the scorn of others if you did." Men compensate for their guilt at the disproportionate burden placed on women through religious rituals: "Yangbum recited one hundred million manis for his mother after she died. This was the only way he could show his gratitude. He was constantly praying that his beloved mother would be reborn in the pure land." The story shows women prematurely aging (Yangbum outlives his wife), their burden replicated by successive generations. After Yangbum gets married, his mother no longer collected dung: "All he and his wife had needed to worry about was making their food; milking the yaks, churning the butter, cleaning out the pen, gathering dung, spinning yarn, weaving—these were hard tasks" (see figure 4.3). Ironically, these "hard tasks" for "he and his wife" are all women's work.

FIGURE 4.3 Yaks are integral to Tibetan nomadic life. Photo by author, June 2007.

What the male sheepherder gains from his relative freedom is the opportunity to ponder the philosophy of existence. In the beginning of the "day," Yangbum placed the "little life" into his bag, which he carries around throughout a "day;" the lives of Yangbum and the lamb(s) are intertwined. Later, Yangbum notices the lamb's bleating strengthening, noting he should find in the bleating a "joy of a growing life," but has doubts on how joyful growing up is, as "whatever grows up will get old. Whatever gets old will die" and "when you die you go to hell" to suffer the "endless torments of freezing and burning." When Yangbum climbs the mountain to admire the scenery he sees the world as "completely still" and "round like an egg" that "kept turning day and night like a wheel." The contrast between the lamb's life, his own, and the continuation of the world after their death reinforces the impersonal environment compared to the animate sentient beings, whose lives last only a day relative to the world's unfathomable endurance. The story thus reinforces an illusory sense of time and material existence, central Buddhist tenets. Yangbum also associates seasons with enmity: he fears the deadly first spring for lambs (when they are often killed by eagles), which is nonetheless preferable to the "brutal and terrifying prospect" of an "eternal winter." Reminiscent of characters in Mandumai's stories (chapter 2), Yangbum repeatedly meditates on perceived paradoxes from a human perspective that appear to dissipate or resolve within the wider ecocentric perspective offered by the narrative structure.

Jangbu's story "Odd Boots" (1998) challenges the status quo in Amdo Tibetan nomadic cultures even more directly than Takbum Gyel's "Illusion of a Day." Jangbu is the pen name of Dorje Tsering Chenaktsang (b. 1963), a prominent Tibetan poet and filmmaker. Like Tsering Döndrup, he was raised in Malho Mongolian Autonomous County in Qinghai Province, a locale with a rich tradition of fierce fighters and strong sense of independence. In her introduction to her translation of Jangbu's works, Tibetan scholar Helen Stoddard also attributes Jangbu's strong character to his illiterate Tibetan mother, "who adopted a fundamental approach to raising her nine children: that they be allowed to follow their natural inclinations in all things."[35] Jangbu has published poems, stories, and essays since 1980, and his works have been translated into Mongolian, Chinese, French, and English. He has been awarded more than a dozen major Tibetan literary prizes, including the most prestigious prize for Tibetan-language literature, the Jomolangma Award, in 2001. He taught Tibetan language and chemistry in the Malho Middle School from 1981 to 1984, then majored in Tibetan language and literature at the Northwest University for Nationalities (Xibei minzu daxue) in Lanzhou from 1984 to 1988. After graduation, he became editor of the Tibetan-language literary journal *Bod kyi rtsom rig sgyu rtsal* (Tibetan Literature and Art) in Lhasa from 1989 to 2006. He also taught Tibetan at the National Institute for Oriental Languages and Civilizations in Paris from 2002 to 2008. Though he has lived in France since 2005, he frequently returns to Tibet, often to shoot his films, which include *Tantric Yogi* (2005), *Kokonor* (2008), *Ani Lachem* (2005), *Yartsa Rinpoche* (2014), and *Voices of the Stone* (2018), the last on mining in Qinghai.

"Odd Boots" opens the same way as "Illusion of a Day," with a young boy awakening to his mother's admonitions to get up, but rather than herding, this child's morning task is to light a fire in the schoolhouse. Chaklo (like Yangbum) places his mother's griddlecakes in his knapsack, reflecting on the landscape geomancy of the mountainous plateau:

> The sunlight made the "mountain" in front of the village that everyone called the "Dozing Dzomo" look at present exactly like a

white half-breed female yak, with a large humped back—even though it was just a hill. She was held to be the foundation from which the "three excellent white substances" [milk, butter, and yoghurt] flowed. That is why everyone made offerings to her with great veneration. The old people said that the "vital essence" of the entire community was provided by this one dome, and that it still keeps on flowing even today. So who would dare say that the construction of the new Silden ("Cool Land") Primary School at the foot of this important mountain was not a great joy for all, teachers and schoolchildren alike?[36]

Yangbum's parallel reflections on landscape read: "He drove the flock past the edge of their camp, and they came upon a small hill. This was the route he always took to the pastures, and he knew the land like the back of his hand. Every land has its peaks and canyons—that's the way of the world. It seemed to him that if there were no valleys and hills on the land, it would be as dull as a flat stone, wouldn't it?"[37]

While both writers convey geocosmic presumptions, reinforced by rhetorical questions, Chaklo's ironic question undermines societal norms, while Yangbum's question reinforces his emplacement on the plateau. Here the stories diverge greatly, not so much due to Chaklo's potential for social mobility via schooling (which, in the story, merely seems to reinforce disciplinary strictures), but due to his extraordinarily high degree of individual autonomy. Although Yangbum grows, weds, and ages, generational cyclicality engages with the replication of seasons, and the rising and setting of the sun in one day. The time frame in "Odd Boots," on the other hand, is one mere day in Chaklo's boyhood, yet the dynamics of this day are unique. They resist replication. This child will wander far from the plateau. Chaklo walks to school imagining the joy of having the wings of a vulture, "his dream appearing fantastic, marvelous, astonishing, even wildly boastful" (137). His subsequent encounters challenge such daring reveries, as person after person recoils from him with a battery of curses. Puzzled as to why he is considered "such a troublemaker," Chaklo eventually realizes he is wearing one red and one blue boot. By nightfall, as he returns to his mother, the matter of his "odd boots" has escalated:

FIGURE 4.4 Livestock, prayer flags, prayer wheels integral to Tibetan lifeways. Photo by author, June 2007.

In the village of Silden, the news of Chaklo's odd boots spread in secret whispers from one person to the next. They gaped and opened their eyes wide, stuck out their tongues, shook their heads and sighed long sighs. The whole matter had to be discussed!

Some were afraid. "The world is topsy-turvy! It's getting worse from one generation to the next!"

Chaklo's mother was sick with anguish. She could not sit still. Pacing to and fro in the square room half lit by a butter lamp, she prayed incessantly. (139)

Although Chaklo surprises his mother by resolving the problem (he had rubbed both his boots with red ocher-colored earth), the story ends by trailing off humorously: "Odd boots ... odd ..." (139). The story mocks social strictures that sanction an individual's natural curiosity, imagination, and idiosyncrasies. While expressed via humor, independence is a deadly serious theme for Jangbu. Ecocriticism considers how humans imagine relations to natural environments, and this story illustrates that far from static, individuals from tight-knit Indigenous communities can dream big and range far (see figure 4.4).

The ideal of maintaining an independent spirit permeates Jangbu's work. For example, his lyrical trilogy "Three Animal Stories" (2001) allegorizes the social complexities faced by Sinicized Tibetans. Like marginalized writers in the Chinese tradition, such as the exiled Tang dynasty literati Han Yu and Liu Zongyuan, who often used animals in poems or stories as metaphors for unsavory human relationships, Indigenous writers also adopt animal characters, yet their aims extend beyond those of exiled Han officials. In their zoomorphic depictions of humans in animal form, writers such as Takbum Gyel in his humorous dog tales and Memtimin Hoshur in his humorous pig tales (chapter 3) use animal allegories to represent suppressed minorities. Beyond allegory, they decenter the human agent by questioning her supposed clear distinction from nonhuman animals. In *When Species Meet*, Donna Haraway writes of the "entanglement" of the human and nonhuman worlds, the "naturecultures" which have evolved from them, and the anxiety this produces for anthropocentric speciesism.[38]

Species entanglement is evident in the Chinese proverb cited in the first of Jangbu's three animal stories, "The Lamb" (Lu gu). It also situates the relationship between Tibetans and Chinese in the all-too-familiar terms of Confucian kinship ties, where the subordinate is beholden to the nurturing elder.

As Emily Yeh explains, the Chinese Communist Party engineers indebtedness via Confucian familial metaphors: "The trope of Tibetans as children of the patriarchal parent-state is persuasive in Tibet, with Han and Tibetans portrayed both as 'daughters of our one mother—China' as well as elder and younger brothers of the broader Chinese (*Zhonghua*) nation."[39]

THE LAMB

All those who give us milk are our mothers. —Chinese proverb

On the day you were born, in the morning,
A female wolf came, brazen and unrestrained.
Brazen and unrestrained, she ate your mother.
But since that wolf too had been a mother

She nourished you with her milk.
In the future, will you be wolf or sheep?
Or a new species of animal?
Is it possible you will eat those of your own kind?[40]

The story belies the nurture; indeed, the wolf ate the lamb's mother prior to nursing the lamb, leaving its future identity, character, and even species indeterminate. Clearly the fable attempts to alert the lamb of the possibility it could become a future sheep-eater, just as Lu Xun's "Madman" tried to "Save the Children" from future cannibalism in his canonical 1918 story.

The second animal story, "The Pheasant and the Chicken" (De pho dang khyim bya), is even more chilling. It recounts an encounter between a pheasant who lives on the snowy mountains (identifying with historical Tibet) and an urban chicken. The submissive chicken refuses to acknowledge the prevalence of "chicken-eating," maintaining willful ignorance of her own inevitable slaughter.

THE PHEASANT AND THE CHICKEN

That pheasant had lived many years in the snowy mountains
Faced with an invitation from a chicken.
One day, the pheasant arrived in town.
He said: "Let's go and find some food!"
The chicken laughed out loud.
She said: "The master will feed us with leftovers."
The pheasant said: "Let's go and find a place to sleep."
The chicken laughed: "The master has everything ready."
The pheasant then said: "Let's go for a walk."
The chicken said: "That will not do. The master will scold us."
The pheasant said: "Well. Let's sing and dance."
The chicken said: "We must ask permission from the master."
The pheasant said: "Then what shall we do?"
The chicken replied: "There's no need for us to think about that! The master organized everything long ago."
The pheasant said: "So where is this master?"
"He is everywhere. There is nowhere he does not reach."

The chicken pronounced these words softly in fear.
The pheasant asked: "Then please show me your master."
The chicken discretely pointed to an eagle in the distance
Looking carefully, the talons of the eagle were bloody.
He was in the act of eating a chicken's leg.
The pheasant exclaimed in surprise: "Over there! Over there! He's eating one of your kind!"
The chicken declared with an air of great assurance: "That sort, they are the very few who do not obey."
The pheasant asked: "The countless corpses of chickens all around, what are they?"
The chicken pretended to reflect: "That is what happens when one does harm to the environment."
The pheasant went back to the snowy mountains.
Many years passed, when one day he came face to face with fleeing chickens.
He asked for news of his friend, the chicken.
They replied: "The master ate your friend. He's gone."
"Why? For what reason?" the pheasant asked immediately.
"Because he had a pheasant friend who lived on top of the mountain."[41]

The story ends on an ironic note, with a group of fleeing chickens rationalizing that *this* chicken is slaughtered because she associated with the pheasant interlocutor. The logic of the terrorist state is to incite terror by continually moving the goal posts, keeping its subjects in perpetual fear and gaslighting them into thinking if they behave in a particular way their lives will be spared.[42]

"He who Died in a Trap" (Gzeb nang nas shi ba'i), is the most explicit in Jangbu's "Three Animal Stories" series. It is no longer necessary to adopt an animal allegory. Imbibing the "free gift" of another mother's milk, in the first story, results, in the third animal story, in lifelong entrapment and complete dehumanization.

HE WHO DIED IN A TRAP

Ribs of guns
Cunning of iron thorns

> Vacillation of a storm
> Terror that touches neither earth nor sky
> Cruel lies and calumny.
> What else do you have, Trap?
> Ruminating on these, he died.
> They say the story of his death
> For some special reason
> Could not come out of the trap for many long years.[43]

While the entrapped is usually animal prey, the person who dies in this trap had ruminated on terror to the point of self-destruction. In these three poems Jangbu warns his readers not to fall into the trap of adopting the dominator's logic stream: although the benefactor's gifts appear free, disinterested, and generous, they are always constraining and intentional, entrapping their recipients in a relationship of obligation and dependence. Axel Goodbody explains that "cultural animal studies is concerned with the ways in which culture shapes individual experiences, everyday life, and social and power relations. Animals in literature are historically determined and culturally motivated constructions, by means of which conceptions of the human and the animal are negotiated."[44] The first two stories use animals to allegorize human relations, while the third does not require it. The third story illustrates that the process of dehumanization is complete, as the colonized have fully internalized the colonizers' logic (see figure 4.5).

Takbum Gyel's "Notes on the Pekingese" (2009), a surrealist story about ethnic politics and social climbing set in a local government office in Tibet, replicates the themes in Jangbu's fables. Like Memtimin Hoshur's "Festival of the Pigs" (chapter 3), the story is a tongue-in-cheek account of discrimination encountered by Indigenes attempting to exert agency within Chinese culture. It also illustrates how assimilating to the ways of colonizers invariably results in doing violence to one's own "species." The first-person narrator is an unnamed urban official who adopts a Pekingese (likely symbolizing a Sinicized Tibetan).

> In some places, *hapa* is a generic term for dogs. But where I come from, the word *hapa* refers not to the wild, ferocious Tibetan mastiffs kept by nomads, but to a Pekingese: one of those squat, fluffy,

FIGURE 4.5 Police surveillance at Tibetan cultural heritage festival in Lhasa. Photo by author, June 2007.

snub-nosed, flat-faced, stout-legged little Chinese dogs that shuffles about the house and the yard. Though Pekingese have neither the ability of the mastiff to fight off wolves and jackals nor the courage to stop a burglar, they're very good at notifying you when a visitor arrives and keeping you company during your leisure hours, and they're skilled at entertaining important dignitaries and high officials too. They really are adorable little things. For a while, I myself had a little Pekingese just like this.[45]

The Pekingese eventually ingratiates itself into the life of the official, initially by licking his shoes clean after a long day at work, and next by managing affairs in the office. In contrast to the "wild, ferocious Tibetan mastiffs kept by nomads" (non-Sinicized Tibetans), his success at social climbing leads the Pekingese to feel he is on par with (or superior to) humans, so he proposes to the official's secretary, who eventually concedes to marry him. Finally, the clever Pekingese charms the official's superior, the county governor, and the official is left dogless. As the official walks home with the Pekinese, having just gifted him to the county governor, who had treated them to a banquet of his slaughtered Tibetan mastiff, he waxes philosophical:

> "You ate dog meat tonight, didn't you? Do dogs eat their own kind?"
> The Pekingese snorted and put on his lecturing voice. "So what if I did? Don't people eat other people when they're starving?"—he swayed slightly, then raised a paw to the sky—"*however*, dogs eating dogs is a direct relationship, people eating people is an indirect relationship. First and foremost, you must understand *that*. And another thing, there's only one way for a dog to eat a dog. People are the opposite—there are lots of ways for a person to eat a person."[46]

The Pekingese states the obvious, exposing the violence belying illusions of civilizational superiority which reinforces eugenics thought. The notion of speciesism is called into question, with "humans" presented as more inhumane than those to which they claim superiority.[47] The moral of Takbum Gyel's story resembles that of Jangbu's "Three Animal Stories": adopting the "civilized" logic of the colonizer ultimately rationalizes cannibalism. As Jangbu says in "The Lamb," "Is it possible you will eat those of your own kind?" Again, this calls to mind Lu Xun's critique of violent civilizational tenets in his classic story, "Diary of a Madman" (*Kuangren riji* 狂人日記, 1918), where the titular "Madman" fears being literally eaten by his fellow villagers. Even before he wrote his story "New Year's Sacrifice" (*Zhufu* 祝福, 1924), where the tragedy does not lie in the wolf eating her son Ah mao, but in traditional morality devouring Xianglin's Wife,[48] Lu Xun had come to question the rationality of modern "civilization."[49] In the words of Qinghai Tibetan elder, Aku Sonam Tashi, "If people say we are lagging behind, then we are only lagging behind in destroying the earth."[50]

ONE WITH THE COSMOS IN TIBETAN ECOPOETRY

As a corpus of work, modern Tibetan ecopoetry powerfully exposes dynamics precipitating cultural and ecological genocide on the Tibetan Plateau and globally. One way that Tibetan writers counter Hanspace cosmologies of center and periphery is by radically centering Tibetan origin myths, narrative traditions, religion, language, and relations to the land. For example, Ju Kalsang's poetry, which he writes in Tibetan and translates into Chinese, while often considered apolitical, powerfully centers the Tibetan subject in time and space by evoking origin stories, nomadic practices, and religious worldviews that challenge the reader to reexamine agency and positionality. One of the most prominent poets and intellectuals in Tibet, Ju Kalsang (Ju Kelzang, b. 1960) was born into a nomadic family in Golok Prefecture in Qinghai Province. He holds a master's degree in Tibetan Studies from Qinghai Nationalities Institute. Since his return to Golok in 1987 he has worked as a civil servant and is now director of the nationalities section of the Golok prefecture translation bureau. His mastery of both classical poetry and free verse is evident in his three acclaimed poetry collections.

His poem, "Night Ecology," describes the grassland sounds and sensations during a bout of insomnia within "a half-asleep tent shrouded in moon haze." It begins:

夜生态一草原印象之二	NIGHT ECOLOGY: GRASSLAND IMPRESSIONS II
失眠是一粒种子	Insomnia is a seed
种在夜里它会发芽	Planted at night it will sprout
夜风微微	Gentle night breezes
从帐篷底下边缘的缝隙	From a slit at the bottom edge of the tent
偶尔传来来自外界的	Occasionally come from the outside
介于凉爽与寒冷之间的信息	A message between cool and cold."[51]

The reader is invited to slow down and identify the insomniac (the tent? the person within the tent?), the role of consciousness, and cosmic agency (Do the breezes enter to awaken the insomniac? Does the insomniac's wakened state beckon the breezes? Who conveys the temperature to whom?). Like those of the Tang dynasty Buddhist nature poet Wang Wei (699–759), Ju Kalsang's poems feature intransitive verbs that obfuscate to enlighten.

Tibetologist Françoise Robin points out that the nomad's black tent is a key image in Tibetan poetry. Frequently personified and addressed in honorific terms, the tent is "endowed with blood and flesh, its structure

FIGURE 4.6 Traditional Tibetan black tent. Photo by author, June 2007.

is reminiscent of the maternal body."[52] In his prose poem "The Call of the Black Tent," Ju Kalsang writes, "Indeed, it is from under the skirt of your robe that my little body fell gracelessly among men. It is within your shelter that my hesitant little legs first explored, surfing on the waves of samsara. It was equally in you that, heart pounding, my small mind threw the first lassoes of its gaze. It is all this love that makes me reluctant to let you go."[53] The nomad's tent is central: the child is born, learns to walk, learns to love his mother within its folds, manifesting *samsara* (Tb. *'khor ba*), the Buddhist cycle of transmigration and rebirth. The poet mourns the forced relocations of Tibetan nomadic families, asking the personified tent "Why do I see you less and less? . . . Once, you were the place where we dwelt, the reason for our pride. You were our restaurant. Bedroom. Hotel. Sanctuary. Meeting place. School. And also workplace. Stage. Samsara. World. Flag. And even, vital force" (see figure 4.6).[54]

Water, another prominent image in Tibetan ecopoetry, also has cosmic associations. Ju Kalsang's poem series "On Water" ("Shui jilu" 水记录), composed for a 2016 Qinghai poets forum on "Water and River: The Origin of Human life and Poetry," includes the following poem:

水珠	DROP OF WATER
水珠，水的帐篷	A drop of water, the tent of water
澄澈剔透	Crystal clear
多想永久地安睡在这里面	How I would like to sleep in it permanently
要埋藏就埋藏在这里吧	If burial is required, then bury here
留有一点点慧性和灵气的空域	Leaving a little space for insight and spirituality
我还要带着一丝羞涩 因为	I have to be a little bit shy because
我一贯以此鉴别人性的纯度	This is how I assess purity of human nature.⁵⁵

The structure of the drop functions like a tent, encompassing cosmic worlds. "Leaving a little space for insight and spirituality" evokes Buddhist notions of emptiness (*kongyu* 空域), wisdom (*huixing* 慧性), and power or anima (*lingqi* 灵气). Humility (*xiuse* 羞涩) facilitates perception. Another poem in the series, "The Center of Water," ties Tibetan origin stories to maternal birth rituals and Buddhist cosmologies that center the subject in time and space:

水中央	THE CENTER OF WATER
据说在很遥远的年代	It's said that once upon a time
第一个生命孕育在水中	The first life was born in the water
在一片汪洋中飘摇	Drifting in the ocean
像卵 或像半条鱼	Like ovum Or a half fish
这不大关我的事	It's none of my business
这高原	This plateau
说原先又是汪洋一片	Was originally an ocean
故,我的祖先视贝亮为宝	So my ancestors see shells as treasure
当红珊瑚为最美的装饰品	And regard red coral as the prettiest decoration
戴上它 高原的女人们立刻	When wearing it plateau women immediately

跃居为世间最漂亮女人的行列	Leap into the ranks of the most beautiful women in the world
尽管喜马拉雅山脉攀升不息	Although the Himalayas continue to rise
一再拉远我们与海的距离	Further distancing us from the sea
但天地作证	Yet heaven and earth bear witness
她们最喜欢的装饰品还是红珊瑚	That red coral is still their favorite decoration
我要说的是	What I'm trying to say is
那时裹着胎衣	Wrapped in the afterbirth of that time
我确确实实在水的中央	I am really in the center of water
铺水盖水 天地为水	Surrounded by covered by heaven and earth as water
在水中第一次我聆听	I heard in the water for the first time
阿妈梵音般的胎教：	My mother's prenatal teaching as Sanskrit intonations:
孩儿阿	Child
你的降临是我莫大的荣幸	Your birth is my great honor
妈妈愿你一世平安	I wish you a lifetime of peace
但这世界不只你有我	But this world is not just you and me
还有六道有情	There are also the sentient beings in the Six Realms
人间苦乐	Life is bittersweet
愿一切众生无灾无难	May all beings be peaceful and happy
唵 嘛 呢 叭 咪 吽！	Om Mani Padme Hum!
懂得那句祝愿的美好	I understand the beauty of this blessing
我痴情心路延伸的	At each plot detail extended by
每一个情节	My enamored mind
在水中听到的那个语音	How I long to hear once again
我多么渴望再次听到一次！	The voice I heard in the water![56]

This poem begins with the Buddhist cosmological notion that the origin of life is "none of my business" in that our universe is but one among many millions existing in infinite space and in time measured in many millions of years. The poem then immediately centers the poet in time and space, exhibiting a Tibetan's characteristic "keen sensitivity to place, position, and relative location, both geographical and cosmographic."[57] The poet evokes the Tibetan creation myth of the world covered by water, and a natural history of tectonic plates rising to form the Tibetan Plateau, leaving red coral shells buried in its crevices. His mother's prenatal invocation informs him of the Six Realms of sentient beings, a reference to being born into the lowest of the three realms in the tripartite and vertically ordered universe, centered on an *axis mundi*.[58] This lower realm, a horizontal terrestrial plane, constitutes only an insignificant part of the cosmos as a whole. While the poet does not explicitly name Mount Kailash (Meru, Sumeru, or Ri-rab), both Buddhist and pre-Buddhist Bön cosmology considers the sacred peak to be situated in the Cosmic Ocean, at the center of all the physical, metaphysical, and spiritual universes.[59] The poet ends with his wish to hear once again the voice in the water, the amniotic fluid of birth, evoking a cosmology where the universe, like all animate creatures within it, goes through cycles of emergence, decline, dissolution, and rebirth.

Dekyi Drolma (b. 1967) evokes more direct nature imagery in her powerful poetry, which often enacts ecofeminist critique. Like Jangbu and Tsering Döndrup, she was raised in a herding family in Malho Mongolian Autonomous County of Qinghai. She received a BA in Tibetan language and literature from Northwest University for Nationalities in 1990. Dekyi Drolma chairs the Writers Association of Huangnan Tibetan Autonomous Prefecture and is chief editor of the journal *Renzhuo* 仁卓. She has won many literary prizes, including on the environment, has published four anthologies of poetry and a prose anthology, and her poems have been translated into Mongolian, English, Chinese, French, and Japanese.

In "There is Running Water from Henan: To Jingdu," a poem dedicated to the 2016 Qinghai Forum's host town in her native Malho County, she personifies the river as a natural, playful goddess: "melting in the purity of snow / flourishing in the fragrance of flowers / permeating the mountain crevices / playing the music of life from beginning to end." Although this poem primarily features idealized natural images, it ends with a subtle analogy evoking a darker history: "She / the holy water of Shenmu Spring / dripping through mother's fingertips / moistening the story of my childhood / even washing the blind area of stone / until the light kisses the darkness / and the land takes on a new look."[60] Her poem, "Straight and Bent," contains a sharper critique. Superficially she describes the shape and functions of bows and arrows, but she concludes:

在直与弯的国度里	In the nation of straight and bent
一切　直	Everything　straight
来自弯的使命	Comes from the mission of the bent
一切　弯	Everything　that bends
隐藏于直的巢穴	Hides in the nest of the straight.[61]

While obviously open to interpretation, the concerns of the minority (e.g., women, Tibetans), those that "bend," are hidden and subordinated to "the mission of the straight." In her poem "Young Brother Searched for the Missing Cow," a woman remains alone in the tent, anxiously picking up cow dung (collected by women in nomadic communities for fuel), dreaming of the missing cow, knowing their impoverished livelihood depends on the man finding their asset.

In Drolma's "Sheep Turd," the poetic persona is dung itself, which bears silent witness to a rapidly disappearing nomadic lifestyle by imbuing the individual with cosmic powers. The sheep manure, an important source of fuel and building material for winter shelters in nomadic households, observes green grassland trampled upon, changes in snow cover, yet while "Everything tries to cover up today's hypocrisy, / rarely do people expose my secret." The seemingly powerless dung pronounces triumphantly: "I have a dream for the grassland and it burns more vigorously than coal / In the Land of Snows I determine to dedicate my all / Who cares if no one knows about me / A tiny sheep turd."[62] The expression "Land of Snows" (*gangs ljongs, gangs can,* or *kha ba can,* "the snow region") is an epithet for Tibet found in traditional Tibetan literature. The term invokes a larger, cultural Tibet that consists of the entire plateau and that includes all Tibetan people, without necessarily suggesting any political conception. Expressing wholehearted dedication to Tibet despite one's ostensible insignificance subtly echoes the nationalist sentiments of the popular 1985 Chinese folk song "Little Grass" (小草). Like the tiny blade of grass in "Little Grass," which does its part to serve the nation alongside its many compatriots, the sheep turd in the poem burns most strongly when gathered with its many companions. Yet, unlike the Chinese folk song, the Tibetan poet also attributes spiritual power to incarnate individuals ("My story is ordained by the gods").[63] Drolma further emphasizes the cosmological identity of the self in her poem, "Losing Myself":

丢失的我	LOSING MYSELF
突然有一天	Suddenly one day
手机没有信号	My cell phone had no signal
稿子上的文字也消失得无影无踪	The text on the manuscript also disappeared without a trace
松石耳坠和珊瑚项链撒落一地后	After my turquoise earrings and coral necklace scattered all over the floor
脚上的鞋子也开始没入泥土中	The shoes on my feet began to sink into the mud
渐渐地我的脑子化为虚无	Gradually my mind turned into nothingness
身躯与空气融为一体	My body became one with the air.[64]

Like many Tibetan poets, Dekyi Drolma expresses the transient nature of matter and self. This is not the same as the disembodied notion of "village as chronotope" in Liu Liangcheng's idealized Hansspace metaphysics of Xinjiang (chapter 3). Rather than reinforcing the status quo and naturalizing destruction, Drolma's Buddhist metaphysics asserts oneness with natural elements.

Far from embracing quietism, Drolma's ecofeminist poetry sharply denunciates worldly violence. Her most biting critique of environmental degradation and social injustice is in the poem "Grassland Feelings," which she contains within a Buddhist ethics of compassion:

草原情怀	GRASSLAND FEELINGS
给我吧！	Give it to me!
找不到营养而分散四处的黑白畜群	The scattered black and white herds lacking nutrition

遭受化学气体污染切流通不畅的空气	The poorly circulating air suffering chemical pollution
被工厂有毒烟雾熏得无处躲藏的云朵	The clouds unable to hide from the toxic factory smog
茂密的原始森林中恐惧不安的野生动物	The fearful wildlife in the dense primeval forests
让飞来的子弹击毁温馨巢穴的幼鸟们	The baby birds in warm nests shattered by flying bullets
落入水泥与钢筋设计的圈套中的石子们	The stones entrapped by designs of cement and steel
因而狭窄的瓶罐里失去自由的美丽鲜花	The beautiful flowers enslaved by narrow bottles
来自江河引入管道却白白流失的水滴	The water piped from the river only to drip in vain
炎热干早中焦渴难耐垂下头颅的庄稼	The thirsty drooping crops enduring scorching arid heat
所有这一切都给我吧！	Give me all of this!
我要把淳朴的爱化作绿色的种子	I will turn my simple love into green seeds
让大自然重新勃发生机与活力	To make nature revitalize and come back to life
给我吧！	Give it to me!
艰难地生长于深港里受人蔑视的乞丐们	The scorned beggars living in Shenzhen and Hong Kong
被外侵和内战的火箭炮迁出家园踏上拥挤的逃亡之路的难民们	The refugees crowded on escape routes, displaced from their homes by invasions and civil war
徒峭阶梯上气喘呼呼的疲倦不堪的肢残者们	The weary disabled, panting for breath on steep stairs
饥荒与蒙昧中等待援助的穷苦者们	The poor, waiting for help amidst famine and ignorance
食不果腹居无定所的孤儿	The famished and homeless orphans
年迈体柔遭到儿女抛弃的老人们	The feeble elderly, abandoned by their children

心中千言万语却不能表达喜怒哀乐的哑巴们	The dumb who cannot express the words in their hearts
无缘欣赏人间喧嚣和吵闹的聋子们	The deaf unable to appreciate the noise of life
所有这一切都给我吧！	Give me all of this!
我要把博大的爱均匀地摊开	I will spread expansive love equitably
以愧意和慈悲尽力满足众生的需求	And try, with a sense of shame and compassion, to satisfy the needs of all beings[65]

The poet posits cosmic love as the remedy for the global suffering endured by all entities (animals, birds, humans, vegetation, clouds, water, stones, etc.) due to the greed causing climate change, extraction capitalism, warfare, poverty, disability. While "Grassland Feelings" does not explicitly locate the suffering in Tibet, its title indicates sentiments emanating from the plateau.

Because of the potential backlash from critiquing government policy, Tibetan poets often publish online, and often anonymously, as a means of expressing a communal state of disempowerment experienced not in exile but in their own homeland. The introduction to Françoise Robin's translated series of anonymous Tibetan poems claims, "the yearning of Tibetan poets for a fuller, more authentic life is connected to both the imaginative recovery of a nomadic culture and the idea of a rooted Tibetan identity."[66] But beyond imaginary nostalgia, the following examples demonstrate that these Tibetan poets are also protesting, anonymously due to the real dangers involved, their dispossession from the land and their chosen lifestyles.

POET 3 CHAPTER: FEAR

The act of a magician

Give me your lofty meadow
Give me your horses, yaks and sheep

Give me your pure rivers
And give me too your black tent, which lasted so many generations

Go to the city
Go to the city and eat plants
Go to the city and eat worms and bugs
Go and pay homage in harmony with the modern
Distance yourself from tradition

Once you are in town
Wait for death in the chemical breeze
Wait for death while in awe of earth and water, fire and wind.[67]

In "Chapter: Fear" the forcefully repeated commands ("give me," "go to," "wait for") speak to genuine structural disparities in power between the government and the disenfranchised nomads. A "magician" commands them to exchange heritage and health for toxins and death. Rather than note tactical sleights of hand, they should "harmonize," feigning awe of modernity. Another poem describes with biting clarity the internalized racism produced by subjection to monolithic logics of development and assimilation, or what Dekyi Drolma calls "the straight":

POET 5 "CHANGES" IN MY HOMELAND

> This morning, a girl, a young relative of mine, ran up to me and said, "Elder sister, help me write an essay. The teacher said we must write something called 'Changes in My Homeland,' but I don't know what to write." I sent her away telling her that it was impossible for me to write on command, and besides one should always do one's homework without help. Then, by myself, I thought again about the "changes" in our homeland.

1

Fierce dogs that even wolves dare not attack
Do not bow their heads when cars drive by
Nor blink an eye when facing machine-horses

But if they see the head of a rider or someone on a yak
It is as if a demon had them by the throat
They roam the passes and valleys, hair standing on end

2

A young relative, who does not know a word of Chinese,
Was married into a Chinese family, the two sides communicating through gestures alone
The very last words her people told her as she was leaving for her new home
Were: "Chinese husbands treat their wives better than Tibetan husbands"

3

The river that flowed noisily at the foot of the village
Has been diverted by piles of dug-up earth and stone
Now if you want drinking water
You must wait by the roadside night and day
As water trucks loaded with minerals drive by
One following the next, like beads in a rosary

4

On my family's land, there is not one piece of coal
Nor one stalk of valuable *yartsa* fungus
People who feel a deep love for cattle and earth
Say this is the making of the Three Jewels of Buddhism
Can it be true that a relative made rich by minerals
Looked at them in disgust, saying,
"You black herders, blame yourself for your misery?"

5

My uncle whose nomad camp is close to the coal mine
Came into my family's tent
He squatted on the ground, his back erect
And said, "Ah, truly this is what I call mountains, green grass,
Pure gushing rivers, meadows
This is how nomads should live

I once had such meadows, some years back . . ."
The words choking in his throat

6

And thanks to this coal mine
A macadam road divides the community in half
Sister Drolma's leg got broken
Uncle Tenpa lost his life
Little Tharlo became an orphan
Is it right to call all these
"Changes" in my homeland?[68]

The poem presents a microcosm of the effects of forced assimilation into extractive market capitalism. Dogs police would-be nomads; Tibetan men (presumed to be abusive, lazy, addicted, unfaithful, poor) rank below Chinese husbands; freely accessible river water is diverted, processed, sold; other Tibetans shame herders for failing to bioprospect for minerals or medicinal fungus; Tibetans become crippled, orphaned, displaced, diseased due to coal mining. Anthropologist Huatse Gyel agonizes, "What pained me the most during my research was the realization that many Tibetan pastoralists had internalized their externally-imposed inferiority."[69] When we compare the anonymously published themes of " 'Changes' in my Homeland" to Dekyi Drolma's poem, "Grassland Feelings," it becomes clear that the globalized sentiments of the latter speak to specific local conditions. The cosmic compassion expressed in "Grassland" likely sublimates the poet's rage at the unspeakable violations endured by a persecuted community.

Because of censorship and exigency, artistic expression of Tibetan outrage at environmental injustice is often sublimated or globalized. However, the 2008 documentary film *Kokonor* (青海湖 Qinghai Lake), directed by Jangbu, powerfully indicts the Chinese government for inflicting atrocious harms upon a nomadic community by displacing them for ecotourism. In the film, the government tortures nomads and incarcerates them for protesting violations of their legal land use rights and fines them for trespassing when they attempt to revitalize the polluted environment surrounding their sacred lake, ravaged by climate change and the tourist industry. Others are crippled or chronically ill owing to botched or aborted surgeries and lack of health insurance, or by cancer caused by radiation from the nuclear testing conducted in the region in the 1960s.[70] In the documentary, the Tibetan community suffers financial loss due to structural discrimination: when they attempt to compete in the tourist industry by building their own hotel, they have their construction permit revoked after laying a hotel foundation, draining all their savings. Prohibited from engaging in their traditional pastoral economy or from competing in the new tourist economy, the nomads pull their children from school to make money by posing with Han Chinese tourists, replicating the cycle of generational poverty. During a 2018 screening of his film at Emory University, Jangbu broke down sobbing: it was the first time he had viewed his film in many years, and a decade after its filming most of the subjects had died.[71]

Clearly one reason the cosmos features so prominently in Tibetan ecoliterature is that the actual landscape on the Tibetan Plateau is increasingly subjected to devastation, and Tibetans are severely restricted from going on pilgrimage to sacred sites such as Lake Kokonor and Mount Kailash. On the other hand, in 2020, the internationally renowned Chinese artist Zhang Huan (b. 1966) created a "high tech environmental protection" performance and installation on Mount Kailash, sponsored by Dior and LV. In response, prominent Han-Tibetan poet and environmental activist Woeser (b. 1966) posted the blog "Our Sacred Land, Their Rubbish Dump: Chinese Artist Zhang Huan's 'Land Art' Installation on Mount Kailash," writing:

> Tibetans are restricted from entering Lhasa; Tibetans are even more severely restricted from going on a pilgrimage to the holy Mount Kailash and other sacred places—mainly because they are not given a "border permit"—but at the same time, this so-called artist who claims to have been Tibetan in a former life and the only Han Chinese Sky Burial Master in his current life, he is not only able to freely come and go, he is even allowed to set up a "high tech environmental protection project" on the holy mountain to satisfy his lust for performance and to win the support from the industry.[72]

What was for centuries a sacred site for four Asian religions was desecrated, politicized, and monetized in the name of high-tech green governance.

邝老五：强烈反对张洹在神山冈仁波齐实施"大地艺术"装置作品

 邝老五 10-09 21:07

冈仁波齐（Kangrinboqe）是世界公认的神山，被誉为神山之王。

同时被印度教、藏传佛教、西藏原生雍仲本教以及古耆那教认定为世界的中心。

冈仁波齐，位于东经81.3°，北纬31°（西藏阿里地区普兰县巴嘎乡北部，巴嘎乡也是转山的起点和终点）。海拔6638米（另说海拔6714米），是冈底斯山的主峰。

FIGURE 4.7 Tibetan artist Kuang Laowu's deleted Weibo post protesting Zhang Huan's desecration of Mount Kailash. Woeser's blog, October 2020, http://woeser.middle-way.net/2020/10/blog-post_19.html

Woeser reproduces Tibetan artist Kuang Laowu's critique on Weibo (immediately censored), which initially alerted her to the "incident" (see figure 4.7):

> Mount Kailash's environment is likely to be seriously polluted next month under the smokescreen of "advanced technology," in the name of "biodegradable plant fiber composites" and based on the promise of being "very environmentally friendly." The notion of being "very environmentally friendly" is merely wishful thinking and not very realistic. The plateau environment is already very vulnerable (to make it very clear: it is hardly possible for any kind of fabric that is left on Mount Kailash to degrade within the next one hundred years). I strongly oppose this "land art" installation on the sacred mountain, because whenever humans interfere with nature on such a large scale, a certain degree of damage and loss is inevitable.[73]

Zhang Huan's art unquestionably desecrates Mount Kailash not only through his insensitive appropriation of the locale but also by leaving a large amount of nonbiodegradable materials within the sensitive ecosystem. Tibetan literature on the environment foregrounds such sharp contrasts between Tibetans forbidden from adapting their historically environmentally sustainable livelihoods and lifestyles and the deadly superficiality of neoliberal Han settler-colonial policies.

CHAPTER FIVE

Island Excursions and Indigenous Waterways in Activist Taiwan

> Born into a world of mutual, uncertain, and unequal conditions of relation, humans survive through labors of care pressured by energies of coercion and domination.
> —LAURA DOYLE, *INTER-IMPERIALITY*

An island with a population of nearly twenty-four million people, the Republic of China is one of the most ecologically diverse regions on earth, and its writers engage an island ecology in a context where environmental activism, art, and scholarship are intimately integrated. Most Taiwanese literature, whether written by a Han, Hakka, or Hoklo or a writer from one of the sixteen officially recognized Indigenous groups, is written in Mandarin Chinese, though it often incorporates terms from other languages or dialects.[1] After Germany, the island generates more "nature writing" per capita than any other locale; Taiwan has long been recognized as one of the epicenters of international ecocriticism.[2] Ecocritics Chia-Ju Chang and Scott Slovic locate Taiwan in the Global South, saying that as a society "at once developing and highly advanced . . . this island illustrates the ironic, multifaceted identities of a society teetering between postcolonial exploitation and first-world power."[3] As such, Taiwan offers unique opportunities to better understand how environmentally conscious writers engage an island ecology, how environmental activism is intimately integrated into ecocritical art and scholarship, how Southern trajectories of development differ from Western ones, and how inter-imperial dynamics manifest (see figure 5.1).

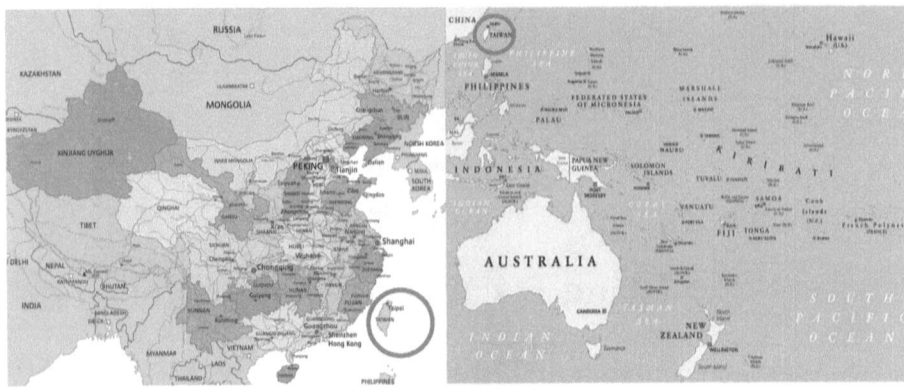

FIGURE 5.1 Two very different island imaginations of Taiwan. *Left*: As an island near southeastern China. *Right*: In an archipelago in Oceania.

Unlike the other regions examined in this book, Taiwan's geopolitical history mitigates against the possibility of setting a "Beijing western" on this island. Yet like the PRC, Taiwan has a history of settler colonialism. This affords us an opportunity to explore an alternative expression of Hanspace cosmology, one I call the "South Seas Dreamscape." Dominated by Han Chinese, Taiwan is a place of complicated ethnic identities, histories, and affiliations to place. In one sense, Taipei has similar strategic motivations to those of Beijing for celebrating indigeneity. As Taipei moves its development regime southward, it replicates trajectories of the earlier empire of Japan as it competes with Beijing for markets in Southeast Asia. On the other hand, after taking office as president of the Republic of China in 2016, Tsai Ing-wen conveyed a different political imagination than Beijing of relations between the nation-state and indigeneity by apologizing to Indigenous Peoples for the discrimination they had endured for centuries.

Inhabited by Austronesian Indigenes for thousands of years, the island was partially colonized by the Dutch in the south (1624–1662, 1664–1668) and the Spaniards in the north (1626–1642), followed by partial rule as a prefecture of the Qing dynasty. By the eighteenth century the island had been transformed by settlers into "an outpost of China's agrarian civilization," yet the plains Indigenes on Taiwan's western coast retained land rights and sustained an export trade in deer products.[4] The Japanese occupied Taiwan between 1895 and 1945, and after the Nationalist Party (KMT, Kuomintang) lost the civil war to the Communists, it moved its governance as Republic of China to Taiwan, even as Beijing continues to view Taiwan as one of its provinces. While Japanese military tutelage was harsh, many Taiwanese experienced more autonomy under Japanese colonial policies than under the KMT's explicitly assimilationist and eliminationist settler-colonialist practices.

With strong ties to the United States and Europe, Taiwan's rapid economic growth under the military dictatorship of the KMT led to extreme environmental degradation, including radical deforestation, irreversible changes to biodiversity, and unprecedented pollution of water, air, and soil with devastating effects on human health. Issues of the environment, Indigenous rights, labor rights, and gender equity dominated the 1980s Taiwanese social movements that brought about the end of martial law and the four-decade dominance of KMT rule. The ravages wrought by landslides, food safety, deforestation, soil and water contamination, air pollution, nuclear waste, and landfills affected the entire population, but they disproportionately affected the most socially marginal. As many Taiwanese works of ecofiction depict, Indigenous peoples in Taiwan continue to experience discrimination, which often manifests as environmental racism. For example, in 1974 the government deceived the Tao by building a nuclear waste-disposal facility on Orchid Island, claiming it was building a fish cannery.

By the 2000s, the political discourse of Taiwanese independence bolstered Indigenous rights, where Indigenes, together with "native Taiwanese" (本省人 *bensheng ren*), whose ancestors migrated to Taiwan from southern China in the eighteenth century, represent the core of genuine Taiwanese-ness, in opposition to the so-called Mainlanders (外省人 *waisheng ren*), the minority KMT population who fled China at the end of the 1945–1949 civil war against the Communists. As Jin-Yung Wu puts it, "for pro-independence Taiwanese, *waisheng ren* are counterposed to *bensheng ren* as interlopers and colonialists, [for which reason] Indigenous groups, which account for less than five percent of Taiwan's population, occupy a central position."[5] The Taiwanese nativist movement in the 1970s found expression in literature written in Taiwanese (Hokkien or Minnan hua) and Hakka, the two dialects spoken by *bensheng ren*. This has allowed Indigenous peoples on the island to leverage the exoticism that they evoke in the minds of many Han Chinese and exploit their ideological centrality as supposedly authentic Taiwanese, both in ecoliterature and in realpolitik. Indigenous literary expression and activism were intertwined. For example, 1984 marked both the establishment of the Association for the Promotion of the Rights of the Indigenous People in Taiwan and the publication of the first special issue of Indigenous literature in the poetry journal *Spring Breeze* (Chunfeng 春風).[6]

Taiwanese did not always identify with the Global South. In fact, until the mid-1990s, most intellectuals had identified themselves with advanced, first-world countries. While Taiwanese industrial development in the 1980s included westward (toward mainland China) and southward (toward Southeast Asia) flows of capital, it was mostly by small or medium businesses motivated by access to cheap labor. But in 1994, the KMT government announced a policy called "moving southward" (*nanxiang* 南向) to encourage Taiwanese companies to invest in Southeast Asia as a counterbalance to the existing overinvestment in mainland China, a move applauded by the opposition party, the Democratic Progressive Party (DPP). The Taiwanese critical theorist Chen Kuan-hsing deems this state-sanctioned southward advance a "sub-empire," a lower-level empire dependent on an empire at a higher level in the imperialist hierarchy. He elaborates: "unlike the earlier colonial imperialism, which depended on invasion, occupation, and usurpation of sovereignty to further economic interests, neocolonial imperialism uses military force as a support mechanism and employs it only as a last resort."[7]

To illustrate Taiwan's emerging imperial consciousness, Chen analyzes a special issue on the southward advance in the March 2, 1994, literary supplement of the *China Times* newspaper, published in the wake of Taiwan President Lee Teng-hui's and Academia Sinica President Lee Yuan-tseh's separate trips to Nanyang (Southeast Asia). The editor notes, "Taking into consideration Taiwan's cultural and historical connections with Nanyang countries, we launch this special issue, in part, to echo—or make a preliminary start toward realizing—the plan of President Lee [of Academia Sinica] to make Taiwan the center of Southeast Asian historical studies within ten years."[8] Similar to "Chinese western" cultural initiatives from Beijing, this effort successfully steered the academy through research funding that directed scholars to reposition Taiwan along a new political horizon and rediscover its "genuine" connections to the South. Chen Kuan-hsing suggests its success stemmed from investment in a uniquely Hanspace mode of thought, the Chinese *yin-yang* logic of bipolar complementarity, manifest in the "double-Lee structure"[9] of politics/economy versus culture and current policies versus historical connections. In Chen's words, "the southward-advance special issue has its impetus in the need to recover the forgotten past so as to complete the present, in order to secure a stable future."[10] In this sense it replicates strategies motivating the root-seeking impetus in the 1980s in the PRC.

To naturalize Taiwan's rightful place as an original part of the Southeast Asian black-tide cultural sphere, a term which refers to an ocean current that has formed around the Indochinese peninsula, Yang Changzhen, an author in the *China Times* special issue, argues that archaeological and anthropological evidence indicates that Taiwan's Pingpu aboriginal tribe belonged to the Malay race and was incorporated into "the Chinese system" only after the Han invasions during the Ming dynasty. He presents nature versus human, original versus alien, and Southeast Asia versus China, binary oppositions that resolve themselves in the figure of Taiwan's Austronesian aborigine, who serves to connect Han Chinese Taiwan with Southeast Asia. While symbolically celebrating Indigeneity, Yang fails to reflect on the Han Chinese colonization of Taiwan's aboriginal population, ironically rendering their historical experience invisible. Two decades later Wu Ming-yi's cli-fi novel *The Man with the Compound Eyes* (2011) explicitly employs these binary tropes, only to complicate them in fascinating ways. The strategic invisibility and ahistorical figuring of Indigenous experience allows Yang to valorize empire. Yang claims that Japan's vaunted Greater East Asia Co-Prosperity Sphere was once "welcomed by Southeast Asian nationalists and intellectuals as its salvation" and successfully destroyed the European colonial structure "that was oppressing Southeast Asian nationalism," in what Chen denounces as "a discursive exoneration of the invaders."[11] Finally, Yang argues that "Southeast peoples favor[ed] nationalism over socialism," without naming the antisocialist interventions of the United States. Like Beijing's rhetoric of ecological civilization, which rationalizes neocolonial expansion with a back-to-nature call, Taiwanese 1990s discourse naturalized the southern advance. Ironically, Taiwanese nationalism became a mirror image of the KMT's "Great China" (Da Zhongguo) discourse, the exact ideology it attempted to resist.

The Taiwanese nationalism of the 1990s was, like most nationalisms, predicated upon resentment against the colonial outsider or the imaginary Other (in this instance, Communist China), often expressing itself in the form of ethnocentrism or racism. Interestingly, Chen Kuan-hsing advocates decolonizing subjectivity by applying a distinctly Hanspace-inflected cosmology of critical syncretism. His decolonial project combines Western poststructuralist identity politics with a neo-Confucianist emergence of consciousness that mixes elements of Buddhism, Daoism, and Confucianism, where subjectivity is composed of body (*shen*), mind (*xin*), and desire (*qi*):

> The intent is to become others, to actively interiorize elements of others into the subjectivity of the self so as to move beyond the boundaries and divisive positions historically constructed by colonial power relations in the form of patriarchy, capitalism, racism, chauvinism, heterosexism, or nationalist xenophobia. Becoming others is to become female, aboriginal, homosexual, transsexual, working class, and poor; it is to become animal, third world, and African. Critical syncretism is a cultural strategy of identification for subaltern subject groups.[12]

This method calls to mind the neo-Confucian process of subject-entity formation expressed in Beijing westerns, especially Gao Xingjian's novel *Soul Mountain* (chapter 1). Like Gao's novel, Chen's project appears motivated by utopian, pseudo-scientific impulses premised on inherently discriminatory hierarchies. Indeed, in his epilogue to *Asia as Method* titled "The Imperial Order of Things, or Notes on Han Chinese Racism," Chen acknowledges "the mind-set, the psychic structure, and the ideological practice of the formula 'we are equal, yet you are not quite human enough' was and is entrenched in the political unconscious [of Han Chinese]."[13] He also imagines that if a European or American were to address Han Chinese racism it would be quickly cast aside by Chinese readers, just as Americans may discount Chinese pronouncements on white supremacy as stemming from a failure to understand the United States. He concludes, what does this reflect if not the fact that "the rules of the game were set by the empire?"[14]

Because of the global dominance of psychic structures of empire, or what I have been calling imperial cosmologies based on naturalism and agrilogistics, Chen Kuan-hsing's call for Asians to engage in subjective decolonization is presented as a method transferable to other regional contexts. This book is, in part, an attempt to analyze in detail the extent to which empire is dismantled in ecoliterature of various Asian communities to make visible aspects of the political unconscious. On the one hand, the rise in cross-straits nationalism in the 1990s resonates with cosmologies in Taiwanese and Chinese ecoliterary works that "borrow the contemporary discourse of environmentalism, and incorporate the language of science, with an emphasis on taxonomy."[15] For example, the unusual exactness with which nature is described in *Soul Mountain* shares similarities with the Taiwanese nature writing and ecodocumentary movement that emerged in the early 1980s and which, by the 1990s, had come to include a variety of genres including travel and historical reports, ecological essays, and ecological fiction, drama, and poetry. This early Taiwanese nature literature records, in scientific detail and without explicit recourse to cosmology, the radically changing habitats of plants, mangrove swamps, birds, insects and shellfish, estuaries, rivers, coasts, harbors, and coastal villages. It was only in the 1990s, with the incorporation of Indigenous cosmologies into Taiwanese ecocriticism, that cosmological formulations became more explicit. The dominant strand of ecoliterature in the PRC over the past four decades, on the other hand, has consistently interpreted scientific knowledge of environmental degradation via explicit cosmological understandings of how humans should relate to their environment. While the prominent Taiwanese ecowriter Liu Ka-shiang denounces the application of classical Chinese philosophy to contemporary environmental issues as "naïve," Chinese ecoliterature from the PRC regularly synthesizes scientific rationalism and less anthropocentric philosophies within neo-Confucian cultural epistemes.[16] Nonetheless, Taiwan's prioritization of scientific rationalism in its 1980s–1990s nature writing was also a product of capitalist knowledge constructs that have been challenged by global ecocritical investment in Indigenous modes of thought in the twenty-first century.

Taiwan has a rich and diverse forty-year history of contemporary ecoliterature (*shengtai wenxue* 生態文学) or nature writing (*ziran xiezuo*

自然寫作). Many prominent scholars and ecocritics, including Chen Sihe 陳思和, Wu Ming-yi 吳明益, Chiu Kuei-fen 邱貴芬, and Chang Chia-ju 張嘉如田园, have analyzed its development in considerable depth. Wu Ming-yi describes "nature writing" as "a type of writing that manifests the interaction between humans and nature, enigmatic dialogues with its disparate temporal and spatial realms, resulting in a unique literary style expressing the varied experiences and vocabularies of authors from different periods."[17] He distinguishes modern nature writing from classical landscape (*shanshui* 山水) or pastoral (*tianyuan* 田園) literature, calling the former "intellectualized writing" (*zhixing shuxie* 知性書寫), an evolutionary effect of a civilization structured by the postindustrial technological metropolis, which gives rise to deviations and regressions in its own biological character. This kind of writing, he suggests, can help us reassess our relationship to the "myriad things" (*wanwu* 萬物): are we tyrants, managers, or merely one among many? Chen Sihe contrasts Taiwan's intensely realistic environmentalist reportage writing of the 1980s with its nature writing of the 1990s, whose dominant representatives are essays and scientific sketches that are specialized, appreciative, and expressive and emphasize maritime literature. Chen characterizes the narrative viewpoint of 1990s ecoliterature as "a consciousness of one's position among the people" (*minjian gangwei yishi* 民間崗位意識); that is, the narrator is of the people yet writes from a professional standpoint (such as environmental and marine science or the fishery industry).[18]

LIU KA-SHIANG: FROM NATURE WRITING TO URBAN ECOLOGY

By all accounts, Liu Ka-shiang (劉克襄, b. 1957) is the pioneer of contemporary nature writing in Taiwan.[19] Liu was born in Taichung and worked as a journalist in Taipei. He was initially known as a political poet, publishing three prize-winning poetry collections from 1980 to 1985, including poems on the February 28 (1947) massacre of *bensheng ren* by *waisheng ren*. At the same time, he was intensely interested in Taiwan's ecology and first became interested in birds during his mandatory navy training:

> As our ship traveled along Taiwan's coastal waters, we would occasionally come across large flocks of sea birds. I also recall that,

when I started writing, Taiwan was more or less bereft of experts in the botanical sciences and outdoor fieldwork. I often had to seek material in traditional Chinese literature and history. My sources of inspiration included: flora and fauna named in the *Book of Odes*, images of birds in Tang and Song Dynasty poetry, even traditional medical texts such as Li Shizhen's *Compilation of Herbal Remedies*. That's more or less how I finished my first collection of prose, *Letters from Lodgings*, a book centered on bird themes.[20]

His later prose poems collected in *Views of a Flying Squirrel* (*Xiao wushu de kanfa*, 1988) present a vast expanse of space and time, focusing on a wide range of creatures living in the natural world. Written from 1984 to 1987, this collection contains seventy-six poems and presents the physical world in realist detail. Many scholars have analyzed Liu's anthropomorphism, illustrated by lines depicting green tortoises as "discoverers," Irish elks and seaturtledoves as having "children," or progeny of gray whales referred to as "grandchildren."[21] At the same time, Liu switches back and forth between his viewpoint and the creatures, so that "I" might be a stag or pig perspective: they are interchangeable. This dissolution of boundaries between nature and culture, human and nonhuman, and the emergence of identification and commonality is what causes scholars to attribute to Liu the qualities of "becoming-animal" in the sense advocated by Gilles Deleuze and Félix Guattari, in which "it is no longer the subject of the statement who is a dog, with the subject of the enunciation remaining 'like' a man," but "a circuit of states that forms a mutual becoming."[22]

Wu Ming-yi edited a 2003 anthology of Taiwanese nature writing in which Liu's early work figures prominently. In it, he follows a schema developed in his dissertation, published in 2004 as his monumental book *Liberate Nature by Writing*, dividing the first two decades of Taiwanese nature writing into three parts, deeming 1980–1985 a period where writers "listened to the sounds of the earth," 1986–1995 as the "gradual evolution of diversity," and 1996–2002 as "approaching new theories and forms of nature writing."[23] In his early 1982 prose poem "Journey of the Gull," Liu relies heavily on the Chinese classics to write about nature. He quotes the *Gazetteer of Southern Yue* (*Nanyue zhi* 南越志) (ca. 1127–1279 CE), which identifies different types of gulls, noting that some of the observations of the ancients seem accurate, others lack specificity, and others are simply incorrect. But he aspires to observe in that "muddled" (*mihu* 迷糊) way of the ancients, and having once been a sailor, he can vouch for the importance of tracking gulls when lost in order to reorient to land. Liu bemoans the fact that today sailors depend only on sonar, radar, lighthouses, and so forth to find their way home.[24] In his analysis of Liu's poem, Wu Ming-yi writes:

> Liu's nature writing, from its inception, forms a rhythm between human history and natural history. He synthesizes extracts from gazetteers, poetic fragments, empirical observations of the natural environment, and ecological knowledge, in a gentle, detached tone. This "intellectualized beauty" (*zhixing zhi mei* 知性之美) comes from combining literati lyricism with natural science lyricism.... It is not an embellished literary style, and is full of extraneous nonmelodic tones, directly hinting at the increasing gap between the intimacy between humans and creatures in a highly technically developed era.[25]

As Liu continues to develop his nature writing, he is increasingly informed by direct observations and less mediated by literati knowledge. In "Sandpiper" (1982), Liu starts by quoting a 1982 book on ornithology, but he quickly turns to his present birdwatching expedition:

> I slowly grasped my superzoom lens camera, and moved forward in the dense clumps of grass, my hands at my side like a snake's, gliding forward without a sound. Finally, I poked my lens through the grass... This time I finally succeeded. None of the sandpipers noticed the movement in the grass. They continued breathing, standing on the beach. I was less than two centimeters away.... At that moment my only desire was that our proximity—that my proximity to all wild birds, would always be this close.
>
>   Do you know what I'm doing?[26]

Liu proceeds to inform the reader that the previous autumn he went to the largest marsh in northern Taiwan, called Guandu. Initially he hadn't noted the sandpipers in his journal. He had noted only airborne water birds because sandpipers are some of the latest birds to migrate, usually arriving in the late fall or early winter. Liu indicates that they became his primary object of investigation at that time and proceeds to provide three full pages of detailed observations. In his final paragraph he speculates on where they may have migrated from: The Mongolian grasslands? Somewhere else? Liu concludes his lyrical essay with the following reflections:

> Like other waterfowl, sandpipers have no national boundaries. They come from the south and return north following natural evolutionary principles, their ancestors' sky is also their sky, they do not have boundless desire, and do not passionately acquire due to desire, they only live to eat, migrate, and propagate the next generation. They have never wrangled with time.
>
> When I retracted my lens, I accidentally knocked over a mound of dirt, and finally startled them. To my regret, all the sandpipers flew away, leaving an empty shore.
>
> They circled above in the sky, with the whole flock abruptly changing direction to the east, then to the west, with no leader, and no followers. This is a silent contract, impossible to explain using scientific methods or from study. Every sandpiper was his own operator while also belonging to a group. None fell behind, separated, or sped ahead to lead. They flew away, preserving their silent, orderly formation, gradually disappearing on the horizon.
>
> I knew that late March was their last period for migrating home. I was alone on the beach watching the sandpipers disappear in the sky and felt as though I had lost something. I suddenly felt cold. But I didn't find it strange, because whenever I contact birds, and they leave, it's always like this.[27]

While he no longer cites classical Chinese essayists, Liu's rhetorical style in this 1985 eco-essay resembles 1990s lyrical essays by Han Chinese Xinjiang writers Liu Liangcheng and Li Juan (Chapter 3). The fact that their essays are set in landlocked plateaus, deserts, and grasslands as opposed to an oceanic island is irrelevant. What links their aesthetic sensibilities is how humans ultimately experience an existential sense of loneliness once conscious of their difference from other creatures. Each of these nature writers responds to technological advances by conveying a sense of lack in the human, a sense that their overdeveloped consciousness and mental capacities have alienated them from their environment and instincts. On the other hand, the Kazakh Xinjiang writer Yerkesh Hulmanbek, in her acclaimed lyrical essay "Eternal Lamb," while acknowledging difference between herself and the lamb she raises, imagines an "eternal" connection to the lamb via a spiritual perception of shamanic reincarnation that is lacking in the Chinese essayists. In this sense, Liu Ka-shiang inherits, perhaps unwittingly at this stage of his writing, the aesthetic style of the literati nature writers he so assiduously worked to displace.

In the 1990s Taiwanese nature writing became infused with a more sensory experience of the observation process, moving into what David Hall calls an "aesthetic ordering" as opposed to scientific "rational ordering" of the cosmos.[28] For his part, Liu Ka-shiang began writing urban ecology, his observations fully embedded in the Taipei metropolis of his home. Liu's lyrical essays in the "Little Green Mountain Series" (1995) "leaves behind the aesthetic of the sole backpacker on the marshes and deep mountain forests, and instead are long-term observations based on his walks in his garden and everyday excursions from home."[29] For example, "Discovering the Pond" reads, in part:

> It's late autumn, and a gentle morning breeze is blowing. Looking out my back window I see that on the mountaintop five reddish-brown flowers are already in full bloom. A few days ago, a brown shrike [*Lanius cristatus*] arrived on this desolate plain, which made me very excited for a while, and every day I would look for it, observing every movement it made. But it's already been gone now for two days, and I feel depressed, so I decided to climb over the acacia forest hill bordering my apartment and look for it in the inner ranges. In the past I would carry my child while climbing quite a few nearby large mountains, but never to this small mountain because its forest is mysterious, the incline is steep, and there are many insects.
>
> At the entrance of the hill stands a phoenix tree about the size someone could hug in a broad embrace. It stood out amongst the others. When kids see it, they all think of that big phoenix tree in *My Neighbor Totoro*.[30] Of course it's not that huge. But at present it's not that easy to find such a majestic tree in the center of Taipei.

There are also rare forests and unseen sights in the mountain trails nearby. Last month, outside the forest, I saw a crested fly being chased by a bird. So, I paid close attention to any movement in the forest. But all I heard were a few bird cries and didn't even sight one bird. This kind of outcome is very disappointing.

I quickly arrived at the mountaintop. I followed the mountain ridge where it split into three trails. Only one was somewhat distinct. I tried following that path, which was nearly swallowed up by dense foliage, trying to go from one end of the mountain peak to the other, certain that brown shrike was hiding there. However, I soon encountered dense foliage and spider webs and couldn't get through. So before long, I gave up my plan.

I followed the larger path downhill, soon coming to a paved road, and before long saw a huge black water pipe. It was a stinky light industrial pipe over two meters tall. The thickest part of its structure was the size of my wrist. Just as I was observing it through the binoculars it began to spit out snakes that slowly left the path and disappeared into the neighboring black bamboo grove.[31]

Eventually Liu discovers a pond, sees a white bird, and feels he is the luckiest guy in the city.

Rather than feeling alienated from chemical pollutants or estranged due to his difference from other creatures, Liu Ka-shiang embeds himself in his urban environment and delights in small discoveries. The interpenetration of human technology and nonhuman phenomena is even more evident in "Brown Hawk-Owl," another entry in Little Green Mountain Series:

One uses time to measure perseverance, and monotonous, repetitive work to measure patience. If one only seeks the answer to a biological behavior, the outcome can be predicted. What can't be anticipated, in its infinite depth, probably happens at another level of inspiration, experience, practice. I long for such gifts from observing Little Green Mountain.

It is early morning, and I'm sleeping with my two sons in their room. The cry of the brown hawk-owl sounds from Xinhai Hill across the wilderness for the third day in a row, calling out a

FIGURE 5.2 He Huaren's woodcut of a brown hawk-owl in Taipei. Feiye Bookstore blog, April 25, 2019, http://blog.udn.com/012book/126118728.

resonant "bo . . . bo" from the hidden forest opposite Xinhai Elementary School. Before dawn, this sound mixes with the sound of cars on Wanmei Street.

But at times when there are no cars on Wanmei Street, that empty and melodious cry pierces the slight chill of the night with a bleak and clear beauty. This is primitive declaring itself to civilization, the calm protest of nature in the face of development. With this beautiful chirping sound, the moonlight at the same time streamed through the window, filled the room, and lit up the wall where He Huaren's woodblock print illustration of a brown hawk-owl was hanging [see figure 5.2]. What a fortuitous and beautiful experience![32]

The children were sleeping soundly, snoring rhythmically, in sync with the brown hawk-owl's "bo . . . bo" sound. Because of this beautiful sound, I couldn't go back to sleep. The last time I had insomnia the owl's cry wasn't as clear as this time. And that bout of insomnia was probably because it was the first time I heard the owl hoot, so I was very excited! But this time was different. This time was completely peaceful and harmonious. It didn't matter that I couldn't find it. I once again embraced a feeling of great satisfaction and lay down to sleep.[33]

The popularity of such nature writing by Liu and other Taiwanese nature writers who unequivocally embrace urban ecology, complete with hidden contaminants and noise pollution, led to widespread understandings among the population that global warming was real and environmental initiatives were imperative.[34] Yet as Taiwan entered the twenty-first century, even though certain global agreements had been signed (such as the Kyoto Protocol, adopted in 1997, and the Earth Charter, finalized in 2000), environmentally destructive development projects intensified, creating clashes with the ecological awareness raised by widespread environmental protests, popular nature writing, and the advent of ecotourism.[35] Wu Ming-yi considers the Little Green Mountain Series a maturation in Liu Ka-shiang's nature writing aesthetics. According to Wu, the main points Liu tries to express in his series are first the idea that everyday surroundings are filled with a bounty of creatures and birds that we can interact with via long-term observations in order to educate the next generation about its ecological home. Wu cites Liu's stated intent (in 1985) that he wants to "relinquish baseline melancholic sensibilities. Give up poetry. This is an active act of abandonment and a decision reached after a long period of reflection."[36] In other words, Liu did not want his works to be regarded as literary works only. Liu wants his writing to alert readers to on-the-ground realities and spur people to action. While he realizes this intention a decade later, Liu's lyricism in the Green Mountain Series essays indicates that he does not fully relinquish his poetic sensibilities. Still, Liu is adamant about his active attempts to eradicate the influence of classical Chinese ecopoetics in his 1990s works. He says:

> Earlier writers of nature can no longer sustain their creativity through reliance on the ideas of Laozi, Zhuangzi or other naïve modes of thinking. In similar fashion, their descendants, [confronted as they are with such a diversity of issues and rapidly changing environment,] find little sustenance in traditional Chinese pastoralism and ecological views.

In response to such turbulent change, in the 90s my own writings shifted abruptly away from the style of my earlier works. During this time, the content of my prose narratives and articles was no longer strictly limited to birds or other animals. Instead, I began to focus more on ecological education, localized field studies, and ecotourism. Just as with my younger nature writing colleagues, this change reflected a change in consciousness and content, an unambiguous move closer to "the real world."[37]

By the 1990s, Liu succeeds in his aims by embedding his nature writing within the urban ecology of a highly industrialized, technological society. In the twenty-first century, his writing matures even further, particularly in the way he expresses animal sensibilities in the city. Liu's series of novels on urban animals span three decades, including *Pinuocha, the Plover* (*fengniao pinuocha* 風鳥皮諾查, 1991), *He-lien-mo-mo the Humpback Whale* (*Zuotoujing Helianmomo* 座頭鯨赫連麼麼, 1993), *Hill of Stray Dogs* (*Yegou zhi qiu* 野狗之丘, 2007), *Eternal Albatross* (*Yongyuan de xinweng* 永遠的信翁, 2008), *Bean Mouse Goes Home* (*Doushu huijia* 豆鼠回家, 2011), and *Tiger Land Cats* (*Hudi mao* 虎地貓, 2016).[38] As an amateur bird researcher nicknamed "bird-man" by his friends in the Taiwanese literary circle for the writings about birds which initiated his career as a nature writer, Liu's inaugural novel also featured birds, but his subsequent novels extended to stories of whales, stray dogs, mice, and street cats. His aesthetic approach combines field notes from his careful observations of the species in question and fictional stories framed by the power structure of the actual world. He insists that the "profound allegorical meanings" in animal novels derive from situating species within their local environments, given that they are necessarily implicated within national and cultural "borders."[39]

For example, in Liu's novella *Hill of Stray Dogs*, he imagines the lives of stray dogs in Taipei, which he documents by photographing, researching, and observing their behavior. With the aid of a monocular telescope, he spends 655 days documenting his observations of strays that congregate on a hill near his apartment. He subsequently writes a multifaceted novella focusing on twelve of the dogs, comprising his journal entries, paintings, sketches, maps, and photographs, expressing their consciousness and his own.⁴⁰ According to Huang Tsung-Huei, Liu's approach is not one of straightforward anthropomorphism, but rather that of "becoming animal" by engaging in dialogue with individuals in the pack.⁴¹ A specialist in animal studies in the Department of Foreign Languages and Literatures at National Taiwan University, Huang summarizes the context for Liu's novella. In 1994, the Taipei municipal government implemented a new garbage disposal program that ended up severely reducing food sources for stray dogs. At the same time, the city began systematically killing high volumes of strays to control the population. Liu Ka-shiang wrote a 2006 op-ed protesting the culling of strays, maintaining they are also citizens of the city: "valorizing safety and hygiene of the city, we ignore the fact that the city does not belong exclusively to human beings; what is more, we fail to reflect on the historical determinants that bring strays into existence"⁴²

What Liu takes issue with, fundamentally, is the anthropocentrism of municipal policies. His novella, published a year after his op-ed, attempts to make visible other citizens of the city. Huang considers Liu to be a "Deulozo-Guattarian writer" in that he "enters into alliance to become-animal" by expressing the consciousness of "the Anomalous," in this case interpolated along the human borderline with pack animals.⁴³ The majority of the book centers on the breeding behavior of Little Winter Melon and how she trains progeny, such as Potato and Teeny, to survive a harsh environment. Liu recounts various behaviors of the pack, including foraging, eating, play, seeking refuge, and burial of the dead, embedding them in their elemental and temporal environments so that each stray in the assemblage is "inseparable from an hour, a season, an atmosphere, an air."⁴⁴ In his 2016 preface to the second edition of the novella, Liu insists that his ethic of writing about animals is primarily governed by long-term, careful observation and that he avoids inducing negative sentiments when narrating animal stories. He adds that although government policies toward strays are continually being refined and improved, many people still treat them with cruelty, and he insists that his relationship with strays will continue beyond this publication; it is integrated into his daily life.⁴⁵

Liu's *Tiger Land Cats* (2016), a novella on street cats, adopts a similar methodology to that of *Hill of Stray Dogs*. The opening chapter is titled "Cat on a Roof":

> Once I learned that President Ying was a "cat slave" I couldn't help but laugh. It seems that no matter how rational, once such a person returns home and embraces her kitty, the gentleness of her innermost heart is revealed. The status of cats in the hearts of many people is clear, incomparable to that of other animals. Yet I am sorry to say I am not yet a full-fledged member of the cat slave clan. When I encounter a street cat on my way home, it always feels like an illusion, as though I'm on the African savannah encountering a lonely lion. The first question I always have is, are you alone or a member of a group?[46]

The narrator acknowledges that many street cats, like nomads, have migrated to the city from the countryside or are house cats abandoned by their owners. Like his other works, Liu's intent is to help his readers "see" these cats and understand that they, too, are citizens of the city: "When I happen to see a cat perched erect on a rooftop, it is my favorite scene in the city."[47]

While his earlier novels featured "suicidal" humpback whales or preyed-upon mice, Liu's later animal ecologies orient humans toward an animal perspective in ways that elevate them to equal citizenry within our shared environment rather than mere victims of our cruelty. Such literature engages subalterns in imaginative futures imbued with creative forms of power and agency.

Over the past four decades, Liu Ka-shiang's nature writing has evolved from neo-Confucian aesthetic ordering merged with scientific rationalism to sentient urban ecology (see figure 5.3). Liu's hybrid modes of "becoming-animal" create new ways of seeing and being with "others" in technologically complex environments, aimed at mitigating modes of thought and praxis that bifurcate "nature" and "culture." In this sense, Liu exhibits the Anthropocene consciousness that geological time and human time are no longer two separate systems. Like a Möbius strip generating disparate vectors to the naturalist episteme governing the closed system of global capitalism, Liu's ecoliterature enacts

FIGURE 5.3 Liu Ka-shiang leading urban ecology tours in 2015. Lin Kuo-hsien 林國賢, "Lüxing zuojia Liu Ka-hsiang dailingzhe dajia manyou Yunlin" 旅遊作家劉克襄帶領著大家慢遊雲林 (Travel Writer Liu Ka-Hsiang Leads Everyone on a Tour of Yunlin), *Ziyou shibao* 自由時報 (Liberty Times) (October 8, 2015).

contemporary small-scale resonances (*ganying* 感應) between early Chinese metaphysical categories of *qi* (器 technics) and *dao* (道 the Tao). The philosopher of science Yuk Hui advocates such an approach, concluding his monograph-length essay on comparative cosmotechnics in the Anthropocene with this statement:

> One finds an entropic becoming driven by capitalism (the dominant cosmotechnics) leading nowhere, and with no resonance—the universalization of naturalism in Descola's sense. This is the danger posed to all of us in the Anthropocene.... The "internal resonance" we seek here is the unification of the metaphysical categories of *Qi* and *Dao*, which must be endowed with new meanings and forces proper to our epoch.... This is where imagination should take off and concentrate its efforts.[48]

While Yuk Hui is inspired by idealist Confucian imaginations of a moral metaphysics of technology, which Liu Ka-shiang generally eschews as naïve, Liu is unquestionably motivated by an ethical desire to integrate materiality, aesthetics, and praxis in order to influence social change. His literary efforts and environmental activism influence countless

Island Excursions and Indigenous Waterways 207

readers, writers, students, and citizens to engage in a more sentient, just, and sustainable ecological society.

WANG CHIA-HSIANG'S INTIMATE ENMESHMENTS WITH ECOLOGICAL HISTORY

While Liu Ka-shiang is the pioneer of Taiwanese nature writing, and the most prolific, there are a tremendous number of other influential writers. In his monumental scholarly monograph on the first two decades of contemporary Taiwanese nature writing, Wu Ming-yi identifies thirty-four writers.[49] One of these prominent ecowriters, Wang Chia-hsiang (王家祥, b. 1966), was born in Kaohsiung, graduated from the Department of Forestry of National Chung Hsing University, and initially worked as chief editor for the *Taiwan Times* supplement while producing award-winning ecoliterature.[50] In his college days, he joined a bird watching society and hiked through mountain forests and river estuaries, taking field notes and witnessing industrialization defacing the wilderness at an alarming rate. Before age twenty, Wang determined to change society with in-depth environmental reportage.[51] Wang subsequently engaged in rural ecological conservation and activism, serving as leader of "Promoting Ape Hill Nature Park Society" (1992) and "Green Association" (1994), and is currently an independent writer and painter. Initially lauded as a nature writer specializing in botany and animal representations, Wang has also produced a series of historical fantasies.[52] Wang's first major publication, *Civilizational Wilderness* (文明荒野, 1990), is a collection of four entries featuring animals as their main protagonists, where conflict with human society disrupts or destroys the animal world. A hybrid of scientific observation, lyrical praise of natural phenomenon, and personal reflection on social ills wrought by rapid development and political corruption, the essays exude disappointment: "The Taiwanese only care for economic value. When it comes to matters of aesthetics, affection, and historical understandings of the land, we discard of all of it."[53] His subsequent writings ranged from emotive treatises outlining engagement with "the wild," conflicted responses to the zero-sum logic of eating or being eaten, and concern for the preservation of natural habitats. Some essays reveal activist sentiments and denounce anthropogenic damage, while others meditate on benefits of nature for humanity.⁵⁴ Like Liu Ka-shiang, Wang insists on urban ecology, or what he calls "looking for wilderness in civilization." In *Prayer for Nature* (1992) he states:

> Wilderness exists in multiple forms; wilderness, a general name, has its origin in humanity's deep inner primitive feelings, the desire for the primeval. Wilderness can be a forgotten little ditch in the backyard; it need not be as big as an open prairie. Wilderness can exist in the charm of a modern city: in Europe and America, in Japan, Singapore, and New Zealand, such ideas have been recognized and implemented. Wild Bird Park is an artificial work, able to connect human society with the wild. It is a restored wilderness through human efforts.⁵⁵

While he persists in his activism and writing, Wang's nature writing exudes a pervasive sense of grief, ambivalence, and despair, sentiments which motivated him to engage a new mode of writing to reimagine Taiwan's ecological history. Written from 1995 to 1999, these imaginative histories are intricate meditations on interethnic and species identifications intended to compensate for island's lost connections. His stories fictionalize not only Taiwan's environmental and colonial relations, but also how the premodern past and modern present speak to each other to inform imaginative futures. As Payne puts it, Wang's "narrative worlds overlap heterarchically and not hierarchically," and do not "divest the modern world of a future, but rather suggests that such a future can only be possible through this fictional blending of past and present."⁵⁶ Like Lu Xun's first-person narrators whose complicit social positionality (as young male elite intellectuals) is often called into question, Wang's stories present characters situated in ambiguous interstitial spaces. Payne associates this form of consciousness as dialogic, in a Bakhtinian sense, calling it the "other-another," in which "that which is Other, outside the same, separated by a diachronic measuring of time, but still an another, is still the filial companion that remains answerable to all the many others."⁵⁷

His novel *On Lamatasinsin and Dahu Ali* (*Guanyu Lamadaxianxian yu Lahe Alei* 關於拉馬達仙仙與拉荷阿雷, 1995) illustrates this positionality. Wang states his motivation in its preface, declaring "Taiwan, like a tribe deprived of its ancestral dreams and totem, has now lost its way. Great literature, great myths, and inspiring totems are what Taiwan really needs."[58] The fascinating story that ensues features as central protagonist the historical figure of Japanese amateur ethnographer Mori Ushinosuke 森丑之助 (1877–1926). Like Guo Xuebo's use of the Danish amateur ethnographer Henning Haslund-Christensen (1896–1948) as a central protagonist in his ecological novel in search of Mongol identity (see chapter 3), Wang adopts a character who longed to reject his colonial status and fully identified with his research subjects. The historical Mori, who was sympathetic to the plight of Taiwan's aboriginal population, vocally promoted more conciliatory policies for "managing" (*lifan* 理蕃) Taiwan's mountain peoples.[59] As Robert Tierney argues in his study on Japanese colonial policy concerning Taiwan's "savages," "in his later years, Mori excoriated the colonial policies of the Japanese state" for effectively "eliminating the very object the ethnographers wished to study, that is, the aborigines themselves."[60] When the government refused his suggestions, Mori resigned his posts and, dejected and humiliated, drowned himself in the sea.

The conceit of Wang's short story is a diary, written in Japanese, which an Indigenous Bunun tribesman gives to the contemporary (1990s) narrator, a Han ethnographer, to translate. After doing so, the ethnographer surmises that it was likely Mori's diary discovered by his Bunun son, yet he hesitates to reveal this. Christopher Payne summarizes his dilemma as follows:

> Publicising his discovery would, on the one hand, breathe new life into an important yet neglected figure in Taiwan's environmental and colonial history. On the other hand, it would figuratively "return" Mori—if indeed the diarist is Mori Ushinosuke—to Japaneseness. In a manner of speaking, it would subsume and subvert the diarist's entire effort to be a Bunun warrior by reasserting a Japanese identity he had disavowed; an identity, moreover, that the diarist could only ironically describe as "savage" (and this is to say nothing of the impact it would have on the now old Bunun warrior who gave the young Taiwanese man the diary to translate in the first place).[61]

As such, Mori is "interstitially situated between the Bunun, the Japanese, the Han Taiwanese (and Wang Chia-hsiang himself, if we allow for Mori to represent the author's own awareness and hesitancy about futilely trying to 'go native')."[62] Payne correctly identifies Wang Chia-hsiang's discomfort with the deeper implications of "go South" identity politics; he hesitates at his historical complicity in the subjugation of the Indigenous peoples and his contemporary attempts to identify with them as a type of amends. Payne calls this ethical awareness the "another": "the fictional character is the another that has stepped outside and has become answerable to the Bunun; he has seen the invisible, both the peoples and the land, and the imperial destruction that is laying waste to it, but he has not been absorbed into the same."[63] What is fascinating about Payne's analysis, however, is that to be able to "step out-side" is to have agency. To be able to "see" without being "absorbed into the same" entails the *privilege* of not being enmeshed by overwhelming power dynamics.

Wang Chia-hsiang also attempts to navigate neocolonial subjectivities in his 1997 novel *Daofeng Inland Sea* (*Daofeng neihai* 倒風內海), a novel being adapted to film by filmmaker Wei Te-sheng 魏得聖 (b. 1969) as part of a Taiwan Trilogy series (*Taiwan sanbuqu* 台灣三部曲).[64] It recounts how the Dutch East India Company settled on Taiwan from 1625 to 1662 and how, along with Han Chinese pirates and refugees, Dutch traders altered sustainable Indigenous ways of farming, fishing, and foraging, deforesting the landscape to create a flat plain of profitable agricultural crops that radically transformed the marshy ecosystem on Taiwan's southwestern coast. Written from the perspective of the Siraya (西拉雅族), plains Indigenous peoples who first settled near today's Tainan City and Taitung County, Wang weaves a tale based on diverse anthropological, historical, ecological, and linguistic sources. Whereas some Han writers of Indigenous peoples, such as Chi Zijian's novel of Evenki reindeer herders in Manchuria, *Last Quarter of the Moon* (*E'erguna he you'an* 額爾古納河右岸, lit. *The Right Bank of the Argun*, 2005), or Wu Ming-yi's ecological history of Taiwan, *The Stolen Bicycle* (*Danche shiqie ji* 單車失竊記, 2015), directly incorporate Indigenous and foreign loan words, leaving the reader to interpret the meaning from context, Wang consistently glosses Sirayan terms with Mandarin definitions throughout his novel.[65]

For his film adaptation of the novel, Wei Te-sheng consulted with linguists to accurately reconstruct Sirayan dialect.

The novel follows the coming of age of the seventeen-year-old hero, Sanan, who is initially sailing on a bamboo canoe spearing fish but soon witnesses gigantic ships transporting cannons, priests, exotic goods, black slaves, poor Han Chinese workers, and cattle. Wang poignantly conveys the rich sensorium of the male Sirayan hunter: salty wind on bare flesh while fishing, violent sounds of withered grass devoured by autumn fires set to drive out deer as game, the smell of rain revitalizing the grass for the deer in the spring. After invading, the Dutch order their Han Chinese conscripts to turn the grassy fields into tillable lands. In historical records by Dutch merchants, they claim that "Formosa is a very fruitful island, but it lies untilled; as its inhabitants are very lazy."[66] Interestingly, according to environmental economist Jason Moore, it was the sinking of the Netherlands peat bogs in the sixteenth century that motivated Dutch farmers to venture overseas for other sources of capital.[67]

Wang's novel portrays the Sirayans as adaptive agents of such incursions rather than hapless victims. Sanan becomes a plains trader, yet scenes of environmental devastation continually shock him and his business partner, Daluoje. As the Sirayan hunters approach Chihkan village (today's Tainan) to barter deer hides, Sanan and his friends are astonished to see "a skinny Han Chinese pulling a huge grey horned beast with an arrow-shaped wooden stick tied with flax strings attached to his shoulder, that can "dig deeply into the earth full of deep-rooted weed" (91). Witnessing the violence of large-scale farming to soil, vegetation, animals, and laboring humans, their disbelief was greatest when they encountered extensive clearing of the mangrove forests. "Ever since the ancestors landed and settled in the estuaries, swamps, and lakes, at least in Daluoje's memory, the forests on both sides of the waterways have always been there silently protecting and guarding them. No one ever imagined that one day these massive water trees would disappear" (190).[68] Although the Indigenous peoples actively adapt to rapid change, they experience the scale and speed of the devastation as "suffocating" and "evil" and hear the wind in the bamboo as "grieving" (191). Throughout the novel, the dire warning of the female shaman, Inibs, echoes ominously: "The giant tree falls, and a great flood comes! We will lose our land to the Han Chinese!" (191). Wang concludes the novel in a section entitled "The Real Owners" (*zhenzheng de zhuren* 真正的主人) with a proclamation of historical fact: "In 1822, the Zenwen River flooded; its riverbank collapsed. Half of the Daofeng Inland Sea disappeared, and none of our homes or fisheries at Mattauw were spared" (274).

The ending of *Daofeng Inland Sea* is apocalyptic, with Dutch and Han Chinese agrarian imperialism ending millennia-long Indigenous livelihoods based on waterways. Despite Wang's respect for the ecological wisdom of the Indigenous peoples, their narratives are ultimately those of decline. Unlike genres of Afrofuturism or Indigenous speculative futurism, where the ravages of the past and present are acknowledged yet lack future determinism, many narratives by non-Indigenous writers sympathetic to Indigenous concerns follow this familiar story arc, known in North American literature as "last-Indian laments." North American authors frequently wrote "fictional and allegedly genuine last-Indian laments" to "obtain a form of catharsis," and "while last Indians always forgave white Americans, these melancholy figures also increasingly reminded the conquerors of their own loss." Such narratives allowed readers to "mourn[ed] Native America's passing, even as they reassured themselves that it was inevitable, [believing] "their decay is the natural, inevitable result of the progress of society, [and] we are not necessarily responsible ... for the extinction of the Indian race."[69] Wang's fiction acknowledges Indigenous ecological knowledge, yet in romanticizing Sirayan expressions of the familial (for example, relations between Sirayans and deer, fish, trees) and recounting legends of Sirayan sea crossings, he perhaps unwittingly replicates imperial thinking. Like Chi Zijian's and Jiang Rong's nostalgic depictions of the "inevitable" demise of the Indigenous Evenki and Mongol ways of life in northeastern China, Wang's portrayal of the colonization of the Sirayan people ultimately reifies the Indigene akin to the "ecological Indian" that is destined to perish.[70]

The storyline suggested by *Daofeng Inland Sea* reinforces the southern advance narrative promoted by the Taiwanese government in that it indulges what Shu-fen Tsai calls a "dark blue fantasy" whereby the Sirayans are encouraged to overcome their fears of crossing the ocean. In the novel, the Sirayan elders bemoan the fact that "we have forgotten the skills of building big ships and have become too acclimated to life on land" (15). In interpreting this passage, Tsai claims that all Islanders long to know the wild sea and reconnect to their origins, yet "for those Taiwanese [raised] under the Kuomintang's regime, similar desires and doubts were harshly suppressed."[71] Taiwanese scholar Chiu Kuei-fen explains further that in the new Taiwanese cultural imaginary, the notion of "ocean" is taken to signify an open attitude toward cultural interchanges, whereas land denotes an introverted cultural imagination that stresses agrarian rootedness.[72] Narratives of settlers attempting to invigorate themselves via identifications with Indigenous practices are familiar. Powell writes of "emasculated" urban Americans "Indianizing themselves" during the U.S. conservation movement.[73] Whether the message is "go West" or "go South," such narratives can be seen to replicate neocolonial logics.

Further, Shanghai literary critic Chen Sihe stresses that Beijing has also promoted this same expansionist, globalizing ocean discourse since 1988, exemplified by the television series *Heshang* (River Elegy), which contrasted a "yellow earth civilization" to a "blue civilization." He says, "the transformative model of going from a continental culture to a maritime culture is not merely the particular aspiration of the Taiwanese, but rather is related to the establishment of a global capitalist economic system, intensifying competition, control, and reallocation of the ocean."[74] It was Hegel's *Philosophy of World History* (1837), claims Chen, that reified the ocean-colonizing mindset by promoting the respective development of the three "civilizations" of the "high plateau," "plains and river valley," and "ocean and coastal regions."[75]

In *Why Indigenous Literatures Matter*, Daniel Heath Justice tells stories written by American Indian and First Nations writers that feature "trickster" characters and duplicitous leaders, stories that rarely romanticize Indigenous peoples. They have complex relations with each other and their environments. For example, in "This Is a Story," Okanagan writer and language teacher Jeannette Armstrong introduces readers to Kyoti—Coyote—the Okanagan trickster-transformer, who returns to the lands of the People after a long absence in full expectation of a reunion and a celebratory salmon dinner, only to find that the once-teeming rivers have been dammed, the salmon no longer run in clear waters, and he has been forgotten. He confronts a "headman" (an Indian Act Leader), who responds to his entreaty to destroy the dams with the fear and derision of one broken by Canadian policy: "We gotta work with them now even if we don't exactly like what they do. We gotta survive. We gotta get money to buy food and other things. We gotta have jobs to live. That's how it is now, we can't go back to the old times."[76] Unlike narratives of inevitable decline, however, stories such as Armstrong's infuse life into young community members who have inherited seemingly empty social roles (such as "Salmon Chief"). The role of the trickster character is to activate potentialities in the community's youth, who end up actualizing the inherent power of their ancestral legacies. Indigenous stories matter, says Justice, because they "tell us something that we do not know."[77] The implication is clearly that stories by non-Indigenous writers often tell Indigenous peoples what they already know. Indigenous literature matters because it activates alternative futures.

Another example of an Indigenous story that challenges narratives of inevitable decline is "The Last Hunter" ("Zuihou de lieren" 最後的獵人, 1987), by Bunun writer Topas Tamapima (b. 1960).[78] While hardly optimistic, the story does the hard work of countering prevalent narratives of Indigene decadence and marital discord by elucidating structural pressures brought to bear on the modern Bunun community. Topas Tamapima was born in the Bunun village of Loloko in Nantou County in central Taiwan. He first rose to literary prominence when he won the second prize in Nan-hsing Literature Award for his story "Topas Tamapima" (拓拔斯·塔瑪匹瑪, 1981), written while in medical school at Kaohsiung Medical College. After winning the Wu Chuo-liu Literature Award for "The Last Hunter," Morning Star Press published them in a story collection that also included "Sunset Cicadas" ("Xiyang chan" 夕陽蟬) and "The Pygmy Tribe" ("Zhuru zu" 侏儒族), followed by a second collection, *Lovers and Prostitutes* (*Qingren yu jinü* 情人與妓女, 1992). He also worked nearly four years as a doctor among Tao Indigenes on Orchid Island, resulting in an essay collection, *Tales of Medical Practice on Orchid Island* (*Lanyu xingyi ji* 蘭嶼行醫記, 1988), which won the Lai Ho Literary Prize, and is translated into French.

"The Last Hunter" describes Bunun hunter Biyari's three-day winter hunting expedition in the mountains and forests to actualize ancestral practices and escape domestic troubles. It opens with him absentmindedly chopping wood for a fire to warm his wife, Pasula, who is irritated by their poverty, frustrated at his refusal to work an industrial job, and blames his shamanic ancestors for their recent miscarriage.

A work of psychological realism, the story details Biyari's resentment at his wife's incriminations, his ambivalence over the influence of his hunter father's rigid principles (our ancestors only hunt or farm) and rage at Han discrimination. The story does not romanticize Indigenous ecological knowledge; rather, it contextualizes it. On the one hand, the Bunun villagers are ignorant of the pollutants caused by their woodstove fires, believing the smoke merged with the clouds (5), on the other hand, they are astonished at the ignorance of the Forestry Bureau, which decimates whole forests by cutting the timber, setting fire to the stumps, and replanting; they know "life in the forest account[s] for half the life on earth" (9).[79] While deep in the forests, Biyari meditates on how officials have ruined the forests:

> Biyari felt lonely and uneasy about the future of the forest. Well-off government employees should be brought to the forest to probe its secrets. Perhaps they were afraid of its mysteries the way a boss fears his employees growing healthy, wealthy, and wise. They should come and listen to the birds and beasts and winds and falling leaves; they should go to the valley to see the magnificent cliffs; they should take off their shoes and put their feet in the water and watch the fish swimming in unpolluted water, unafraid of people. They would unravel the enigma of the forest, and like sinners condemned to hell, they would regret their previous lack of understanding in seeing the forest as nothing but a source of timber. (15–16)

After finally shooting a large muntjac, Biyari returns home, triumphantly, only to be stopped by a Han policeman at a checkpoint. Addressing Biyari as "savage," he opines "you mountain people are cruel by nature. The government takes care of you people so that you don't have a care. But you people are lazy and dirty and break the law. Don't you know what the law is? It would be better to lock all you hunters up to teach you a lesson" (19). He confiscates the muntjac for his own meals, just as he had taken Biyari's fellow tribesman's squirrel for his breakfast. The story powerfully details the internalized racism and persistent emasculation of a policed settlement community estranged from traditional Indigenous practices and ecological relations.[80]

Topas Tamapima wrote "The Last Hunter," like most Indigenous literature of Taiwan, in Mandarin Chinese, in part to ensure a larger audience, yet it reads somewhat awkwardly both syntactically and with its interspersed Bunun terms and Hakka dialect. Translator John Balcom claims this is because "the native language of an author impacts or 'interferes' with the [Chinese] style," attributing this to the fact that Austronesian languages largely use the verb-subject-object structure as opposed to the Chinese subject-verb-object structure.[81] Richard Rongbin Chen, on the other hand, argues that Balcom's "smoothed-out" English translation may not do justice to "the political agenda of Topas as an Indigenous Taiwanese writer: using Mandarin texts that read 'unnaturally' to subvert the hegemonic framework of the Chinese language in Taiwan."[82] In fact, Chen points out, due to Taiwan's long history of colonization, many writers before Topas, including Wang Chen-ho and Huang Chun-ming, would mix Hoklo, English, and Japanese, while Chen Ying-chen's syntax is often characterized as replicating English structure. Postcolonial theorists refer to this method of "syntactic fusion" as an "interlanguage," a "separate but genuine linguistic system" unrelated to the mother tongue and second language of a postcolonial writer, with a "separate linguistic logic."[83] Salmon Rushdie, for example, in *Midnight's Children* (1981), and Wu Ming-yi in *The Stolen Bicycle* (2015), both adopt "interlanguage."

SYAMAN RAPONGAN AND INDIGENOUS WATERWAYS

Syaman Rapongan (b. 1957), a Tao Indigene from Orchid Island, located twenty-five miles (40 km) southeast of Taiwan, is considered by ecocritic Peter I-min Huang to be "Taiwan's most distinguished Aboriginal poet, writer, and activist."[84] As a teenager he left Orchid Island for schooling and work in urban Taiwan, remaining there for decades before moving back to Orchid Island with his wife and children to learn the Austronesian culture and oceanic way of life of his tribal elders. Living close to the path of the Kuroshio Current and nurtured by the richness of the Pacific ecosystem, the Tao people lived for centuries as an affluent society. After the Chinese Nationalist regime (KMT) moved to Taiwan, in the 1950s it set up four labor camps, ten veteran farms, and the command headquarters for a garrison on Orchid Island. Nonetheless, the Tao preserved their indigenous knowledge through songs, myths, and stories. Ecocritic Hsinya Huang conveys in detail the sustainable practices of Tao culture:

> Based on egalitarian concepts of resource distribution and environmental governance, the Tao has become a prominent model of ecological sustainability. The tribal people alternate seasonally between migratory fishing and coral reef fishing. Wet taro fields with irrigation channels are supplemented by shifting cultivation (firing and fallowing) of dry taro, yams and millet. Fish are classified into three types, one each for men, women, and the elders, so as to conserve the ocean and maintain the biodiversity of the surrounding waters. The Tao also practice a unique way of reckoning time at night based on the rhythm of the moon and waves. The Tao cultivate forests and plant trees (*Mi mowamowa*), leaving the lands to their offspring as an invaluable inheritance. Forest timber is harvested from the interior mountains for their traditional houses and boats, and the wood selected and ranked as appropriate for building decorative (*Mivatek*) and non-decorative boats. Using their adroit boat-building skills (*Mi tatala*) and incorporating their rudimentary knowledge of waves, the Tao produce streamlined carriers of traditional beauty. They anticipate that their boats will become good friends to the fish. The *Mi tatala* bespeaks a symbolic order of the Tao's intimate relationship with the ocean; their assembled boats become the medium for significant connections between the Tao, the sea, and their blood relations in the sea. Tao people observe these customary regulations of everyday life and include ecological conservation on their tribal management agenda.[85]

Despite this rich cultural heritage, in a 2014 speech Rapongan gave at National Sun Yat-sen University in Kaohsiung, he spoke of the discrimination that Indigenes faced in Taiwan, including the fact that as a boy and teenager the government used to hire him to perform "aboriginal" dances for foreign and domestic tourists. He recounted the degrading experience of having mostly middle-class Taiwanese and Chinese tourists touch his body all over. Peter Huang recounts, "At the conference,

FIGURE 5.4 Tao author Syaman Rapongan rows a traditional canoe off Orchid Island. Chen Cheng-wei 陳政偉, "Xiaman Lanbo'an: Laizi dahai shenchu de shuxie" 夏曼・藍波安：來自大海深處的書寫 (Syaman Rapongan: Writing from the Ocean Depths" *Zhongyang Tongxun She* 中央通訊社 (Central News Agency), (December 21, 2019). Photo by Wang Feihua 王飛華, https://www.cna.com.tw/culture/article/20191221w005.

he said to us he can never be Taiwanese or Han Chinese. He has never considered himself to be anything other than Aboriginal."[86] Rapongan's unambiguous Indigenous identity undermines assimilationist Hanspace ideals of a homogenized nation-state (see figure 5.4).

A prolific writer, Rapongan first achieved acclaim for his 1997 novel *Deep Love for the Cold Sea*. In this autobiographical novel comprising twelve sections, or what Chen Sihe calls a "novel in essay form,"[87] Rapongan provides intimate vignettes of his experience, after receiving a college education in Mandarin in Taiwan and working on the main island for a while, of returning to his home island of Orchid to try to learn the ways of his elders and eke out a living for his family by spearfishing: "I am aware that wisdom comes from many accumulated life experiences, and collective wisdom from many people's accumulated life experiences is culture. This is the special civilization harbored by my clan on Lanyu Island. Losing my job gave me an opportunity to explore my ancestors love-hate relationship with the sea . . . This work is dedicated to my dear family, and to the illiterate elders, as a way of expressing their stories."[88] Indeed, in the late 1990s, following indigenous trends globally, many educated Indigenous adults made intentional choices to actively learn the customs of their elders and disseminate this knowledge to the next generation and to mainstream culture more generally.[89] Further, Tao Indigenous knowledge directly informed the environmental movement in Taiwan. Lanyu, known as Orchid Island or Pongso no Tao ("island of human beings") in the Tao language, was the site of antinuclear protests in the 1980s. The Tao people were active in these protests and shaped political strategy resisting the radioactive waste depository the government established on the island. Again in 2007, as Syaman Rapongan details in his 2012 novel *The Eyes of the Sky*, Tao activists blocked invading fishing vessels and prevented an impending flying fish extinction.

The primary framing conceit of *Deep Love for the Cold Sea* is how to decolonize one's mind and way of life. The colonizer, by the late twentieth century, no longer solely and externally imposes the challenges; they arise instead from modes of thought internalized within the community itself. Unlike the domestic tensions implicitly conveyed within Topas Tamapima's "The Last Hunter," which Syaman Rapongan cites in *Deep Love*, Rapongan is explicit about his domestic stress in the preface to his novel:

> When I was unemployed for several years in middle age my wife said, "you get a job, I'll plant vegetables, OK?" I said, "no, you'll lose your beauty." The kids said, "we need money." I said, proudly, "the fish I spear each night for dinner is money." My grandparents said, "the sea isn't as good as it used to be, you should go to the mainland to find a job." But I couldn't bear to leave my family and even less the island of Lanyu itself. (11–12)

This tension between modern economic demands and the narrator's desire to connect to Indigenous lifeways plays out powerfully in the first vignette of the novel. On a stormy winter afternoon, the narrator ventures out on a solo spearfishing expedition, to the dismay of his elders owing to a taboo against returning home after dark: "I was well aware that as dusk approached children all went home to eat and sleep, and men still out in the dark could not go home in case the evil spirits followed them to their homes" (21). Despite his stated desire to learn from his elders, not only does the narrator flaunt their taboo, but he also ironically engages in all-too-modern psychoanalytic cogitation once he escapes into the gray ocean, "my deepest love," where "I felt relaxed, distanced from the quarreling women at home. Am I pursuing a traditional livelihood or avoiding modern responsibilities?" (24). Diving to the depths of the stormy ocean synthesizes his tumultuous emotions: "I looked up at the rain patterns on the surface of the water above, and knew that the sea was alive, has feelings, and is the gentlest partner. Only those that love the sea can appreciate her in her naked beauty" (26). Despite his fear of the raging storm, after spearing nearly a dozen large fish, he felt a sense of accomplishment: "I had turned a scene of fear into intimate affection" (27), a metaphor for the domestic challenges he faced at home.

Triumphing over the natural elements and overcoming his fear of the raging sea pale in comparison to his challenges on the home front. His male relatives send a search party to the beach. On the home front, his mother wails prayers that the evil spirits release his soul and return him to life. His wife is enraged beyond pacifying. The scene closes with a lengthy ritual in which his male elders engage in a wine-fueled song duel aimed at reconciliation: "The sacred music of Bofu's poem-song caused hundreds of feelings to intertwine. This song was made for me. It was an exhortation. In principle, according to Tao custom, I must reply in kind. But my father responded to his brother on my behalf" (37):

> I face the sea and wail, Brother
> I am ashamed and full of regret
> The children's father
> Caused us to cry over and over
> How do I discipline him, dear brother?
> No one is older than us
> Only the children's father
> Frustrates us in the ocean
> Ocean ... ocean ... helped us grow up
> My tears cannot stop flowing
> The joys of a child's love of the sea
> Never defeated by dark night or waves
> Brother, I'm so ashamed

> We can only face the sea, look at the sea
> The watery expanse was once our partner in heroics
> It made us rich with wisdom
> We experienced the substance of life
> Let us rest, brother (37–38)

After his father's song, the narrator reflects that "father, his elder brother, and younger brother tried to wipe away tears. I downed some wine to repress my pain and desire to cry. These three men have never rebuked me before, they were using words from inner peace to enlighten me. I loved them deeply. The room was very quiet. Outside it was also very solemn. I had created this environment." (38) A younger cousin breaks the tension by telling a joke and asking the elders to sing stories of their own fishing exploits in their youth.

The Tao male social practices provide space for the narrator to experience his complex emotions with loved ones in a relatively safe space, and eventually he apologizes for causing so his family so much anxiety. Contrary to the reader's expectation, however, the narrator is not easily pacified. As he burrows into a sleeping bag on the landing, he overhears his mother's incessant curses and coughing (she had refused to eat the fish he caught, including the medicinal fish soup), and his wife's persistent urging that he get a job in Taiwan. Throughout the entire event his resentment resurges again and again, like the ocean waves, activated by female dissatisfaction with his choices. The next morning, he ponders, "The Tao are a very happy people; they are fortunate to see the sea upon waking. But over the past forty years our happiness has been sullied by 'evil spirits' of materialism" (47). His elder daughter asks him to help her prepare for an exam. His wife holds their baby daughter and gazes at the sea, commenting, "It's such a bleak day, such a lonely sea." To which he responds, "Yes, it's a very cold feeling" (47).

Yet the secular understanding of the sea that frames the novel becomes mythologized as it proceeds. In one vignette, Rapongan's father tells his son a story implying that human and nonhuman are intimately related in a circle of ecological interdependence. In the distant past, flying fish jumped out of the ocean and landed on the reef, letting the Tao ancestors learn their diverse kinds. "In this way, the chief of the flying fish, Black Wing, educated our ancestors how to eat flying fish, how to catch them, and how to offer sacrifices to them" (75). Many of Rapongan's subsequent novels, which include *Black Wings* (*Heise de chibang* 黑色的翅膀, 1999), *Memory of Waves* (*Hailang de jiyi* 海浪的記憶, 2002), and (after sailing across the South Pacific on a canoe in 2005), *The Eyes of the Sky* (*Tiankong de yanjing* 天空的眼睛, 2012), *The Eyes of the Sea* (*Dahai zhiyan* 大海之眼, 2018), and *The Man Without a Mailbox* (*Meiyou Xinxiang de nanren* 沒有信箱的男人, 2022), demonstrate his extensive knowledge of the stars, the ocean, and the multispecies world of the Pacific.[90] This knowledge was passed down by his forefathers through storytelling and singing and the physical techniques of fishing, canoeing and boat building. He underscores the fact that fishermen lack agency in catching fish. Rather, in Tao cosmology, the flying fish offer themselves to the humans as a seasonal ritual when predatory fish chase them; thus the Tao fisherman fish only during this season. They then switch to coral reef fishing, waiting for the flying fish to return with the north-flowing Kuroshio Current, which transports warm, tropical water to sustain microbes and coral reefs, thus bringing a variety of marine organisms that migrate in the eddies.[91]

What Rapongan points to in his writing is what Fijian scholar Epeli Hau'ofa theorized as "The Way of the Ocean." In his two seminal essays, "Our Sea of Islands" (1994) and "The Ocean in Us" (1998), Hau'ofa argues for an Oceanian cosmology that centers long-standing practices of traversing indigenous maritime waterways that create transnational networks as opposed to settler colonial mappings of Pacific island states and territories as isolated islands.[92] Inspired by Hau'ofa's scholarship, a whole school of cultural study in Taiwan links Taiwanese indigenous studies to both the Native American transnational frameworks of "trans-Indigenous" belonging and to a contemporary connection with oceanic frameworks. Hsinya Huang argues that "the Indigenous bloodlines originating in Taiwan and spreading across the Pacific open up a large world in which Indigenous peoples intermingle along numerous, interconnecting water routes unhindered by the boundaries erected by imperial powers."[93] An ocean-centered imagination can decolonize ecocriticism and reterritorialize trans-indigeneity from a South Seas perspective.[94] The fact that trans-Indigenous connections predate imperialism was scientifically validated in 2020 by a high-density genome-wide DNA study showing that intermingling between Indigenes of Polynesia and the Americas (pre-Columbian Zenú people) occurred between 1150 and 1380 CE.⁹⁵ Yet scholars such as Chen Kuan-hsing, Chiu Kuei-fen, and Chen Sihe have also challenged this genealogical and narrative recuperation of the sea as a trope intended to deterritorialize land-based epistemes of empire, suggesting that it rationalizes neoimperialist agendas. As Chiu Kuei-fen puts it,

> The struggle to be recognized by his community as a T'au man implicitly undercuts Rapongan's claim to be an Indigenous writer. As his writing shows him in the process of becoming a genuine Indigenous man again, his Indigenous identity is at stake, seen as something in the future rather than a mission accomplished... This in-between-ness of Rapongan in the process of becoming an Indigenous person makes it possible for him to stand for all Taiwanese in the new Taiwanese narrative. For in this discourse, the Taiwanese are also reaching out for their matrilineal Indigenous roots.⁹⁶

WU MING-YI AND THE PRODUCTION OF TRANS-INDIGENEITY

Wu Ming-yi (b. 1971) is a multitalented artist, photographer, environmental activist, nature writer, and professor specializing in ecoliterature, with extensive knowledge of entomology, biology, and ecology. He first became renowned through his works on butterflies, including *The Book of Lost Butterflies* (*Midie zhi* 迷蝶誌, 2000) and *The Tao of Butterflies* (*Die dao* 蝶道, 2003). Later he began writing novels that situate ecological Taiwan in transnational historical perspectives, including *Routes in the Dream* (*Shuimian de hangxian* 睡眠的航線, 2007), *The Man with the Compound Eyes* (*Fuyan ren* 複眼人, 2011), *The Stolen Bicycle* (*Danche shiqie ji* 單車失竊記, 2015), nominated for the 2018 Man Booker International Prize, and *The Land of Little Rain* (*Kuyu zhidi* 苦雨之地, 2019).

When I ask my students how they feel about *The Man with the Compound Eyes*, most respond with some version of the term "uncanny," in the sense discussed by Amitav Ghosh in *The Great Derangement*. Ghosh says, "the uncanny and improbable events that are beating at our doors seem to have stirred a sense of recognition, an awareness that humans were never alone, that we have always been surrounded by beings of all sorts who share elements of that which we had thought to be most distinctively our own: the capacities of will, thought, and consciousness."[97] Ghosh argues further that the modern novel fails to convey the deeply unsettling effects of climate change, especially "the freakish weather events of today," except in the "less serious" and futuristic genre of science fiction.[98] Yet my students said they feel unsettled by Wu's novel because it is so clearly situated in the here and now.

In *The Man with the Compound Eyes* the incessantly torrential rains, floods, typhoons, earthquakes, soil erosions, mountain tunnel cave-ins, and, most notably, the Great Pacific Garbage Patch are as ubiquitous as human, other mammals, insect, fish, and reptilian characters. Three islands—The Island (Taiwan), Wayo Wayo (symbolizing the origins of Taiwan's Austronesian Indigenous tribes), and the Great Pacific Garbage Patch (a real thing, and present remnants of our past)—provide the physical setting for much of the story, although the narrative also traverses Norwegian whaling ships, German universities, Brazilian coastlines, and Danish campgrounds. The human characters all live or meet in Haven (H-county in the original, referring to Hualian County), a town on the east coast of The Island (Taiwan). They include Atilei'i, a teenager from Wayo Wayo; Rasula, his teenaged lover; Alice, a suicidal Taiwanese literature professor; Thom, her Danish mountain-climbing husband; Toto, Alice and Thom's insect-loving son; Dahu, a Bunun tribe forestry expert; Hafay, a Pangcah tribe café owner; Ohiyo, Alice's cat; Jung-hsiang Li, a Taiwanese tunnel engineer; Detlef, a German engineering professor; and Sara, a Norwegian environmental activist. In near-death moments, human characters encounter The Man with the Compound Eyes, a being who "observes without intervening," whose compound eyes (like those of an insect) are made up of repeating units, the ommatidia, each of which function as a separate visual receptor.[99]

The novel begins with a one-page chapter called "The Cave." A team of Taiwanese and German engineers are trying to bore through a mountain. Halfway through the novel a passage makes clear that, after a decade of effort, the engineers have finally succeeded:

> When he was younger Detlef would have described it as a triumph, no question about it. But these past few years he was not so sure. Now he often told his classes that each mountain had its own

unique 'heart.'" "My job is to design a tool that will bore through the 'heart' of a mountain." Detlef looked his students in the eyes one by one. "But now I sometimes have my doubts. I wonder whether we shouldn't just go around . . . We thought we were making a scientific judgment, but actually we were making a lifestyle choice." (245–46; 203)

Wu Ming-yi might say the engineers were telling themselves a particular story and calling it science to rationalize their choices.

The novel's themes of selective memory, storytelling, colliding islands, and compound eyes invite the reader to view reality from different perspectives. We learn, late in the novel, that Alice is "writing to save a life." Like Wu Ming-yi, she has written a novel and short story (all titled "The Man with the Compound Eye"). These world-building media creations allow her, and her husband, to sustain the myth of Toto's life (he had died from a snakebite years before). Writing "saves a life" (his own, his characters) by allowing the author to construct a world where traumatized individuals heal through cathartic connection with others in the midst of global climate catastrophe and the Sixth Great Extinction. Similar compensatory actions to forgo mourning overwhelming loss and the powerlessness that accompanies it pervade the entire novel: Hafay sees evidence of her beloved "Spider" on her client's back; Hafay replaces Dahu's Millet; the environmental activism of his namesake in the novel redeem the ravages of the great explorer Roald Amundsen, colonizer of the South Pole. The novelist himself took an unpaid leave from his deadly bureaucratic academic position to write, to "save a life."

As such, *The Man with the Compound Eyes* is a study of consuming practices. As a monument to human folly and wisdom, the novel depicts architectural space (such as Anu's Forest Church and Alice's Sea House) and the trash vortex as ways to understand consumption, grief, and sedimented layers of stories, displacement, and loss. Its magical realist tropes evoke the fused triad of coloniality, indigeneity, and technomodernity. For example, Indigenes view the congenital defects of the Earth Sage and Rasula's child as spiritually empowering, while scientific rationalists attribute disability to environmental exposure to toxins.[100] Thom Jacobsen is portrayed as a "good colonizer" (an adventurer and lover who comes and goes), producing Toto, a mixed-race boy with different-colored eyes, a characteristic shared by Ohiyo, a signifier of Taiwan's colonial past. The islands are memorials of grief, wiped out by tsunamis caused by the volcanic eruptions of human violence. The man with the compound eyes requires us to see all of this, in an ethical call to action. We (readers, characters) rely on trash disposal systems but put them outside our frame of vision; what happens when "trash" is brought within our vision? The "man" is neither fully human (yet is an anthropomorphization of nature), nor fully divine (lacking omnipotence he only observes and does not act) nor fully cyborg (a product of technocapitalism, his eyes are described as television screens or liquid crystal displays). Humanity in Wu's novel remains within nature, itself actively resistant to humanity. Translator Darryl Sterk argues the man with the compound eyes, who represents the subjectivity of nature as a whole, "can be said to be a hypersubject," engaging both intersubjectively and ecosystemically, where "all subjects are looking at one another at once in a sort of holistic gaze that does not cancel out the gazes of individuals."[101]

Citing Shiuhhuah Serena Chou, who suggests that James Cameron's 2009 film *Avatar* inspired Wu's novel, Sterk also implies that we can read Alice as Wu Ming-yi's alter ego inside a MMORPG, a massively multiplayer online role-playing game. Neither scholar pursues this line of analysis, however. Sterk merely concludes that "Wu's novel appeals to ecologically concerned media-savvy citizens, using a metaphor of videomosaic montage that "gives gaze" to nature."[102] To me, the metafictional postmodern aspects of the novel resonate with themes in early modern Chinese science fantasy, emerging as a new form of Indigenous futurism or speculative fantasy cli-fi. In his analysis of this genre in late Qing fiction, David Der-wei Wang insists the fantastic exceeds Tzvetan Todorov's definition of it as an effect of narrative that tantalizes the reader by straddling the realm of the intelligible and that of the speculative. Instead, Wang emphasizes that the fantastic is part of the knowledge system of a given culture, namely, the traditional acceptable way of imagining the uncanny.[103] While Sterk also historizes the uncanny in Wu Ming-yi's novel, his central interpretation posits the "videomosaic gaze as postmodern eco-sublime" through analysis firmly rooted in Western philosophical aesthetics. He summarizes theories of the mediated sublime from Kant to Jameson, only to conclude that an ecological sublime, unlike Western aesthetics that have rendered nature mute, would give voice to nature. However Wu Ming-yi is not merely countering Western philosophical traditions. He is transmitting Indigenous ecological knowledge and paradigms in which all components of the cosmos exhibit subjectivity. Shamanist roots of Daoist cosmology locate this in *qi* and early Chinese cosmological thought in *ganying* (anthropocosmic resonance); however, philosophical Daoism does not account for the subjectivity of technology *per se.*

In this sense, Wu Ming-yi, like late Qing science fantasy writers who fused motifs of new Western technology with *"the all-too-familiar* actants and topoi of a narrative tradition of the unknown," absorbs the overwhelming impact of global technomodernity into (increasingly familiar) knowledge paradigms of Taiwanese Indigeneity. In other words, the "terror" evoked by uncanny new structural formations of the subject resulting from technologically mediated compressions of time and space (viscerally experienced at a global scale during the Covid-19 pandemic) becomes ethically manageable in Wu Ming-yi's fiction via speculative fantasy and Indigenous futurism. The novel, while largely dystopian, is not without hope and healing. Like the Möbius strip featured in Timothy Morton's *Dark Ecology*, small pockets of society, individual points on the "strip," find healing despite the overwhelmingly dark context of climate catastrophe and the Sixth Mass Extinction, which the novel never soft-pedals.

> Ignored, unseen, mislaid with ease, a tiny millet grain,
> might fall away in the faintest breeze,
> beneath the August rain.
> You passed on by, you passed on out, my wristwatch read 6:10,
> the time the grain was set to sprout,
> interred, to live again. (195; 159)

Midway through the novel, Hafay sings a song suggesting the grain (her name means "Millet" in Pangcah) might sprout and live again. At the end of the novel, Dahu tells his daughter, Umav, to allow "Auntie Hafay" her time along in the cave (319; 268), and Atile'i tells Alice "the mountain will cure you" (320; 270). Then the crying begins. Alice cries as she sends Atilei'i, her surrogate "son," out to sea, acknowledging that he is a figment of her literary imagination and her real son is dead (346; 292).

Dahu finally acknowledges his emptiness as he hears Hafay singing Bob Dylan's "A Hard Rain's A-Gonna Fall" (350–53; 296–97). A Swiss cetologist weeps himself to death, evoking collective weeping in Chile after the sperm whale avatars of the second sons of Wayo Wayo explode on the shores of Valparaiso (359–60; 300). Yet the novel ends with Ohiyo, responding to Alice's call, meeting her gaze directly with her one blue and one brown eye. They have kept each other alive.

Students often report that *The Man with the Compound Eyes* is dystopian, yet oddly hopeful. The Indigenous practices of relationality practiced in Haven are contagious, bringing Sarah and Detlef together despite their epistemic differences, transforming Jung-Hsiang Li's Cartesian rationalism into grief for his brother. The Indigenous community lends money to Anu to allow him to operate the Forest Church as a site of ecotourism, stemming further land grabs from transnational corporations. According to feminist philosopher and scientist Karen Barad, Indigenous forms of embedded care and reciprocity also operate within quantum field theory, theorized not as epistemological uncertainty but ontological indeterminacy, the indeterminacy of nature, of being, itself. Because matter itself is constitutively inhabited, constituted in relationality and agential, Western notions of ontology are radically undone. Barad elaborates:

> The void is far from empty. It is flush with yearning and possibilities. It can hardly be thought of as that which does not matter. It is a womb that births existence. Matter is constituently inseparable from the void. It is a dynamic relationality. It is not fixed, given, instantiated, essential. Even the smallest bits of matter are an enormous multitude made up of material relations, sedimented histories of interactions with itself and all others across space and time. There is no such thing as a discrete individual. The other is always already within. Matter is an ongoing enactment of the undoing of individuality, self, other, property, and kind.[104]

Barad makes these remarks after showing the powerful video *Anointed*, by the Indigenous Marshall Islands poet Kathy Jetñil-Kijiner, who powerfully denounces colonial epistemologies of "radioactive racism" premised on the notions of Pacific islands as "empty" of life, hence rife ground for the U.S. military to conduct sixty-seven nuclear test explosions during the Cold War.[105] Like Hau'ofa Epeli, who argues that colonial mappings of the void must be replaced by an archipelago imagination of Oceania rife with mobility, agency, and connection, Barad denounces colonial epistemes based on Newtonian physics of the void that rationalize scientific applications of quantum field theory as "politically neutral." On the contrary, Barad finds material traces of injustices written inside the theory: "the bomb inhabits the physics all the way down into the equations themselves."[106] While the colonial story is one of nuclear deterrence and a future threat of nuclear apocalypse, the actual material practices of nuclear destruction are ongoing: 2,100 of the 2,115 nuclear explosions since 1945 have been on the sovereign nations of Indigenous peoples. As Jetñil-Kijiner writes about the nuclear aftermath of the Eniwetok and Bikini atolls in *Anointed*:

> How shall we remember you?
> You were a whole island, once. You were breadfruit trees heavy with green globes of fruit whispering promises of massive canoes. Crabs dusted with white sand scuttled through pandanus roots. Beneath looming coconut trees beds of ripe watermelon slept still, swollen with juice. And you were protected by powerful *irooj*, chiefs birthed from women who could swim pregnant for miles beneath a full moon.
> Then you became testing ground. Nine nuclear weapons consumed you, one by one by one, engulfed in an inferno of blazing heat. You became crater, an empty belly. Plutonium ground into a concrete slurry filled your hollow cavern. You became tomb. You became concrete shell. You became solidified history, immoveable, unforgettable.[107]

The mythology informing the logic of the void as opposed to material agency of the cosmos is what Wu Ming-yi highlights in his novel. It ends with an underwater nuclear test that creates an earthquake, activating a tsunami wave that sends a piece of the Trash Vortex hurling toward Wayo Wayo: "In three minutes and thirty-two seconds, it would, like a gargantuan carpenter's plane, peel away everything on the island, the living and the nonliving, into the sea" (357; 298). In this sense, Wu Ming-yi is not writing magical realism so much as hyperrealism.

Epilogue

Indigenous Entanglements in Techno Hypersubjectivity

> If something is stolen, that means people want it.
> —WU MING-YI, *THE STOLEN BICYCLE*

At the end of *Death's End*, the final volume in Liu Cixin's monumental science fiction trilogy *The Three-Body Problem*, a man and a woman must make a choice after Earth and most of humankind have been destroyed. They can remain safely in their isolated pocket universe or return their mass to the cosmos, trusting that enough others will independently make the same choice, potentially triggering a new Big Bang to catalyze a rich ten-dimensional multiverse and stop the continuous, alienating cosmic expansion. The man and woman cannot communicate with the other pocket universes, and their contribution of mass is so small that it will make no difference to the outcome either way. Nonetheless, they return themselves and the mass of their private universe to the grand universe. We readers never learn the outcome of their decision.[1]

For the most part, the acclaimed trilogy appears to be a stark reaffirmation of a world politics based in zero-sum logics of power. In its final pages, however, Liu introduces a radical challenge to the seemingly settled dynamics of interstellar conflict. He reveals that acts of agency produced the basic properties of his interstellar system, susceptible to change by further acts. This destabilizes key aspects of the zero-sum thought system that, for the great majority of the trilogy, drives the narrative of Liu's fictional world. The system is revealed to be historical rather than universal, created by powerful actors rather than a natural state. It is the result of and can be changed by conscious action.[2]

While some readers find the final pages of Liu's trilogy to be unsatisfactory, it reveals a prevalent "Chinese" understanding of ecological aesthetics and the operations of the cosmos. Liu's entire trilogy indulges Kenneth Waltz's neorealist theory that the anarchic structure of the international system is the root cause of war over limited resources, suggesting the need for a sovereign body governing the interactions between autonomous nation-states. Yet its concluding pages overturn the theory by suggesting that only by recognizing human limitations while also celebrating human agency might humans sustainably coexist within the "Dark Forest" of the cosmos. Greatly inspired by Arthur C. Clarke, Liu nonetheless differs from the British writer in that he does not distrust matter, and ultimately eschews mysticism.

This book contends that the ways in which climate-crisis literature imagines human relations to nonhuman animals, organic and inorganic entities, and regional ecosystems matter. It understands contemporary ecoliterature to emerge in contexts of inter-imperiality that express complex entanglements of colonizer and Indigenous cosmologies. While this regional study scrutinizes ecoliteratures from Taiwan and the PRC, it argues that similar patterns of Indigenous visions embedded within imperial cosmologies are globally prevalent and suggests that the ability of humans to decolonize their cosmologies has potentially global ramifications.

Liu Cixin's lingering investment in early Chinese cosmological beliefs in anthropocosmic resonance (*ganying* 感应) and *tianxia* (天下), whereby humans imbue the cosmos with a form of moral material agency, is reminiscent of film scholar Victor Fan's understanding of karmic agency in *Cinema Illuminating Reality* and Yuk Hui's comparative intellectual history of technics in *The Question Concerning Technology in China*, along with the essays in *Embodied Memories, Embedded Healing*.[3] While each presents unique derivations of human relations to materiality, these writers share underlying assumptions about ethical-material agency. This book has attempted to make those assumptions visible. Chapter 1, for example, examined how Han Chinese ecoliterature in the form of Beijing westerns synthesizes dialectics in what Ge Zhaoguang calls the historical metamorphosis of an imaginary utopia of "all under Heaven."[4]

Ecoliterature written by ethnic minority or Indigenous writers imagines different ways in which humans activate potentiality within matter. Writers expressing Indigenous forms of embedded care and reciprocity often come from cultures that historically privileged nomadic pastoralism, swidden agriculture, foraging, or fishing.[5] Such livelihood practices are more sustainable than those of the expansionist agrarian-based civilizations supporting empire, now bent on extracting Indigenous resources in new regimes of green governmentality.[6] Physicist Karen Barad's ideas of agential realism resonate with many Indigenous cosmologies in that they challenge conceptualizations of matter as apolitical and neutral. She argues that neocolonial scientism rationalizes the nonexistent ethical-material concept of the void, "a way of offering justification for claims of ownership in the 'discovery' of 'virgin' territory—the particular notion that 'untended,' 'uncultivated,' 'uncivilized' spaces are *empty* rather than plentiful, has been a well-worn tool used in the service of colonialism, racism, capitalism, militarism, imperialism, nationalism, and scientism."[7] Expansionist desires inherent in colonialist, capitalist, consumerist systems induce death from pandemics, toxins, drought, sea-level rise, loss of biodiversity, policing of climate refugees, and the sixth mass extinction.

Wa poetry by Burao Yilu (chapter 1) is one example of Indigenous ecoliterature that centers rituals and geographic formations in ways which defy both scientist cosmologies of the void and Hanspace cosmologies of peripheral exoticism. Rather than a subjective remembering of a past assumed to be left behind, embodied bordering re-members the material present. Her poems dynamically manifest the ontological indeterminacy of time-being: "The Wa people play instruments of joy—the calabash reed-pipes / And dance before the river, / Invoking no irreverence from their people."[8] Indigenous joy befuddles the imperial logic that engulfs it. It emerges from its own dynamic, embodied history. Anthropologist Magnus Fiskesjö emphasizes this potentiality in Wa mythology:

> We must underline again that the fabled Sigang aperture—expounded in origin myths, ubiquitous in everyday parlance as the endpoint that every genealogy is traced back to—signifies the legitimating claim that the Wa rightfully possess the lands where they live today. The Wa appeared first on earth and stayed around where

they had emerged; non-Wa latecomers on earth had to move farther away (to China, America, etc.), and such modern-era outsiders moving into Wa lands to appropriate its riches are intruders.⁹

The Sigang myth legitimizing centrality and land rights is no more constructed than Hanspace resonance theories of center and periphery or Western-derived evolutionist concepts of the void. The only difference is that the Wa are marginalized as "primitive" and "superstitious," while the latter are naturalized as "scientific" and "civilized."

Imperial cosmologies that eradicate the local histories of Indigenes and other marginalized peoples obscure anthropogenic damage to ecosystems. Indigenous-environmentalist synergies matter not because of imagined pristine purities but because marginalized histories and alternative environmental relations manifest real force in the world. They exist. They evolve. They have not disappeared. And they can enact change. Wu Ming-yi conveys this sensibility in his 2015 novel *The Stolen Bicycle*, a microhistory of Taiwan and the larger Pacific region. Ranging among themes of ecology, memory, and identity, the protagonist is the Taiwanese writer Ch'eng, a fictionalized version of the author, who had written a novel about the disappearance of his father. As Wu Ming-yi told me at a 2018 dinner in Cambridge, Massachusetts, his own father, who died in his youth, likely hid his Indigenous heritage from the family out of shame and exigency.

In what is ostensibly a study of Taiwan's bicycles set in World War II, Ch'eng embarks on an obsessive journey to locate his father's stolen bike based on the serial number on the seat post. At the same time, *The Stolen Bicycle* explores the island's landscape of colonization and the Japanese conscription of Indigenous peoples to join their Silverwheel Squad in the Burmese jungle. Searching for his father's bike in antique stalls and on message boards, Ch'eng encounters colorful characters who illuminate the island's landscape of colonization and wars, where humans, bicycles, cultures, and nature have collectively endured. When an elephant travels through the dense Burmese jungle in the Pacific theater of World War II, we view the war through its eyes and emotions, placing the horrors wrought by humans into sharp relief. Wu Ming-yi's novel engages the multispecies, multiethnic, multilingual complexities of contemporary Taiwan, a microcosm of our globalized world. Wu writes:

> In the world I grew up in, the word a person used for "bicycle" told you a lot about them. Jiten-sha ("self-turn vehicle") indicated a person had received a Japanese education. Thih-bé ("iron horse") meant he was a native speaker of Taiwanese, as did Khóng-bîng-tshia ("Kung-ming vehicle"), chiao-t'a-ch'e ("foot-pedaled vehicle") or tsu-hsing-ch'e ("auto-mobile vehicle") told you they were from the south of China. But everyone uses these terms now, so they're no longer a reliable way to tell how old someone is or where they come from.[10]

Linguistic purity is nonexistent, and ethnic identities are indistinct. Bloodlines are overrated. Tribalist ethnonationalist sentiments are eschewed. Wu Ming-yi reimagines borders, taking decolonization seriously. Readers of such ecoliterature can enlarge capacities for empathy and change perspectives, an ongoing project for all humanity. These tales expose the lies in imperialist cosmologies that insist nonhuman animals lack emotional depth and understanding, or that Indigenous cultural traditions lack conscious agency.

Ultimately, this book espouses Édouard Glissant's right to opacity. It claims the right to be valued even if *not* transparent or perfectly understood by others. It embraces the precivilizational, prelinguistic notions in the southern shamanism informing Laozi's *Daodejing*. Syaman Rapongan's song-ritual processing of emotional tensions in *Deep Love for the Cold Sea* (chapter 5) differs from the disembodied, philosophical resolution to the dichotomies featured in Gao Xingjian's *Soul Mountain* (chapter 1). Inspired by Derrida's *différance*, Gao's attention to subaltern elements in society is important because it questions reductive ideas of racial or geographic superiority rooted in deterministic notions of bodies and environments. And still the hierarchical complementarities synthesized by neo-Confucian and poststructuralist dialectics fail to acknowledge embodied opacities. This failure of recognition inevitably results in violence.

In his analysis of headhunting in Wa society, Magnus Fiskesjö provides an example of how imperialist logics do violence to Indigenous bodies. He contends that the Wa copied long-standing Chinese head-taking practices when they took them up as part of their own warfare. Yet "headhunting" as a nineteenth-century, Western-derived evolutionist concept denies official Chinese records that "beginning in pre-imperial times, the first millennium BCE, enemy heads were brought home by Chinese war chiefs and 'presented' at ancestral temples as a victory report to the ancestors."[11] Further, Fiskesjö characterizes "skull avenues" in Wa society as "an almost completely erased genre of unwritten historical records" transmitted via oral tradition.[12] Chinese ethnographers of the 1950s recognized these local forms of "historiography without writing," yet Wa memory was still deemed illegible in official records.

While peoples such as the Wa and Tao have largely manifested their histories in the natural and built environment, transmitted through storytelling by elders, other Indigenes (particularly Tibetans, Mongols, Uyghurs, and Kazakhs) discussed in this book have strong literary traditions and vast bodies of written historiography. In fact, literacy has always been higher among the Mongols than the Chinese in Inner Mongolia from the Republican era to the present.[13] When Guo Xuebo, Yerkesh Hulmanbek, or Alai evoke oral traditions of historiography in *Moŋgoliya* (chapter 2), *Eternal Lamb* (chapter 3), or *As the Dust Settles* (chapter 4), that is a positioning born of their restrictions within the twenty-first-century PRC; it is not something their nineteenth-century ancestors would have necessarily recognized or seen as useful.[14]

In general, reading stories about embodied relations to environments can sensitize us to our own interconnectedness with organic and inorganic matter. As the title character of Wu Ming-yi's *The Man with the Compound Eyes* puts it, "no life can survive without other lives, without the ecological memories other creatures have, memories of the environments in which they live. People don't realize they need to rely on the memories of other organisms to survive."[15] Inspired by such literature, I try to learn the memories of others.

A casual remark by a scholar of Southeast Asia at an academic conference planted the seeds for this book: "You China scholars are so Sinocentric." I was shocked. I needed to decolonize my mind. Six years later, a different Southeast Asian specialist reiterated a similar critique: your "borders" are Beijing-centric. My default thought is imperialist, anthropocentric, and agrarian. From my education in Chinese literature, from my Dutch farming ancestors, from my indoctrination into U.S. militarism, I have unwittingly absorbed Chinese and Western imperialist cosmologies. I need to decolonize my relational practices. For me this is not an academic exercise. Nor a solo one. Our lives depend upon it.

Acknowledgments

I am most grateful to David Der-wei Wang, Ursula Heise, Yomi Braester, and Ralph Litzinger for their generous and unflagging support of this project. The University of North Carolina at Chapel Hill Carolina Asia Center provided invaluable funding for multiple summers of field research. I also received vital support from a National Humanities Center Fellowship (NEH Fellowship and Walter Hines Page Fellowship of the Research Triangle Foundation), a UNC-Chapel Hill Institute of Arts and Humanities Fellowship, and a UC-Berkeley Faculty Fellowship for a summer workshop called Bordering China: Modernity and Sustainability. I give thanks to the directors, librarians, staff, and fellows at all three institutes, where research assistance and stimulating conversations over meals and walks helped shape this book.

In addition to the authors featured in this book, many others contributed to its creation, including Christopher Ahn, Nasan Bayer, Mark Bender, Uffe Bergeton, Darren Byler, Cheng Xiangzhan, Kuei-fen Chiu, Mark Driscoll, Joshua Freeman, Gong Haomin, Huatse Gyal, Stevan Harrell, HasErdene, Yerkesh Hulmanbek, Jangbu (Dorje Tsering Chenaktsang), Ju Kalsang, Christian Lentz, Liao Hongji, Liu Ka-hsiang, Long Qilin, Christopher Peacock, Mandumai, Mei Hua, Menghejiligu, Mei Chia-ling, Morton Pedersen, Morgan Pitelka, Ou Ning, Sakuliu Pavavaljung, Peng Hsiao-yen, Guldana Salimjan, Shuang Shen, Song Lili,

Tang Huisheng, Rian Thum, Timothy Thurston, Tung Chien-hung, Julie Velasquez-Runk, Wang Chia-hsiang, Wang Qianqian, Thomas White, Wu Ming-yi, Nadia Yaqub, Gang Yue, Yuyunbilige, and many other unnamed souls.

A special thanks to my students, a particularly helpful anonymous reviewer, members of the Justin Wolfe Pandemic Online Writing Group, Wade and Denise Baynham, and Christine Dunbar and her colleagues at Columbia University Press. Each of you made this possible.

My deepest gratitude, as always, goes to Zoe Ahn Ren, Jordan Shan Ren, and Takoda Lei Ren.

Notes

INTRODUCTION: ECOLITERATURES INHABITING BORDERS

1. Walter Mignolo, "Foreword: On Pluriversality and Multipolarity," in *Constructing the Pluriverse: The Geopolitics of Knowledge*, ed. Bernd Reiter (Durham, NC: Duke University Press, 2018), xii.
2. Ecocriticism is the branch of environmental humanities scholarship dedicated to the study of human/nature relationships through textual analysis.
3. Édouard Glissant, *Caribbean Discourses: Selected Essays*, trans. J. Michael Dash (Charlottesville: University Press of Virginia, 1981), 2.
4. Mignolo, "Foreword," x.
5. Édouard Glissant, *Poetics of Relation*, trans. Betsy Wing (Ann Arbor: University of Michigan Press, 1997), 62.
6. Yuk Hui, *The Question Concerning Technology in China: An Essay in Cosmotechnics* (Cambridge, MA: MIT Press, 2016).
7. See, for example, Miles Powell, *Vanishing America: Species Extinction, Racial Peril, and the Origins of Conservation* (Cambridge, MA: Harvard University Press, 2016).
8. Uffe Bergeton makes this argument in *The Emergence of Civilizational Consciousness in Early China: History Word by Word* (New York: Routledge, 2019).
9. Glissant, *Poetics of Relation*, 146.
10. Meredith DeBoom, "Climate Necropolitics: Ecological Civilization and the Distributive Geographies of Extractive Violence in the Anthropocene," *Annals of the American Association of Geographers* 111, no. 3 (2021): 904.

11. Bryan K. M. Mok, "Reconsidering Ecological Civilization from a Chinese Christian Perspective," *Religions* 11, no. 5 (2020): 261.
12. Guldana Salimjan, "Naturalized Violence: Affective Politics of China's 'Ecological Civilization' in Xinjiang," *Human Ecology* 49 (2021): 60.
13. Shinjilt, "Introduction: Remote Regions of Western China and 'Ecological Migration,'" in *Ecological Migration: Environmental Policy in China*, ed. Masayoshi Nakawo, Yuki Konagaya, and Shinjilt (Bern: Peter Lang, 2010), 12.
14. Mette Halskov Hansen, Hongtao Li, and Rune Svarverud, "Ecological Civilization: Interpreting the Chinese Past, Projecting the Global Future," *Global Environmental Change* 53 (2018): 195–203. In its Fourteenth Five-Year Plan (2021–25), the Chinese Communist Party (CCP) promises to lower the energy consumption per unit of gross domestic product (GDP) and carbon dioxide emissions per unit of GDP by 13.5 percent and 18 percent, respectively, and strives to peak carbon dioxide emissions by 2030 and achieve carbon neutrality by 2060. See "Man-Nature Harmony, An Essential Part of China's Modernization," *Xinhua*, April 27, 2021, http://www.xinhuanet.com/english/2021-04/27/c_139908104.htm.
15. Wei Guo, Peina Zhuang, "Ecophobia, 'Hollow Ecology,' and the Chinese Concept of *Tianren Heyi* (天人合一)," *ISLE: Interdisciplinary Studies in Literature and Environment* 26, no. 2 (Spring 2019): 430. See also Jialuan Li and Qingqi Wei, "Planetary Healing through the Ecological Equilibrium of *Ziran*: A Daoist Therapy for the Anthropocene," in *Embodied Memories, Embedded Healing: New Ecological Perspectives from East Asia*, ed. Xinmin Liu and Peter I-min Huang (Lanham, MD: Lexington Books, 2021), 55–69; rather than idealize human/nature relations, Daoism asks us to "rethink human aspirations, social ambitions, and ultimately 'man's way,'" 64.
16. 天地與我並生，而萬物與我為一 in *Zhuangzi*, Qiwulun 莊子齊物論 (The Sorting Which Evens Things Out). I use Burton Watson's translation: *The Complete Works of Zhuangzi* (New York: Columbia University Press, 2013), 38.
17. Dong Zhongshu 董仲舒, *Chunqiu fanlu* 春秋繁露, quoted in Guo and Zhuang, "Ecophobia," 436.
18. Guo and Zhuang, "Ecophobia," 436.
19. See, for example, Mark Elvin, *The Retreat of the Elephants: An Environmental History of China* (New Haven, CT: Yale University Press), 2004; Ling Zhang, *The River, the Plain, and the State: An Environmental Drama in Northern Song China, 1048–1128* (Cambridge: Cambridge University Press, 2016); Ian Miller, *Fir and Empire: The Transformation of Forests in Early Modern China* (Seattle: University of Washington Press, 2020), David A. Bello, *Across Forest, Steppe, and Mountain: Environment, Identity, and Empire in Qing China's Borderlands* (Cambridge: Cambridge University Press, 2016); Peter B. Lavelle, *The Profits of Nature: Colonial*

Development and the Quest for Resources in Nineteenth-Century China (New York: Columbia University Press, 2020); Judith Shapiro, *Mao's War Against Nature: Politics and Environment in Revolutionary China* (Cambridge: Cambridge University Press, 2001).

20. Jinping Xi, "Secure a Decisive Victory in Building a Moderately Prosperous Society," speech delivered at the 19th National Congress of the Communist Party of China, October 18, 2017, http://www.xinhuanet.com/english/download/Xi_Jinping's_report_at_19th_CPC_National_Congress.pdf.
21. Alice C. Hughes et al., "Horizon Scan of the Belt and Road Initiative," *Trends in Ecology & Evolution* 35, no. 7 (July 2020): 584.
22. See "Belt and Road Portal" (中国一带一路网), www.yidaiyilu.gov.cn, and "Countries of the Belt and Road Initiative," https://greenfdc.org/countries-of-the-belt-and-road-initiative-bri/.
23. Cecilia Han Springer, "Policies for an Ecological Civilization," PhD diss., University of California at Berkeley, 2019, 88.
24. Hughes et al., "Horizon Scan of the Belt and Road Initiative," 583–93.
25. For a summary of the ontological literature see Julie Velásquez Runk, Chindío Peña Ismare, and Toño Peña Conquista, "Animal Transference and Transformation Among Wounaan," *Journal of Latin American and Caribbean Anthropology* (2019): 3–5.
26. Philippe Descola, *Beyond Nature and Culture*, trans. Janet Lloyd (Chicago: University of Chicago Press, 2013), 9.
27. In Western philosophy, perspectivism is often equated with relativism; however, while Zhuangzi sees all knowledge as perspective-dependent, he holds that some perspectives are broader and more accurate than others. These superior perspectives, or "greater knowledge" (*da zhi* 大知), aim to ensure human survival and well-being. See Tim Connolly, "Perspectivism as a Way of Knowing in the Zhuangzi." *Dao* 10 (2011): 487–505.
28. Fernando Santos-Granero, "Beinghood and People-Making in Native Amazonia: A Constructional Approach with a Perspectival Coda," *HAU: Journal of Ethnographic Theory* 2, no. 1 (2012): 204.
29. Uradyn E. Bulag, *The Mongols at China's Edge: History and the Politics of National Unity* (Lanham, MD: Rowman & Littlefield, 2002), 18.
30. Bulag, *The Mongols at China's Edge*, 6.
31. Thomas Karl Alberts, *Shamanism, Discourse, Modernity* (London: Ashgate, 2015), 100.
32. For example, the Law of the People's Republic of China on Regional National Autonomy, revised in 2001, modified the subject of autonomy from "ethnic group" (*minzu*) to "area" (*diqu*), i.e., an ethnic autonomous region. "This revision

clearly exposes the Chinese government's belief that ethnic minorities should study Chinese and become assimilated with the mainstream culture of the country." Shinjilt, "Introduction," 26.
33. Para 65, quoted in Alberts, *Shamanism, Discourse, Modernity*, 104.
34. Alberts, *Shamanism, Discourse, Modernity*, 99.
35. Benedict Anderson, *Imagined Communities: Reflections on the Origins and Spread of Nationalism* (London: Verso, 1991), 86.
36. Kuan-Hsing Chen, *Asia as Method: Toward Deimperialization* (Durham, NC: Duke University Press, 2010).
37. See, for example, Karen Barad, "After the End of the World: Entangled Nuclear Colonialisms, Matters of Force, and the Material Force of Justice," *Theory & Event* 22, no. 3 (July 2019): 524–50.
38. See Ursula Heise, *Imagining Extinction: The Cultural Meanings of Endangered Species* (Chicago: University of Chicago Press, 2016).
39. In both Taiwan and the PRC, the first wave of ecocriticism started in 1980s with concerns by writers, literary scholars, journalists, and activists over environmental degradation. In the PRC, 1990s writers and prominent academics such as Wang Nuo, Lu Shuyuan, and Zeng Fanren established ecocritical centers and academic concentrations at university campuses in Xiamen, Suzhou, and Shandong. Taiwanese environmental humanities scholarship is equally rich, with journal issues and conferences devoted to ecocriticism and postcolonialism at National Taiwan University, National Chung Hsing University, Tamkang University, Tunghai University, and Academia Sinica. The Association for the Study of Literature and the Environment (ASLE)–Taiwan formed in 2010.
40. Karen Thornber, *Ecoambiguity: Environmental Crises and East Asian Literature* (Ann Arbor: University of Michigan Press, 2012); Simon Estok and Won-Chung Kim, eds., *East Asian Ecocriticisms: A Critical Reader* (New York: Palgrave Macmillan, 2013).
41. Riccardo Moratto, Nicoletta Pesaro, and Di-kai Chao, eds., *Ecocriticism and Chinese Literature: Imagined Landscapes and Real Lived Spaces* (London: Routledge, 2022); Xinmin Liu and Peter I-min Huang, eds., *Embodied Memories, Embedded Healing: New Ecological Perspectives from East Asia* (Lanham, MD: Lexington Books, 2021); Chia-ju Chang, ed., *Chinese Environmental Humanities: Practices of Environing at the Margins* (New York: Palgrave Macmillan, 2019); Chia-ju Chang and Scott Slovic, eds., *Ecocriticism in Taiwan: Identity, Environment, and the Arts* (Lanham, MD: Lexington Books, 2016).
42. Mark Bender, "Introduction: Poems from Borderlands in Asia," in *The Borderlands of Asia: Culture, Place, Poetry*, ed. Mark Bender (Amherst, NY: Cambria Press, 2017), 1–52.

43. Peter I-min Huang, *Linda Hogan and Contemporary Taiwanese Writers: An Ecocritical Study of Indigeneities and Environment* (Lanham, MD: Lexington Books, 2015).
44. Bergeton, *The Emergence of Civilizational Consciousness in Early China*, 135–36.
45. Bergeton, *The Emergence of Civilizational Consciousness in Early China*, 136.
46. 《孟子·尽心上》君子之于物也，爱人而弗仁；于民也，仁之而弗亲，亲亲而仁民，仁民而爱物。"A virtuous man is caring toward animals but is not benevolent toward them; he is benevolent toward the people but is not devoted to them. He is devoted to his parents but is merely benevolent toward the people; he is benevolent toward the people but is merely caring to animals." *Mencius* 7A45, trans. D. C. Lau (New York: Penguin Books, 1970), 192.
47. Mark Edward Lewis and Mei-yu Hsieh, "Tianxia and the Invention of Empire in East Asia," in *Chinese Visions of World Order: Tianxia, Culture, and World*, ed. Ban Wang, (Durham, NC: Duke University Press, 2017), 25–48.
48. Nasan Bayar, "A Discourse of Civilization/Culture and Nation/Ethnicity from the Perspective of Inner Mongolia, China," *Asian Ethnicity* 15, no. 4 (2014): 442.
49. There is a "long history of linguistic sedimentation bound up with the fundamentally hierarchical, non-Westphalian character of the Chinese world order," Haiyan Lee, *The Stranger and the Chinese Moral Imagination* (Stanford, CA: Stanford University Press, 2014), 247. Lee cites William Callahan, "in a hierarchical world order, foreigners are by definition barbarians," *China: The Pessoptimist Nation* (Oxford: Oxford University Press, 2010), 23. She adds that graphs designating non-Hua-Xia peoples outside of the "central states" (Zhongguo) or "central plains" (Zhongyuan) often carry animal radicals denoting their inferior, beastly status on a Chinese-style great chain of beings, 247, citing Magnus Fiskesjö, "The Animal Other: China's Barbarians and their Renaming in the Twentieth Century," *Social text* 29, no. 4 (2012): 61–68, and Lien-sheng Yang, "Historical Notes on the Chinese World Order," in *The Chinese World Order: Traditional China's Foreign Relations*, ed. John King Fairbank (Cambridge, MA: Harvard University Press, 1968), 20–33.
50. Historian Ibram X. Kendi defines assimilationist and segregationist racism in *Stamped from the Beginning: The Definitive History of Racist Ideas in America* (New York: Nation Books, 2016).
51. 非我族類其心必異。《左傳·成公四年》https://ctext.org/chun-qiu-zuo-zhuan/cheng-gong-si-nian. Though the northern Rong and western Di ("outer barbarians") were initially recognized by Zhou kings as equals, they were later disparaged as rapacious marauders to be driven to the civilizational peripheries "reserved for barbarians, ferocious animals, and evil spirits." See Yang, "Historical Notes on the Chinese World Order," 27.

52. Summarized by Hoyt Cleveland Tillman, "Proto-Nationalism in Twelfth-Century China? The Case of Ch'en Liang," *Harvard Journal of Asiatic Studies* 39, no. 2 (December 1979): 407.
53. 夷狄之與華夏,所生異地,其地異,其氣異矣;氣異而習異,習異而所知所行蔑不異焉。乃於其中亦自有其貴賤焉,特地界分、天氣殊,而不可亂;亂則人極毀,華夏之生民亦受其吞噬而憔悴。Wang Fuzhi 王夫之. "Ai Di" 哀帝 (Mourning the Emperor), in *Dutong jianlun* 讀通鑑論 (On *Zizhi Tongjian*), 14:9 (Beijing: Zhonghua shuju, 1975).
54. Bello, *Across Forest, Steppe, and Mountain*, 24. *Yin* is the principle of feminine, dark, moon, receptivity; *yang* that of male, light, sun, agency.
55. 夷狄者,殲之不為不仁,奪之不為不義,誘之不為不信 。何也?信義者,人與人相於之道,非以施之非人者也。Wang Fuzhi 王夫之 "Han Zhao Di" 漢昭帝 (Han Emperor Zhao), in *Dutong jianlun*, 1:75.
56. Frank Dikötter, *The Discourse of Race in Modern China* (Hong Kong: Hong Kong University Press, 1992), 28.
57. "Orders to Clear Wilderness for Cultivation" ("Ken Ling" 墾令) chapter *Book of Lord Shang* (商君书 *Shangjunshu*). Cited in Bello, *Across Forest, Steppe, and Mountain*, 42.
58. Bello, *Across Forest, Steppe, and Mountain*, 42.
59. Elvin, *Retreat of the Elephants*, 87.
60. For example, in a 1698 edict to "educate Mongols," the Kangxi emperor asserted "the Mongol character is indolent. Once seed is sown on the fields they go to various places to herd and, although the grain ripens, do not attend to reaping its harvest. Nor when frost falls do they gather in the harvest, but instead declare a bad year." Quoted in Bello, *Across Forest, Steppe, and Mountain*, 46.
61. William M. Campbell, *Formosa Under the Dutch: Described from Contemporary Records with Explanatory Notes and a Bibliography of the Island* (Taipei: SMC Publishing, 1992), 254. Cited in Shu-fen Tsai, "Taiwan is a Whale: The Emerging Oneness of Dark Blue and Human Identity in Wang Chia-hsiang's Historical Fiction," in *Ecocriticism in Taiwan*, 47.
62. Timothy Morton, *Dark Ecology: For a Logic of Future Coexistence* (New York: Columbia University Press, 2016), 43.
63. Morton, *Dark Ecology*, 23.
64. Charles Sanft, "Environment and Law in Early Imperial China (Third Century BCE–First Century CE): Qin and Han Statutes Concerning Natural Resources," *Environmental History* 15 (October 2010): 701–21.
65. For example, "The Duke of Zhou assisted King Wu of the Zhou dynasty . . . He drove the tigers, leopards, rhinoceroses, and elephants far away, and the world was greatly delighted." *Mencius* 3B9, trans. D. C. Lau (New York: Penguin Books, 1970), 113.
66. *Mencius* 1A3, 5.

67. In *Fir and Empire: The Transformation of Forests in Early Modern China* (Seattle: University of Washington Press, 2020), Miller argues that from 1000 to 1600 there was a "silvicultural revolution" in South China, a privatized and market-based forestry regime without foresters or a centralized forestry bureau.
68. Meng Zhang, *Timber and Forestry in Qing China: Sustaining the Market* (Seattle: University of Washington Press, 2021).
69. "The original graph for *tian* 天 seems to depict a large person striding across the sky . . . and from the very beginning of the written record in China *tian* is portrayed as issuing commands and sending down mandates." Edward Slingerland, "Conceptual Blending, Somatic Marking, and Normativity: A Case Example from Ancient Chinese," *Cognitive Linguistics* 16, no. 3 (2005): 570.
70. Slingerland, "Conceptual Blending," 569.
71. Peter B. Lavelle, *The Profits of Nature: Colonial Development and the Quest for Resources in Nineteenth-Century China* (New York: Columbia University Press, 2020), 168.
72. Ling Zhang, "Treating One's Neighbor Like a Gully 以鄰為壑: Environmental Ethics and Yellow River Management of the Chinese State," abstract for lecture at the University of Michigan, January 30, 2018, https://lsa.umich.edu/asian/news-events/all-events.detail.html/47853-11033230.html. 白圭曰："丹之治水也愈于禹。" 孟子曰："子過矣。禹之治水，水之道也，是故禹以四海為壑。今吾子以鄰國為壑。水逆付謂之洚水，洚水者，洪水也，仁人之所惡也。吾子過矣。" Mencius 孟子, Gaozi Pt 2 告子下, in *Xinhua Chengyu Cidian* 新华成语词典 Xinhua Idiom Dictionary, ed. Xu Zhensheng 许振生 (Beijing: Shangwu yinshuguan, 2002).
73. Ling Zhang, *The River, the Plain, and the State: An Environmental Drama in Northern Song China, 1048–1128* (Cambridge: Cambridge University Press, 2016), 6.
74. David Bello defines Hanspace as "the reductive and apprehensive ethnic-ecological expression of imperial China proper's arablism in comparative isolation from other environmental relations as a type of (super)natural habitat for agrarian Han Chinese." *Across Forest, Steppe, and Mountain: Environment, Identity, and Empire in Qing China's Borderlands* (Cambridge: Cambridge University Press, 2016), 23.
75. Kang Liu, "Chinese Exceptionalism: Linguistic Construction of a Superpower," in *The Routledge Handbook of Chinese Language and Culture*, ed. Liwei Jiao (London: Routledge, 2024.
76. Robert Weller, *Discovering Nature: Globalization and Environmental Culture in China and Taiwan* (Cambridge: Cambridge University Press, 2006), 33.
77. Weller, *Discovering Nature*, 33.
78. Mark Bender, *The Borderlands of Asia*, 5.

79. See, for example, Benjamin Hopkins's analysis of nineteenth century colonial governmentality of "peripheries" in Arizona, Afghanistan, and Argentina via "encapsulation" of Indigenous nomadic peoples in *Ruling the Savage Periphery: Frontier Governance and the Making of the Modern State* (Cambridge, MA: Harvard University Press, 2020). Uradyn E. Bulag argues Mongols were similarly governed in the formation of the Chinese nation-state in *The Mongols at China's Edge*.
80. Xuetong Yan, *Ancient Chinese Thought, Modern Chinese Power* (Princeton, NJ: Princeton University Press, 2013).
81. Zhao Tingyang 赵汀阳, *Tianxia tixi: Shijie zhidu zhexue daolun* 天下体系：世界制度哲学导论 (The Tianxia System: An Introduction to the Philosophy of a World Institution) (Nanjing: Jiangsu Jiaoyu Chubanshe, 2005). Summarized in Ban Wang, "Introduction," in *Chinese Visions of World Order: Tianxia, Culture, and World*, ed. Ban Wang (Durham, NC: Duke University Press, 2017), 2.
82. Ge Zhaoguang summarizes the past decade of Sinocentric discourse on tianxia in "Imagining 'All Under Heaven': The Political, Intellectual, and Academic Background of a New Utopia," trans. Michael Duke and Josephine Chiu-Duke, in *Utopia and Utopianism in the Contemporary Chinese Context: Texts, Ideas, Spaces*, ed. David Der-wei Wang, Angela Ki Che Leung, and Zhang Yinde (Hong Kong: Hong Kong University Press, 2020), 15–35.
83. Summarized in Hiroko Sakamoto, "The Cult of 'Love and Eugenics' in May Fourth Movement Discourse," trans. Rebecca Jennison, *positions* 12, no. 2 (Fall 2004): 333.
84. Sakamoto, "The Cult of Love," 333–34.
85. Cited in Sakamoto, "The Cult of Love," 336.
86. Sakamoto, "The Cult of Love," 337.
87. Ban Wang, "The Moral Vision in Kang Youwei's *Book of the Great Community*," in *Chinese Visions of World Order*, 100.
88. Sakamoto, "The Cult of Love," 337.
89. Andrew Jones, *Developmental Fairy Tales: Evolutionary Thinking and Modern Chinese Culture* (Cambridge, MA: Harvard University Press, 2011), 29.
90. See Sakamoto, "The Cult of Love," 331, 356. Zhou Zuoren, "Funü yundong yu changshi" (The Women's Movement and Common Sense), *Funü zazhi* (Women's Journal) 9, no. 1 (1923): 9; Andrew Jones, "The Child as History in Republican China: A Discourse on Development," *positions: east asia cultures critique* 10, no. 3 (Winter 2002): 713–14.
91. Lydia Liu, "Life as Form: How Biomimesis Encountered Buddhism in Lu Xun," *The Journal of Asian Studies* 68, no. 1 (February 2009): 26–27.
92. Liu, "Life as Form," 21.
93. Lu Xun, "Women xianzai zenyang zuo fuqin" 我們現在怎樣做父親 (What We Need to Do to Become Better Fathers Today), *Xin qingnian* 新青年 6 (1919): 558–59.

94. Zhou Jianren 周建人, "Chan'er zhiqian gaishuo" (What Must Be Said Before Giving Birth), 產兒之前該說 *Eastern Miscellany* 東方雜誌 19, no. 7 (1922): 18.
95. Zhou Jianren 周建人, "Lian'ai jiehun yu jianglai de renzhong wenti" 戀愛結婚與將來的人種問題 (Love, Marriage, and the Future of Our Race), *Funü zazhi* 婦女雜志 (Women's Journal) 8 (1922): 4. Quoted in Sakamoto, "The Cult of Love," 354.
96. Sakamoto, "The Cult of Love," 359.
97. Liu, "Life as Form," 23.
98. Sakamoto, "The Cult of Love," 361.
99. Pan Guangdan 潘光旦, "Zhongguo zhi yousheng wenti" 中國之優生問題 (The Eugenics Problem in China), *Dongfang zazhi* 東方雜誌 (Eastern Miscellany) no. 22 (1924): 15–33; "Ershinian lai shijie zhi yousheng yudong." 二十年來世界之優生運動 (The Eugenics Movement Around the World in the Last Twenty Years); *Dongfang zazhi* 東方雜誌 (Eastern Miscellany) no. 22 (1925): 60–85; "Yousheng gailun" 優生概論 (An Overview of Eugenics). *Liumeixuesheng jibao* 留美學生季報 (The Chinese Students Quarterly) 11, no. 4 (1927): 51–69. See also Leon Antonio Rocha, "Quentin Pan 潘光旦 in the *China Critic*," *China Heritage Quarterly* 30–31 (June–September 2012), http://www.chinaheritagequarterly.org/features.php?searchterm=030_rocha.inc&issue=030.
100. Yuehtsen Juliette Chung, "Better Science and Better Race? Social Darwinism and Chinese Eugenics," *Isis* 105 (December 2014): 800.
101. Rocha, "Quentin Pan."
102. Li Chonggao 李崇高, "Yousheng kexue de youlai yu fazhan" 优生科学的由来与发展 (The Origin and Development of Eugenics Science), in *Xing jiaoyu yu yousheng* 性教育与优生 (Sex Education and Eugenics) (Shanghai: Shanghai kexue jishu chubanshe, 1987), 198–201. See also Dikötter, *The Discourse of Race*, 174; Sakamoto, "The Cult of Love," 367.
103. Sakamoto, "The Cult of Love," 367.
104. Chung, "Better Science," 801.
105. Kai-wing Chow, "Imagining Boundaries of Blood: Zhang Binglin and the Invention of the Chinese Race in Modern China," in *Racial Identities in East Asia*, ed. Barry Sautman (Hong Kong: Hong Kong University of Science and Technology, 1995), 34–52.
106. Mao Zedong, "On the Ten Major Relationships," quoted in Thomas Mullaney, *Coming to Terms with the Nation: Ethnic Classification in Modern China* (Berkeley: University of California Press, 2011), 18.
107. Mullaney, *Coming to Terms with the Nation*, 57.
108. Joseph Stalin, *Marxism and the National and Colonial Question* (San Francisco: Proletarian Publishers, 1975). Summarized by Mullaney, *Coming to Terms with the Nation*, 73. See also Francine Hirsch, *Empire of Nations: Ethnographic Knowledge and the Making of the Soviet Union* (Ithaca, NY: Cornell University Press, 2005).

109. Mullaney, *Coming to Terms with the Nation*, 83–85.
110. Judith Shapiro, *Mao's War Against Nature*, 4.
111. David M. Lampson, "The Implementation Problem in Post-Mao China," in *Policy Implementation in Post-Mao China*, ed. David M. Mapson (Berkeley: University of California Press, 1987), 161.
112. Naktsang Nulo, *My Tibetan Childhood: When Ice Shattered Stone*, trans. Angus Cargill and Sonam Lhamo (Durham, NC: Duke University Press, 2014).
113. Naktsang Nulo, "Response to Questions by Tehor Lobsang Choephel and Others," posted January 15, 2013, on his website bodrigs.com. Translation from https://highpeakspureearth.com/a-tibetan-intellectual-naktsang-nulo-shares-his-thoughts-on-self-immolations-in-tibet/.

1. BEIJING WESTERNS AND HANSPACE ELIXIRS IN SOUTHWEST CHINA

Portions of this chapter appeared in an earlier form in "Anthropocosmic Resonance in Post-Mao Chinese Environmental Literature," *Wenyi lilun yanjiu* 文藝理論研究 (Theoretical Studies in Literature and Art) 33, no. 4 (2013): 34–44.

1. Zhong Dianfei 钟惦棐 "Mianxiang da xibei, kaituo xinxing de 'xibu pian'" 面向大西北,开拓新型的<西部片> (Face the Great Northwest, Develop a New Type of "Western"), *Dianying xinshidai* 电影新时代 (New Film Age) (1984): 61.
2. Daniel Fried, "Riding Off Into the Sunrise: Genre Contingency and the Origin of the Chinese Western," *PMLA* 22, no. 5 (October 2007): 1486.
3. "用电影的犁头耕种大西北这块正待开发的处女地,你们定会获得双培的收成." Zhong Dianfei, "Mianxiang da xibei," 63.
4. Also known as the Heihe-Tengchong Line (黑河–腾冲线). See Zhang Jian, Wei Jie, Chen Quangong, "Mapping the Farming-pastoral Ecotones in China," *J. Mt. Sci.* (2009) 6: 85; and Colum Murphy, "Hu Line: China's Forgotten Frontier," *Sixth Tone* (July 5, 2017) http://www.sixthtone.com/news/1000459/hu-line-chinas-forgotten-frontier.
5. Shinjilt, "Introduction: Remote Regions of Western China and 'Ecological Migration,'" in *Ecological Migration: Environmental Policy in China*, ed. Masayoshi Nakawo, Yuki Konagaya, and Shinjilt (Bern: Peter Lang, 2010), 24. Jarmila Ptackova lists jurisdictions included in the "Great Opening of the West" (*xibu da kaifa*) policies, comprising an astonishing 71 percent of China's total area and 29 percent of its population. See *Exile from the Grasslands: Tibetan Herders and Chinese Development Projects* (Seattle: University of Washington Press, 2020), 20.
6. Shinjilt, "Introduction," 25.
7. Fried, "Riding Off Into the Sunrise," 1485.

8. Judith Shapiro analyzes Maoist environmental policies and practices in *Mao's War Against Nature: Politics and the Environment in Revolutionary China* (Cambridge: Cambridge University Press, 2001).
9. Gang Yue, "The Strange Landscape of the Ancients: Environmental Consciousness in 'The King of Trees,'" *American Journal of Chinese Studies* 5, no. 1 (1998): 68–88.
10. Roger Ames, "Chinese Philosophy," in *The Edinburgh Companion to Twentieth-Century Philosophies*, ed. Constantin V. Boundas (Edinburgh: Edinburgh University Press, 2007), 664.
11. Wu Jingming 吴景明 includes *zhiqing* literature as early examples of ecological literature in his appendix, "Zhongguo dangdai shengtai wenxue zuopin nianbiao" 中国当代生态文学作品年表 (Chronology of Contemporary Chinese Ecological Literature), in "Zouxiang hexie: Ren yu ziran de shuangchong bianzou—Zhongguo shengtai wenxue fazhan lungang" 走向和谐：人与自然的双重变奏——中国生态文学发展论纲 (Toward Harmony: The Double Variation of Man and Nature: An Outline of the Development of Chinese Ecological Literature), PhD diss., Dongbei Shifan Daxue, 2007. Matthias Liehr argues, "these literary works are not driven primarily by a concern for environmental issues." "The Green Leaves of China: Sociopolitical Imaginaries in Chinese Environmental Nonfiction," PhD diss., University of Heidelberg, 2013, 51.
12. The search for the primeval forest remains a prominent theme in 1990s Chinese fiction, such as Qiu Huadong's 1998 novel *Fly Eyes* (Yingyan 蝇眼), where the protagonist dreams he is airlifted to Heilongjiang to live a primitive lifestyle in an old-growth forest. Writers often imagine alternative lifestyles in mountains and forests as an escape from the corruption of urban modernity. See, for example, He Dun's 1998 novel *The Himalayas* (Ximalayashan 喜马拉雅山).
13. The dominant paradigm of anthropocosmic resonance (*ganying* 感应) within 1980s Chinese ecoliterature differs from that in other literary cultures: in North American Indigenous ecoliterature the cosmos is anthropomorphized, in Mongolian ecoliterature the cosmos is sacralized, and Indigenous ecoliterature of Taiwan evokes Derrida's temporal-spatial ontological contiguities: "being *after*, being *alongside*, being near (près) would appear as different modes of being, indeed as *being-with*." Jacques Derrida, *The Animal That Therefore I Am*, ed. Marie-Louise Mallet, trans. David Wills (New York: Fordham University Press, 2008), 10.
14. Karen Thornber, *Eco-Ambiguity: Environmental Crises and East Asian Literatures* (Ann Arbor: University of Michigan Press, 2012), 147.
15. The setting appears to be a border village populated by Yi Indigenes in Guizhou, Yunnan, or Sichuan: "People said the Yelang people were conceited (*Yelang zida* 夜郎自大) but if they lived on mountains between Sichuan and Guizhou they had reason for it," Ah Cheng, *The King of Trees*, 11. The Yi are possibly modern-day

descendants of the Yelang kingdom, referred to in Chinese histories *Shiji* (史记) and *Hanshu* (汉书) as having supernatural skills, wearing their hair up, farming, and having strong armies. While Ah Cheng describes much of the landscape generically, he identifies bears, leopards, wild boar, wild oxen, snakes, pheasants, bamboo rats, muntjac, red deer, and muskrats, soon to disappear due to the Maoist deforestation project. See Ah Cheng, *The King of Trees*, 10.

16. In-text page references cite, respectively, Ah Cheng 阿城, *Ah Cheng Xiaoshuo: Qiwang shuwang haiziwang* 阿城小説: 棋王樹王孩子王 (Taipei: Haifeng, 1988), and Ah Cheng, *The King of Trees*, trans. Bonnie McDougall (New York: New Directions, 2010).
17. Edward Slingerland, "Conceptual Blending, Somatic Marking, and Normativity: A Case Example from Ancient Chinese," *Cognitive Linguistics* 16, no. 3 (2005): 568.
18. My interpretation of the novella differs from that of other ecocritics, including Gang Yue, "The Strange Landscape of the Ancients," and Karen Thornber, *Eco-Ambiguity*, 146–54. Both scholars provide an excellent analysis of the ambivalence and awakening consciousness of the sent-down youth; however, neither foregrounds the philosophical roots of Hanspace civilizational ideology or its emphasis on energizing the core from the periphery. Thornber concludes that "*King of Trees* demonstrates how easily appreciation and reverence of ecosystems can be accompanied by indifference to them or even satisfaction at their destruction" (149), while my reading reveals how violence inherent in agrilogistics is rationalized by synthesizing such contradictions via neo-Confucian metaphysics.
19. Qin Legal Code "Statutes on Fields" (*tianlu* 田律), in Charles Sanft, "Environment and Law in Early Imperial China (Third Century BCE–First Century CE): Qin and Han Statutes Concerning Natural Resources." *Environmental History* 15 (October 2010): 704.
20. Sanft, "Environment and Law in Early Imperial China," 704.
21. Wu Jingming identifies two 1982 short stories as the earliest examples of ecoliterature: "It's a Magical Land" 这是一片神奇的土地 by Liang Xiaosheng 梁晓声 (Han) in *Xiaoshuo yuebao* 11 (1982), and *The Black Steed* 黑骏马 by Zhang Chengzhi 张承志 (Hui) in *Shiyue* 6 (1982). See "Zhongguo dangdai shengtai wenxue zuopin nianbiao, 184. Most chronologies also omit "Source of Fortune" (1981) by Mandumai (Mongol) (see chapter 2).
22. Zhang Chang 张长, "Xiwang de lüye" 希望的绿叶 (The Green Leaves of Hope) *Renmin wenxue* 9 (1980): 94–102. Zhang Chang (b. 1938) is a prolific writer from Yunnan, formerly a country doctor, journal editor, and librarian, who rose to prominence with his 1979 story "Empty Valley Orchid" (空谷兰), which won the National Fiction Award (later named the Lu Xun Literary Award).

23. Sha Qing 沙青 (pen name of CCP member Li Shaqing 李沙青), "Beijing Loses Its Balance" 北京失去平衡 *Baogao wenxue* 4 (1986): 3. For overviews of eco-reportage see Yang Jianlong 杨剑龙 and Zhou Xufeng 周旭峰, "Lun Zhongguo dangdai shengtai wenxue chuangzuo" 论中国当代生态文学创作 (On Contemporary China's Writing of Ecoliterature)," *Shanghai shifan daxue xuebao* 上海师范大学学报 34, no. 2 (2005): 38–43; Zhang Xiaoqin 张晓琴 "Zhongguo 复眼人 shengtai baogao wenxue zongshu" 中国生态报告文学总数 (Summary of Chinese Eco-Reportage), *Xibei chengren jiaoyu xuebao* 西北成人教育学报 6 (2008): 28–29; Luo Zongyu 罗宗宇, "Dui shengtai weiji de yishu baogao: Xin shiqi yilai de shengtai baogao wenxue jianlun" 对生态危机的艺术报告：新时期以来的生态报告文学兼论 (Artistic Reportages on the Ecological Crisis: Brief Comments on Eco-Reportages since the New Era)," *Wenyi lilun yu piping* (2002): 636–42; and Liehr, "The Green Leaves of China."

24. Xu Gang 徐刚, *Famuzhe, xinglai!* 伐木者，醒来！(Woodcutter, Wake up!) (Changchun: Jilin renmin chubanshe, 1997), 6. Translation by Liehr in "The Green Leaves of China," 71–72.

25. Xu Gang, *Famuzhe, xinglai!* 16. Translation by Liehr, "The Green Leaves of China," 72–73.

26. Charles Sanft, "Progress and Publicity in Early China: Qin Shihuang, Ritual, and Common Knowledge," *Journal of Ritual Studies* 22, no. 1 (2008): 21–37.

27. Thomas Moran, "Lost in the Woods: Nature in Soul Mountain," *Modern Chinese Literature and Culture* 14, no. 2 (Fall 2002): 214.

28. Bai Indigene Zhang Chang's "Green Leaves of Hope" on deforestation in Yunnan and Mongol Indigene Guo Xuebo's 1980s stories of desertification in Inner Mongolia (see chapter 2) are two other exceptions.

29. Kam Louie, "Review Essay: In Search of the Chinese Soul in the Mountains of the South," *The China Journal* 45 (January 2001): 145.

30. According to Jeffrey Kinkley, Gao Xingjian feared being sent to labor reform camps in Qinghai and thus fled Beijing. "Gao Xingjian in the 'Chinese' Perspective of Qu Yuan and Shen Congwen," *Modern Chinese Literature and Cultures* 14, no. 2 (2002): 137.

31. Kinkley, "Gao Xingjian," 136.

32. Kam Louie, "Review Essay," 146.

33. Andrea Bachner, "The Remains of History: Gao Xingjian's *Soul Mountain* and Wuhe's *The Remains of Life*." *Concentric: Literary and Cultural Studies* 37, no. 1 (March 2011): 109, and Moran, "Lost in the Woods," 229.

34. Karen Thornber, *Ecoambiguity*, 222.

35. In-text page references cite, respectively Gao Xingjian 高行健, *Lingshan* 灵山 (Soul Mountain) (Taipei: Lianjing chubanshe, 1990), and Gao Xingjian, *Soul Mountain*, trans. Mabel Lee (New York: Harper, 2001).

36. David L. Hall, "On Seeking a Change of Environment," in *Nature in Asian Traditions and Thought: Essays on Environmental Philosophy*, ed. J. Baird Callicott and Roger Ames (Albany: State University of New York Press, 1989), 105.
37. Translated by Shan Chou, "Beginning with Images in the Nature Poetry of Wang Wei," *Harvard Journal of Asiatic Studies* 42, no. 1 (1982): 118–19.
38. Hall, "On Seeking a Change of Environment," 106.
39. Alfred North Whitehead, *The Concept of Nature* (Cambridge: Cambridge University Press, 1964), 28.
40. Alfred North Whitehead, *Science and the Modern World* (New York: Free Press, 1967), 83.
41. Donald W. Sherburne, "Whitehead, Alfred North," in *The Cambridge Dictionary of Philosophy*, ed. Robert Audi (Cambridge: Cambridge University Press, 1995), 852.
42. Alfred North Whitehead, *Process and Reality: An Essay in Cosmology (Corrected Edition)*, ed. David Ray Griffin and Donald W. Sherburne (New York: Free Press, 1979), 88.
43. Ames, "Chinese Philosophy," 664.
44. Sin Yee Chan, "Tang Junyi: Moral Idealism and Chinese Culture," In *Contemporary Chinese Philosophy*, ed. Chung-Ying Cheng and Nicholas Bunnin (Malden, MA: Blackwell, 2007), 306.
45. Quoted in John Zijiang Ding, "Li Zehou: Chinese Aesthetics from a Post-Marxist and Confucian Perspective," *Contemporary Chinese Philosophy*, ed. Chung-Ying Cheng and Nicholas Bunnin (Malden, MA: Blackwell, 2007), 247.
46. Louie, "Review Essay," 147.
47. Louie, "Review Essay," 148.
48. Kinkley, "Gao Xingjian," 141.
49. Kinkley, "Gao Xingjian," 141. Ge Zhaoguang, "Imagining 'All Under Heaven:' The Political, Intellectual, and Academic Background of a New Utopia," trans. Michael Duke and Josephine Chiu-Duke, in *Utopia and Utopianism in the Contemporary Chinese Context: Texts, Ideas, Spaces*, ed. David Der-wei Wang, Angela Ki Che Leung, and Zhang Yinde (Hong Kong: Hong Kong University Press, 2020), 32.
50. Ralph Litzinger, *Other Chinas: The Yao and the Politics of National Belonging* (Durham, NC: Duke University Press, 2000), 238.
51. See Robin Visser, "Ecocriticism and Indigenous Anti-Epics of China," in *The Epic World*, ed. Pamela Lothspeich (New York: Routledge, 2024).
52. In imperial times the Wa, like the Yi and Yao, were classified under the broad category of "southern barbarians" (*nan man*) due to the nomadic lifestyle of swidden cultivators. Swidden agriculture, also known as shifting cultivation, refers to a technique of rotational farming in which land is cleared for cultivation (normally by fire) and then left to regenerate after a few years. Governments worldwide have

long sought to eradicate swidden agriculture, which is often pejoratively called "slash-and-burn" through a mistaken belief that it is a driver of deforestation. For an extensive historicization of Wa headhunting, also briefly discussed in the epilogue of this book, see Magnus Fiskesjö, *Stories from an Ancient Land: Perspectives on Wa History and Culture* (New York: Berghahn Books, 2021).

53. Burao Yilu 布饶依露 "Yueliang shan" 月亮山 (Moon Mountain), *Minzu wenxue* 民族文学 4 (2002): 58. The translation is mine, adapted from Mark Bender, "Echoes from *Si Gang Lih:* Burao Yilu's 'Moon Mountain,'" *Asian Highlands Perspectives* 10 (2011): 99–128.
54. Burao Yilu, "Yueliang shan," 58.
55. Bender, "Echoes from *Si Gang Lih*," 115.
56. The Drum Dance shares certain similarities with the Mongol shamanistic ritual of the Andai Dance, described in Guo Xuebo 郭雪波 *Damo hun* 大漠魂 (Desert Soul) (Beijing: Zhongguo wenlian chubanshe, 2002). See chapter 2.
57. For example, in his study of the Yao, Ralph Litzinger recounts that Han county officials expressed "both fascination and contempt for the increased boisterousness (*renao*) of Yao community ritual." *Other Chinas*, 196.
58. Burao Yilu, "Four Generations of Va Women," in *Chinese Women Writers on the Environment: A Multi-Ethnic Anthology of Fiction and Non-Fiction*, ed. Dong Isbister, Xiumei Pu, Stephen D. Rachman, trans. Alexandra Draggeim (Jefferson, NC: McFarland and Company, 2020), 14.
59. Burao Yilu, "Four Generations of Va Women," 18.
60. Litzinger, *Other Chinas*, 231.
61. Burao Yilu, "Four Generations of Wa Women," 24. Some minorities have been unable to get desirable jobs because of discrimination. For example, Anar Sabit, a Uyghur woman who had been an excellent student, was unable to land a job in 2004 in Shanghai: "Some people, believing that 'barbarians' lived in Xinjiang, expressed surprise that she spoke Mandarin fluently. Just before she completed her degree, the tech company Huawei hosted a job fair, and Sabit and her friends applied. She was the only one not offered an interview—because of her origins, she was sure." Raffi Khatchadourian, "Surviving the Crackdown in Xinjiang," *The New Yorker*, April 5, 2021, https://www.newyorker.com/magazine/2021/04/12/surviving-the-crackdown-in-xinjiang.
62. Burao Yilu, "Mengdong River," trans. Mark Bender, in *The Borderlands of Asia: Culture, Place, Poetry*, ed. Mark Bender (Amherst, NY: Cambria, 2017), 229–30.
63. Bamo Qubumo 巴莫曲布嫫, "The Origin of Patterns," in Mark Bender, *The Borderlands of Asia*, 195–96. An alternate translation, "Patterns of the Sun," is in Isbister, Pu, and Rachman, *Chinese Women Writers on the Environment*, 11–12.
64. Bender, *The Borderlands of Asia*, 17.

65. Bamo Qubumo, "Water Lines," trans. Mark Bender, in *The Borderlands of Asia*, 197–98.
66. Aku Wuwu 阿库乌雾 (Chinese name 罗庆春) learned Chinese at age seven in the Liangshan Yi Autonomous Prefecture in southern Sichuan Province. He graduated from the Southwest University for Nationalities in Chengdu, where he is currently Dean of the Yi Studies Institute. He has published many volumes of poetry in both Nuosu and Chinese. See also *Tiger Traces: Selected Nuosu and Chinese Poetry of Aku Wuwu*, ed. Aku Wuwu and Mark Bender, Columbia, OH: Foreign Languages Publications, 2006, and *Coyote Traces: Aku Wuwu's Poetic Sojourn in America*, trans. Aku Wuwu, Wen Peihong and Mark Bender, Beijing: The Ethnic Publishing House/Columbus: The Ohio State University National East Asian Resource Center, 2015.
67. Aku Wuwu 阿库乌雾, "Spring Water," trans. Mark Bender, in *The Borderlands of Asia*, 191–193.
68. The date of the *Hnewo teyy* (Book of Origins), a Nuosu Yi folk epic from the Liangshan region in southwest Sichuan Province, is unknown. The earliest extant samples of Yi writing date from 1485, but Aki 阿畸 is said to have invented the Yi script during the Tang dynasty (618–907 CE). See *The Nuosu Book of Origins: A Creation Epic from Southwest China*, trans. Mark Bender and Aku Wuwu with Jjivot Zopqu (Seattle: University of Washington Press, 2019).
69. Aku Wuwu 阿库乌雾, "Black Bear," trans. Mark Bender, in *The Borderlands of Asia*, 187–88. The Yi version of "Black Bear" was published in *Aku Wuwu Zuopin Xuan* (Selected Works of Aku Wuwu) (Chengdu: Sichuan minzu chubanshe, 2019), 60–61.

2. GRASSLAND LOGIC AND DESERT CARBON IMAGINARIES IN INNER MONGOLIA

Portions of this chapter appeared in an earlier form in "Ecology as Method," *Prism: Theory and Modern Chinese Literature* 16, no. 2 (October 2019): 320–45.

1. Thomas Karl Alberts coins this expression and historicizes the alliance in *Shamanism, Discourse, Modernity* (London: Ashgate, 2015).
2. Other IMAR ecostories featuring Beijing-based Han sent-down youth include Ma Bo's memoir *Blood Red Sunset*, trans. Howard Goldblatt (New York: Penguin Books, 1996), Liu Cixin's science-fiction novel *The Three-Body Problem*, trans. Ken Liu (New York: Tor Books, 2016), and Hui-Han writer Zhang Chengzhi's novella *The Black Steed* (Beijing: Panda Books, 1990). Of these *The Black Steed* in particular replicates Beijing western "last Indian" laments. See Allesandra Pezza, "Environmental Nostalgia from Idyll to Disillusionment: Zhang Chengzhi's

Inner Mongolia from Short Stories to Essays," *Ecocriticism and Chinese Literature: Imagined Landscapes and Real Lived Spaces*, ed. Riccardo Moratto, Nicoletta Pesaro, and Di-kai Chao (London: Routledge, 2022), 167–79.

3. David A. Bello, *Across Forest, Steppe and Mountain: Environment, Identity, and Empire in Qing China's Borderlands* (Cambridge: Cambridge University Press, 2016), 128.
4. Bello, *Across Forest, Steppe and Mountain*, 129.
5. Bello, *Across Forest, Steppe and Mountain*, 150.
6. See Masoyoshi Nakawo, Yuki Konagaya, and Shinjilt, eds., *Ecological Migration: Environmental Policy in China* (Bern: Peter Lang, 2010), for detailed case studies on effects of such policies in IMAR and other "western" locales.
7. Thomas Richard Edward White, "Transforming China's Desert: Camels, Pastoralists and the State in the Reconfiguration of Western Inner Mongolia," PhD diss., University of Cambridge, 2016, 8.
8. Ling Zhang, *The River, the Plain, and the State: An Environmental Drama in Northern Song China, 1048–1128* (Cambridge: Cambridge University Press, 2016), 20. See also Li Xianglan 李香兰, "Xibu dakaifa yu Nei Menggu huanbao shengchanye de fazhan" 西部大开发与内蒙古环保产业的发展 (Western Development and the Development of Environmental Protection Industries in Inner Mongolia), *Nei Menggu Daxue Xuebao* (Journal of Inner Mongolia University) 34, no. 5 (2002): 19–24.
9. Uradyn Erden Bulag, *The Mongols at China's Edge: History and the Politics of National Unity* (Lanham, MD: Rowman & Littlefield, 2002), 6.
10. 幼小時候，我知道中國在"盤古氏開辟天地"之后，有三皇五帝，……宋朝，元朝，明朝，"我大清"。到二十歲，又聽說"我們"的成吉思汗征服歐洲，是"我們"最鬧氣的時代。到二十五歲，才知道所謂這"我們"最鬧氣的時代，其實是蒙古人征服了中國，我們做了奴才。Lu Xun 魯迅. "Suibian fanfan" 隨便翻翻 (A Random Glance), in *Qiejie ting zawen ji* 且介亭雜文集 (Essays from the Qiejie Pavilion) (Shanghai: Sanxian Shuwu, 1937), quoted in Bulag, *The Mongols at China's Edge*, 6, and in Anran Wang, "The Sino-Mongolian Contention over the Legacy of Chinggis Khan," *Studies in Ethnicity and Nationalism* 16, no. 3 (2016): 359.
11. Nasan Bayar, "A Discourse of Civilization/Culture and Nation/Ethnicity from the Perspective of Inner Mongolia, China," *Asian Ethnicity* 15, no. 4 (2014): 449.
12. Nicola Di Cosmo, *Ancient China and Its Enemies: The Rise of Nomadic Power in East Asian History* (Cambridge: Cambridge University Press, 2002), 57.
13. Bayar, "A Discourse of Civilization," 451.
14. Bayar, "A Discourse of Civilization," 451. Italics mine.
15. Elizabeth Povinelli, *Geontologies: A Requiem to Late Liberalism* (Durham, NC: Duke University Press, 2016), 5.
16. Povinelli, *Geontologies*, 9.

17. A Mongol-Han graduate student told me her Han grandmother often characterized her Mongol grandfather's perspectives as "suicidal." Such Mongol ecocentrism arises "because shamanic belief in the transformation of different spirits presupposes recognition of the eternity of the animistic world, in which individual human life is considered transient and unimportant when compared with the perpetuity of holistic existence." Lili Song, "Toward an Ecocriticism of Cultural Diversity: Animism in the Novels of Guo Xuebo and Chi Zijian," in *Embodied Memories, Embedded Healing: New Ecological Perspectives from East Asia*, ed. Xinmin Liu and Peter I-min Huang (Lanham, MD: Lexington Books, 2021), 81.
18. Wu Lan 乌兰, "Zhi duzhe" 致读者(To the Reader), in *Junma, canglang, guxiang* 骏马·苍狼·故乡 (*Horse, Wolf, Home*), by Mandumai 满都麦, 2 vols. (Beijing: Zuojia chubanshe, 2015), 1:i.
19. Bulag, *The Mongols at China's Edge*, 189.
20. Jiang Rong, *Wolf Totem: A Novel*, trans. Howard Goldblatt (New York: Penguin Books, 2009), 377. 如果中国人能在中国民族精神中剜去儒家的腐朽成分，再在这个精神空虚的树洞里，移植进去一个狼图腾的精神树苗。Jiang Rong 姜戎, *Lang tuteng* 狼图腾 (Wolf Totem) (Wuhan: Changjiang wenyi chubanshe, 2004), 253.
21. Miles Powell, *Vanishing America: Species Extinction, Racial Peril, and the Origins of Conservation* (Cambridge, MA: Harvard University Press, 2016), 147.
22. Mandumai, *Junma, canglang, guxiang*, 1:12. Subsequent in-text page references cite this edition.
23. Cao Yu 曹禺, "Wang Zhaojun," 王昭君 (Wang Zhaojun). *Renmin wenxue* 人民文学 (1978): 55.
24. Quoted in Prasenjit Duara, *Rescuing History from the Nation: Questioning Narratives of Modern China* (Chicago: University of Chicago Press, 1995), 59.
25. Carolyn Merchant, *The Death of Nature: Women, Ecology, and the Scientific Revolution* (New York: HarperCollins, 1980), 3.
26. Morten Pedersen, *Not Quite Shamans: Spirit Worlds and Political Lives in Northern Mongolia* (Ithaca, NY: Cornell University Press, 2011), 217.
27. Many ecocritics see Han nature aesthetics in the *Shijing*. See Zeng Fanren 曾繁仁, *Shengtai meixue daolun* 生态美学导论 (Introduction to Ecological Aesthetics) (Beijing: Shangwu yinshu guan, 2010); Chen Wangheng, *Chinese Environmental Aesthetics*, ed. Gerald Cipriani, trans. Feng Su (London: Routledge, 2015); Karen Thornber, "Environments of Early Chinese and Japanese Literatures," in *A Global History of Literature and the Environment*, ed. John Parham and Louise Westling (Cambridge: Cambridge University Press, 2016), 37–51; Mark Elvin, *The Retreat of the Elephants: An Environmental History of China* (New Haven, CT: Yale University Press, 2004).

28. Anthropocosmic "resonance" (*ganying* 感應) posits that humans are in a mutually dependent relationship with the world. Confucian resonance theories are one of the three most important ecological cosmologies that still influence Han Chinese today, along with Buddhist compassion and an image of power that radiated from the margins to the center. See Robert P. Weller, *Discovering Nature: Globalization and Environmental Culture in China and Taiwan* (New York: Cambridge University Press, 2006), 23–25; Weiming Tu, "Beyond the Enlightenment Mentality," in *Confucianism and Ecology: The Interrelationship of Heaven, Earth, and Humans*, ed. Mary Evelyn Tucker and John Berthrong (Cambridge, MA: Harvard University for the Study of World Religions, 1998), 17–19; and Robin Visser, "Anthropocosmic Resonance in Post-Mao Chinese Environmental Literature," *Wenyi lilun yanjiu* 文藝理論研究 (Theoretical Studies in Literature and Art) 33, no. 4 (2013): 34–44.
29. For example, Liu Shi claims that Mandumai is warning wolves not to behave like humans in "Deep in the Woods," and Guo Peng interprets "The Four-Eared Wolf" via Mencian ideas about compassion for animals. Ma Mingkui 马明奎, ed., *Youmu wenming de yousi* 游牧文明的忧思 (Troubled Thoughts on Nomadic Civilization) (Hohhot: Neimenggu chuban jituan, yuanfang chubanshe, 2013), 171–72, 181.
30. Shantarakshita, *The Adornment of the Middle Way: Shantarakshita's Madhyamakalankara with Commentary by Jamgon Mipham* (Boston: Shambhala, 2005), 304.
31. Urantsatsral Chimedsengee, Amber Cripps, Victoria Finlay, Guido Verboom, Ven Munkhbaatar Batchuluun, and Ven Da Lama Byambajav Khunkhur, *Mongolian Buddhists Protecting Nature: A Handbook on Faiths, Environment and Development* (Bath: The Alliance of Religions and Conservation, 2009), 15.
32. For historical background on similar agrarian communities formed of sedentarizing herders and displaced migrant farmers in eastern Inner Mongolia, see Burensain Borjigin, *The Agricultural Mongols: Land Reformation and the Formation of Mongolian Village Society in Modern China*, trans. Thomas White, ed. Uradyn E. Bulag (Yokohama: Shumpushu Publishing, 2017).
33. Ji Cheng, "Spring on the Horqin Sandland," in *The Desert Wolf*, by Xuebo Guo, trans. Chiying Wang (Beijing: Chinese Literature Press, 1996), 348.
34. Guo is one of the few writers in this book to explicitly identify as an ecowriter. See Lili Song, "Toward an Ecocriticism of Cultural Diversity," 75. Guo received Taiwanese literary prizes for his early ecofiction but was largely overlooked by PRC ecocritics until Li Changzhong's 李长中 edited *Ecocriticism and Ethnic Literary Studies* 生态批评与民族文学研究) (Beijing: Academy of Social Sciences Press, 2012). See Cheng Li, "Echoes from the Opposite Shore: Chinese Ecocritical

Studies as a Transpacific Dialogue Delayed," *Interdisciplinary Studies in Literature and Environment* 21, no. 4 (Autumn 2014): 825.
35. Timothy Morton, *Dark Ecology: For a Logic of Future Coexistence* (New York: Columbia University Press, 2016), 23.
36. Morton, *Dark Ecology*, 43.
37. Guo Xuebo 郭雪波, *Damo hun* 大漠魂 (Desert Soul) (Beijing: Zhongguo wenlian chubanshe, 2002), 84; Guo, *The Desert Wolf*, 86. Subsequent in-text page references are, respectively, to *Damo hun* and *The Desert Wolf*.
38. Dee Mack Williams, "Patchwork, Pastoralists, and Perception: Dune Sand as a Valued Resource Among Herders of Inner Mongolia," *Human Ecology* 25, no. 2 (June 1997): 299. Italics mine.
39. Dee Mack Williams, "Patchwork, Pastoralists, and Perception," 302–303.
40. Povinelli, *Geontologies*, 14.
41. Povinelli, *Geontologies*, 16.
42. Dubiously comparing prominent Chinese ecocritic Lu Shuyuan to Timothy Morton, who denounces agrilogistics, Chia-ju Chang celebrates Lu's promotion of Tao's spirit, seen as the collective unconscious of Chinese agricultural civilization. Lu contends that "an industrial civilization cannot sever itself from agricultural civilization and that urbanization cannot destroy pastoral traditions." Chia-ju Chang, "Building a Post-Industrial Shangri-La: Lu Shuyuan, Ecocriticism, and Tao Yuanming's 'Peach Blossom Spring,'" in *Chinese Environmental Humanities: Practices of Environing at the Margins*, ed. Chia-ju Chang (New York: Palgrave Macmillan, 2019), 50.
43. "Living with Wolves," *Guardian*, November 22, 2007.
44. Karen Thornber notes these stark contrasts in her analysis of *Wolf Totem* but does not critique the representations, rather focusing on Han Chinese blindness to ecological evidence presented by Mongols. See *Ecoambiguity: Environmental Crises and East Asian Literatures* (Ann Arbor: University of Michigan Press, 2012), 310–17.
45. Haiyan Lee, for example, concludes that the novel subscribes to "an ideologically repackaged totemism that recruits animals to naturalize racist notions of human differences and hierarchies." See *The Stranger and the Chinese Moral Imagination* (Stanford, CA: Stanford University Press, 2014), 100.
46. Jiang, *Lang tuteng*, 23; Jiang and Goldblatt, *Wolf Totem*, 34. In-text page references cite, respectively, these two editions.
47. Mandumai 滿都麥, *Aobao: Caoyuan shengtai wenming de shouhu shen—Youmu wenhua ganwu lu* 敖包：草原生态文明的守护神—游牧文化感悟录 (Ovoos: Protector Spirits of Grassland Ecological Civilization—On Nomadic Cultural Sensibilities) (Hulunbeir: Neimenggu chuban jituan, 2013).

48. 狼从来不是蒙古人图腾。蒙古所有文史中从未记载过狼为图腾！这是一汉族知青在草原只待三年，生生嫁祸蒙古人的伪文化！蒙古人最早信萨满后佛教。狼是蒙古人生存天敌，狼并无团队精神两窝狼死磕，浪贪婪自私冷酷残忍，宣扬狼精神是反人类法西斯思想。"Mengguzu zuojia pi *Lang tuteng*: Lang conglai bushi Mengguren tuteng" 蒙古族作家批《狼图腾》狼从来不是蒙古人图腾 (Mongol Author Criticizes *Wolf Totem*: Wolves Have Never Been a Mongol Totem), Morningpost.com.cn (February 25, 2015).

49. In her trenchant analysis of *Wolf Totem*, Haiyan Lee says, "One cannot but be puzzled by the incongruity between [Chen Zhen's] wistful admiration for the Mongol cavalries laying waste to the cities and villages of Eurasia and his lamentation over the state-sponsored destruction of the Mongolian grasslands," *The Stranger and the Chinese Moral Imagination*, 109. Yet this kind of "last Indian" lament characterizes settler-colonialist narratives worldwide. Miles Powell, for example, recounts how U.S. social scientists considered Indian extirpation inevitable, nostalgically eulogizing still-living species and races while proposing models of progress that adopt successful strategies used by Indians and wild animals. *Vanishing America*, 15–16.

50. A scientific account of Mongol grassland ecology, recommended by Inner Mongol scholars, is Han Nianyong 韩念勇, *Caoyuan de luoji* 草原的逻辑 (*Grassland Logic*), 4 vols. (Beijing: Beijing kexue jishu chubanshe, 2011).

51. See Weller, *Discovering Nature*, and Steven Harrell, "The Role of the Periphery in Chinese Nationalism," in *Imagining China: Regional Division and National Unity*, ed. Shu-min Huang and Cheng-kuang Hsu (Nankang, Taiwan: Institute of Ethnology, Academia Sinica, 1999), 139–43.

52. Bayar, "A Discourse of Civilization," 452.

53. Wolfgang Kubin, "Deguo hanxue quanwei ling yizhiyan kan xiandangdai Zhongguo wenxue" 德国汉学权威另一只眼看现当代中国文学 (German Sinology Expert Looks at Contemporary Chinese Literature with Another Eye), Interview by Xin Ping, Deutsche Welle, November 26, 2006, https://p.dw.com/p/9R8g.

54. Anonymous, Interviews with Inner Mongolia University faculty, Hohhot, August 28, 2017.

55. Anonymous, Interviews, 2017.

56. Anonymous, Interviews, 2017.

57. Anonymous, Interviews, 2017. 为什么《狼图腾》那么出名，它是汉族作家写蒙古族的故事讲给汉族听。一方面是环境保护和人与生态之际和谐的关系的需求，另一方面他是不是要强调一个汉族一定要怎样强大起来，怎样往外，用狼的精神去克服目前这个国际国内各种各样的地位的问题呢？一方面觉得很自豪，又另一方面觉得很不好意思.

58. Li Xianglan 李香兰, "Xibu dakaifa yu Nei Menggu huanbao shengchanye de fazhan" 西部大开发与内蒙古环保产业的发展. (Western Development and the

Development of Environmental Protection Industries in Inner Mongolia), *Nei Menggu Daxue Xuebao* (Journal of Inner Mongolia University) 34, no. 5 (2002): 19–24.
59. Alberts, *Shamanism, Discourse, Modernity*, 205.
60. Ursula Heise, *Imagining Extinction: The Cultural Meanings of Endangered Species* (Chicago: University of Chicago Press, 2016), 90.
61. Bello, *Across Forest, Steppe and Mountain*, 266.
62. Amy Qin, "As China Hungers for Coal, 'Behemoth' Studies the Ravages at the Source," *New York Times*, December 28, 2015, https://www.nytimes.com/2015/12/29/world/asia/china-film-zhao-liang-inner-mongolia-coal-behemoth.html.
63. Bruce Humes, "Borderland Fiction: 'The Mongol Would-be Self-Immolator.' An Excerpt from Guo Xuebo's '*Mongoliya*,'" February 17, 2019, https://bruce-humes.com/category/guo-xuebos-mongolia-蒙古里亚/. In-text citations are to Guo Xuebo 郭雪波, *Mengguliya* 蒙古里亚 (*Mongoliya*) (Beijing: Beijing shiyue wenyi chubanshe, 2014).
64. In her analysis of *The Great Shaman's Golden Sheep Cart* (大萨满之金羊车, 2011), Lili Song says, "The search for shamanic culture has been Guo Xuebo's distinctive narrative perspective in his shaman story series, in which the narrator is always the 'I' looking for the ancient shaman culture long thought to have disappeared from northern China in the wake of modernization. Each story develops against the background of a local environmental problem, such as mine drilling, desertification, or the loss of prairie." "Toward an Ecocriticism of Cultural Diversity," 75.
65. Though Manchukuo is often referred to as a "puppet state" of the Empire of Japan established in northeast China and Inner Mongolia from 1932 to 1945, the Manchoukuo-era Hinggan Province and Prince De's "Autonomous Mongol State" were, in fact, the institutional precursors of the Inner Mongolian Autonomous Region. See Liu Xiaoyuan's *Reins of Liberation: An Entangled History of Mongolian Independence, Chinese Territoriality, and Great Power Hegemony, 1911–1950* (Palo Alto, CA: Stanford University Press, 2006) and Prasenjit Duara, *Sovereignty and Authenticity: Manchukuo and the East Asia Modern* (Lanham, MD: Rowman & Littlefield, 2004).
66. Guo Xuebo tacitly acknowledged his belief that he has inherited his family's shamanic powers in an interview I conducted with him on July 27, 2019, in Beijing.
67. From 2011 to 2013 more than one hundred Tibetans enacted political self-immolation. See Robert Barnett, "Introduction: A Note on Context and Significance," in *My Tibetan Childhood: When Ice Shatters Stone*, by Naktsang Nulo, trans. Angus Cargill and Sonam Lhamo (Durham, NC: Duke University Press, 2014), xxxiv–xxxv.

68. The novel reveals that the woman and her husband were poor rural migrants from southeastern Jiangxi Province. More than one in ten people in eastern rural China are Christians.
69. The *-liya* suffix is also a version of the Russian name for Mongolia (Mongoliya), which creates an implicit reference to the international dimension of Mongolia.
70. Dee Mack Williams, "Grazing the Body: Violations of Land and Limb in Inner Mongolia," *American Ethnologist* 24, no. 4 (1997): 763–85.
71. Pedersen, *Not Quite Shamans*, 174.
72. Pedersen, *Not Quite Shamans*, 35.

3. SACRED ROUTES AND DARK HUMOR IN GROUNDED XINJIANG

1. According to the 2020 census, Uyghurs comprise 45 percent and Han comprise 42 percent of 26 million total residents of Xinjiang, 57 percent of whom reside in cities or towns. In 1949, just 6 percent of its population were Han Chinese and 75 percent were Uyghur. See Qing-Li Yuan, "Population Changes in the Xinjiang Uighur Autonomous Region (1949–1984)," *Central Asian Survey* 9, no. 1 (1990): 49–73.
2. A professor from Inner Mongolia University told me his doctoral student in ethnography had done summer field research in Xinjiang without problems, but after a visit in 2017, ten of his contacts were detained and sent to "reeducation" camps. When I returned to Hohhot in 2019, most of my previous Mongol contacts avoided meeting, since sensitivities had heightened in IMAR.
3. Guldana Salimjan, "Naturalized Violence: Affective Politics of China's 'Ecological Civilization' in Xinjiang," *Human Ecology* 49 (2021): 60.
4. Guldana Salimjan in Nurila Qizihan, "A Houseful of Birds," trans. Guldana Salimjan, *Chinese Women Writers on the Environment: A Multi-Ethnic Anthology of Fiction and Non-Fiction*, ed. Dong Isbister, Xiumei Pu, and Stephen D. Rachman (Jefferson, NC: McFarland and Company, 2020), 81n1.
5. Gulidana Shalimujiang (Guldana Salimjan), "Finding Kazakh Women in the Chinese State: Embodiment and the Politics of Memory" (PhD diss., University of British Columbia, 2018), 175.
6. Nurila Qizihan, "A Houseful of Birds," 83.
7. Guldana Salimjan in Nurila Qizihan, "A Houseful of Birds," 83n5.
8. Nurila Qizihan, "A Houseful of Birds," 83.
9. In *Animals in the Qur'an* (Cambridge: Cambridge University Press, 2012), Sarra Tlili claims the Qur'an depicts humans as *mukallaf* ("accountable persons,"

adult, sane, given the Islamic message) that bear responsibilities other creatures do not. Summarized in Anna M. Gade, *Muslim Environmentalisms: Religious and Social Foundations* (New York: Columbia University Press, 2019), 103.

10. The 1956–1967 National Programs for Agricultural Development Article XVII states, "starting from 1956, within 12 years, substantially eliminate the most serious hazards animals that can damage production in all possible places." Quoted in Guldana Salimjan in Nurila Qizihan, "We Have Surpassed the Bears," 84n2.

11. Similar laws were passed in Taiwan around the same period, as reflected in Indigenous Bunun writer Topas Tomapima's "The Last Hunter" (1987) (see chapter 5).

12. Nurila Qizihan, "We Have Surpassed the Bears," 86.

13. Many Confucian texts establish human superiority over animals, both analogizing animal behavior as natural moral philosophy and animals as worthy of compassion while exhorting humans to be more *humane* than "beasts." Muslim ecophilosophy posits humans as superior to other animals due to *accountability*, yet esteems animal nature.

14. Her essays are set in her childhood home in Qitai County 奇台县 in the northwest Xinjiang border region of the Baitag Bogd range 北塔山, part of the Altai mountain range 金山.

15. A 2010 documentary film adaptation, *Eternal Lamb* (*Yongsheng yang* 永生羊), produced by Gao Feng 高峰 (head of the CCTV documentary channel) and directed by Gao Chang 高厂, retains documentary verisimilitude regarding local customs and music, yet the story was altered in typically exoticizing ways: the main character of the film was a little boy, and the story featured a thwarted love story typical of a soap opera. See Brigitte Duzan, "Yerkesh Hulmanbek 叶尔克西·胡尔曼别克 Présentation par Brigitte Duzan, 12 juin 2016" (On Yerkesh Hulmanbek, June 12, 2016), http://chinese-shortstories.com/Auteurs_de_a_z_Yerkesy_Hulmanbiek.htm.

16. Yerkesh Hulmanbek 叶尔克西·胡尔曼别克, *Caoyuan huomu* 草原火母 (Fire Mother of the Grassland) (Ürümchi: Xinjiang renmin chubanshe, 2006); Yerkesh Hulmanbek 叶尔克西·胡尔曼别克, trans., *Hasakesitan shixuan: "Yidai yilu" yanxian guojia jingdian shige wenku* 哈萨克斯坦诗选"一带一路"沿线国家经典诗歌文库 (Selected Kazakhstan Poetry: Library of Poetry Classics from Countries along the "Belt and Road") (Beijing: Zuojia chubanshe, 2019).

17. James A. Millward, "Positioning Xinjiang in Eurasian and Chinese History: Differing Visions of the 'Silk Road,'" in *China, Xinjiang, and Central Asia: History, Translation and Crossborder Interaction into the 21st century*, ed. Colin Mackerras and Michael Clarke (New York: Routledge Contemporary China Series, 2009), 55.

18. Yerkesh Hulmanbek 叶尔克西·胡尔曼别克, *Yongsheng yang* 永生羊 (Eternal Lamb) (Ürümchi: Xinjiang remin chubanshe, 2012), 208–9. Subsequent in-text parenthetical page references are to this edition. In "Memories" she recounts the famous 1947 Battle of Baitag Bogd Mountain (北塔山事件), where Kazakh heroes

fought with their Chinese counterparts to defeat Russian-backed Mongolian invaders. She recalls a huge festival, held in the early 1960s, that celebrated friendship between China and Mongolia. In 2002 few remembered the festival, and its namesake stream had dried up, its now-desolate locale "resting in peace." The essay collection ends by exhorting local Kazakh schoolchildren to "learn to be thankful."

19. Aydos Amantay, "The Failure," trans. Canaan Morse, in *Chutzpah! New Voices from China*, ed. Ou Ning and Austin Woerner (Norman, OK: Chinese Literature Today Book Series, 2015), 116.
20. The second page number for the in-text parenthetical citations refers to a translation of "Yongsheng yang" by Nicky Harman, "Eternal Lamb," *Peregrine: An English Companion to Chutzpah! Magazine* (December 2012): 19–24.
21. Shen Wei 沈苇, *Xinjiang cidian* 新疆词典 (Dictionary of Xinjiang), bilingual excerpt, trans. Eleanor Goodman, *Ninth Letter* 10, no. 2 (Fall/Winter 2013–14): 139. Subsequent in-text parenthetical page references are to this translation.
22. According to Guldana Salimjan, "*sende jaziq joq, mende aziq joq* expresses respect and graduate to the sheep's sacrifice for the human need for food. It's often said as part of the Islamic prayer 'Bismillah. . . .' Kazakhs say this every time before a sheep is sacrificed for feasts." Personal communication, October 7, 2021.
23. The biblical text, which refers to Christ as "The Lamb," reads: "The city had no need of the sun or of the moon to shine in it, for the glory of God illuminated it. The Lamb *is* its light." Rev 21:23 KJV.
24. Yerkesh Hülmanbek, "Painless," trans. Roddy Flagg, *Read Paper Republic*, September 3, 2015, http://paperrepublic.org/pubs/read/painless/. Yerkesh Hülmanbek 叶尔克西·胡尔曼别克, "Wutong" 无痛 (Painless) *Qingchun* 青春 (Youth) 8 (2005): 29–32.
25. Dee Mack Williams also details extreme dissociation from bodily pain among IMAR herders in "Grazing the Body: Violations of Land and Limb in Inner Mongolia," *American Ethnologist* 24, no. 4 (1997): 763–85. He attributes alcoholic numbing, accidents, and death to government policies inducing poverty, despair, and cultural alienation.
26. Yerkesh Hülmanbek, "Painless," np.
27. Nurbergen, a government-licensed Kazakh imam, illustrates the "maternal betrayal" of the state, which trained them to be loyal and patriotic, only to ultimately jail most of them in the recent crackdowns: "'They raised us like sheep," Nurbergen says. "They took us all around the country, trained us. And then, having fattened us up, slaughtered us." Quoted in Gene A. Bunin, "From Camps to Prisons: Xinjiang's Next Great Human Rights Catastrophe," Art of Life in Chinese Central Asia, October 5, 2019, https://livingotherwise.com/2019/10/05

/from-camps-to-prisons-xinjiangs-next-great-human-rights-catastrophe-by-gene-a-bunin/.

28. Nathan Ruser and James Leibold, "Cultural Erasure and Re-writing: How China is Using State Cultural Protection to Erase Islamic and Indigenous Cultures from Xinjiang," September 1, 2021, https://www.youtube.com/watch?v=AcF-nG5xays Presentation at The Xinjiang Crisis: Genocide, Crimes Against Humanity, Justice, Newcastle University, September 1–3, 2021. See also Rian Thum, "The Spatial Cleansing of Xinjiang: *Mazar* Desecration in Context," Made in China, August 24, 2020, https://madeinchinajournal.com/2020/08/24/the-spatial-cleansing-of-xinjiang-mazar-desecration-in-context/. Magnus Fiskesjö claims that "the razing of Uyghur cultural heritage is actually an important further piece of evidence of the systematic intention to destroy the native peoples *as such*—which clearly is what drives the Chinese regime's campaign, and which is the core element of genocide in the 1948 Genocide Convention [the five criteria for which have been met] (they target the Uyghur and other peoples in question with killings, mass trauma, livelihood destruction, mass birth prevention, mass removal of children)." "China Ravages Xinjiang Cultural Heritage," Modern Chinese Literature and Culture Blog Post, August 25, 2020, https://u.osu.edu/mclc/2020/08/25/china-ravages-xinjiang-cultural-heritage-1/#more-34956.

29. Italics mine. Nearly four years after Rahile Dawut disappeared, confirmation came that she was arrested and sentenced by Chinese authorities, although the charge and length of sentence are unclear. See "Uyghur Professor Rahile Dawut Confirmed to be Imprisoned by Chinese Authorities," Pen America, July 16, 2021, https://pen.org/press-release/uyghur-professor-rahile-dawut-confirmed-to-be-imprisoned-by-chinese-authorities/, and "Noted Uyghur Folklore Professor Serving Prison Term in China's Xinjiang," Radio Free Asia, July 13, 2021, https://www.rfa.org/english/news/uyghur/rahile-dawut-07132021175559.html.

30. Dilmurat Mahmut, Jo Smith Finley, "Corrective 'Re-Education' as (Cultural) Genocide in the Uyghur Region: Content Analysis of Children's Textbook *Til-Ädäbiyat* (rev. 2018)," September 1, 2021, presentation at The Xinjiang Crisis, https://www.youtube.com/watch?v=AcF-nG5xays.

31. In-text pages cite Perhat Tursun, *The Backstreets: A Novel from Xinjiang*, trans. Darren Byler and Anonymous (New York: Columbia University Press, 2022). Byler's anonymous cotranslator, who disappeared in 2017, is presumed to be in the reeducation camp system in northwestern China. Perhat Tursun was detained in 2018 and reportedly given a sixteen-year sentence. The original was published in an online digital Uyghur language salon called kitaphumar.com ("book craving/desire"). Like most Uyghur-language websites, the entire website was completely erased in 2017. Darren Byler directed me to this archived version: Perhat Tursun, *Chong Sheher: Birinchi Bap, Arqa Kocha* (Big City: The First Chapter,

The Backstreets), in *Perhat Tursun Eserliri* (Works of Perhat Tursun) (2013), https://web.archive.org/web/20140322013840/http://kitaphumar.com/.

32. Rian Thum writes of southern Xinjiang identity, "Altishahris clearly differentiated themselves from Han Chinese by calling them Khitay, from Turkic and Mongolic nomadic groups whom they called Kirghiz and Qalmaq, and even from settled Turkic speakers of Western Turkestan with whom they shared language, religion, and way of life." *The Sacred Routes of Uyghur History* (Cambridge, MA: Harvard University Press, 2014), 135.

33. Darren Byler, "The Disappearance of Perhat Tursun, One of the Uyghur World's Greatest Authors," SupChina, February 5, 2020, https://supchina.com/2020/02/05/disappearance-of-perhat-tursun-uyghur-worlds-greatest-author/. Uyghur poet Tahir Hamut Izgil describes Tursun's writing as "truly unique." In January 2018, Tursun was seized by Chinese authorities from Ürümchi and was later reported to have been sentenced to sixteen years' imprisonment.

34. Darren Byler, *Terror Capitalism: Uyghur Masculinity in a Chinese City* (Durham, NC: Duke University Press, 2022), 148–49.

35. Liu Liangcheng, "One Man's Village," excerpt trans. Joshua Dyer, *Pathlight: New Chinese Writing* (October 2015): 60. Liu Liangcheng 刘亮程, *Yigeren de cunzhuang* 一个人的村庄 (One Man's Village) (Shenyang: Chunfeng wenyi chubanshe, 2006).

36. Georg Simmel, "The Metropolis and Mental Life," in *The Sociology of Georg Simmel*, ed. Kurt H. Wolff (New York: Free Press, 1950), 409.

37. Yan Lianke 阎连科, Zhang Xuexin 张学昕, *Wode xianshi, wode zhuyi: Yan Lianke wenxue duihua lu* 我的现实，我的主义: 阎连科文学对话录 (My Reality, My "Ism:" Notes on a Dialogue About Yan Lianke's Literature) (Zhongguo Renmin Daxue Chubanshe, 2011), 42, italics mine.

38. Yan Lianke 阎连科, *Faxian xiaoshuo* 发现小说 (Discovering Fiction) (Tianjin: Nankai Daxue Chubanshe, 2011).

39. Thum, *The Sacred Routes of Uyghur History*, 106.

40. "The Failure," by Beijing-based Kazakh writer Aydos Amantay, like Gao Xingjian's journey west in *Soul Mountain*, details a root-seeking journey via a two-month visit to Xinjiang as a Chinese teacher. Amantay's awakened identity is mostly epistemological, although "the smell of cow's milk" on his nomadic students' bodies does work its way into his consciousness.

41. In his introduction to *The Backstreets*, vii–viii, Darren Byler explains how Han settlers in Xinjiang cities frequently discriminate against Uyghurs in hiring and housing practices.

42. Darren Byler, *Terror Capitalism*, 150.

43. Nathan Light, "Cultural Politics and the Pragmatics of Resistance: Reflexive Discourses on Culture and History," in *Situating the Uyghurs Between China and Central Asia* (2007), 51.

44. Memtimin Hoshur, "Burut Majrasi," *Tarim* (ch. 塔里木) 1 (1991): 20–30. See, also, Memtimin Hoshur 买买提明·吾守尔, "Huxu fengbo" 胡须风波 (Mustache Dispute), trans. Aikebaier 艾克拜尔, *Minzu wenxue* 民族文学 (May 1991): 75–80+82, and Memtimin Hoshur, "The Mustache Dispute (An Excerpt)," trans. Darren Byler and Mutellip Enwer, *Pathlight* (2014): 87–93.
45. Darren Byler and Enwer, "Translator's Note," *Pathlight* (2014): 93
46. Hoshur, "Burut Majrasi," 29; Hoshur, "Huxu fengbo," 82.
47. Carolyn L. Burke and Joby G. Copenhaver, "Animals as People in Children's Literature," *Language Arts* 81, no. 3 (January 2004): 205–13.
48. A noteworthy exception in English is the Freddy the Pig series (1927–1958) for children by Walter R. Brooks.
49. Axel Goodbody, "Animal Studies: Kafka's Animal Stories," in *Handbook of Ecocriticism and Cultural Ecology*, ed. Hubert Zapf (Berlin: De Gruyter, 2016), 256.
50. Memtimin Hoshur, "Festival for the Pigs," trans from Uyghur by Darren Byler and Mutellip Enwer, *Guernica Magazine* (December 1, 2014), np., https://www.guernicamag.com/festival-for-the-pigs/.
51. Memtimin Hoshur, "Festival for the Pigs," np.
52. Memtimin Hoshur, "Festival for the Pigs," np.
53. Australian philosopher Peter Singer, in his 1975 book *Animal Liberation*, popularized the term "speciesism" (discrimination against animals, coined by analogy with racism) for the thinking in which our treatment of animals differently from humans and our systematic, institutionalized killing of them are grounded.
54. Memtimin Hoshur, "Festival for the Pigs," np.
55. Azati Suritan 阿扎提·苏里坦, "Youmo shi zuigao de fengci—qiantan Memtimin Hoshur de fengci yishu 幽默是最高明的讽刺–浅谈买买提明·吾守尔的讽刺艺术 (Humor is the Highest Satire: A Brief Discussion on the Satire Art of Memtimin Hoshur), in *Minzu wenxue de shuxie yu goujian* 民族文学的书写与构建 (The Writing and Construction of Ethnic Literature), ed. Azati Suritan, 205–8 (Shanghai: Wenlian chubanshe, 2016).
56. Memtimin Hoshur 买买提明·吾守尔, "Zhu de jieri" 猪的节日 (Festival for the Pigs) won the Excellence Award on the fiftieth anniversary (1999) of the founding of the journal, *Minzu Wenxue* 民族文学 (Ethnic Literature).
57. Memtimin Hoshur, "Festival for the Pigs," np.
58. Memtimin Hoshur, "Festival for the Pigs," np.
59. Haraway claims the mutual attraction, manipulation and dependence between humans and domestic species are better understood as instances of symbiosis than simple domination. Donna Haraway, *When Species Meet* (Minneapolis: University of Minnesota Press, 2007).
60. Goodbody, "Animal Studies," 252. Goodbody discusses Kafka's importance as a precursor of contemporary critics of speciesism, including Deleuze and

Guattari as a model for their project of unsettling the human/animal divide, Derrida's references to Kafka's "zoopoetics," and J. M. Coetzee's tribute to him in *The Lives of Animals*.

61. Yang Yang, "A Poetic Way to Decode Xinjiang," *China Daily*, August 26, 2015, http://www.china.org.cn/arts/2015-08/27/content_36428378.htm.
62. Miles Powell, *Vanishing America: Species Extinction, Racial Peril, and the Origins of Conservation* (Cambridge, MA: Harvard University Press, 2016), 123.
63. Blog by Don Hanlon, emeritus professor of architecture at the University of Wisconsin at Milwaukee: "The Case of Turpan, China: How to Destroy a Culture," October 3, 2019, https://agslibraryblog.wordpress.com/2019/10/03/the-case-of-turpan-china-how-to-destroy-a-culture/.
64. Hanlon, "The Case of Turpan, China."
65. Hanlon, "The Case of Turpan, China."
66. Mérceles, also transliterated musällăs or muselles, means "homemade wine," and is one of the oldest wines in Altishahr. A Uyghur from Xinjiang's rural south recalled a folk song that describes the process of making it by adding a couple of drops of pigeon blood, so she was unwilling to try it. She also recalled a Uyghur documentary film that shows the production of muselles in a workshop (without pigeons). Personal communication, August 8, 2022. See also a blog post by a Han visitor describing muselles: https://www.laitimes.com/en/article/ceqz_chmt.html.
67. The title of this poem refers to the sometimes province of Liangzhou, first formed as part of the Han conquest of parts of the Xiongnu empire of the 120s BCE, in the Han-Xiongnu War. The Hexi Corridor served to connect China proper with the Western Regions, which helped secure important parts of the Silk Road into Central Asia. This was paralleled in the Sui-Tang dynastic era and is also a key transport route in modern times.
68. 涼州詞   A SONG OF LIANGZHOU
    葡萄美酒夜光杯， From a jade cup I'm about to drink the finest grape wine,
    欲飲琵琶馬上催。 But they strum pipas on horses, urging me to fall in line.
    醉臥沙場君莫笑， Don't laugh if I lay drunk on the battle ground.
    古來征戰幾人回？ After this campaign how many of us will still be around?
    Ying Sun and Ssu-Yu Huang, "Poems of Tang Dynasty with English Translations," 2008, http://musicated.com/syh/TangPoems.htm.
69. Bruce Humes, "The Success of Shen Wei's *A Dictionary of Xinjiang*," comment on Paper Republic blog, August 27, 2015, https://paper-republic.org/links/the-success-of-shen-weis-a-dictionary-of-xinjiang/.
70. Li Juan 李娟. *Jiu pian xue* 九篇雪 (Nine Stories on Snow), 2003, 2nd ed. (Nanjing: Jiangsu wenyi chubanshe, 2013); Li Juan 李娟, *Aletai de jiaoluo* 阿勒泰的角落 (Altay Corner) (Beijing: Lianhe chubanshe, 2010); Li Juan 李娟, *Wode Aletai*

我的阿勒泰 (My Altay) (Kunming: Yunnan renmin chubanshe, 2010); Li Juan 李娟, *Dong muchang* 冬牧场 (Winter Pasture) (Beijing: Xinxing chubanshe, 2012); Li Juan 李娟, *Yangdao: Sanbuqu* 羊道三部曲 (The Way of Sheep Trilogy) (Beijing: Zhongxin chubanshe, 2017); Li Juan 李娟, *Yaoyuan de xiangrikui di* 遥远的向日葵地 (Distant Sunflower Fields) (Guangzhou: Guangdong huacheng chubanshe, 2017); Li Juan, *Distant Sunflower Fields*, trans. Christopher Payne (London: Sinoist Books, 2021); Li Juan, *Winter Pasture: One Woman's Journey with China's Kazakh Herders* (New York: Astra House, 2021).

71. Li Juan, *Aletai de jiaoluo*, 17–37.
72. See Daniel Abramson and Yu Qi, "'Urban-Rural Integration' in the Earthquake Zone: Sichuan's Post-Disaster Reconstruction and the Expansion of the Chengdu Metropole," *Pacific Affairs* 84, no. 3 (September 2011): 495–523.
73. Li Juan, "Shuyu wo de ma" 属于我的马 (The Horse That Belonged to Me), in *Wode Aletai*, 8.
74. Li Juan, "Shuyu wo de ma," 8.
75. Ou Ning 欧宁, "Meiyou zuihao de difang, ye meiyou zuihuai de difang: Li Juan zhuanfang" 没有最好的地方, 也没有最坏的地方: 李娟专访 (Neither the Best nor Worst Place: Interview with Li Juan), Jintian, September 13, 2012, https://www.jintian.net/today/html/69/n-38669.html.
76. Ou Ning, "Meiyou zuihao de difang."
77. Li Juan, "Li chuntian zhiyou ershi gongfen de xuetu" 離春天只有二十公分的雪兔 (A Snowshoe Hare Merely Twenty Centimeters from Springtime), *Aletai de jiaoluo*, 5. Subsequent parenthetical citations in-text.
78. Li Juan 李娟, "Motuoche chuanguo chuntian de huangye" 摩托车穿过春天的荒野 (Motorcycling Through the Wilderness of Spring), *Wode Aletai*, 16–17.
79. Liu Zhirong 刘志荣, "Dadi yu tiankong de liaokuo yu wenmi" 大地与天空的辽阔与隐秘—李娟散文漫谈 (The Vastness and Secrets of Earth and Sky: On Li Juan's Essays), *Wenyi zhengming* (September 2011): 133–37. Xu Zhaoshou 徐兆寿, "'Jie diqi' he 'jie tianqi'–jiantan dui 'renxue' de chaoyue" '接地气'和'接天气'–兼谈对'人学'的超越 (Connect to the Vital Energies of Heaven and Earth: Transcend the Human), *Xiaoshuo pinglun* (2012): 57–63.
80. Her style has also been compared to that of the 1930s writer Xiao Hong, particularly her attention to close emotional ties between humans and animals and her deep empathy for those she describes. Yet the narrative voice in Xiao Hong's 1934 novel *Field of Life and Death* is more detached from her subjects, and while empathetic, also conveys mild cynicism, while the humor in Li Juan's narrative voice is as easily directed toward self as others.
81. Zhang Yan 张岩 and Zhang Shuqun 张书群, "Shouwang xiangtu de shengming zhiwu" 守望乡土的生命之悟: 对《一个人的村庄》的解读 (Life Intuition from

Watching the Countryside: An Interpretation of *One Man's Village*), *Dangdai wenxue* 当代文学 (November 2009): 66.

82. Liu emphasizes the difference between *xiangcun* 乡村, which he writes about, and *nongcun* 农村, which he does *not* write about. See Jiang Guangping 姜广平, "Wo buhuang bumangde shuxuzhe renlei jiuwei de ziran shengcun: Yu Liu Liangcheng duihua" 我不慌不忙地叙述着人类久违的自然生存：与刘亮程对话 (I Leisurely Recount the Long-Lost Natural Existence of Human Beings: A Dialog with Liu Liangcheng), *Wenxue jiaoyu* 3 (2011): 4–9.

83. Xu Yongquan 徐永泉 and Jiang Wei 隆伟, "Ni bie wuxuanze: *Yigeren de cunzhuang* zhong de shengcun kunjing tanxi 你别无选择：《一个人的村庄》中的生存困境探析 (You Have No Choice: An Analysis of the Dilemma of Survival in *One Man's Village*), *Tangshan shifan xueyuan xuebao* 31, no. 6 (November 2009): 22–24. Liu Hanhua 刘涵华, "Nongye wenming de gezhe: Wei An, Liu Liangcheng sanwen chuangzuo bijiao 农业文明的歌者：苇岸、刘亮程散文创作比较 (Eulogists of Agricultural Civilization: A Comparison of Prose Creation by Wei An and Liu Liangcheng), *Changji xueyuan xuebao* 3 (2010): 46–49.

84. Liu Liangcheng 刘亮程, *Yige ren de cunzhuang* 一个人的村庄 (One Man's Village) (Shenyang: Chunfeng wenyi chubanshe, 2006), 5. Subsequent in-text pages cite this edition. Some translations adapted from Thomas Moran, "Bringing It All Back Home: Ecocriticism and Liu Liangcheng's (刘亮程) *One Man's Village* (一个人的村庄)," Presentation at the Association of Asian Studies Annual Meeting, Chicago, March 2012.

85. Moran, "Bringing It All Back Home."

86. *sende jaziq joq, mende aziq joq* (n21). For a variety of translations into Chinese and English, see Hulmanbek, *Yongsheng yang*, 152: "你生不为罪时，我生不为挨饿"; Hulmanbek, "Eternal Lamb," 9: "you were not born for sin and I was not born to go hungry;" Li Juan, *Dong Muchang*, 44: "你不因有罪而死；我们不为挨饿而生"; Li Juan, *Winter Pasture*, 66: "a Kazakh writer that I like, Sister Yerkesh Hulmanbek, once said, 'you shouldn't die for your sins, we aren't born to go hungry.'"

87. Astrid Møller-Olsen, "Take the Elevator to Tomorrow: Mobile Space and Lingering Time in Contemporary Urban Fiction," Lund University Publications, August 30, 2018, https://lup.lub.lu.se/record/87b5ebbb-8507-45ca-a362-9d8a6 bd3dc19. Møller-Olsen coins the term "time-space" to "to describe discrete 'blocks' of spacetime, a term that recognizes the inseparability of space and time (so place will not do) and can be used to describe everyday scenes."

88. Liu Liangcheng lived from 1962 to 1982 in two different villages in Shawan County 沙湾县, 150 kilometers west of Ürümchi. Liu's father was killed in 1970, and his stepfather relocated the family to Taiping Village 太平乡. *One Man's Village*

conflates experiences in Liu's two different childhood villages into the single village of Huangshaliang 黄沙梁, a place name that refers to all of northern Shawan County. Moran, "Bringing It All Back Home."

89. Alfred North Whitehead, *Science and the Modern World* (New York: Free Press, 1925), 69.

90. Adam C. Scarfe, "James Mark Baldwin with Alfred North Whitehead on Organic Selectivity: The 'Novel' Factor in Evolution," *Cosmos and History: The Journal of Natural and Social Philosophy* 5, no. 2 (2009), https://cosmosandhistory.org/index.php/journal/article/view/136/247.

91. Whitehead, *Science and the Modern World*, 107.

92. James Mark Baldwin, *Development and Evolution: Including Psychophysical Evolution, Evolution by Orthoplasy, and the Theory of Genetic Modes* (New York: Macmillan, 1902), 119.

93. James Mark Baldwin, *Mental Development in the Child and the Race: Methods and Processes* (New York: Macmillan, 1894), 221.

94. Baldwin states, "What appears to be new ... in Organic Selection is, first, the emphasis laid upon the almost unlimited powers of individual adaptation; second, the extension of such adaptation without any effect upon heredity for long periods of time; third, that heredity slowly adapts itself to the needs of a race [e.g., species] in a new environment along lines anticipated by individual adaptation, and therefore alone definite and determinate lines." *Development and Evolution*, 339–40.

95. Jim Welden, trans., "Liu Liangcheng: Literature Only Begins Where the Story Ends—Interview with Shu Jinyu," *Pathlight* (Spring 2015): 69.

96. Welden, "Liu Liangcheng," 69.

97. Welden, "Liu Liangcheng," 69.

98. Moran, "Bringing It All Back Home," 20. See a similar quote in Welden, "Liu Liangcheng," 71. Tom Moran said Liu told him that *One Man's Village* has been translated into Uyghur, and Uyghur readers responded well to the book because of its universality, but neither I nor Moran have been able to verify that claim.

99. "The fact that [animals] can observe us has lost significance. They are the objects of our ever-extending knowledge. What we know about them is an index of our power, and thus an index of what separates us from them. The more we know, the further away they are." John Berger, "Why Look at Animals?" in *About Looking* (London: Penguin Books, 1980), 14. And yet, "meeting the look of animals, their gaze on us and the world, reveals our human limitations. By attuning to animals, we can overcome some of the limitations of our so-called 'rational' condition." Goodbody, "Animal Studies," 254.

4. COSMIC ECOLOGIES AND TRANSCENDENT TRICKSTERS ON THE TIBETAN PLATEAU

1. The Tusi 土司 chieftain system, initiated during the Yuan dynasty, adapted the Jimi system 羈縻制度 first implemented during the Tang dynasty.
2. David Bello, "The Chinese Roots of Inner Asian Poppy," *Cahiers d'études sur la Méditerranée orientale et le monde turco-iranien* 32 (July–December 2001): 39–68.
3. Gang Yue, "As the Dust Settles in Shangri-La: Alai's Tibet in the Era of Sino-Globalization," *Journal of Contemporary China* 17, no. 56 (August 2008): 547.
4. Jason Moore coins the term "Capitalocene" in *Capitalism in the Web of Life: Ecology and the Accumulation of Capital* (London: Verso, 2015).
5. Alai, *Red Poppies*, trans. Howard Goldblatt and Sylvia Li-chun Lin (New York: Houghton Mifflin, 2002), 81. Based on Alai 阿来, *Chenai luoding* 尘埃落定 (*Chenai luoding* As the Dust Settles) (Beijing: Renmin wenxue chubanshe, 1998). Subsequent in-text page references are to *Red Poppies*.
6. Mark Driscoll, *The Whites Are Enemies of Heaven: Climate Caucasianism and Asian Ecological Protection* (Durham, NC: Duke University Press, 2020), 21.
7. *As the Dust Settles* was adapted as a Sichuan local theater play in 2009.
8. Carl Trocki, *Opium, Empire, and the Global Political Economy: A Study of the Asian Opium Trade, 1750–1950* (London: Routledge, 1999), 3–4.
9. Nathaniel Isaacson, "Science Fiction for the Nation: Tales of the Moon Colony and the Birth of Modern Chinese Fiction," *Science Fiction Studies* 40, no. 1 (March 2013): 49.
10. Ran Yunfei 冉云飞 and Alai 阿来, "Tongwang keneng zhilu – yu Zangzu zuojia Alai tanhua lu" 阿来,通往可能之路—与藏族作家阿来谈话录 (A Pathway to Possibilities: A Dialogue with Tibetan Author Alai), *Xinan minzu xueyuan xuebao* 西南民族文学学报 20, no. 2 (September 1999): 9.
11. Kun Mchog Dge Legs, Dpal Ldan Bkra Shis, and Kevin Stuart, "Tibetan Tricksters," *Asian Folklore Studies* 58 (1999): 7.
12. According to a 1999 survey of fifty-three Tibetan students studying at Qinghai Education College in Xining, all the students had heard Aku Tonpa stories, and twenty-one said they were sexual. However, the 1966 Chinese publication *Akou dengba de gushi* 阿叩登巴的故事 (Aku Tonpa Stories), purportedly based on three hundred stories collected in Sichuan Province, criticize landlords, religious personalities, and feudalism, while "none of these stories show the seamier side of A khu bstan pa, e.g., his sexual exploits." See Kun Dpal, and Stuart, "Tibetan Tricksters," 6–7.

13. Lama Jabb, *Oral and Literary Continuities in Modern Tibetan Literature: The Inescapable Nation* (Lanham, MD: Lexington Books, 2015), 6.
14. Yue, "As the Dust Settles in Shangri-La," 551.
15. Wang Qianhai 王前海, "Shangwu shijiao nengfo kanqing Chen'ai luoding: Yu diwujie Mao Dun wenxuejiang huodezhe Alai duihua" 商务视角能否看清《尘埃落定》—与第五届茅盾文学奖获得者阿来对话 中国信息报 (Can a Commercial Angle Provide a Better View on Red Poppies: A Dialogue with Alai, Winner of the Mao Dun Literature Prize), *Zhongguo xinxi bao* 中国信息报 (China Information) (December 21, 2000): 1–4.
16. Yue, "As the Dust Settles in Shangri-La," 552.
17. Li Jian 李建, "*Chenai luoding* de shenmi zhuyi shushi yu Zangzu benjiao wenhua"《尘埃落定》的神秘主义叙事与藏族苯教文化 (Tibetan Bön Religious Culture and Mysticism Narratives in *As the Dust Settles*), *Qilu Journal* 5 (2008): 148–51.
18. Causal vehicles of Bön engage (1) gross or raw elements (exorcism, spirits, and rituals that overlap with shamanism); (2) energetic elements of *qi* (vital energy, overlapping with Daoist, Tantric, and yogic practices); (3) light (manifesting as five pure lights, with white as the highest form of wisdom). Tenzin WanGyel Rinpoche, "Bön and Shamanism," 2014 interview by Guildo Ferrari, https://www.youtube.com/watch?v=BTLROrUqq5E.
19. The six-volume series comprises *Scattered in the Wind, Celestial Fire, Dase and Dage, Desolation, Gentle Thunder,* and *Empty Mountain*. Subsequent in-text parenthetical pages cite Alai 阿来, *Kongshan: Jicun chuanshuo yi* 空山–机村传说壹 (Empty Mountain: Legends of Ji Village I), *Juan yi: Suifeng piaosan; Juan er: Tianhuo* 卷一:随风飘散; 卷二:天火 (Vol. 1: Scattered in the Wind; Vol. 2: Celestial Fire) (Beijing: Renmin wenxue chubanshe, 2005).
20. Emily Yeh, *Taming Tibet: Landscape Transformation and the Gift of Chinese Development* (Ithaca, NY: Cornell University Press, 2013), 55. "The Foolish Old Man Who Moved the Mountain" (*yugong yishan* 愚公移山) is a Chinese myth about the virtues of perseverance and willpower in altering nature. Chairman Mao cited it in a famous speech in 1945.
21. Yeh, *Taming Tibet,* 69.
22. Xiaofei Kang and Donald Sutton, *Contesting the Yellow Dragon: Ethnicity, Religion, and the State in the Sino-Tibetan Borderland, 1379–2009* (Leiden: Brill, 2016), 252. See also Naktsang Nulo's account of the violent 1958 "Democratic Reform" in *My Tibetan Childhood: When Ice Shattered Stone,* trans. Angus Cargill and Sonam Lhamo (Durham, NC: Duke University Press, 2014).
23. Tim Thurston analyzes trickster and social outcast characters in Alai's novels, including in *Empty Mountain*, though he does not discuss the dominant roles of these marginalized women. See Timothy O'Connor Thurston, "Tricksters

and Outcasts in Modern Tibetan Literature: An Examination of Folkloric Character Types in Alai's Novels," MA thesis, Ohio State University, 2007.
24. Christopher Peacock, "Introduction: Corrupt Lamas, Reliable Yaks—The Fictional World of Tsering Döndrup," in Tsering Döndrup, *The Handsome Monk and Other Stories*, trans. Christopher Peacock (New York: Columbia University Press, 2019), 1–16.
25. Helen Stoddard, "Introduction," *The Nine-Eyed Agate: Poems and Stories*, by Jangbu and Helen Stoddard (Lanham, MD: Lexington Books, 2010), 13.
26. For a fascinating discussion of identity politics in Malho, see Yangdon Dhondup, "Writers at the Crossroads: The Mongolian-Tibetan Writers Tsering Dondup and Jangbu," *Inner Asia* 4, no. 2 (2002): 225–40.
27. Tsering Döndrup, "Black Fox Valley," in *The Handsome Monk and Other Stories*, trans. Christopher Peacock (New York: Columbia University Press, 2019), 169–96. In-text parenthetical page references are to this edition.
28. Michael Goldman, "Eco-Governmentality and Other Transnational Practices of a 'Green' World Bank," in *Liberation Ecologies: Environment, Development, and Social Movements*, ed. Richard Peet and Michael Watts (London: Routledge, 2004), 167.
29. Emily Yeh, "Green Governmentality," *Nomadic Peoples* 9, nos. 1–2 (2005): 13–14.
30. Huatse Gyal, "Our Indigenous Land Is Not a Wasteland," *American Ethnologist* website, February 6, 2021, https://americanethnologist.org/features/reflections/our-indigenous-land-is-not-a-wasteland.
31. This passage evokes the 2008 Wenchuan earthquake in Qiang-Tibetan Sichuan, where 5,600–8,000 children died in schools that collapsed because of substandard construction. See "Sichuan Earthquake Killed More Than 5,000 Pupils, Says China," *Guardian*, May 7, 2009, https://www.theguardian.com/world/2009/may/07/china-quake-pupils-death-toll.
32. Jarmila Ptackova, *Exile from the Grasslands: Tibetan Herders and Chinese Development Projects* (Seattle: University of Washington Press, 2020), 14.
33. Ptackova, *Exile from the Grasslands*, 19.
34. Takbum Gyel, "Nyin gcig gi cho 'phrul," *Gangs rgyan me tog* 2 (1990): 13–21, trans. Christopher Peacock, "The Illusion of a Day," *Two Lines* 31 (Fall 2019), https://www.catranslation.org/online-exclusive/the-illusion-of-a-day/. In-text quotations cite Peacock's translation.
35. Stoddard, "Introduction," *The Nine-Eyed Agate*, 13.
36. In-text citations are to Jangbu, "Odd Boots," trans. Heather Stoddard, in *The Nine-Eyed Agate*, 136–39. Originally published as Ljang bu (Jangbu), "Cha mi 'grig pa'i lham," in *Bod rtsom gsar ba bdams bkod dang de dag gi bshad pa*, ed. Bdud lha rgyal (Lanzhou: Gansu Nationalities Publishing House, 1998), 133–40.

37. Takbum Gyel, "The Illusion of a Day," np.
38. Donna Haraway, *When Species Meet* (Minneapolis: University of Minnesota Press, 2008).
39. Yeh, *Taming Tibet*, 327.
40. Ljang bu (Jangbu), "Srog chags kyi gtam rgyud gsum" (Three Animal Stories), *Snyan rtsom gzi mig dgu pa* (Zhang kang: Gyi ling dpe skrun kung zi, 2001), 46–49. Translation by Heather Stoddard in Jangbu, "Three Animal Stories," *The Nine-Eyed Agate*, 31–32.
41. Translation by Heather Stoddard in Jangbu, "Three Animal Stories," 32–33.
42. Translation by Heather Stoddard in Jangbu, "Three Animal Stories," 33.
43. Similar themes appear in the popular Uyghur short story "The Wild Pigeon," *Kashgar Literature* 5 (2004), by Nurmuhemmet Yasin (b. 1977). When a wild pigeon encounters a caged pigeon, the latter says: "Everyone says we are not as brave as you, that we think no further than the branches on which we rest and the cages in which we sleep. I have always lived here and have ventured no farther out—and why should I? Here I have a branch for resting and a cage for living, and everything is ready-made for me. Why would we leave here—to suffer? Besides, I am married. I have a family. Where would I go? My hosts treat me well." Trans. Dolkun Kamberi, *Radio Free Asia* (June 27, 2005), https://www.rfa.org/NS/ENG/ebooks/Caged.pdf.
44. Axel Goodbody, "Animal Studies: Kafka's Animal Stories," *Handbook of Ecocriticism and Cultural Ecology*, ed. Hubert Zapf (Berlin: De Gruyter, 2016), 256.
45. Takbum Gyel and Christopher Peacock, "Notes on the Pekingese," *Ploughshares* 45, no. 3 (Fall 2019): 162.
46. Takbum and Peacock, "Notes on the Pekingese," 185–86.
47. Takbum Gyel speaks of his love of dogs in "Pema Tseden Interviews Takbum Gyal: 'In my Previous Life I may Have Been a Dog,' " High Peaks Pure Earth, December 12, 2016, https://highpeakspureearth.com/pema-tseden-interviews-takbum-gyal-in-my-previous-life-i-may-have-been-a-dog/.
48. Xu Shoushang, quoted in William Lyell, *Lu Hsun's Vision of Reality* (Berkeley: University of California Press, 1976), 144.
49. As early as 1908 Lu Xun critiqued technocratic elites who fetishized science and technology by trashing "superstition" to gain power, prestige, and profit: "Having paged through books of physiology, they talked about the human body in terms of molecule biology, proclaiming that the body is only 'composed of cells' and 'how can there be a soul?'" "Po e'sheng lun" 破惡聲論 (Toward a Refutation of Malevolent Voices), in *Lu Xun quanji* (Complete Works of Lu Xun) (Beijing: Renmin wenxue, 1981), 8:28–29. See Ban Wang's analysis in "Old Dreams Retold: Lu Xun as Mytho-Ecological Writer," *Prism: Theory and Modern Chinese Literature* 17, no. 2 (2020): 225–43.

50. Quoted in Huatse, "Our Indigenous Land Is Not a Wasteland," np.
51. Ju Kalsang 居·格桑. "Ye Shengtai—Caoyuan yinxiang zhier" 夜生态—草原印象之二 (Night Ecology: Grassland Impressions II). Ju Kalsang gave the author his Chinese translation of his Tibetan poem on June 26, 2020.
52. Françoise Robin, "Introduction," *Human Rights and the Arts in Global Asia: An Anthology*, ed. Theodore W. Goossen and Anindo Hazra (Lanham, MD: Lexington Books, 2014), 15.
53. Ju Kalsang, "The Call of the Black Tent," trans. Françoise Robin, in Goossen and Hazra, *Human Rights and the Arts in Global Asia*, 124.
54. Ju, "The Call of the Black Tent," 124.
55. Ju Kalsang 居·格桑, in *Shui heliu—renlei zhi shengming zhi yuan yu shige* 水河流—人类之生命之源与诗歌 (Water and River: Origin of Human Life and Poetry), 2016 Zhongguo Jingdu Qinghai guoji shiren tanfang yuanzhuo huiyi shiwen xuan, 2016 中国渌都青海国际诗人毡房圆桌会议诗文选 (Poems and Essays of China Jingdu 2016: Qinghai International Poets Mongolian Yurt Roundtable Forum), ed. Jidi Majia 吉狄马加 (Xining: Qinghai renmin chubanshe, 2016), 207.
56. Ju Kalsang 居·格桑, "Shui Zhongyang" 水中央 (The Center of Water), in *Water and River*, 204–5.
57. Joseph E. Schwartzberg, "Maps of Greater Tibet," in *The History of Cartography*, ed. J. B. Harley and David Woodward (Chicago: University of Chicago Press, 1994), 2:614.
58. In Tibetan Buddhism the essential structure of the universe is tripartite, consisting of a lowermost realm, the Kamadhatu, or Realm of Desire; a middle realm, the Rupadhatu, or Realm of Form; and an uppermost realm, the Arupyadhatu, or Realm of Nonform. See Schwartzberg, "Maps of Greater Tibet," 619.
59. Mount Kailash is a 21,778-foot (6,638m)-tall peak in the Kailash Range, which forms part of the Transhimalaya in Ngari Prefecture, Tibet Autonomous Region. Located near Lake Manasarovar, Lake Rakshastal, and the Indus, Sutlej, Brahmaputra, and Karnali Rivers, Mount Kailash is considered sacred in Hinduism, Bön, Buddhism, and Jainism.
60. Dekyi Drolma 德吉卓玛, "You yizhong huoshui laizi tianhe zhi nan—zhi Jingdu" 有一种活水 来自天河之南—致渌都 (There Is Running Water from Henan: To Jingdu), in *Water and River*, 272–73.
61. Dekyi Drolma 德吉卓玛, "Zhi yu wan" 直与弯 (Straight and Bent), in *Water and River*, 273.
62. Dekyi Drolma 德吉卓玛, "Yang fendan" 羊粪蛋 (Sheep Turd), in *Water and River*, 275.
63. "Wo you shenling jicun de gushi" 我有神灵寄存的故事, Drolma "Sheep Turd," 275.
64. Dekyi Drolma 德吉卓玛, "Shiqu de wo" 丢失的我 (Losing Myself), in *Water and River*, 278.

65. Dekyi Drolma 德吉卓玛, "Caoyuan qinghuai" 草原情怀 (Grassland Feelings), in *Water and River*, 276–77.
66. Theodore W. Goossen and Anindo Hazra, "Introduction," in Goossen and Hazra, *Human Rights and the Arts in Global Asia*, 16.
67. Translated from Tibetan by Françoise Robin, in Goossen and Hazra, *Human Rights and the Arts in Global Asia*, 129.
68. Translated from Tibetan by Françoise Robin, in Goossen and Hazra, *Human Rights and the Arts in Global Asia*, 130–31.
69. Huatse Gyal, "Our Indigenous Land Is Not a Wasteland," np.
70. Dee Mack Williams addresses similar problems among "downwardly mobile" Mongol herders in "Grazing the Body: Violations of Land and Limb in Inner Mongolia," *American Ethnologist* 24, no. 4 (1997): 763–85.
71. I attended the March 29, 2018, screening of *Kokonor* and talk by Jangbu (Dorje Tsering) at the Michael C. Carlos Museum at Emory University. http://www.khabar.com/events-calendar/Film-Kokonor. This remarkable film was produced in collaboration with Workshop Now in Xining, Qinghai Province, and Purple Productions in Paris.
72. Woeser, "Our Sacred Land, Their Rubbish Dump: Chinese Artist Zhang Huan's 'Land Art' Installation on Mount Kailash," High Peaks, Pure Earth, December 10, 2020, https://highpeakspureearth.com/our-sacred-land-their-rubbish-dump-part-1-chinese-artist-zhang-huans-land-art-installation-on-mount-kailash-by-woeser/.
73. Kuang Laowu, quoted in Woeser, "Our Sacred Land, Their Rubbish Dump."

5. ISLAND EXCURSIONS AND INDIGENOUS WATERWAYS IN ACTIVIST TAIWAN

1. In the eighteenth century, an influx of Han Chinese migrants from China's southeastern coast came primarily from southern Fujian Province (known as Hoklo or Hokkien), and from northern Guangdong Province (predominantly Hakka peoples). The sixteen recognized Indigenous Peoples are Amis (Pangcah), Atayal, Bunun, Hla'alua, Kanakanavu, Kavalan, Paiwan, Puyuma, Rukai, Saisiyat, Tao, Thao, Tsou, Truku, Sakizaya, and Sediq.
2. Chia-ju Chang and Scott Slovic provide an overview of Taiwan ecocriticism in "Introduction," in *Ecocriticism in Taiwan: Identity, Environment, and the Arts*, ed. Chia-ju Chang and Scott Slovic (Lanham, MD: Lexington Books, 2016), ix–xi.
3. Chang and Slovic, "Introduction," xii.
4. John Robert Shepherd, *Statecraft and Political Economy on the Taiwan Frontier, 1600–1800* (Stanford, CA: Stanford University Press, 1993), 1–2.

5. Jin-Yung Wu, "Amis Aborigine Migrants' Territorialization in Metropolitan Taipei," *East Asian History and Culture Review* 1, no. 1 (May 2012): 107, 116.
6. See Basuya Boyijernu 巴蘇亞・博伊哲努, "Taiwan yuanzhu minzu de guoqu xianzai yu weilai" 台灣原住民族的過去現在與未來 (The Past, the Present, and the Future of Indigenous Literature in Taiwan), in *Ershiyi shiji Taiwan yuanzhumin wenxue* 21世紀台灣原住民文學 (Taiwan Indigenous Literature in the 21st Century), ed. Huang Linghua 黃鈴華 (Taipei: Taiwan yuanzhumin wenjiao jijinhui, 1999), 13.
7. Kuan-hsing Chen, *Asia as Method: Toward Deimperialization* (Durham, NC: Duke University Press, 2010), 18. In general, Chen's approach to cultural studies calls for multiplying points of reference within Asia to deemphasize preoccupations with the West.
8. Quoted in Chen, *Asia as Method*, 27.
9. This is a play on the shared surnames of Taiwan President Lee Teng-hui and Academia Sinica President Lee Yuan-tseh, whose trips to *Nanyang* inaugurated the special issue, and who respectively represent political-economy and culture.
10. Chen, *Asia as Method*, 27.
11. Chen, *Asia as Method*, 31–32. While Chen denounces Yang's analysis as pure propaganda, scholars such as Jeremy Yellen in *The Greater East Asia Co-Prosperity Sphere: When Total Empire Met Total War* (Ithaca, NY: Cornell University Press, 2019) have challenged the long-standing view that the Sphere was little more than a facade for Japan's predatory imperialism and that Asian leaders who collaborated with Japan were traitors to their countries.
12. Chen, *Asia as Method*, 99.
13. Chen, *Asia as Method*, 265.
14. Chen, *Asia as Method*, 268.
15. Thomas Moran, "Lost in the Woods: Nature in Soul Mountain," *Modern Chinese Literature and Culture* 14, no. 2 (Fall 2002): 214.
16. Liu writes, "Earlier writers of nature books can no longer sustain their creativity through reliance on the ideas of Lao Zi and Zhuang Zi or other naïve modes of thinking. In similar fashion, their descendants [confronted as they are with such a diversity of issues and rapidly changing environment] find little sustenance in traditional Chinese pastoralism and ecological views." Liu Kexiang, "A Nature Writer in Taiwan," trans. Nick Kaldis (2012). Wu Ming-yi's econovel *The Man with the Compound Eyes* (2011), analyzed in this chapter, does not indulge Hanspace nature aesthetics. Like post-Mao ecoliterature, however, the symbolic return to nature in this dystopian novel is also via a forest, here a grove of consecrated trees dubbed "the Forest Church."
17. Wu Ming-yi 吳明益, *Taiwan ziran xiezuo xuan* 台灣自然寫作選 (Selected Taiwan Nature Writings) (Taipei: Eryu wenhua, 2003), 11.

18. Chen Sihe, "Taiwanese Writings with a Maritime Theme in the 1990s," trans. Robert Smitheram, *Taiwan Literature: English Translation Series* 8 (2000): 149, a translation of Chen Sihe 陳思和, "Shilun 1990 niandai Taiwan haiyang ticai de chuangzuo" 試論1990年代台灣海洋題材的創作 (Taiwan Writings with a Maritime Theme in the 1990s), presented at the Liang'an wenxue fazhan yantaohui 兩岸文學發展研討會 (Conference on the Development of Literature in the PRC and Taiwan), National Chung-Hsing University Chinese Literature Department, September 16–17, 2000. An excerpt of his talk was published as Chen Sihe 陳思和, "Shilun 1990 niandai Taiwan haiyang ticai de chuangzuo" 試論1990年代台灣海洋題材的創作 (Taiwan Writings with a Maritime Theme in the 1990s), *Xueshu yuekan* 學術月刊 11 (2000): 91–98.
19. Liu Ka-shiang's impact on Taiwanese ecological consciousness is monumental. Scores of academic articles and over forty academic theses have analyzed his works. See "Liu Kexiang shuwei zhuti guan: Yanjiu lunwen" 劉克襄數位主題館: 研究論文 (Liu Kexiang Digital Subject Archive: Research Theses), http://www.liukashiang.campus-studio.com/thesis.php.
20. Liu Kexiang, "A Nature Writer in Taiwan."
21. See Michelle Yeh, "From Surrealism to Nature Poetics: A Study of Prose Poetry from Taiwan," *Journal of Modern Literature in Chinese* 3.2 (2000): 145–53. See also Sun Chieh-Liang on Liu's anthropomorphism in "Animal Contact in Liu Ka-shiang's *He-lien-mo-mo the Humpback Whale*," *Tamkang Review* 42, no. 2 (June 2012): 33–58; Fang Binxiu 方賓秀, "Liu Kexiang dongwu xiaoshuo zhi zhuti yishi ji xiezuo tese xilun" 劉克襄動物小說之主題意識及寫作特色析論 (An Analysis of the Theme Consciousness and Writing Characteristics of Liu Kexiang's Animal Novels), *Taiwan shiyuan xuesheng xuekan* 台南師院學生學刊 20 (February 1999): 101–13; and Li Yulin 李育霖, "Dongwu zhengzhi: Liu Kexiang de niao ren xuecheng" 動物政治: 劉克襄的鳥人學程 (Animal Politics: Liu Kexiang's Writing Apprenticeship on Birds), in *Nizao xindiqiu—Dangdai Taiwan ziran shuxie* 擬造新地球——當代臺灣自然書寫 (Create a New World: Contemporary Taiwan Nature Writing) (Taipei: Guoli Taiwan Daxue chuban zhongxin, 2015), 115–39.
22. Giles Deleuze and Félix Guattari, *Kafka: Toward a Minor Literature*, trans. Dana Polan (Minneapolis: University of Minnesota Press, 1986), 22. Quoted in Tsung-Huei Huang, "Anthropomorphism or Becoming-Animals? Ka-shiang Liu's *Hill of Stray Dogs* as a Case in Point," *Transtext(e)s Transcultures: Journal of Cultural Studies* 5 (2009): 2. See also Yu-lin Lee, "Becoming-Animal," in Chang and Slovic, *Ecocriticism in Taiwan*, 155–62.
23. Wu Ming-yi, *Taiwan ziran xiezuo xuan*, and Wu Ming-yi 吳明益, *Yi shuxie jiefang ziran—Taiwan xiandai ziran shuxie de tansuo* 以書寫解放自然—台灣現代自然書寫的探索 (Liberate Nature by Writing: An Exploration of Modern Nature Literature of Taiwan) (Taipei: Da'an chubanshe, 2004).

24. Liu Ka-shiang 劉克襄, "Ou zhi lu" 鷗之路 (Journey of the Gull), in Wu, *Taiwan ziran xiezuo xuan*, 29–31.
25. Wu, *Taiwan ziran xiezuo xuan*, 32–33.
26. Liu Ka-shiang 劉克襄, "Binyu" 濱鷸 (Sandpiper), in Wu, *Taiwan ziran xiezuo xuan*, 71.
27. Liu Ka-shiang, "Binyu," 78–79.
28. David L. Hall, "On Seeking a Change of Environment," in *Nature in Asian Traditions and Thought: Essays on Environmental Philosophy*, ed. J. Baird Callicott and Roger Ames (Albany: State University of New York Press, 1989), 105.
29. Wu, *Taiwan ziran xiezuo xuan*, 222.
30. This is a very popular 1988 Japanese anime film.
31. Liu Ka-shiang 劉克襄, "Faxian chitang" 發現池塘 (Discovering the Pond), in Wu, *Taiwan ziran xiezuo xuan*, 213–14.
32. He Huaren 何華仁 (1958–2021) specialized in woodblock prints of urban birds. See "He Huaren huibenli de kexue, wenxue, yu meixue—*Wa! Gongyuan you ying* xinshu fenxiang zuotanhui 何華仁繪本裡的科學、文學與美學—《哇！公園有鷹》新書分享座談會 (Science, Literature and Aesthetics in He Huaren's Picture Books—*Wow! Eagle in the Park* New Book Launch), Feiye Bookstore 飛頁書房, April 25, 2019, http://blog.udn.com/012book/126118728.
33. Liu Ka-shiang 劉克襄, "He yingxiao" 褐鷹鴞 (Brown Hawk-Owl), in Wu, *Taiwan ziran xiezuo xuan*, 217–18.
34. Peter I-min Huang discusses Taiwan urban ecocriticism in "Junkspace and Nonplace in Taiwan's New Ecoliterature," in *Embodied Memories, Embedded Healing: New Ecological Perspectives from East Asia*, ed. Xinmin Liu and Peter I-min Huang (Lanham, MD: Lexington Books, 2021), 101–19.
35. Wu, *Taiwan ziran xiezuo xuan*, 210–12.
36. Liu Ka-shiang 劉克襄, *Sui niao zou tianya* 隨鳥走天涯 (Follow the Birds) (Taipei: Hongfan chubanshe, 1985). Quoted in Wu, *Taiwan ziran xiezuo xuan*, 223.
37. Liu, "A Nature Writer in Taiwan."
38. Liu's animals novels include *Fengniao pinuocha* 風鳥皮諾查 (Pinuocha, the Plover) (Taipei: Yuanliu chubanshe, 1991); *Zuotou jing He Lian Ma Ma* 座頭鯨赫連麼麼 (He-lien-mo-mo, the Humpback Whale) (Taipei: Yuanliu chubanshe, 1993); *Yongyuan de xintianweng* 永遠的信天翁 (The Eternal Albatross) (Taipei: Yuanliu chubanshe, 2008); *Doushu huijia* 豆鼠回家 (Bean Mouse Goes Home) (Taipei: Yuanliu, 2011); *Hu di mao* 虎地貓 (Tiger Land Cats) (Taipei: Yuanliu, 2016); and *Yegou zhi qiu* 野狗之丘 (The Hill of Stray Dogs) (Taipei: Yuanliu, 2016).
39. Lee, "Becoming-Animal," 157–58.
40. Liu, *Yegou zhi qiu*, 156–57.
41. Huang, "Anthropomorphism or Becoming-Animals?" 5. See also Tsung-Huei Huang 黃宗慧, "Baohu dongwu jiu biran xishengdiao baohu rende quanyi ma?"

保護動物就必然犧牲掉保護人的權益嗎？(Does Protecting Animals Necessarily Sacrifice Human Rights?), TedxTaipei (2019), https://www.ted.com/talks/tsung_huei_huang_deconstructing_the_animal_human_binary.

42. Liu Ka-shiang 劉克襄, "Yegou xiaoshi shier nian" 野狗消失十二年 (Stray Dogs Have Been Out of Sight for Twelve Years) *China Times*, January 28, 2006. Quoted in Huang, "Anthropomorphism or Becoming-Animals?" 3. Liu has also protested the concentration of petrochemical plants in Kaohsiung. See Peter I-min Huang, *Linda Hogan and Contemporary Taiwanese Writers: An Ecocritical Study of Indigeneities and Environment* (Lanham, MD: Lexington Books, 2016), 137–38.

43. Gilles Deleuze and Félix Guattari, *A Thousand Plateaus: Capitalism and Schizophrenia*, trans. Brian Massumi (Minneapolis: University of Minnesota Press, 1987), 244. Quoted in Huang, "Anthropomorphism or Becoming-Animals?" 5.

44. Liu, *Yegou zhi qiu*, 38.

45. Liu, *Yegou zhi qiu*, 4.

46. Liu, *Hudi mao*, 4.

47. Liu, *Hudi mao*, 6.

48. Yuk Hui, *The Question Concerning Technology in China: An Essay in Cosmotechnics* (Cambridge, MA: MIT Press, 2016), 311–12.

49. Wu, *Yi shuxie jiefang ziran*, 603–9.

50. Wang has won the *Taiwan Times* 時報, *United Press* 聯合報, Lai Ho 賴和, and Wu Zhuoliu 吳濁流 literary prizes.

51. Shu-fen Tsai, "Taiwan Is a Whale: The Emerging Oneness of Dark Blue and Human Identity in Wang Chia-hsiang's Historical Fiction," in Chang and Slovic, *Ecocriticism in Taiwan*, 43.

52. Wang's nature writings include *Wenming huangye* 文明荒野 (Civilizational Wilderness) (Taichung: Chenxing chubanshe, 1990); *Ziran daogaozhe* 自然禱告者 (Prayer for Nature) (Taichung: Chenxing chubanshe, 1992); *Guanyu Lamadaxianxian yu Lahe Alei* 關於拉馬達仙仙與拉荷阿雷》(On Lamatasinsin and Dahu Ali) (Taipei: Yushanshe, 1995); *Shan yu hai* 山與海 (Mountains and Seas) (Taipei: Yushanshu, 1996); *Xiao airen zhi mi* 小矮人之謎 (Mystery of the Little People) (Taipei: Yushanshe, 1996); *Siji de shengyin* 四季的聲音 (The Sounds of Four Seasons) (Taipei: Chenxing chubanshe, 1997); *Yujian yike huhuan ni de shu* 遇見一棵呼喚你的樹 (Meet a Tree That Calls to You) (Taipei: Fangzhi chubanshe, 2001); *Wo zhuzai Hamaxing de yuren matou* 我住在哈瑪星的漁人碼頭 (I Live on Hamasen Fisherman's Wharf) (Gaoxiong: Chuanmen chubanshe, 2002); *Moshen zi* 魔神仔 (Devil's Son) (Taipei: Yushan chubanshe, 2002); and *Tubu* 徒步 (On Foot) (Taipei: Tianpei wenhua gongsi, 2004). His historical fiction includes *Daofeng neihai* 倒風內海 (Daofeng Inland Sea) (Taipei: Yushanshe, 1997); *Haizhong guiying: Sairen* 海中鬼影：鰓人 (Sea Ghosts: The Gill Men) (Taipei: Yushanshe, 1999); *Shenlan*

深藍 (Dark Blue) (Taipei: Jiuge, 2000); and *Jinfulou yehua* 金福樓夜話 (Jinfu Tower Night Talks) (Taipei: Xiaozhitang, 2003).

53. Wang, *Wenming huangye*, 29.
54. Summarized by Christopher Payne, "In/Visible Peoples, In/Visible Lands: Overlapping Histories in Wang Chia-hsiang's Historical Fantasy," *International Journal of Taiwan Studies* 2 (2019): 4.
55. Wang, *Ziran daogaozhe*, 78.
56. Payne, "In/Visible Peoples, In/Visible Lands," 26.
57. Payne, "In/Visible Peoples, In/Visible Lands," 26.
58. Wang, *Guanyu Lamadaxianxian yu Lahe Alei*, 14.
59. Mori Ushinosuke 森丑之助, *Shengfan xingjiao: Sen Chouzhizhu de Taiwan tanxian* 生蕃行腳：森丑之助的台灣探險 (Travels with Savages: Mori Ushinosuke's Taiwan Expedition), trans. Yang Nangun 楊南郡 (Taipei: Yuanliu, 2012).
60. Robert Tierney, *Tropics of Savagery: The Culture of Japanese Empire in Comparative Frame* (Berkeley: University of California Press, 2010), 87.
61. Payne, "In/Visible Peoples, In/Visible Lands," 16.
62. Payne, "In/Visible Peoples, In/Visible Lands," 19.
63. Payne, "In/Visible Peoples, In/Visible Lands," 19.
64. On October 21–22, 2021, Wei Te-sheng discussed his adaptation of Wang's novel at the University of British Columbia "Indigenous Taiwan: Transpacific Connections" speaker series (https://www.youtube.com/watch?v=2lfaTFpm5tE).
65. The Siraya and Macatao are the two main branches of Taiwan's Pingpu (plains) Indigenous peoples, whose language and culture are nearly extinct today. The Austronesian language family from which Sirayan belongs includes some of the most spoken languages in the western Pacific, particularly Bahasa Indonesia, Javanese, Tagalog (or standardized as Filipino), and Malay.
66. William M. Campbell, *Formosa Under the Dutch: Described from Contemporary Records with Explanatory Notes and a Bibliography of the Island* (Taipei: SMC Publishing, 1992), 254. Cited in Shu-fen Tsai, "Taiwan Is a Whale," 47.
67. Jason Moore, *Capitalism in the Web of Life: Ecology and the Accumulation of Capital* (New York: Verso Books, 2015).
68. In-text pages reference Wang Chia-hsiang 王家祥, *Daofeng neihai* 倒風內海 (Daofeng Inland Sea) (Taipei: Yushanshe, 1997).
69. Miles Powell, *Vanishing America: Species Extinction, Racial Peril, and the Origins of Conservation* (Cambridge, MA: Harvard University Press, 2016), 123–24.
70. See Jiang Rong 姜戎, *Lang tuteng* 狼图腾 (Wolf Totem) (Wuhan: Changjiang wenyi chubanshe, 2004); *Wolf Totem: A Novel*, trans. Howard Goldblatt (New York: Penguin Books, 2009); and Chi Zijian 迟子建, *E'ergu neihe you'an* 额尔古纳河右岸 (The Right Bank of the Argun) (Beijing: Beijing Shiyue wenyi chubanshe, 2006);

The Last Quarter of the Moon, trans. Bruce Humes (New York: Penguin Books, 2013).

71. Shu-fen Tsai, "Taiwan Is a Whale," 48–49.
72. Kuei-fen Chiu, "Aboriginal Literature and the Rise of the Taiwanese New Cultural/ Historical Imaginary in Contemporary Taiwan," Lecture at the School of Oriental and African Studies (2008), https://www.soas.ac.uk/taiwanstudies/eats/eats2008/file43155.pdf.
73. Powell, *Vanishing America*, 137.
74. Chen Sihe, "Taiwanese Writings with a Maritime Theme in the 1990s (Robert Smitheram, trans.)," in *Taiwan Literature: English Translation Series* 8 (2000): 144–45. Originally published as 陳思和〈試論1990年代台灣海洋題材的創作〉「兩岸文學發展研討會」中華發展基金管理委員會、國立中央大學中國文學系所，2000年9月16–17日, in *Xueshu Yuekan* 學術月刊 11 (2000): 91–98.
75. Chen, "Taiwanese Writings with a Maritime Theme in the 1990s," 146.
76. Quoted in Daniel Heath Justice, *Why Indigenous Literatures Matter* (Waterloo, ON: Wilfrid Laurier University Press, 2018), 72.
77. In *Life Among the Qallunaat*, Mini Aodla Freeman (Inuit) says, "I have never forgotten a speech that was made by one of the heads of the Department (of Indian Affairs and Northern Development) when he arrived at the settlement. The Inuit had expected to hear something fantastic since he had come such a long way especially to talk to them. The speech went something like this: 'I am very glad to be here and enjoyed my visit to your homes. I am very pleased to see that they are so clean.' One old woman came over to me and asked if he was really the head of the Department, and if so, why he did not have the intelligence to tell us something that we do not know, instead of telling us what our houses looked like. We lived in them every day and we knew what they were like. How could I tell my elder that he did not think the Inuit have intelligence?" Quoted in Justice, *Why Indigenous Literatures Matter*, 1.
78. Topas Tamapima 拓拔斯·塔瑪匹瑪 (Ch. 田雅各 Tian Yage), "Zuihou de lieren" 最後的獵人 (The Last Hunter) (Taipei: Chenxing, 2012).
79. In-text pages cite Topas Tamapima, "The Last Hunter," trans. John Balcom, in *Indigenous Writers of Taiwan*, ed. John Balcom (New York: Columbia University Press, 2005), 3–20.
80. I disagree with Karen Thornber's analysis in *Ecoambiguity: Environmental Crises and East Asian Literatures* (Ann Arbor: University of Michigan Press, 2012), 132–36. She characterizes Biyari as "sport hunting" (133), concluding, "he worries about the future of the forest only insofar as it is a space of personal rejuvenation and empowerment" (140), while I view his actions as attempts to counter emasculating colonial structures and environmental racism. Darryl Sterk also disagrees with Thornber, historicizing Biyari's behavior within "gift cultures"

of Indigenous hunting communities. See "The Hunter's Gift in Ecorealist Indigenous Fiction from Taiwan," *Oriental Archive* 81 (2013): 555–80.
81. Balcom, "Translator's Introduction," in Balcom, *Indigenous Writers of Taiwan*, xxi.
82. See Richard Rong-bin Chen 陳榮彬, "Between Foreignization and Domestication: On the Four Translations of 'The Last Hunter,'" *Taiwan Lit* 1, no. 2 (Fall 2020), http://taiwanlit.org/articles/between-foreignization-and-domestication-on-the-four-translations-of-the-last-hunter. Other scholars agree that insertion of Indigenous words in Sinophone writing is strategic. See Walis Norgan 瓦歷斯·諾幹, "Taiwan yuanzhumin wenxue de qu zhimin" 台灣原住民文學的去殖民 (The Decolonization of Taiwan Indigenous Literature), in *Taiwan yuanzhumin hanyu wenxue xuanji: Pinglun juan* 台灣原住民漢語文學選集：評論卷 (An Anthology of Chinese-Language Indigenous Literature in Taiwan: Commentaries), ed. Sun Dachuan 孫大川 (Taipei: Yinke chubanshe, 2003), 27–151. See also Fu Dawei, "Bailang senlin li de wenzi liezen" (Word Hunters in the Jungle of Bailang), in Sun, *Taiwan yuanzhuminzu hanyu wenxue xuanji*, 211–46.
83. Bill Ashcroft, Garreth Griffiths, and Helen Tiffen, *The Empire Writes Back* (New York: Routledge, 2002), 65–67.
84. Summarized by Huang, in attendance at the keynote, in Huang, *Linda Hogan and Contemporary Taiwanese Writers*, 8.
85. Hsinya Huang, "Indigenous Taiwan as Location of Native American and Indigenous Studies," *CLCWeb: Comparative Literature and Culture* 16, no. 4 (2014).
86. Huang, *Linda Hogan and Contemporary Taiwanese Writers*, 8.
87. Chen, "Taiwanese Writings with a Maritime Theme in the 1990s," 148.
88. Syaman Rapongan 夏曼·藍波安, *Lenghai qingshen* 冷海情深 (Deep Love for the Cold Sea) (Taipei: Lianhe wenxue chubanshe, 1997), 12.
89. For example, the Paiwan craftsman and artist Sakuliu Pavavaljung (b. 1960) actively sought out stories and legends from his female ancestors and incorporated matrilineal Paiwan religious motifs into his contemporary art. When a Paiwan settlement near Taitung was allocated government funds to renovate, he debated a Han architect from Taitung University at a village council meeting, trying to persuade the community to adopt more sustainable traditional Paiwan design motifs into their plans rather than simply use modern design standards. Sakuliu was to be the sole artist to represent Taiwan at the Venice Biennial 2021 but was accused of sexual assault and was uninvited. Alex Greenberger, "Sakuliu Pavavaljung Dropped as Taiwan's Venice Biennale Artist Following Sexual Assault Allegations," Artnews.com, January 12, 2022, https://www.artnews.com/art-news/news/sakuliu-pavavaljung-venice-biennale-documenta-sexual-assault-allegations-1234615529/.
90. Syaman Rapongan 夏曼·藍波安, *Heise de chibang* 黑色的翅膀 (Black Wings), (Taichung: Chenxing chubanshe, 1999); *Hailang de jiyi* 海浪的記憶 (Memory of

Waves) (Taipei: Lianhe wenxue chubanshe, 2002); *Tiankong de yanjing* 天空的眼睛 (The Eyes of the Sky) (Taipei: Lianhe wenxue chubanshe, 2012); *Dahai zhiyan* 大海之眼 (The Eyes of the Sea), Taipei: Yinke chubanshe, 2018, translated into French as *Les yeux de l'océan*, trans. Damien Ligot (Paris: L'Asiathèque, 2022); *Meiyou Xinxiang de nanren* 沒有信箱的男人 (The Man Without a Mailbox) (Taipei: Lianhe wenxue chubanshe, 2022).

91. Syaman Rapongan, *The Eyes of the Sky*, 30.
92. Epeli Hau'ofa, "Our Sea of Islands," *The Contemporary Pacific* 6, no. 1 (Spring 1994): 148–61, and "The Ocean in Us," *The Contemporary Pacific* 10, no. 2 (Fall 1998): 392–410.
93. Huang, "Indigenous Taiwan as Location of Native American and Indigenous Studies," 2.
94. For example, in *Writing the South Seas: Imagining the Nanyang in Chinese and Southeast Asian Postcolonial Literature* (Seattle: University of Washington Press, 2015), Brian Bernards proposes the South China Sea as an "empty center" of a more balanced comparison between the Sinophone literatures of Southeast Asia. His approach relies on the dual role of the sea as boundary and as zone of cultural and commercial interaction to facilitate analyses that view locality as an ongoing process of cultural cross-fertilization and exchange.
95. Paul Wallin, "Native South Americans were Early Inhabitants of Polynesia" *Nature* 583.7817 (July 23, 2020): 524–25.
96. Kuei-fen Chiu, "The Production of Indigeneity: Contemporary Indigenous Literature in Taiwan and Trans-cultural Inheritance," *The China Quarterly* 200 (2009): 1084–85.
97. Amitav Ghosh, *The Great Derangement: Climate Change and the Unthinkable* (New York: Penguin Books, 2016), 30–31.
98. Ghosh, *The Great Derangement*, 58–59, 32.
99. All subsequent in-text page references are, respectively, to Wu Ming-yi 吳明益, *Fuyan ren* 複眼人 (The Man with the Compound Eyes) (Taipei: Xia'ri chubanshe, 2011), and Wu Ming-yi, *The Man with the Compound Eyes*, trans. Darryl Sterk (New York: Pantheon, 2013).
100. According to Mary Nyangweso, such perspectives are prevalent in African Indigenous communities as well. See "Disability in Africa: A Cultural/Religious Perspective," in *Disability in Africa: Inclusion, Care, and the Ethics of Humanity*, ed. Toyin Falola and Nic Hamel (Rochester, NY: University of Rochester Press, 2021), 115–36.
101. Darryl Sterk, "The Apotheosis of Montage: The Videomosaic Gaze of *The Man with the Compound Eyes* as Postmodern Ecological Sublime," *Modern Chinese Literature and Culture* 28, no. 2 (Fall 2016): 188.

102. Darryl Sterk, "The Apotheosis of Montage," 197. See also Shiuhhuah Serena Chou, "Wu's *The Man with the Compound Eyes* and the Worlding of Environmental Literature," *CLCWeb: Comparative Literature and Culture* 16, no. 4 (2014), https://doi.org/10.7771/1481-4374.2554. Peter I-min Huang argues Wu equates environmental and Indigenous rights, animating materiality with spirits. See "Junkspace and Nonplace in Taiwan's New Ecoliterature," in *Embodied Memories, Embedded Healing*, 107–8.
103. David Der-wei Wang, *Fin-de-Siècle Splendor: Repressed Modernities of Late Qing Fiction, 1849–1911* (Stanford, CA: Stanford University Press, 1997), 263.
104. Karen Barad, "Entangled Nuclear Colonialisms, Matters of Force, and the Material Force of Justice," Lecture for Composite Body Series, Northeastern University, March 10, 2021.
105. Kathy Jetñil-Kijiner, "Anointed," dir. Dan Lin, https://youtu.be/HuDA7i zeYrk.
106. Barad, "Entangled Nuclear Colonialisms." Newtonian physics subscribes to the Democritean notion that nature has but two elements: atoms and the void. In classical Newtonian physics, the void, is mere nothingness; it is that which literally does not matter. See "After the End of the World: Entangled Nuclear Colonialisms, Matters of Force, and the Material Force of Justice," *Theory and Event* 22, no. 3 (2019): 528.
107. Kathy Jetñil-Kijiner, "Dome Poem Part III: Anointed," quoted in Barad, "After the End of the World," 524.

EPILOGUE: INDIGENOUS ENTANGLEMENTS

1. See Liu Cixin 刘慈欣, *Sishen yongsheng* 死神永生 (Death Is Immortal) (Chongqing: Chongqing chubanshe, 2010), and Liu Cixin, *Death's End*, trans. Ken Liu (New York: Tor Books, 2016).
2. Stephen Benedict Dyson develops this line of analysis in "Images of International Politics in Chinese Science Fiction: Liu Cixin's *Three-Body Problem*," *New Political Science* 41, no. 3 (2019): 459–75.
3. Victor Fan, *Cinema Illuminating Reality: Media Philosophy Through Buddhism* (Minneapolis: University of Minnesota Press, 2022); Yuk Hui, *The Question Concerning Technology in China: An Essay on Cosmotechnics* (Cambridge, MA: MIT Press, 2016); Xinmin Liu and Peter I-min Huang, eds., *Embodied Memories, Embedded Healing: New Ecological Perspectives from East Asia* (Lanham, MD: Lexington Books, 2021).
4. Ge Zhaoguang, "Imagining 'All Under Heaven': The Political, Intellectual, and Academic Background of a New Utopia," trans. Michael Duke and Josephine

Chiu-Duke, in *Utopia and Utopianism in the Contemporary Chinese Context: Texts, Ideas, Spaces*, ed. David Der-wei Wang, Angela Ki Che Leung, and Zhang Yinde (Hong Kong: Hong Kong University Press, 2020), 32.

5. For example, Magnus Fiskesjö contends that the Wa in Southwest China did not engage in warfare until impinged upon by colonists: "We should consider that before the Chinese state and other forces pressed into this region during last few centuries (notably to obtain the riches of the land . . .), war must have been uncommon in the Wa lands. There could not have been many reasons for it. Given what we know about Wa history, we must imagine a region with plenty of land where the Wa and other forest farmers could move freely, so there would be no reason for the Wa to take up war until neighboring, menacing states began to circumscribe the Wa area. This engendered frictions and confrontations with outside forces, from whom the Wa defended their autonomy, and also initiated internecine Wa warfare. *Stories from an Ancient Land: Perspectives on Wa History and Culture* (New York: Berghahn Books, 2021), 165.
6. Michael Goldman, "Eco-Governmentality and Other Transnational Practices of a 'Green' World Bank," in *Liberation Ecologies: Environment, Development, and Social Movements*, ed. Richard Peet and Michael Watts (London: Routledge, 2004), 167.
7. Karen Barad, "After the End of the World: Entangled Nuclear Colonialisms, Matters of Force, and the Material Force of Justice," *Theory & Event* 22, no. 3 (July 2019): 529.
8. Burao Yilu, "Mengdong River," trans. Mark Bender, in *The Borderlands of Asia: Culture, Place, Poetry*, ed. Mark Bender (Amherst, NY: Cambria, 2017), 229–30.
9. Magnus Fiskesjö, *Stories from an Ancient Land*, 56.
10. Wu Ming-yi 吳明益, *Danche shiqie ji* 單車失竊記 (The Stolen Bicycle) (Taipei: Maitian chubanshe, 2015), 11. Wu Ming-yi, *The Stolen Bicycle*, trans. Darryl Sterk (Melbourne: Text Publishing, 2018), 8.
11. Magnus Fiskesjö, *Stories from an Ancient Land*, 146.
12. Magnus Fiskesjö, *Stories from an Ancient Land*, 148.
13. Uradyn Bulag elaborates on this fact at length in *The Mongols at China's Edge: History and the Politics of National Unity* (Lanham, MD: Rowman & Littlefield, 2002).
14. I am grateful to an anonymous reader for this insight.
15. Wu Ming-yi 吳明益, *Fuyan ren* 複眼人 (The Man with the Compound Eyes) (Taipei: Xia'ri chubanshe, 2011), 384. Wu Ming-yi, *The Man with the Compound Eyes*, trans. Darryl Sterk (New York: Pantheon, 2013), 281.

Bibliography

Abramson, Daniel, and Yu Qi. "'Urban-Rural Integration' in the Earthquake Zone: Sichuan's Post-Disaster Reconstruction and the Expansion of the Chengdu Metropole." *Pacific Affairs* 84, no. 3 (September 2011): 495–523.
Ah Cheng 阿城. *Ah Cheng xiaoshuo: Qiwang Shuwang Haiziwang* 阿城小說: 棋王樹王孩子王 (Ah Cheng Fiction: The King of Chess, The King of Trees, The King of Children). Taipei: Haifeng, 1988.
Ah Cheng. *The King of Trees*. Trans. Bonnie McDougall. New York: New Directions, 2010.
Aku Wuwu 阿库乌雾. "Hei xiongmao" 黑熊 (Black Bear). In *Aku Wuwu zuopin xuan* 阿库乌雾作品选 (Selected Works of Aku Wuwu), 60–61. Chengdu: Sichuan minzu chubanshe, 2019.
Aku Wuwu. "Black Bear." In Bender, *The Borderlands of Asia*, 187–88.
Aku Wuwu. "Spring Water." In Bender, *The Borderlands of Asia*, 191–93.
Alai 阿来. *Chenai luoding* 尘埃落定 (As the Dust Settles). Beijing: Renmin wenxue chubanshe, 1998.
Alai 阿来. *Kongshan—Jicun chuanshuo yi* 空山–机村传说壹 (Empty Mountain: Legends of Ji Village I). "Juanyi: Suifeng piaosan" 卷一:随风飘散 (Vol. 1, Scattered in the Wind); "Juan'er: Tianhuo" 卷二:天火 (Vol. 2, Celestial Fire). Beijing: Renmin wenxue chubanshe, 2005.
Alai. *Red Poppies*. Trans. Howard Goldblatt and Sylvia Li-chun Lin. New York: Houghton Mifflin, 2002.
Alberts, Thomas Karl. *Shamanism, Discourse, Modernity*. London: Ashgate, 2015.

Amantay, Aydos. "The Failure." Trans. Canaan Morse. In *Chutzpah! New Voices from China*, ed. Ou Ning and Austin Woerner, 109–44. Norman, OK: Chinese Literature Today Book Series, 2015.

Ames, Roger. "Chinese Philosophy." In *The Edinburgh Companion to Twentieth-Century Philosophies*, ed. Constantin V. Boundas, 661–74. Edinburgh: Edinburgh University Press, 2007.

Anderson, Benedict. *Imagined Communities: Reflections on the Origins and Spread of Nationalism*. London: Verso, 1991.

Anonymous. Interviews with Inner Mongolia University faculty, Hohhot. August 28, 2017.

Ashcroft, Bill, Garreth Griffiths, and Helen Tiffen. *The Empire Writes Back*. New York: Routledge, 2002.

Bachner, Andrea. "The Remains of History: Gao Xingjian's *Soul Mountain* and Wuhe's *The Remains of Life*." *Concentric: Literary and Cultural Studies* 37, no. 1 (March 2011): 99–122.

Balcom, John. "Translator's Introduction." In *Indigenous Writers of Taiwan*, ed. John Balcom, xi–xxiv. New York: Columbia University Press, 2005.

Baldwin, James Mark. *Development and Evolution: Including Psychophysical Evolution, Evolution by Orthoplasy, and the Theory of Genetic Modes*. New York: Macmillan, 2005.

Baldwin, James Mark. *Mental Development in the Child and the Race: Methods and Processes*. New York: Macmillan, 1906.

Bamo Qubumo. "The Origin of Patterns." In Bender, *The Borderlands of Asia*, 195–96.

Bamo Qubumo. "Patterns of the Sun." In Isbister, Pu, and Rachman, *Chinese Women Writers on the Environment*, 11–12.

Bamo Qubumo. "Water Lines." In Bender, *The Borderlands of Asia*, 197–98.

Barad, Karen. "After the End of the World: Entangled Nuclear Colonialisms, Matters of Force, and the Material Force of Justice." *Theory & Event* 22, no. 3 (July 2019): 524–50.

Basuya Boyijernu 巴蘇亞·博伊哲努. "Taiwan yuanzhu minzu de guoqu xianzai yu weilai" 台灣原住民族的過去現在與未來 (The Past, the Present, and the Future of Indigenous Literature in Taiwan). In *Ershiyi shiji Taiwan yuanzhumin wenxue 21* 世紀台灣原住民文學 (Taiwan Indigenous Literature in the 21st Century), ed. Huang Linghua 黃鈴華, 13. Taipei: Taiwan yuanzhumin wenjiao jijinhui, 1999.

Bayar, Nasan. "A Discourse of Civilization/Culture and Nation/Ethnicity from the Perspective of Inner Mongolia, China." *Asian Ethnicity* 15, no. 4 (2014): 439–57.

Bello, David A. *Across Forest, Steppe, and Mountain: Environment, Identity, and Empire in Qing China's Borderlands*. Cambridge: Cambridge University Press, 2016.

Bello, David. "The Chinese Roots of Inner Asian Poppy." *Cahiers d'études sur la Méditerranée orientale et le monde turco-iranien* 32 (July–December 2001): 39–68.

Bender, Mark. "Echoes from *Si Gang Lih*: Burao Yilu's 'Moon Mountain.'" *Asian Highlands Perspectives* 10 (2011): 99–128.

Bender, Mark, ed. *The Borderlands of Asia: Culture, Place, Poetry*. Amherst, NY: Cambria Press, 2017.

Bender, Mark, Aku Wuwu, and Jjivot Zopqu, trans. *The Nuosu Book of Origins: A Creation Epic from Southwest China*. Seattle: University of Washington Press, 2019.

Berger, John. *About Looking*. London: Penguin Books, 1980.

Bergeton, Uffe. *The Emergence of Civilizational Consciousness in Early China: History Word by Word*. New York: Routledge, 2019.

Bernards, Brian. *Writing the South Seas: Imagining the Nanyang in Chinese and Southeast Asian Postcolonial Literature*. Seattle: University of Washington Press, 2015.

Bulag, Uradyn E. *The Mongols at China's Edge: History and the Politics of National Unity*. Lanham, MD: Rowman & Littlefield, 2002.

Bunin, Gene A. "From Camps to Prisons: Xinjiang's Next Great Human Rights Catastrophe." Art of Life in Chinese Central Asia. October 5, 2019. https://livingotherwise.com/2019/10/05/from-camps-to-prisons-xinjiangs-next-great-human-rights-catastrophe-by-gene-a-bunin/.

Burao Yilu. "Four Generations of Va Women." Trans. Alexandra Draggeim. In Isbister, Pu, and Rachman, *Chinese Women Writers on the Environment*, 13–25.

Burao Yilu. "Mengdong River." In Bender, *The Borderlands of Asia*, 229–30.

Burao Yilu 布饶依露. "Yueliang shan" 月亮山 (Moon Mountain). *Minzu wenxue* 民族文学 4 (2002): 58

Burensain Borjigin. *The Agricultural Mongols: Land Reformation and the Formation of Mongolian Village Society in Modern China*. Ed. Uradyn E. Bulag; trans. Thomas White. Yokohama: Shumpushu Publishing, 2017.

Burke, Carolyn L., and Joby G. Copenhaver. "Animals as People in Children's Literature." *Language Arts* 81, no. 3 (January 2004): 205–13.

Byler, Darren. "The Disappearance of Perhat Tursun, One of the Uyghur World's Greatest Authors." SupChina. February 5, 2020. https://supchina.com/2020/02/05/disappearance-of-perhat-tursun-uyghur-worlds-greatest-author/.

Byler, Darren. *Terror Capitalism: Uyghur Dispossession and Masculinity in a Chinese City*. Durham, NC: Duke University Press, 2021.

Callahan, William. *China: The Pessoptimist Nation*. Oxford: Oxford University Press, 2010.

Campbell, William M. *Formosa Under the Dutch: Described from Contemporary Records with Explanatory Notes and a Bibliography of the Island*. Taipei: SMC Publishing, 1992.

Cao Yu 曹禺. "Wang Zhaojun" 王昭君 (Wang Zhaojun). *Renmin wenxue* 人民文学 (1978): 37–111.

Chan, Sin Yee. "Tang Junyi: Moral Idealism and Chinese Culture." In *Contemporary Chinese Philosophy*, ed. Chung-Ying Cheng and Nicholas Bunnin, 305–26. Malden, MA: Blackwell, 2007.

Chang, Chia-ju. "Building a Post-Industrial Shangri-La: Lu Shuyuan, Ecocriticism, and Tao Yuanming's 'Peach Blossom Spring.'" In *Chinese Environmental Humanities: Practices of Environing at the Margins*, ed. Chia-ju Chang, 35–58. New York: Palgrave Macmillan, 2019.

Chang, Chia-ju, ed. *Chinese Environmental Humanities: Practices of Environing at the Margins*. New York: Palgrave Macmillan, 2019.

Chang, Chia-ju, and Scott Slovic, eds. *Ecocriticism in Taiwan: Identity, Environment, and the Arts*. Lanham, MD: Lexington Books, 2016.

Chen Cheng-wei 陳政偉. "Xiaman Lanbo'an: Laizi dahai shenchu de shuxie" 夏曼·藍波安：來自大海深處的書寫 (Syaman Rapongan: Writing from the Ocean Depths"). *Zhongyang Tongxun She* 中央通訊社 (Central News Agency). December 21, 2019. https://www.cna.com.tw/culture/article/20191221w005

Chen Kuan-Hsing. *Asia as Method: Toward Deimperialization*. Durham, NC: Duke University Press, 2010.

Chen, Richard Rong-bin 陳榮彬. "Between Foreignization and Domestication: On the Four Translations of 'The Last Hunter.'" *Taiwan Lit* 1, no. 2 (Fall 2020). http://taiwanlit.org/articles/between-foreignization-and-domestication-on-the-four-translations-of-the-last-hunter.

Chen Sihe 陳思和. "Shilun 1990 niandai Taiwan haiyang ticai de chuangzuo" 試論1990年代台灣海洋題材的創作 (Taiwan Writings with a Maritime Theme in the 1990s). *Xueshu yuekan* 學術月刊 11 (2000): 91–98.

Chen Sihe 陳思和. "Shilun 1990 niandai Taiwan haiyang ticai de chuangzuo" 試論1990年代台灣海洋題材的創作 (Taiwan Writings with a Maritime Theme in the 1990s). Liang'an wenxue fazhan yantaohui 兩岸文學發展研討會 (Conference on the Development of Literature in the PRC and Taiwan). National Chung-Hsing University Chinese Literature Department, September 16–17, 2000.

Chen Sihe. "Taiwanese Writings with a Maritime Theme in the 1990s." Trans. Robert Smitheram. *Taiwan Literature: English Translation Series* 8 (2000): 139–66.

Chen Wangheng. *Chinese Environmental Aesthetics*. Ed. Gerald Cipriani; trans. Feng Su. London: Routledge, 2015.

Chimedsengee, Urantsatsral, Amber Cripps, Victoria Finlay, Guido Verboom, Ven Munkhbaatar Batchuluun, Ven Da Lama Byambajav Khunkhur. *Mongolian Buddhists Protecting Nature: A Handbook on Faiths, Environment and Development*. Bath: The Alliance of Religions and Conservation, 2009.

Chiu, Kuei-fen. "Aboriginal Literature and the Rise of the Taiwanese New Cultural/Historical Imaginary in Contemporary Taiwan." Lecture at the School of Oriental and African Studies, 2008. https://www.soas.ac.uk/taiwanstudies/eats/eats2008/file43155.pdf.

Chiu, Kuei-fen. "The Production of Indigeneity: Contemporary Indigenous Literature in Taiwan and Trans-cultural Inheritance." *The China Quarterly* 200 (2009): 1071–87.

Chou, Shan. "Beginning with Images in the Nature Poetry of Wang Wei." *Harvard Journal of Asiatic Studies* 42, no. 1 (1982): 117–37.

Chou, Shiuhhuah Serena. "Wu's *The Man with the Compound Eyes* and the Worlding of Environmental Literature." *CLCWeb: Comparative Literature and Culture* 16, no. 4 (2014). https://doi.org/10.7771/1481-4374.2554.

Chow, Kai-wing. "Imagining Boundaries of Blood: Zhang Binglin and the Invention of the Chinese Race in Modern China." In *Racial Identities in East Asia*, ed. Barry Sautman, 34–52. Hong Kong: Hong Kong University of Science and Technology Press, 1995.

Chung, Yuehtsen Juliette. "Better Science and Better Race? Social Darwinism and Chinese Eugenics." *Isis* 105 (December 2014): 793–802.

Connolly, Tim. "Perspectivism as a Way of Knowing in the *Zhuangzi*." *Dao* 10 (2011): 487–505.

Courtney, Chris. *The Nature of Disaster in China: The 1931 Yangtze River Flood*. Cambridge: Cambridge University Press, 2018.

DeBoom, Meredith. "Climate Necropolitics: Ecological Civilization and the Distributive Geographies of Extractive Violence in the Anthropocene." *Annals of the American Association of Geographers* 111, no. 3 (2021): 900–912.

Deleuze, Gilles, and Félix Guattari. *Kafka: Toward a Minor Literature*. Trans. Dana Polan. Minneapolis: University of Minnesota Press, 1986.

Deleuze, Gilles, and Félix Guattari. *A Thousand Plateaus: Capitalism and Schizophrenia*. Trans. Brian Massumi. Minneapolis: University of Minnesota Press, 1987.

Derrida, Jacques. *The Animal That Therefore I Am*. Ed. Marie-Louise Mallet; trans. David Wills. New York: Fordham University Press, 2008.

Descola, Philippe. *Beyond Nature and Culture*. Trans. Janet Lloyd. Chicago: University of Chicago Press, 2013.

Dhondup, Yangdon. "Writers at the Crossroads: The Mongolian-Tibetan Writers Tsering Dondup and Jangbu." *Inner Asia* 4, no. 2 (2002): 225–40.

Di Cosmo, Nicola. *Ancient China and Its Enemies: The Rise of Nomadic Power in East Asian History*. Cambridge: Cambridge University Press, 2002.

Dikötter, Frank. *The Discourse of Race in Modern China*. Hong Kong: Hong Kong University Press, 1992.

Ding, John Zijiang. "Li Zehou: Chinese Aesthetics from a Post-Marxist and Confucian Perspective." *Contemporary Chinese Philosophy*, ed. Chung-Ying Cheng and Nicholas Bunnin, 246–60. Malden, MA: Blackwell, 2007.

Dong Zhongshu 董仲舒. *Chunqiu fanlu* 春秋繁露 (Spring and Autumn Dew). Taipei: Shangwu yinshuguan, 1975.

Doyle, Laura. *Inter-Imperiality: Vying Empires, Gendered Labor, and the Literary Arts of Alliance*. Durham, NC: Duke University Press, 2020.

Driscoll, Mark. *The Whites Are Enemies of Heaven: Climate Caucasianism and Asian Ecological Protection*. Durham, NC: Duke University Press, 2021.

Duara, Prasenjit. *Rescuing History from the Nation: Questioning Narratives of Modern China*. Chicago: University of Chicago Press, 1995.

Duara, Prasenjit. *Sovereignty and Authenticity: Manchukuo and the East Asia Modern*. Lanham, MD: Rowman & Littlefield, 2004.

Duzan, Brigitte. "Yerkex Hulmanbek 叶尔克西·胡尔曼别克 Présentation." June 12, 2016. http://chinese-shortstories.com/Auteurs_de_a_z_Yerkesy_Hulmanbiek.htm.

Dyson, Stephen Benedict. "Images of International Politics in Chinese Science Fiction: Liu Cixin's *Three-Body Problem*." *New Political Science* 41, no. 3 (2019): 459–75.

Elvin, Mark. *The Retreat of the Elephants: An Environmental History of China*, New Haven, CT: Yale University Press, 2004.

Estok, Simon, and Won-Chung Kim, eds. *East Asian Ecocriticisms: A Critical Reader*. New York: Palgrave Macmillan, 2013.

Fan, Victor. *Cinema Illuminating Reality: Media Philosophy Through Buddhism*. Minneapolis: University of Minnesota Press, 2022.

Fang Binxiu 方賓秀. "Liu Kexiang dongwu xiaoshuo zhi zhuti yishi ji xiezuo tese xilun" 劉克襄動物小說之主題意識及寫作特色析論 (An Analysis of the Theme Consciousness and Writing Characteristics of Liu Kexiang's Animal Novels). *Taiwan shiyuan xuesheng xuekan* 台南師院學生學刊 20 (February 1999): 101–13.

Fiskesjö, Magnus. "The Animal Other: China's Barbarians and Their Renaming in the Twentieth Century." *Social text* 29, no. 4 (2012): 57–79.

Fiskesjö, Magnus. *Stories from an Ancient Land: Perspectives on Wa History and Culture*. Oxford: Berghahn Books, 2021.

Fried, Daniel. "Riding off into the Sunrise: Genre Contingency and the Origin of the Chinese Western." *PMLA* 22, no. 5 (October 2007): 1482–98.

Fu Dawei. "Bailang senlin li de wenzi liezen" (Word Hunters in the Jungle of Bailang). In *Taiwan yuanzhumin hanyu wenxue xuanji* 台灣原住民漢語文學選集 (Anthology of Indigenous Taiwanese Literature in Chinese), ed. Sun Dachuan 孫大川 (T. C. Sun), 211–46. Taipei: Yinke wenxue, 2003.

Gade, Anna M. *Muslim Environmentalisms: Religious and Social Foundations*. New York: Columbia University Press, 2019.

Gao Xingjian 高行健. *Lingshan* 灵山 (Soul Mountain). Taipei: Lianjing chubanshe, 1990.

Gao Xingjian. *Soul Mountain*. Trans. Mabel Lee. New York: Harper, 2001.

Garrard, Greg. *Ecocriticism*. London: Routledge, 2004.

Ge Zhaoguang. "Imagining 'All Under Heaven': The Political, Intellectual, and Academic Background of a New Utopia." Trans. Michael Duke and Josephine Chiu-Duke. In *Utopia and Utopianism in the Contemporary Chinese Context: Texts, Ideas, Spaces*, ed. David Der-wei Wang, Angela Ki Che Leung, and Zhang Yinde, 15–35. Hong Kong: Hong Kong University Press, 2020.

Ghosh, Amitav. *The Great Derangement: Climate Change and the Unthinkable*. New York: Penguin Books, 2016.

Glissant, Édouard. *Caribbean Discourses: Selected Essays*. Trans. J. Michael Dash. Charlottesville: University Press of Virginia, 1981.

Glissant, Édouard. *Poetics of Relation*. Trans. Betsy Wing. Ann Arbor: University of Michigan Press, 1997.

Goldman, Michael. "Eco-Governmentality and Other Transnational Practices of a 'Green' World Bank." In *Liberation Ecologies: Environment, Development, and Social Movements*, ed. Richard Peet and Michael Watts, 153–76. New York: Routledge, 2004.

Goodbody, Axel. "Animal Studies: Kafka's Animal Stories." In *Handbook of Ecocriticism and Cultural Ecology*, ed. Hubert Zapf, 249–72. Berlin: De Gruyter, 2016.

Goossen, Theodore W., and Anindo Hazra. "Introduction." In *Human Rights and the Arts in Global Asia: An Anthology*, ed. Theodore W. Goossen and Anindo Hazra, 8–19. Lanham, MD: Lexington Books, 2014.

Greenberger, Alex. "Sakuliu Pavavaljung Dropped as Taiwan's Venice Biennale Artist Following Sexual Assault Allegations." Artnews.com. January 12, 2022. https://www.artnews.com/art-news/news/sakuliu-pavavaljung-venice-biennale-documenta-sexual-assault-allegations-1234615529/.

Guo, Wei, and Peina Zhuang. "Ecophobia, 'Hollow Ecology,' and the Chinese Concept of *Tianren Heyi* (天人合一)." *ISLE: Interdisciplinary Studies in Literature and Environment* 26, no. 2 (Spring 2019): 430–41.

Guo Xuebo 郭雪波. *Damo hun* 大漠魂 (Desert Soul). Beijing: Zhongguo wenlian chubanshe, 2002.

Guo Xuebo 郭雪波. *Mengguliya* 蒙古里亚 (Moŋgoliya). Beijing: Beijing shiyue wenyi chubanshe, 2014.

Guo Xuebo. *The Desert Wolf*. Trans. Wang Chiying. Beijing: Chinese Literature Press, 1996.

Gyal, Huatse. "Our Indigenous Land Is Not a Wasteland." *American Ethnologist* (February 6, 2021). https://americanethnologist.org/features/reflections/our-indigenous-land-is-not-a-wasteland.

Hall, David L. "On Seeking a Change of Environment." In *Nature in Asian Traditions and Thought: Essays on Environmental Philosophy*, ed. J. Baird Callicott and Roger Ames, 99–111. Albany: State University of New York Press, 1989.

Han Nianyong 韩念勇. *Caoyuan de luoji* 草原的逻辑 (Grassland Logic). 4 vols. Beijing: Beijing kexue jishu chubanshe, 2011.

Hanlon, Don. "The Case of Turpan, China: How to Destroy a Culture" (October 3, 2019). https://agslibraryblog.wordpress.com/2019/10/03/the-case-of-turpan-china-how-to-destroy-a-culture/.

Hansen, Mette Halskov, Hongtao Li, and Rune Svarverud. "Ecological Civilization: Interpreting the Chinese Past, Projecting the Global Future." *Global Environmental Change* 53 (2018): 195–203.

Haraway, Donna J. *When Species Meet*. Minneapolis: University of Minnesota Press, 2008.

Harkin, Michael E., and David Rich Lewis. "Introduction." In *Native Americans and the Environment: Perspectives on the Ecological Indian*, ed. Michael E. Harkin and David Rich Lewis, xix–xxxiv. Lincoln: University of Nebraska Press, 2007.

Harrell, Stevan. "The Role of the Periphery in Chinese Nationalism." In *Imagining China: Regional Division and National Unity*, ed. Shu-min Huang and Cheng-kuang Hsu, 139–43. Nankang, Taiwan: Institute of Ethnology, Academia Sinica, 1999.

Hau'ofa, Epeli. "The Ocean in Us." *The Contemporary Pacific* 10, no. 2 (Fall 1998): 392–410.

Hau'ofa, Epeli. "Our Sea of Islands." *The Contemporary Pacific* 6, no. 1 (Spring 1994): 148–61.

"He Huaren huibenli de kexue, wenxue, yu meixue—*Wa! Gongyuan you ying* xinshu fenxiang zuotanhui 何華仁繪本裡的科學、文學與美學—《哇！公園有鷹》新書分享座談會 (Science, Literature and Aesthetics in He Huaren's Picture Books—*Wow! Eagle in the Park* New Book Launch). Feiye Bookstore 飛頁書房. April 25, 2019. http://blog.udn.com/012book/126118728.

Heise, Ursula. *Imagining Extinction: The Cultural Meanings of Endangered Species*. Chicago: University of Chicago Press, 2016.

Hirsch, Francine. *Empire of Nations: Ethnographic Knowledge and the Making of the Soviet Union*. Ithaca, NY: Cornell University Press, 2005.

Hopkins, Benjamin. *Ruling the Savage Periphery: Frontier Governance and the Making of the Modern State*. Cambridge, MA: Harvard University Press, 2020.

Hoshur, Memtimin. "Burut Majrasi" (The Mustache Dispute). *Tarim* (Ch. 塔里木) Vol 1 (1991): 20–30.

Hoshur, Memtimin. "Festival for the Pigs." Trans. Darren Byler and Mutellip Enwer. *Guernica Magazine*, December 1, 2014. https://www.guernicamag.com/festival-for-the-pigs/.

Hoshur, Memtimin. 买买提明·吾守尔. "Huxu Fengbo" 胡须风波 (The Mustache Dispute). Trans. Akebaier 艾克拜尔. *Minzu wenxue* 民族文学 (May 1991): 75–80+82.

Hoshur, Memtimin. "The Mustache Dispute" (Excerpt). Trans. Darren Byler and Mutellip Enwer. *Pathlight: New Chinese Writing* (June 2014): 87–93

Hsiao, Hsin-Huang Michael. "Environmental Movements in Taiwan." In *Asia's Environmental Movements: Comparative Perspectives*, ed. Yokshiu F. Lee and Alvin Y. So, 31–54. Armonk, NY: M. E. Sharpe, 1999.

Huang Hsinya. "Indigenous Taiwan as Location of Native American and Indigenous Studies." *CLCWeb: Comparative Literature and Culture* 16, no. 4 (2014): 1–9. https://docs.lib.purdue.edu/clcweb/vol16/iss4/2/.

Huang, Peter I-min. "Junkspace and Nonplace in Taiwan's New Ecoliterature." In Liu and Huang, *Embodied Memories, Embedded Healing*, 101–19.

Huang, Peter I-min. *Linda Hogan and Contemporary Taiwanese Writers: An Ecocritical Study of Indigeneities and Environment*. Lanham, MD: Lexington Books, 2016.

Huang, Tsung-Huei. "Anthropomorphism or Becoming-animals? Ka-shiang Liu's *Hill of Stray Dogs* as a Case in Point." *Transtext(e)s Transcultures: Journal of Cultural Studies* 5 (2009): 1–17.

Huang, Tsung-Huei 黃宗慧. "Baohu dongwu jiu biran xishengdiao baohu rende quanyi ma? 保護動物就必然犧牲掉保護人的權益嗎？(Does Protecting Animals Necessarily Sacrifice Human Rights?). TedxTaipei (2019). https://www.ted.com/talks/tsung_huei_huang_deconstructing_the_animal_human_binary.

Hughes, Alice C., et al. "Horizon Scan of the Belt and Road Initiative." *Trends in Ecology & Evolution* 35, no. 7 (July 2020): 583–93.

Hui, Yuk. *The Question Concerning Technology in China: An Essay in Cosmotechnics*. Cambridge, MA: MIT Press, 2016.

Hulmanbek, Yerkesh. "Eternal Lamb." Trans. Nicky Harman. *Peregrine: An English Companion to Chutpah! Magazine* (December 2012): 19–24.

Hulmanbek, Yerkesh. "Painless." Trans. Roddy Flagg. Read Paper Republic. September 3, 2015. http://paperrepublic.org/pubs/read/painless/.

Hulmanbek, Yerkesh 叶尔克西·胡尔曼别克. "Wutong" 无痛 (Painless). *Qingchun* 青春 (Youth) 8 (2005): 29–32.

Hulmanbek, Yerkesh 叶尔克西·胡尔曼别克. *Yongsheng yang* 永生羊 (Eternal Lamb). Ürümchi: Xinjiang renmin chubanshe, 2012.

Humes, Bruce. "Borderland Fiction: 'The Mongol Would-be Self-Immolator,' An Excerpt from Guo Xuebo's '*Mongoliya*.' " February 17, 2019. https://bruce-humes.com/category/guo-xuebos-mongolia-蒙古里亚/.

Humes, Bruce. "The Success of Shen Wei's *A Dictionary of Xinjiang*." Paper Republic. August 27, 2015. https://paper-republic.org/links/the-success-of-shen-weis-a-dictionary-of-xinjiang/.

Isaacson, Nathaniel. "Science Fiction for the Nation: Tales of the Moon Colony and the Birth of Modern Chinese Fiction." *Science Fiction Studies* 40, no. 1 (March 2013): 33–54.

Isbister, Dong, Xiumei Pu, and Stephen D. Rachman, eds. *Chinese Women Writers on the Environment*. Jefferson, NC: McFarland, 2020.

Jabb, Lama. *Oral and Literary Continuities in Modern Tibetan Literature: The Inescapable Nation*. Lanham, MD: Lexington Books, 2015.

Jangbu (Ljang bu). "Cha mi 'grig pa'i lham" (Odd Boots). In *Bod rtsom gsar ba bdams bkod dang de dag gi bshad pa*, ed. Bdud lha rgyal, 133–40. Lanzhou: Gansu Nationalities Publishing House, 1998.

Jangbu. *The Nine-Eyed Agate: Poems and Stories*. Trans. Heather Stoddard. Lanham, MD: Lexington Books, 2010.

Jangbu (Ljang bu). "Srog chags kyi gtam rgyud gsum" (Three Animal Stories), 46–49. *Snyan rtsom gzi mig dgu pa* (Zhang kang: Gyi ling dpe skrun kung zi, 2001).

Ji Cheng. "Spring on the Horqin Sandland." In *The Desert Wolf*, by Xuebo Guo, trans. Chiying Wang, 348–54. Beijing: Chinese Literature Press, 1996.

Jiang Guangping 姜广平. "Wo buhuang bumangde shuxuzhe renlei jiuwei de ziran shengcun: Yu Liu Liangcheng duihua" 我不慌不忙地叙述着人类久违的自然生存：与刘亮程对话 (I Leisurely Recount the Long-Lost Natural Existence of Human Beings: A Dialog with Liu Liangcheng). *Wenxue jiaoyu* 3 (2011): 4–9.

Jiang Rong 姜戎. *Lang tuteng* 狼图腾 (Wolf Totem). Wuhan: Changjiang wenyi chubanshe, 2004.

Jiang Rong. *Wolf Totem: A Novel*. Trans. Howard Goldblatt. New York: Penguin Books, 2009.

Jidi Majia 吉狄马加, ed. *Shui heliu—renlei zhi shengming zhi yuan yu shige* 水河流—人类之生命之源与诗歌 (Water and River: Origin of Human Life and Poetry). Xining: Qinghai renmin chubanshe, 2016.

Jones, Andrew. "The Child as History in Republican China: A Discourse on Development." *positions: east asia cultures critique* 10, no. 3 (Winter 2002): 695–727.

Jones, Andrew. *Developmental Fairy Tales: Evolutionary Thinking and Modern Chinese Culture* Cambridge, MA: Harvard University Press, 2011.

Juan, Rose Hsiu-li. "Imagining the Pacific Trash Vortex and the Spectacle of Environmental Disaster: Environmental Entanglement and Literary Engagement in Wu Ming-Yi's Fuyan ren (The Man with the Compound Eyes)." In Chang and Slovic, *Ecocriticism in Taiwan*, 79–93.

Ju Kalsang. "The Call of the Black Tent." Trans. Françoise Robin. *Human Rights and the Arts in Global Asia: An Anthology*, ed. Theodore W. Goossen and Anindo Hazra, 123–26. Lanham, MD: Lexington Books, 2014.

Ju Kalsang 居·格桑. "Ye Shengtai—Caoyuan yinxiang zhier" 夜生态—-草原印象之二 (Night Ecology: Grassland Impressions II). Personal communication. June 26, 2020.

Justice, Daniel Heath. *Why Indigenous Literatures Matter.* Waterloo, ON: Wilfrid Laurier University Press, 2018.

Kang, Xiaofei, and Donald Sutton. *Contesting the Yellow Dragon: Ethnicity, Religion, and the State in the Sino-Tibetan Borderland, 1379–2009.* Leiden: Brill, 2016.

Kendi, Ibram X. *Stamped from the Beginning: The Definitive History of Racist Ideas in America.* New York: Nation Books, 2016.

Khatchadourian, Raffi. "Surviving the Crackdown in Xinjiang." The New Yorker. April 5, 2021. https://www.newyorker.com/magazine/2021/04/12/surviving-the-crackdown-in-xinjiang.

Kinkley, Jeffrey. "Gao Xingjian in the 'Chinese' Perspective of Qu Yuan and Shen Congwen." *Modern Chinese Literature and Cultures* 14, no. 2 (2002): 130–62.

Kubin, Wolfgang. "Deguo hanxue quanwei lingyizhiyan kan xiandangdai Zhongguo wenxue" 德國漢學權威另一只眼看現當代中國文學 (German Sinology Expert Looks at Contemporary Chinese Literature with Another Eye). Interview by Xin Ping. Deutsche Welle. November 26, 2006. https://p.dw.com/p/9R8g.

Kun Mchog Dge Legs, Dpal Ldan Bkra Shis, and Kevin Stuart. "Tibetan Tricksters." *Asian Folklore Studies* 58 (1999): 5–30.

Lampton, David M., ed. *Policy Implementation in Post-Mao China.* Berkeley: University of California Press, 1987.

Lau, D. C., trans. *Mencius.* New York: Penguin Books, 1970.

Lavelle, Peter B. *The Profits of Nature: Colonial Development and the Quest for Resources in Nineteenth-Century China.* New York: Columbia University Press, 2020.

Lee, Haiyan. *The Stranger and the Chinese Moral Imagination.* Stanford, CA: Stanford University Press, 2014.

Lee, Yu-lin. "Becoming-Animal: Liu Kexiang's Writing Apprenticeship on Birds." In Chang and Slovic, *Ecocriticism in Taiwan*, 155–62.

Lewis, Mark Edward, and Mei-yu Hsieh. "Tianxia and the Invention of Empire in East Asia." In *Chinese Visions of World Order: Tianxia, Culture, and World*, ed. Ban Wang, 25–48. Durham, NC: Duke University Press.

Li Changzhong 李长中, ed. *Shengtai wenxue yu minzu wenxue yanjiu* 生态批评与民族文学研究 (Ecocriticism and Ethnic Literary Studies). Beijing: Academy of Social Sciences Press, 2012.

Li, Cheng. "Echoes from the Opposite Shore: Chinese Ecocritical Studies as a Transpacific Dialogue Delayed." *Interdisciplinary Studies in Literature and Environment* 21, no. 4 (Autumn 2014): 821–43.

Li Chonggao 李崇高. "Youshengxue de weilai yu fazhan" 优生科学的由来与发展 (The Future and Development of Eugenics). In 性教育与优生 第2辑 *Xing jiaoyu yu yousheng Di 2 ji* (Sex Education and Eugenics Series 2), 198–201. Shanghai: Shanghai kexue jishu chubanshe, 1987.

Li Juan 李娟. *Aletai de jiaoluo* 阿勒泰的角落 (Altay Corner). Beijing: Lianhe chubanshe, 2010.

Li Jian 李建. "*Chenai luoding* de shenmi zhuyi shushi yu Zangzu benjiao wenhua." 《尘埃落定》的神秘主义叙事与藏族苯教文化 (Tibetan Bön Religious Culture and Mysticism Narratives in *As the Dust Settles*). *Qilu Journal* 5 (2008): 148–51.

Li Juan. *Distant Sunflower Fields*. Trans. Christopher Payne. London: Sinoist Books, 2021.

Li Juan 李娟. *Dong muchang* 冬牧场 (Winter Pasture). Beijing: Xinxing chubanshe, 2012.

Li Juan 李娟. *Jiu pian xue* 九篇雪 (Nine Stories on Snow). 2nd ed. Nanjing: Jiangsu wenyi chubanshe, 2013.

Li Juan. *Winter Pasture: One Woman's Journey with China's Kazakh Herders*. Trans. Jack Hargreaves and Yan Yan. New York: Astra House, 2021.

Li Juan 李娟. *Wode Aletai* 我的阿勒泰 (My Altay). Kunming: Yunnan renmin chubanshe, 2010.

Li Juan 李娟. *Yangdao: Sanbuqu* 羊道三部曲 (The Way of Sheep Trilogy). Beijing: Zhongxin chubanshe, 2017.

Li Juan 李娟. *Yaoyuan de xiangrikui di* 遥远的向日葵地 (Distant Sunflower Fields). Guangzhou: Guangdong huacheng chubanshe, 2017.

Li, Jialuan, and Qingqi Wei. "Planetary Healing Through the Ecological Equilibrium of *Ziran*: A Daoist Therapy for the Anthropocene." In Liu and Huang, *Embodied Memories, Embedded Healing*, 55–69.

Li Xianglan 李香兰. "Xibu dakaifa yu Nei Menggu huanbao shengchanye de fazhan." 西部大开发与内蒙古环保产业的发展 (Western Development and the Development of Environmental Protection Industries in Inner Mongolia). *Nei Menggu Daxue Xuebao* 34, no. 5 (2002): 19–24.

Li Yulin 李香兰. "Dongwu zhengzhi: Liu Kexiang de niao ren xuecheng" 動物政治：劉克襄的鳥人學程 (Animal Politics: Liu Kexiang's Writing Apprenticeship on Birds). In *Nizao xindiqiu—Dangdai Taiwan ziran shuxie* 擬造新地球———當代臺灣自然書寫 (Create a New World: Contemporary Taiwan Nature Writing), 115–39. Taipei: Guoli Taiwan Daxue chuban zhongxin, 2015.

Liehr, Matthew. "The Green Leaves of China: Sociopolitical Imaginaries in Chinese Environmental Nonfiction." PhD dissertation, University of Heidelberg, 2013.

Light, Nathan. "Cultural Politics and the Pragmatics of Resistance: Reflexive Discourses on Culture and History." In *Situating the Uyghurs Between China and*

Central Asia, ed. Ildikó Bellér-Hann, M. Christina Cesàro, and Joanne Smith Finley, 49–68. Burlington, VT: Ashgate, 2007.

Lin Kuo-hsien 林國賢, "Lüxing zuojia Liu Ka-hsiang dailingzhe dajia manyou Yunlin" 旅遊作家劉克襄帶領著　家慢遊雲林 (Travel Writer Liu Ka-Hsiang Leads Everyone on a Tour of Yunlin), *Ziyou shibao* 自由時報 (Liberty Times). October 8, 2015.

Litzinger, Ralph. *Other Chinas: The Yao and the Politics of National Belonging*. Durham, NC: Duke University Press, 2000.

Liu Cixin. *Death's End*. Trans. Ken Liu. New York: Tor Books, 2016.

Liu Cixin 刘慈欣. *Sishen yongsheng* 死神永生 (Death Is Immortal). Chongqing: Chongqing chubanshe, 2010.

Liu Cixin. *The Three-Body Problem*. Trans. Ken Liu. New York: Tor Books, 2016.

Liu Hanhua 刘涵华. "Nongye wenming de gezhe: Wei An, Liu Liangcheng sanwen chuangzuo bijiao 农业文明的歌者：苇岸、刘亮程散文创作比较 (Eulogists of Agricultural Civilization: A Comparison of Prose Creation by Wei An and Liu Liangcheng). *Changji xueyuan xuebao* 昌吉学院学报 3 (2010): 46–49.

Liu, Kang. "Chinese Exceptionalism: Linguistic Construction of a Superpower." In *The Routledge Handbook of Chinese Language and Culture*, ed. Liwei Jiao. London: Routledge, 2024.

Liu Ka-shiang 劉克襄. "Binyu" 濱鷸 (Sandpiper). In Wu, *Taiwan ziran xiezuo xuan*, 71–79.

Liu Ka-shiang 劉克襄. *Doushu huijia* 豆鼠回家 (Bean Mouse Goes Home). Taipei: Yuanliu chubanshe, 2011.

Liu Ka-shiang 劉克襄. "Faxian chitang" 發現池塘 (Discovering the Pond). In Wu, *Taiwan ziran xiezuo xuan*, 213–15.

Liu Ka-shiang 劉克襄. *Fengniao pinuocha* 風鳥皮諾查 (Pinuocha, the Plover). Taipei: Yuanliu chubanshe, 1991.

Liu Ka-shiang 劉克襄. "He yingxiao" 褐鷹鴞 (Brown Hawk-Owl). In Wu, *Taiwan ziran xiezuo xuan*, 217–18.

Liu Ka-shiang 劉克襄. *Hu di mao* 虎地貓 (Tiger Land Cats). Taipei: Yuanliu chubanshe, 2016.

Liu Ka-shiang 劉克襄. "Ou zhi lu" 鷗之路 (Journey of the Gull). In Wu, *Taiwan ziran xiezuo xuan*, 29–31.

Liu Ka-shiang 劉克襄. *Sui niao zou tianya* 隨鳥走天涯 (Follow the Birds). Taipei: Hongfan chubanshe, 1985.

Liu Ka-shiang 劉克襄. "Yegou xiaoshi shier nian" 野狗消失十二年 (Stray Dogs Have Been out of Sight for Twelve Years). *China Times*, January 28, 2006.

Liu Ka-shiang 劉克襄. *Yegou zhi qiu* 野狗之丘 (The Hill of Stray Dogs). Taipei: Yuanliu chubanshe, 2016.

Liu Ka-shiang 劉克襄. *Yongyuan de xintianweng* 永遠的信天翁 (The Eternal Albatross). Taipei: Yuanliu chubanshe, 2008.

Liu Ka-shiang 劉克襄. *Zuotou jing He Lian Ma Ma* 座頭鯨赫連麼麼 (He-lien-mo-mo, the Humpback Whale). Taipei: Yuanliu chubanshe, 1993.

Liu Kexiang. "A Nature Writer in Taiwan." Trans. Nick Kaldis (2012). Online publication on file with author.

Liu Kexiang shuwei zhuti guan: Yanjiu lunwen 劉克襄數位主題館: 研究論文 (Liu Ka-shiang Digital Subject Archive: Research Theses). http://www.liukashiang.campus-studio.com/thesis.php.

Liu Liangcheng. "One Man's Village." Trans. Joshua Dyer. *Pathlight: New Chinese Writing* (October 2015): 56–65.

Liu Liangcheng 刘亮程. *Yige ren de cunzhuang* 一个人的村庄 (One Man's Village). Shenyang: Chunfeng wenyi chubanshe, 2006.

Liu, Lydia. "Life as Form: How Biomimesis Encountered Buddhism in Lu Xun." *Journal of Asian Studies* 68, no. 1 (February 2009): 21–54.

Liu, Xiaoyuan. *Reins of Liberation: An Entangled History of Mongolian Independence, Chinese Territoriality, and Great Power Hegemony, 1911–1950*. Stanford, CA: Stanford University Press, 2006.

Liu, Xinmin, and Peter I-min Huang, eds. *Embodied Memories, Embedded Healing: New Ecological Perspectives from East Asia*. Lanham, MD: Lexington Books, 2021.

Liu Zhirong 刘志荣. "Dadi yu tiankong de liaokuo yu wenmi" 大地与天空的辽阔与隐秘—李娟散文漫谈 (The Vastness and Secrets of Earth and Sky: On Li Juan's Essays). *Wenyi zhengming* 文艺争鸣 (September 2011): 133–37.

"Living with Wolves." *The Guardian*, November 22, 2007.

Louie, Kam. "Review Essay: In Search of the Chinese Soul in the Mountains of the South." *The China Journal* 45 (January 2001): 145–49.

Lu Xun 鲁迅. "Po e'sheng lun" 破惡聲論 (Toward a Refutation of Malevolent Voices). In *Lu Xun quanji* 鲁迅全集 (Complete Works of Lu Xun), 8:28–29. Beijing: Renmin wenxue, 1981.

Lu Xun 鲁迅. "Suibian fanfan" 随便翻翻 (A Random Glance). In *Qiejie ting zawen ji* 且介亭雜文集 (Essays from the Qiejie Pavilion). Shanghai: Sanxian Shuwu, 1937.

Lu Xun 鲁迅. "Women xianzai zenyang zuo fuqin" 我們現在怎樣做父親 (What We Need to Do to Become Better Fathers Today). *Xin qingnian* 新青年 (New Youth) 6 (1919): 558–59.

Luo Zongyu 罗宗宇. "Dui shengtai weiji de yishu baogao. Xin shiqi yilai de shengtai baogao wenxue jianlun" 对生态危机的艺术报告—新时期以来的生态报告文学简论 (Artistic Reportages on the Ecological Crisis: Brief Comments on Eco-Reportages since the New Era). *Wenyi lilun yu piping* (2002): 636–42.

Ma Bo. *Blood Red Sunset*. Trans. Howard Goldblatt. New York: Penguin Books, 1996.

Ma Mingkui 马明奎, ed. *Youmu wenming de yousi* 游牧文明的忧思 (Troubled Thoughts on Nomadic Civilization). Hohhot: Neimenggu chuban jituan, yuanfang chubanshe, 2013.

Mahmut, Dilmurat, and Jo Smith Finley. "Corrective 'Re-Education' as (Cultural) Genocide in the Uyghur Region: Content Analysis of Children's Textbook *Til-Ädäbiyat* (rev. 2018)." Presentation at the Xinjiang Crisis: Genocide, Crimes Against Humanity, Justice, Newcastle University, September 1–3, 2021. https://www.youtube.com/watch?v=AcF-nG5xays.

Makley, Charlene. *The Battle for Fortune: State-led Development, Personhood, and Power among Tibetans in China*. Ithaca, NY: Cornell University Press, 2018.

"Man-Nature Harmony, An Essential Part of China's Modernization." Xinhua. April 27, 2021. http://www.xinhuanet.com/english/2021-04/27/c_139908104.htm.

Mandumai 滿都麥. *Aobao: Caoyuan shengtai wenming de shouhu shen—Youmu wenhua ganwu lu* 敖包：草原生态文明的守护神—游牧文化感悟录 (Ovoos: Protector Spirits of Grassland Ecological Civilization—On Nomadic Cultural Sensibilities). Hulunbeir: Neimenggu chuban jituan, 2013.

Mandumai 滿都麥. *Junma, canglang, guxiang* 駿馬·蒼狼·故鄉 (*Horse, Wolf, Home*). 2 vols. Beijing: Zuojia chubanshe, 2015.

Marks, Robert B. *Tigers, Rice, Silk, and Silt: Environment and Economy in Late Imperial South China*. Cambridge: Cambridge University Press, 1998.

"Mengguzu zuojia pi *Lang tuteng*: Lang conglai bushi Mengguren tuteng" 蒙古族作家批《狼圖騰》狼從來不是蒙古人圖騰 (Mongol Author Criticizes *Wolf Totem*: Wolves Have Never Been a Mongol Totem). Morningpost.com.cn, February 25, 2015.

Merchant, Carolyn. *The Death of Nature: Women, Ecology, and the Scientific Revolution*. New York: HarperCollins, 1980.

Mignolo, Walter. "On Pluriversality and Multipolarity." In *Constructing the Pluriverse: The Geopolitics of Knowledge*, ed. Bernd Reiter, ix–xv. Durham, NC: Duke University Press, 2018.

Miller, Ian. *Fir and Empire: The Transformation of Forests in Early Modern China*. Seattle: University of Washington Press, 2020.

Millward, James A. "Positioning Xinjiang in Eurasian and Chinese History: Differing Visions of the 'Silk Road.'" In *China, Xinjiang, and Central Asia: History, Translation and Crossborder Interaction into the 21st Century*, ed. Colin Mackerras and Michael Clarke, 55–74. New York: Routledge Contemporary China Series, 2009.

Mok, Bryan K. M. "Reconsidering Ecological Civilization from a Chinese Christian Perspective." *Religions* 11, no. 5 (2020): 261–78.

Møller-Olsen, Astrid. "Take the Elevator to Tomorrow: Mobile Space and Lingering Time in Contemporary Urban Fiction." Lund University Publications. August 30, 2018. https://lup.lub.lu.se/record/87b5ebbb-8507-45ca-a362-9d8a6bd3dc19.

Moore, Jason. *Capitalism in the Web of Life: Ecology and the Accumulation of Capital*. London: Verso, 2015.

Moran, Thomas. "Bringing It All Back Home: Ecocriticism and Liu Liangcheng's (刘亮程) *One Man's Village* (一个人的村庄)." Presentation at the Association of Asian Studies Annual Meeting, Chicago, March 2012.

Moran, Thomas. "Lost in the Woods: Nature in Soul Mountain." *Modern Chinese Literature and Culture* 14, no. 2 (Fall 2002): 207–36.

Moratto, Riccardo, Nicoletta Pesaro, and Di-kai Chao, eds. *Ecocriticism and Chinese Literature: Imagined Landscapes and Real Lived Spaces*. London: Routledge, 2022.

Mori Ushinosuke 森丑之助. *Shengfan xingjiao: Sen Chouzhizhu de Taiwan tanxian* 生蕃行腳：森丑之助的台灣探險 (Travels with Savages: Mori Ushinosuke's Taiwan Expedition). Trans. Yang Nangun 楊南郡. Taipei: Yuanliu, 2012.

Morton, Timothy. *Dark Ecology: For a Logic of Future Coexistence*. New York: Columbia University Press, 2016.

Mullaney, Thomas. *Coming to Terms with the Nation: Ethnic Classification in Modern China*. Berkeley: University of California Press, 2011.

Murphy, Patrick D. *Ecocritical Explorations in Literary and Cultural Studies: Fences, Boundaries, and Fields*. Lanham, MD: Lexington Books, 2009.

Nakawo, Masayoshi, Yuki Konagaya, and Shinjilt. *Ecological Migration: Environmental Policy in China*. Bern: Peter Lang, 2010.

"Noted Uyghur Folklore Professor Serving Prison Term in China's Xinjiang." Radio Free Asia. July 13, 2021. https://www.rfa.org/english/news/uyghur/rahile-dawut-07132021175559.html.

Nulo, Naktsang. *My Tibetan Childhood: When Ice Shattered Stone*. Trans. Angus Cargill and Sonam Lhamo. Durham, NC: Duke University Press, 2014.

Nulo, Naktsang. "Response to Questions by Tehor Lobsang Choephel and Others." High Peaks Pure Earth. February 26, 2013. https://highpeakspureearth.com/a-tibetan-intellectual-naktsang-nulo-shares-his-thoughts-on-self-immolations-in-tibet/.

Nyangweso, Mary. "Disability in Africa: A Cultural/Religious Perspective." In *Disability in Africa: Inclusion, Care, and the Ethics of Humanity*, ed. Toyin Falola and Nic Hamel, 115–36. Rochester, NY: University of Rochester Press, 2021.

Ou Ning 欧宁. "Meiyou zuihao de difang, ye meiyou zuihuai de difang: Li Juan zhuanfang" 没有最好的地方，也没有最坏的地方：李娟专访 (Neither the Best nor Worst Place: Interview with Li Juan). Jintian 今天. September 13, 2012. https://www.jintian.net/today/html/69/n-38669.html.

Pan Guangdan 潘光旦. "Ershinian lai shijie zhi yousheng yudong." 二十年來世界之優生運動 (The Eugenics Movement Around the World in the Last Twenty Years). *Dongfang zazhi* 東方雜誌 (Eastern Miscellany) no. 22 (1925): 60–85

Pan Guangdan 潘光旦. "Yousheng gailun" 優生概論 (An Overview of Eugenics). *Liumeixuesheng jibao* 留美學生季報 (The Chinese Students Quarterly) 11, no. 4 (1927): 51–69.

Pan Guangdan 潘光旦. "Zhongguo zhi yousheng wenti." 中國之優生問題 (The Eugenics Problem in China). *Dongfang zazhi* 東方雜誌 (Eastern Miscellany) no. 22 (1924): 15–33.

Payne, Christopher. "In/Visible Peoples, In/Visible Lands: Overlapping Histories in Wang Chia-hsiang's Historical Fantasy." *International Journal of Taiwan Studies* 2 (2019): 3–31.

Pedersen, Morten. *Not Quite Shamans: Spirit Worlds and Political Lives in Northern Mongolia*. Ithaca, NY: Cornell University Press, 2011.

Pema Tseden. "Pema Tseden Interviews Takbum Gyal: 'In my Previous Life I may Have Been a Dog.'" High Peaks Pure Earth. December 12, 2016. https://highpeakspureearth.com/pema-tseden-interviews-takbum-gyal-in-my-previous-life-i-may-have-been-a-dog/.

Povinelli, Elizabeth. *Geoontologies: A Requiem to Late Liberalism*. Durham, NC: Duke University Press, 2016.

Powell, Miles. *Vanishing America: Species Extinction, Racial Peril, and the Origins of Conservation*. Cambridge, MA: Harvard University Press, 2016.

Ptackova, Jarmila. *Exile from the Grasslands: Tibetan Herders and Chinese Development Projects*. Seattle: University of Washington Press, 2020.

Qin, Amy. "As China Hungers for Coal, 'Behemoth' Studies the Ravages at the Source." *New York Times*, December 28, 2015.

Qizihan, Nurila. "A Houseful of Birds." Trans. Guldana Salimjan. In Isbister, Pu, and Rachman, *Chinese Women Writers on the Environment*, 81–83.

Qizihan, Nurila. "We Have Surpassed the Bears." Trans. Guldana Salimjan. In Isbister, Pu, and Rachman, *Chinese Women Writers on the Environment*, 84–86.

Ran Yunfei 冉云飞 and Alai 阿来. "Tongwang keneng zhilu—yu Zangzu zuojia Alai tanhualu" 通往可能之路—与藏族作家阿来谈话录 (A Pathway to Possibilities: A Dialogue with Tibetan Author Alai). *Xinan minzu xueyuan xuebao* 西南民族文学学报 20, no. 2 (September 1999): 8–10.

Rocha, Leon Antonio. "Quentin Pan in the *China Critic*." *China Heritage Quarterly* 30–31 (June–September 2012). http://www.chinaheritagequarterly.org/features.php?searchterm=030_rocha.inc&issue=030.

Runk, Julie Velásquez, Chindío Peña Ismare, and Toño Peña Conquista. "Animal Transference and Transformation Among Wounaan." *The Journal of Latin American and Caribbean Anthropology* 24, no. 1 (2019): 32–51.

Ruser, Nathan, and James Leibold. "Cultural Erasure and Re-writing: How China Is Using State Cultural Protection to Erase Islamic and Indigenous Cultures from

Xinjiang." Presentation at The Xinjiang Crisis: Genocide, Crimes Against Humanity, Justice, Newcastle University, September 1–3, 2021. https://www.youtube.com/watch?v=AcF-nG5xays.

Sakamoto, Hiroko. "The Cult of 'Love and Eugenics' in May Fourth Movement Discourse." Trans. Rebecca Jennison. *positions* 12.2 (Fall 2004): 329–76.

Salimjan, Guldana. "Naturalized Violence: Affective Politics of China's 'Ecological Civilization' in Xinjiang." *Human Ecology* 49 (2021): 59–68.

Sanft, Charles. "Environment and Law in Early Imperial China (Third Century BCE–First Century CE): Qin and Han Statutes Concerning Natural Resources." *Environmental History* 15 (October 2010): 701–21.

Sanft, Charles. "Progress and Publicity in Early China: Qin Shihuang, Ritual, and Common Knowledge." *Journal of Ritual Studies* 22, no. 1 (2008): 21–37.

Santos-Granero, Fernando. "Beinghood and People-Making in Native Amazonia: A Constructional Approach with a Perspectival Coda." *HAU: Journal of Ethnographic Theory* 2, no. 1 (2012): 181–211.

Scarfe, Adam C. "James Mark Baldwin with Alfred North Whitehead on Organic Selectivity: The 'Novel' Factor in Evolution." *Cosmos and History: The Journal of Natural and Social Philosophy* 5, no. 2 (2009). https://cosmosandhistory.org/index.php/journal/article/view/136/247

Schwartzberg, Joseph E. "Maps of Greater Tibet." In *The History of Cartography*, ed. J. B. Harley and David Woodward, 2:607–85. Chicago: University of Chicago Press, 1994.

Sha Qing 沙青. "Beijing shiqu pingheng" 北京失去平衡 (Beijing Loses Its Balance). *Baogao wenxue* 报告文学 (Reportage Literature) 4 (1986): 3.

Shalimujiang, Gulidana (Guldana Salimjan). "Finding Kazakh Women in the Chinese State: Embodiment and the Politics of Memory." PhD dissertation, University of British Columbia, 2018.

Shantarakshita. *The Adornment of the Middle Way: Shantarakshita's Madhyamakalankara with Commentary by Jamgon Mipham*. Boston: Shambhala, 2005.

Shapiro, Judith. *Mao's War Against Nature: Politics and Environment in Revolutionary China*. Cambridge: Cambridge University Press, 2001.

Shen Wei 沈苇. *Xinjiang cidian* 新疆词典 (Dictionary of Xinjiang). Trans. Eleanor Goodman. *Ninth Letter* 10, no. 2 (Fall/Winter 2013–14): 120–43.

Shepherd, John Robert. *Statecraft and Political Economy on the Taiwan Frontier, 1600–1800*. Stanford, CA: Stanford University Press, 1993.

Sherburne, Donald W. "Whitehead, Alfred North." In *The Cambridge Dictionary of Philosophy*, ed. Robert Audi, 852. Cambridge: Cambridge University Press, 1995.

"Sichuan Earthquake Killed More Than 5,000 Pupils, Says China." *Guardian*, May 7, 2009. https://www.theguardian.com/world/2009/may/07/china-quake-pupils-death-toll.

Simmel, Georg. "The Metropolis and Mental Life." In *The Sociology of Georg Simmel*, ed. Kurt H. Wolff, 409–24. New York: Free Press, 1950.

Singer, Peter. *Animal Liberation: A New Ethics for Our Treatment of Animals*. New York: HarperCollins, 1975.

Slingerland, Edward. "Conceptual Blending, Somatic Marking, and Normativity: A Case Example from Ancient Chinese." *Cognitive Linguistics* 16, no. 3 (2005): 557–84.

Sodango, Terefe Hanchiso, et al. "Review of the Spatial Distribution, Source, and Extent of Heavy Metal Pollution of Soil in China: Impacts and Mitigation Approaches." *Journal of Health and Pollution* 8, no. 17 (2018): 53–70.

Song, Lili. "Toward an Ecocriticism of Cultural Diversity: Animism in the Novels of Guo Xuebo and Chi Zijian." In Liu and Huang, *Embodied Memories, Embedded Healing*, 71–86.

Springer, Cecilia Han. "Policies for an Ecological Civilization." PhD dissertation, University of California–Berkeley, 2019.

Stalin, Joseph. *Marxism and the National and Colonial Question*. San Francisco: Proletarian Publishers, 1975.

Starr, S. Frederick, ed. *Xinjiang: China's Muslim Borderland*. London: Routledge, 2004.

Sterk, Darryl. "The Hunter's Gift in Ecorealist Indigenous Fiction from Taiwan." *Oriental Archive* 81 (2013): 555–580.

Sterk, Darryl. "The Apotheosis of Montage: The Videomosaic Gaze of *The Man with the Compound Eyes* as Postmodern Ecological Sublime." *Modern Chinese Literature and Culture* 28, no. 2 (Fall 2016): 183–222.

Sun Chieh-Liang. "Animal Contact in Liu Ka-shiang's *He-lien-mo-mo the Humpback Whale*." *Tamkang Review* 42, no. 2 (June 2012): 33–58.

Sun, Ying, and Ssu-Yu Huang. "Poems of Tang Dynasty with English Translations." 2008. http://musicated.com/syh/TangPoems.htm.

Suritan, Azati. 阿扎提·苏里坦. "Youmo shi zuigao de fengci—Qiantan Memtimin Hoshur de fengci yishu" 幽默是最高明的讽刺–浅谈买买提明·吾守尔的讽刺艺术 (Humor Is the Highest Satire: A Brief Discussion on the Satire Art of Memtimin Hoshur). In *Minzu wenxue de shuxie yu goujian* 民族文学的书写与构建 (The Writing and Construction of Ethnic Literature), ed. Azati Suritan, 205–8. Shanghai: Wenlian chubanshe, 2016.

Syaman Rapongan 夏曼·藍波安. *Dahai zhiyan* 大海之眼 (The Eyes of the Sea). Taipei: Yinke chubanshe, 2018.

Syaman Rapongan 夏曼·藍波安. *Heise de chibang* 黑色的翅膀 (Black Wings). Taichung: Chenxing chubanshe, 1999.

Syaman Rapongan 夏曼·藍波安. *Lenghai qingshen* 冷海情深 (Deep Love for the Cold Sea). Taipei: Lianhe wenxue chubanshe, 1997.

Syaman Rapongan 夏曼‧藍波安. *Tiankong de yanjing* 天空的眼睛 (The Eyes of the Sky). Taipei: Lianhe wenxue chubanshe, 2012.

Syaman Rapongan 夏曼‧藍波安. *Meiyou xinxiang de nanren* 沒有信箱的男人 (The Man Without a Mailbox). Taipei: Lianhe wenxue chubanshe, 2022.

Syaman Rapongan. *Les yeux de l'océan* (*Mata nu Wawa*) (The Eyes of the Sea). Trans. Damien Ligot. Paris: L'Asiathèque, 2022.

Takbum Gyel. "The Illusion of a Day." Trans. Christopher Peacock. *Two Lines* 31 (Fall 2019). https://www.catranslation.org/online-exclusive/the-illusion-of-a-day/.

Takbum Gyel. "Notes on the Pekingese." Trans. Christopher Peacock. *Ploughshares* 45, no. 3 (Fall 2019): 162–86.

Takbum Gyel. "Nyin gcig gi cho 'phrul" (The Illusion of a Day). *Gangs rgyan me tog* 2 (1990): 13–21.

Tenzin WanGyel Rinpoche. "Bön and Shamanism." Interview by Guildo Ferrari. 2014. https://www.youtube.com/watch?v=BTLROrUqq5E.

Thornber, Karen. *Ecoambiguity: Environmental Crises and East Asian Literature*. Ann Arbor: University of Michigan Press, 2012.

Thornber, Karen. "Environments of Early Chinese and Japanese Literatures." In *A Global History of Literature and the Environment*, ed. John Parham and Louise Westling, 37–51. Cambridge: Cambridge University Press, 2016.

Thum, Rian. *The Sacred Routes of Uyghur History*. Cambridge, MA: Harvard University Press, 2014.

Thum, Rian. "The Spatial Cleansing of Xinjiang: *Mazar* Desecration in Context." *Made in China* (2020 August 24). https://madeinchinajournal.com/2020/08/24/the-spatial-cleansing-of-xinjiang-mazar-desecration-in-context/.

Thurston, Timothy O'Connor. "Tricksters and Outcasts in Modern Tibetan Literature: An Examination of Folkloric Character Types in Alai's Novels." MA thesis, Ohio State University, 2007.

Tierney, Robert. *Tropics of Savagery: The Culture of Japanese Empire in Comparative Frame*. Berkeley: University of California Press, 2010.

Tillman, Hoyt Cleveland. "Proto-Nationalism in Twelfth-Century China? The Case of Ch'en Liang." *Harvard Journal of Asiatic Studies* 39, no. 2 (Dec. 1979): 403–28.

Tlili, Sarra. *Animals in the Qur'an*. Cambridge: Cambridge University Press, 2012.

Topas Tamapima. "The Last Hunter." In *Indigenous Writers of Taiwan*, ed. and trans. John Balcom, 3–20. New York: Columbia University Press, 2005.

Topas Tamapima 拓拔斯‧塔瑪匹瑪. *Zuihou de lieren* 最後的獵人 (The Last Hunter). Taipei: Chenxing, 2012.

Trocki, Carl. *Opium, Empire, and the Global Political Economy: A Study of the Asian Opium Trade, 1750–1950*. London: Routledge, 1999.

Tsai, Shu-fen. "Taiwan Is a Whale: The Emerging Oneness of Dark Blue and Human Identity in Wang Chia-hsiang's Historical Fiction." In Chang and Slovic, *Ecocriticism in Taiwan*, 41–54.

Tsering Döndrup. *The Handsome Monk and Other Stories*. Trans. Christopher Peacock. New York: Columbia University Press, 2019.

Tu, Weiming. "Beyond the Enlightenment Mentality." In *Confucianism and Ecology: The Interrelationship of Heaven, Earth, and Humans*, ed. Mary Evelyn Tucker and John Berthrong, 17–19. Cambridge, MA: Harvard University for the Study of World Religions, 1998.

Tursun, Perhat. *The Back Streets: A Novel from Xinjiang*. Trans. Darren Byler and Anonymous. New York: Columbia University Press, 2022.

Tursun, Perhat. "Chong Sheher: Birinchi Bap, Arqa Kocha" (Big City: The First Chapter, The Backstreets). In *Perhat Tursun Eserliri* (Works of Perhat Tursun). https://web.archive.org/web/20140322013840/http://kitaphumar.com/.

"Uyghur Professor Rahile Dawut Confirmed to Be Imprisoned by Chinese Authorities." Pen America. July 16, 2021. https://pen.org/press-release/uyghur-professor-rahile-dawut-confirmed-to-be-imprisoned-by-chinese-authorities/.

Visser, Robin. "Anthropocosmic Resonance in Post-Mao Chinese Environmental Literature." *Wenyi lilun yanjiu* 文藝理論研究 (Theoretical Studies in Literature and Art) 33, no. 4 (2013): 34–44.

Visser, Robin. "Ecocriticism and Indigenous Anti-Epics of China." In *The Epic World*, ed. Pamela Lothspeich. London: Routledge, 2024.

Visser, Robin. "Ecology as Method." *Prism: Theory and Modern Chinese Literature* 16, no. 2 (October 2019): 320–45.

Walis Norgan 瓦歷斯·諾幹. "Taiwan yuanzhumin wenxue de qu zhimin" 台灣原住民文學的去殖民 (The Decolonization of Taiwan Indigenous Literature). In *Taiwan yuanzhumin hanyu wenxue xuanji: Pinglun juan* 台灣原住民漢語文學選集：評論卷 (Anthology of Indigenous Taiwanese Literature in Chinese), ed. Sun Dachuan 孫大川 (T. C. Sun), 27–151. Taipei: Yinke wenxue, 2003.

Wallin, Paul. "Native South Americans Were Early Inhabitants of Polynesia." *Nature* 583.7817 (July 23, 2020): 524–25.

Wang Chia-hsiang 王家祥. *Daofeng neihai* 倒風內海 (Daofeng Inland Sea). Taipei: Yushan chubanshe, 1997.

Wang Chia-hsiang 王家祥. *Guanyu Lamadaxianxian yu Lahe Alei* 關於拉馬達仙仙與拉荷阿雷》(On Lamatasinsin and Dahu Ali). Taipei: Yushan chubanshe, 1995.

Wang Chia-hsiang 王家祥. *Haizhong guiying: Sairen* 海中鬼影：鯢人 (Sea Ghosts: The Gill Men). Taipei: Yushan chubanshe, 1999.

Wang Chia-hsiang 王家祥. *Jinfulou yehua* 金福樓夜話 (Jinfu Tower Night Talks). Taipei: Xiaozhitang, 2003.

Wang Chia-hsiang 王家祥. *Moshen zi* 魔神仔 (Devil's Son). Taipei: Yushan chubanshe, 2002.

Wang Chia-hsiang 王家祥. *Shan yu hai* 山與海 (Mountains and Seas). Taipei: Yushan chubanshe, 1996.

Wang Chia-hsiang 王家祥. *Shenlan* 深藍 (Dark Blue). Taipei: Jiuge, chubanshe 2000.

Wang Chia-hsiang 王家祥. *Siji de shengyin* 四季的聲音 (The Sounds of Four Seasons). Taipei: Chenxing chubanshe, 1997.

Wang Chia-hsiang 王家祥. *Tubu* 徒步 (On Foot). Taipei: Tianpei wenhua gongsi, 2004.

Wang Chia-hsiang 王家祥. *Wenming huangye* 文明荒野 (Civilizational Wilderness) Taizhong: Chenxing chubanshe, 1990.

Wang Chia-hsiang 王家祥. *Wo zhuzai Hamaxing de yuren matou* 我住在哈瑪星的漁人碼頭 (I Live on Hamasen Fisherman's Wharf). Gaoxiong: Chuanmen chubanshe, 2002.

Wang Chia-hsiang 王家祥. *Xiao airen zhi mi* 小矮人之謎 (Mystery of the Little People). Taipei: Yushan chubanshe, 1996.

Wang Chia-hsiang 王家祥. *Yujian yike huhuan ni de shu* 遇見一棵呼喚你的樹 (Meet a Tree That Calls to You). Taipei: Fangzhi chubanshe, 2001.

Wang Chia-hsiang 王家祥. *Ziran daogaozhe* 自然禱告者 (Prayer for Nature). Taizhong: Chenxing chubanshe, 1992.

Wang Fuzhi 王夫之 "Ai Di" 哀帝. In *Dutong jianlun* 讀通鑑論 (On *Zizhi Tongjian*), 14:9. Beijing: Zhonghua shuju, 1975.

Wang Fuzhi 王夫之 "Han Zhao Di" 漢昭帝 (Han Emperor Zhao). In *Dutong jianlun* 讀通鑑論 (On *Zizhi Tongjian*), 1:74–76. Beijing: Zhonghua shuju, 1975.

Wang Nuo 王诺. *Shengtai piping yu shengtai sixiang* 生态批评与生态思想 (Ecological Criticism and Ecological Thought). Beijing: Renmin chubanshe, 2013.

Wang Qianhai 王前海. "Shangwu shijiao nengfo kanqing Chen'ai luoding: Yu diwujie Mao Dun wenxuejiang huodezhe Alai duihua" 商务视角能否看清《尘埃落定》—与第五届茅盾文学奖获得者阿来对话 中国信息报 (Can a Commercial Angle Provide a Better View on Red Poppies: A Dialogue with Alai, Winner of the Mao Dun Literature Prize). *Zhongguo xinxi bao* 中国信息报 (China Information) (December 21, 2000): 1–4.

Wang, Anran. "The Sino-Mongolian Contention Over the Legacy of Chinggis Khan." *Studies in Ethnicity and Nationalism* 16, no. 3 (2016): 357–77.

Wang, Ban, ed. *Chinese Visions of World Order: Tianxia, Culture, and World Politics*. Durham, NC: Duke University Press, 2017.

Wang, Ban. "Old Dreams Retold: Lu Xun as Mytho-Ecological Writer." *Prism: Theory and Modern Chinese Literature* 17.2 (2020): 225–43.

Wang, David Der-wei. *Fin-de-Siècle Splendor: Repressed Modernities of Late Qing Fiction, 1849–1911*. Stanford, CA: Stanford University Press, 1997.

Wei Te-sheng. University of British Columbia Indigenous Taiwan: Transpacific Connections speaker series, October 21–22, 2021. https://www.youtube.com/watch?v=2lfaTFpm5tE.

Welden, Jim, trans. "Liu Liangcheng: Literature Only Begins Where the Story Ends—Interview with Shu Jinyu." *Pathlight* (Spring 2015): 66–73.

Weller, Robert. *Discovering Nature: Globalization and Environmental Culture in China and Taiwan*. New York: Cambridge University Press, 2006.

White, Thomas Richard Edward. "Transforming China's Desert: Camels, Pastoralists and the State in the Reconfiguration of Western Inner Mongolia." PhD dissertation, University of Cambridge, 2016.

Whitehead, Alfred North. *The Concept of Nature*. Cambridge: Cambridge University Press, 1964.

Whitehead, Alfred North. *Process and Reality: An Essay in Cosmology (Corrected Edition)*. Ed. David Ray Griffin and Donald W. Sherburne. New York: Free Press, 1979.

Whitehead, Alfred North. *Science and the Modern World*. New York: Free Press, 1967.

Williams, Dee Mack. *Beyond Great Walls: Environment, Identity, and Development on the Chinese Grasslands of Inner Mongolia*. Stanford, CA: Stanford University Press, 2002.

Williams, Dee Mack. "Grazing the Body: Violations of Land and Limb in Inner Mongolia." *American Ethnologist* 24, no. 4 (1997): 763–85.

Williams, Dee Mack. "Patchwork, Pastoralists, and Perception: Dune Sand as a Valued Resource among Herders of Inner Mongolia." *Human Ecology* 25, no. 2 (Jun. 1997): 297–317.

Woeser. "Our Sacred Land, Their Rubbish Dump: Chinese Artist Zhang Huan's 'Land Art' Installation on Mount Kailash." High Peaks Pure Earth. December 10, 2020. https://highpeakspureearth.com/our-sacred-land-their-rubbish-dump-part-1-chinese-artist-zhang-huans-land-art-installation-on-mount-kailash-by-woeser/.

Wu Jingming 吳景明. *Zouxiang hexie: ren yu ziran de shuangchong bianzou: Zhongguo shengtai wenxue fazhan lungang* 走向和諧：人與自然的雙重變奏——中國生態文学发展论纲 (Toward Harmony: The Double Variation of Man and Nature: An Outline of the Development of Chinese Ecological Literature). PhD dissertation, Dongbei Shifan Daxue, 2007.

Wu Lan 烏蘭. "Zhi duzhe" 致讀者 (To the Reader), 1:i–ii. In Mandumai 滿都麥. *Junma, canglang, guxiang* 駿馬·蒼狼·故鄉 (*Horse, Wolf, Home*). 2 vols. Beijing: Zuojia chubanshe, 2015.

Wu Ming-yi 吳明益. *Danche shiqie ji* 單車失竊記 (The Stolen Bicycle). Taipei: Maitian chubanshe, 2015.

Wu Ming-yi 吳明益. *Fuyan ren* 複眼人 (The Man with the Compound Eyes). Taipei: Xia'ri chubanshe, 2011.

Wu Ming-yi. *The Man with the Compound Eyes*. Trans. Darryl Sterk. New York: Pantheon, 2013.

Wu Ming-yi. *The Stolen Bicycle*. Trans. Darryl Sterk. Melbourne: Text Publishing, 2018.

Wu Ming-yi 吳明益. *Taiwan ziran xiezuo xuan* 台灣自然寫作選 (Selected Taiwan Nature Writings). Taipei: Eryu wenhua, 2003.

Wu Ming-yi 吳明益. *Yi shuxie jiefang ziran—Taiwan xiandai ziran shuxie de tansuo* 以書寫解放自然—台灣現代自然書寫的探索 (Liberate Nature by Writing: An Exploration of Modern Nature Writing of Taiwan, 1980–2002). Taipei: Da'an chubanshe, 2004.

Wu, Jin-Yung. "Amis Aborigine Migrants' Territorialization in Metropolitan Taipei." *East Asian History and Culture Review* 1, no. 1 (May 2012): 102–31.

Xi, Jinping. "Secure a Decisive Victory in Building a Moderately Prosperous Society." Speech Delivered at the 19th National Congress of the Communist Party of China, October 18, 2017. http://www.xinhuanet.com/english/download/Xi_Jinping's_report_at_19th_CPC_National_Congress.pdf.

Xu Gang 徐刚. *Famuzhe, xinglai!* 伐木者：醒来！(Woodcutter, Wake Up!). Changchun: Jilin renmin chubanshe, 1997.

Xu Yongquan 徐永泉 and Jiang Wei 隆伟. "Ni bie wuxuanze: *Yigeren de cunzhuang* zhong de shengcun kunjing tanxi 你别无选择：《一个人的村庄》中的生存困境探析 (You Have No Choice: An Analysis of the Dilemma of Survival in *One Man's Village*). *Tangshan shifan xueyuan xuebao* 唐山师范学院学报 31, no. 6 (November 2009): 22–24.

Xu Zhaoshou 徐兆寿. "'Jie diqi' he 'jie tianqi'—jiantan dui 'renxue' de chaoyue" "接地气"和"接天气"—兼谈对"人学"的超越 (Connect to the Vital Energies of Heaven and Earth: Transcend the Human). *Xiaoshuo pinglun* 小说评论 (2012): 57–63.

Yan Lianke 阎连科. *Faxian xiaoshuo* 发现小说 (Discovering Fiction). Tianjin: Nankai Daxue Chubanshe, 2011.

Yan Lianke 阎连科 and Zhang Xuexin 张学昕. *Wode xianshi, wodezhuyi: Yan Lianke wenxue duihualu*. 我的现实，我的主义：阎连科文学对话录 (My Reality, My "Ism": Notes on a Dialogue About Yan Lianke's Literature). Beijing: Zhongguo Renmin Daxue chubanshe, 2011.

Yan Xuetong. *Ancient Chinese Thought, Modern Chinese Power*. Princeton, NJ: Princeton University Press, 2013.

Yang Jianlong 杨剑龙 and Zhou Xufeng 周旭峰. "Lun Zhongguo dangdai shengtai wenxue chuangzuo" 论中国当代生态文学创作 (On Contemporary China's

Writing of Ecoliterature). *Shanghai shifan daxue xuebao* 上海师范大学学报 34, no. 2 (2005): 38–43.

Yang, Lien-sheng. "Historical Notes on the Chinese World Order." In *The Chinese World Order: Traditional China's Foreign Relations*, ed. John King Fairbank, 20–33. Cambridge, MA: Harvard University Press, 1968.

Yang Yang. "A Poetic Way to Decode Xinjiang." *China Daily*, August 26, 2015.

Yasin, Nurmuhemmet. "The Wild Pigeon." *Kashgar Literature* 5 (2004). Trans. Dolkun Kamberi. Radio Free Asia, 2005. https://www.rfa.org/NS/ENG/ebooks/Caged.pdf.

Yeh, Emily. "Green Governmentality." *Nomadic Peoples* 9, nos. 1–2 (2005): 9–30.

Yeh, Emily. *Taming Tibet: Landscape Transformation and the Gift of Chinese Development*. Ithaca, NY: Cornell University Press, 2013.

Yeh, Michelle. "From Surrealism to Nature Poetics: A Study of Prose Poetry from Taiwan." *Journal of Modern Literature in Chinese* 3, no. 2 (2000): 145–53.

Yellen, Jeremy. *The Greater East Asia Co-Prosperity Sphere: When Total Empire Met Total War*. Ithaca, NY: Cornell University Press, 2019.

Yuan Qing-Li. "Population Changes in the Xinjiang Uighur Autonomous Region (1949–1984)." *Central Asian Survey* 9, no. 1 (1990): 49–73.

Yue, Gang. "As the Dust Settles in Shangri-La: Alai's Tibet in the Era of Sino-Globalization." *Journal of Contemporary China* 17, no. 56 (August 2008): 543–63.

Yue, Gang. "The Strange Landscape of the Ancients: Environmental Consciousness in 'The King of Trees.'" *American Journal of Chinese Studies* 5, no. 1 (1998): 68–88.

Zeng Fanren 曾繁仁. *Shengtai meixue daolun* 生态美学导论 (Introduction to Ecological Aesthetics). Beijing: Shangwu yinshu guan, 2010.

Zhang Chang 张长. "Xiwang de lüye" 希望的绿叶 (The Green Leaves of Hope). *Renmin wenxue* 人民文学 (People's Literature) 9 (1980): 94–102.

Zhang Chengzhi. *The Black Steed*. Trans. Stephen Fleming. Beijing: Panda Books, 1990.

Zhang Chengzhi 張承志. *Hei Junma* 黑駿馬 (The Black Steed). In *Zhang Chengzhi daibiao zuo* 張承志代表作 (Representative Works by Zhang Chengzhi), ed. Zhang Caixin, 177–243. Zhengzhou: Henan renmin chubanshe, 1988.

Zhang Jian, Wei Jie, and Chen Quangong. "Mapping the Farming-Pastoral Ecotones in China." *Journal of Materials Science* 6 (2009): 78–87.

Zhang, Ling. *The River, the Plain, and the State: An Environmental Drama in Northern Song China, 1048–1128*. Cambridge: Cambridge University Press, 2016.

Zhang, Ling. "Treating One's Neighbor Like a Gully 以鄰為壑: Environmental Ethics and Yellow River Management of the Chinese State." Abstract for Lecture at

University of Michigan, January 30, 2018. https://lsa.umich.edu/asian/news-events/all-events.detail.html/47853-11033230.html.

Zhang, Meng. *Timber and Forestry in Qing China: Sustaining the Market.* Seattle: University of Washington Press, 2021.

Zhang Wanfu, ed. 張萬福主編. *Taiwan niaolei caise tulan* (A Field Guide to the Birds of Taiwan). Taizhong: Taizhong kexue, 1982.

Zhang Xiaoqin 张晓琴. "Zhongguo shengtai baogao wenxue zongshu" 中国生态报告文学综述 (Summary of Chinese Eco-Reportage). *Xibei chengren jiaoyu xuebao* 西北成人教育学报 6 (2008): 28–29.

Zhang Yan 张岩 and Zhang Shuqun 张书群. "Shouwang xiangtu de shengming zhiwu" 守望乡土的生命之悟：对《一个人的村庄》的解读 (Life Intuition from Watching the Countryside: An Interpretation of *One Man's Village*). *Dangdai wenxue* 当代文学 (November 2009): 66.

Zhao Tingyang 赵汀阳. *Tianxia Tixi: Shijie zhidu zhexue daolun* 天下体系：世界制度哲学导论 (The Tianxia System: An Introduction to the Philosophy of a World Institution). Nanjing: Jiangsu Jiaoyu Chubanshe, 2005.

Zhong Dianfei 种㤠棐. "Mianxiang da xibei, kaituo xinxing de 'xibu pian'" 面向大西北，开拓新型的"西部片" (Face the Great Northwest, Develop a New Type of "Western"). *Dianying xin shidai* 电影新时代 (New Film Age) (1984): 59–63.

Zhou Jianren 周建人. "Chan'er zhixian gaishuo" 產兒之前該說 (What Must Be Said Before Giving Birth). *Dongfang zazhi* 東方雜志 (Eastern Miscellany) 19, no. 7 (1922): 18.

Zhou Jianren 周建人. "Lian'ai jiehun yu jianglai de renzhong wenti" 戀愛結婚與將來的人種問題 (Love, Marriage, and the Future of Our Race). *Funü zazhi* 婦女雜志 (*Women's Journal*) 8 (1922): 4.

Zhou Zuoren 周作人. "Funü yundong yu changshi" 婦女運動與常識 (The Women's Movement and Common Sense). 婦女雜志 *Funü zazhi* (Women's Journal) 9, no. 1 (1923): 9.

Zhuangzi: Qiwulun 莊子·齊物論 (Zhuangzi: The Sorting Which Evens Things Out). https://ctext.org/zhuangzi/adjustment-of-controversies.

Zhuangzi. *The Complete Works of Zhuangzi.* Trans. Burton Watson. New York: Columbia University Press, 2013.

Zuozhuan: Chenggong sinian 左傳·成公四年 (Chunqiu zuozhuan: The Fourth Year of Duke Cheng). https://ctext.org/chun-qiu-zuo-zhuan/cheng-gong-si-nian.

Index

Aba Prefecture. *See* Ngawa [Aba] Tibetan and Qiang Autonomous Prefecture
abortions, forced, 30
Academia Sinica, 192, 277n9
Africa, 7, 25, 63
agency, 141, 142, 144, 211; ethical-material, 232; material agency of the cosmos, 230; suicidal, 153
agriculture, 21, 23, 131; "casual cultivation" of Mongol nomads, 71; deforestation and, 154; desertification and, 92; ecological civilization concept and, 5; farmers reverting to hunting/fishing and gathering, 21; Hu Line and, 35; industrialization of, 134; metaphor of conquest applied to cinema, 35; nonfarmers denounced as "lazy," 20–21, 244n60; rationalization of violence and, 22, 23; swidden, 58, 233, 252–53n52; in Taiwan, 211
agrilogistics, 21–23, 37, 70, 83, 87, 140, 150, 156, 195, 250n18, 285n42;

Anthropocene and, 21, 83; imperialist, 37; origin of, 22; reforestation and, 23
Ah Cheng (Zhong Acheng), 15, 35, 36, 39, 43, 250n15
Aku Sonam Tashi, 173
Aku Tonpa (figure in Tibetan oral folk tales), 152, 271n12
Aku Wuwu (Apkup Vytvy), 15, 37, 67–68, 69, 254n66; "Black Bear" (2016), 68; "Spring Water" (2015), 67–68
Alai, 147, 149, 152, 236; *As the Dust Settles* [*Chenai luoding*] (1998), 147–58, 160; *Empty Mountain* [*Kongshan*] (2009), 148, 154–58, 272n23; *The Epic of Gesar* [*Gesa'er Wang*] (2009), 148; *In the Clouds* [*Yunzhong ji*] (2019), 148, 155
Alberts, Thomas Karl, 254n1
Altai Mountains, 107, 111
Altay (northern Xinjiang), 12–13, 102; Indigenous Kazakh knowledge of Altay grasslands, 103–16; Li Juan's essays set in, 133–40

Altay Corner [*Aletai de jiaoluo*] (Li Juan, 2010), 133
Altishahr (southern Xinjiang), 100, 102, 117, 265n32, 267n65; map, *101*; Six Cities (oases) of, 119
Amantay, Aydos, 109, 265n40
Amdo (Qinghai), 148, 158–73; map, *149*; nomadic dialect of, 33
Ames, Roger, 38
Amis (Pangcah) people, 15, 225, 228, 277n5
Amundsen, Roald, 226
analogism, 9, 13
ancestor worship, 24, 47
Anderson, Benedict, 12
Ani Lachem (Jangbu, film, 2005), 165
Animal Farm (Orwell), 126
Animal Liberation (Singer, 1975), 266n52
animals, nonhuman, 1, 18, 243n46, 268n79; animal studies, 8; anthropocosmic resonance between humans and animals, 79, 257n28; anthropomorphization of, 79, 125–28, 133; "becoming-animal," 197, 205, 206; in children's literature and fables, 125, 128; Chinese medicine and, 25; cruelty toward, 87; domesticated, 21, 145; habitat destruction from deforestation, 157, 250n15; Han civilization's "war on animals," 22; human/animal relations in Qizihan's *Hunter's Stories*, 103; Liu Ka-shiang's series of novels on urban animals, 204, 279n38; mutual gaze between humans and animals, 145–46, 270n98; parity with humans, 102; yaks in Tibetan nomadic life, *164*
Animal That Therefore I Am, The (Derrida), 146
animism, 9, 12, 13, 37, 58, 69

Anointed (Jetñil-Kijiner, video poem, 2018), 229–30
Anthropocene, 3, 4, 15, 37, 68, 75; agriculture, 83; agrilogistics and, 21–23, 83; anti-epic of, 57, 155, 160; biopolitics and, 74; capitalism and, 147, 207; carbon imaginary of, 70; "dark ecology" and, 70; extinction and, 88; global apocalypse and, 152; impotence of organized religion and science in, 99; merging of human and geological time, 206
anthropocentrism, 50, 81, 236, 249n13; of Confucian philosophy, 6, 39; of Maoism, 38; of rational ordering, 50; of speciesism, 141, 168; of municipal policies in Taiwan, 205
anthropocosmic resonance (*ganying*), 39, 42, 228, 249n13, 257n28; Guo Xuebo and, 88; Liu Cixin and, 232; Mandumai and, 79
anthropomorphism, 113, 125, 133; Hoshur and, 127; Liu Ka-shiang and, 197, 205; Mandumai and, 79
Apache, Western, 124
Arctic ice cap, thawing of, 8
Aristotle, 28, 53
Armstrong, Jeannette, 214, 215
Art of Suicide, The (Tursun, 1999), 117
Asia as Method (Chen Kuan-hsing), 13, 194
assimilation, forced, 115, 161, 185
As the Dust Settles [*Chenai luoding*] (Alai, 1998), 147–58, 160, 236
August Torch Festival, of Yi people, 67
Austronesian Indigenes (Taiwan), 10, 12, 189, 190, 210, 225, 276n1. *See also* people, Amis (Pangcah); Bunun; Macatao; Paiwan; Pingpu; Sirayan; Tao
Avatar (Cameron, film, 2009), 227

Bachner, Andrea, 49, 53
Backstreets, The [*Chong Sheher*] (Tursun, 2013), 15, 116–23, 124, 264n31, 265n41
Bai people, 2, 15, 37, 44, 251n28. *See also* Zhang Chang
Bakhtin, Mikhail, 142, 209
Balcom, John, 217
Baldwin, James Mark, 143, 144, 270n93
Bamo Qubumo, 15, 37, 64–66; *Mountain Patterns: The Survival of Nuosu Culture in China* (2000), 64; "The Origin of Patterns," 64–66; "Water Lines," 66, 67
Barad, Karen, 13, 229, 230, 233
"barbarians," 17, 18; foreigners defined as, 243n49; Southwest minority peoples as, 59, 252n52; nomads as, 71; northern Rong and western Di, 243n51; "raw" and "cooked," 19; Uyghurs as, 253n61; "war on animals" and, 22
Basso, Keith, 124
Bayambajav, Da Lama, 81
Bayar, Nasan, 19, 72–74
Bean Mouse Goes Home [*Doushu huijia*] (Liu Ka-shiang, 2011), 204, 279n38
Behemoth [*Beixi moshou*] (Zhao Liang, film, 2015), 95, 96
"Beijing Loses Its Balance" (Sha Qing, 1986), 44
Beijing westerns (film and literary genre), 15–16, 17, 43, 69, 190; ecocriticism and rhetorical logic of, 139; Indigenous ecological perspectives appropriated in, 37, 70; neo-Confucian subject-entity formation and, 194. *See also* neo-Confucianism

Bello, David, 21, 245n74
Belt and Road Initiative (BRI), 4, 7–8, 108
Bender, Mark, 14, 60
Berger, John, 270n98
Bergeton, Uffe, 17, *18*
Bernards, Brian, 284n94
Beyond Nature and Culture (Descola), 9
biodiversity, 8, 103, 191, 218, 233
biogenetics, 28
biological determinism, 27
biometrics, 29, 31, 38
biophilia, 6
biopiracy, 5
biopolitics, 74, 121
biopower, 31, 99
bird migratory routes, 8
birds, 8, 48, 195, 208, 209, 216, in Dekyi Drolma's poetry, 181–82; deforestation and, 45; in Guo's desert fiction, 85, 88; He Huaren's woodcuts of, 202; Liu Ka-hsiang's essays on, 196–204; 279n32; Mongol taboos against disturbing nests of, 79; nests of as exotic Chinese foods, 25; Qizihan's essays on, 104–106. *See also Flight Ways*
"Black Fox Valley" (Tsering Döndrup, 2012), 159–61
Black Steed, The [*Hei Junma*] (Zhang Chengzhi, 1982), 250n21, 254n2
Black Wings [*Heise de chibang*] (Syaman Rapongan, 1999), 223
Blood Red Sunset [*Xuese huanghun*] (Ma Bo, 1988, 1996), 254n2
Bod kyi rtsom rig sgyu rtsal [Tibetan Literature and Art] (journal), 165
Bolivia, 95
Bön, 147, 153, 155, 178, 272n18, 275n59
Book of Changes [*Yijing*], 46

Index 315

Book of Lord Shang [*Shangjunshu*], 20–21
Book of Lost Butterflies, The [*Midie zhi*] (Wu Ming-yi, 2000), 224
Book of Odes (*Book of Poetry, Book of Songs, Classic of Poetry*) [*Shijing*], 22, 39, 79, 197
Book of Origins [*Hnewo teyy*] (Nuosu Yi epic), 68, 254n68
Borderlands of Asia, The (Bender, ed.), 14
borders, 1, 15, 47, 137, 204; Beijing-centric, 236; Belt and Road Initiative (BRI) and, 7; "border" as fraught term, 12; "borderlands," geopolitical, 2–3; centered as place of home, 37, 57, 69; core/center–periphery metaphysics and, 14; created by Hanspace cosmology, 70; multiethnic frontier regions, 148; Pakistani, 102; racially infused ideologies and, 25; reimagined, 235; Soviet-Chinese, 104; Wa people along Burma border, 57, 58, 62; of Xinjiang, 133
Brazil, 71, 95, 225
British Eugenics Education Society, 29
Buddhism, 12, 37, 176, 178; Chan (Zen), 40, 53; as a civilization, 74; cycle of transmigration and rebirth, 175; doctrine of dual nature of reality (*satya*), 80, 81; ethics of compassion, 180; Gandan Monastery (Ulaanbaatar), 81; in *The King of Trees*, 40, 41; Mongolian, 69, 79, 81, 90; Mount Kailash as sacred peak, 178, 275n59; nature poetry, 50, 174; neo-Confucianist syncretism and, 194; radical nonattachment to life, 75; Wa people and, 58

Buddhism, Tibetan, 69, 100, 147, 154, 156, 164; Geluk school, 150; Karma Kagyu school, 152; Nyingma school, 150; tripartite structure of the universe in, 275n58
Bulag, Uradyn E., 10
Bunun people, 2, 14, 17, 210, 211, 215–17; 225; 262n11; 276n1. *See also* Soqluman, Neqou; Tamapima, Topas
Burao Yiling, 59, 62–63
Burao Yilu (Ilu Buraug), 15, 37, 57–64, *61*, 69, 233; "Four Generations of Wa Women" ["Wazu sidai nüren"] (1995), 59, 60–62; "Language of Bauhinia Flower" ["Zijing hua wuyu"] (2018), 59; "Mengdong River" ["Mengdong he"] (2016), 63; "Moon Mountain" ["Yueliang shan"] (2002), 59; *Pledge to the Sacred Tree: Song from the Heart of a Wa Woman* [*Shenshu de yueding: Wazu nüren xinzhong de ge*] (2010), 59
Burke, Carolyn L., 125
Byler, Darren, 117, 122–23, 124, 265n41

"Call of the Black Tent, The" (Ju Kalsang), 175
Cameron, James, 227
Campanella, Tommaso, 28–29
Canada, 214–15
cannibalism, 115, 169, 173
Cantonese identity, 9
Caohai Nature Reserve, 48
Cao Yu, 78
capitalism, 140, 147, 194, 206, 211, 233; Anthropocene and, 207; in evolutionary stages of civilization, 32; resource extraction and, 74, 94, 98, 182, 185; technocapitalism, 227
"Capitalocene," 150, 160, 271n4

carbon dioxide emissions, 7, 240n14
carbon imaginary, 70, 83, 89, 95
censorship, 95, 96, 185, 188
center–periphery. *See* core/center-periphery metaphysics
Central Asia, 7, 107, 267n66; China's Belt and Road Initiative (BRI) in, 4; "restoration" of natural ecosystems in, 8
Central Plain, of North China, 19
Chang, Chia-ju, 189, 196, 257n42, 276n2
"'Changes' in My Homeland" (Anonymous Tibetan Poet), 183–85
"Chapter: Fear" (Anonymous Tibetan Poet), 182–83
Chen, Richard Rongbin, 217
Chen Danling, 14
Cheng Xiangzhan, 9
Chen Kuan-hsing, 13, 192–93, 194, 195, 224, 277n7
Chen Liang, 19, 20
Chen Ran, 119
Chen Sihe, 196, 214, 224
Chen Ying-chen, 217
China, dynastic/imperial: Five Dynasties, 19; Jin, 19; Ming, 20, 23, 193; Northern Song, 24; Qin, 22, 43; Southern Song, 19, 23; Sui, 83; Tang, 79, 132, 174; Yuan, 19. *See also* Han dynasty; Qing (Manchu) dynasty
China, People's Republic of (PRC), 10, 236; Anti-Rightist Movement (1956), 30; assimilation policy for ethnic minorities, 241–42n32; autonomous regions, 2; economic reform era, 45; environmental law of, 44; "Go West" policies, 4, 70; Great Leap Forward, 32–33, 85; "minority nationalities" (*shaoshu minzu*), 10; as multinational country, 10, 13;

national unity ideal of, 10, *11*; neoliberal strategies in, 71; "Open up the West" campaign, 159; Spiritual Pollution Campaign (1983), 47; "urban-rural integration" regional policies, 134–35; Wild Animal Protection Law (1988), 104, 106. *See also* Communist Party, Chinese (CCP); Cultural Revolution
China, pre-Qin, 4, 19, 26; concept of civilization, 17–18; Shang dynasty, 17, 26; Warring States period, 17, 32; Zhou kings, 17, 26, 243n51
China, Republic of, 10, 72, 104, 189, 190, 191. *See also* KMT; Taiwan
Chinese Dream, 25
Chinese Western Literature (journal), 35
"Chinese westerns" (film genre), 35
Chinese Writers Association, 75, 83, 107, 148
Chiu Kuei-fen, 196, 214, 224
Chi Zijian, 211, 213
Chou, Shiuhhuah Serena, 227
Chow, Kai-wing, 31
Christianity, 58, 97–98, 113, 261n68, 263n23
Chung, Yuehtsen Juliette, 30
Chunqiu, 19
Cinema Illuminating Reality (Fan, 2022), 232
City of the Sun, The [*La Città del Sole*] (Campanella, 1602), 29
civilization, 4, 12, 13, 17, 93, 106, 107, 139, 214; agrilogistics and, 21; borders of Han civilization, 47, 71, 190; cannibalistic violence of, 150, 169, 173; "clash of civilizations," 74; comparison of European and pre-Qin concepts of, 18; "Grassland Culture" and, 72, 73; hierarchies

civilization (*continued*)
within, 19, 27, 173; industrial, 5; nomadic culture incorporated into, 75, 76; nomads as barrier to expansion of, 71; racist constructions of, 19, 25, universalizing cosmologies of, 1, 3, 23, 25. *See also* ecological civilization (*shengtai wenming*); *tianxia* ("all under Heaven")

Civilizational Wilderness [*Wenming huangye*] (Wang Chia-Hsiang, 1990), 208–9, 280n52

Clarke, Arthur C., 232

cli-fi (climate change fiction, rooted in science fiction), 17, 193, 227

climate change/crisis, 1, 2, 4, 14, 17, 225

coastal reclamation, 8

Cobo Report (UN Report on Indigenous Populations), 10, 11

Cold Spring Harbor Station for Experimental Evolution, 29

Cold War, 13, 230

Collected Works of Pan Guangdan, The (Pan Naimu, ed., 1993), 30

colonialism. *See* imperialism and colonialism; settler-colonial policies

Communist Party, Chinese (CCP), 5, 72, 95, 157, 240n14; "Democratic Reform" in Ngawa, 154–58; ecology of northwest Xinjjiang altered by, 103; indebtedness engineered via Confucian family metaphors, 168; mandates to develop western regions, 36; Mandumai's membership in, 75, 79; taxonomy of ethnic minorities, 31–32; univeralism and, 25–26. *See also* China, People's Republic of (PRC)

Compilation of Herbal Remedies [*Bencao gangmu*] (Li Shizhen), 197

Concept of Nature, The (Whitehead), 51

Confucian philosophy, 24, 73, 79, 139; agrilogistics and, 23; anthropocentrism of, 6, 39; Chinese exceptionalism and, 24; classics, 22; ethic of moderation, 40; eugenics and, 27; exertion of moral pressure on central authorities, 46; on human/animal relations, 107, 262n13; neo-Confucianist syncretism and, 194; resonance theories, 257n28; rural cultural matrix of, 144. *See also* neo-Confucianism

Confucius, 27, 30

"Connect to the Vital Energies of Heaven and Earth: Transcend the Limits of the Human" (Xu Zhaoshou, 2012), 139

Conrad, Joseph, 151

conservation movement, U.S., 4, 214

Copenhaver, Joby G., 125

core/center–periphery metaphysics, 14, 15, 17, 73, 173–74; agrilogistics and, 23; core fortified with reproductive potency from periphery, 25; core reinvigorated with energy from periphery, 69, 70, 93; grain and, 24–25; infusion of exoticism from peripheries, 47; Yellow River floods and, 24; *yin-yang* complementarity and, 40. *See also* Hanspace cosmology

cosmologies, 2, 13; Han Chinese, 15, 24, 47, 228, 232; imperial(ist), 4, 127, 234, 235; Indigenous, 3, 4, 12–13; 75, 195, 232; Mongolian, 79; shamanistic, 4, 88; Tibetan, 16, 147; universality

318   *Index*

and, 1, 3, 23, 25; Western and non-Western, 9
cosmotechnics, 3
Covid-19 pandemic, 228
Cultural Revolution, 39, 44, 47, 55, 88, 125; as setting in fiction, 36, 76, 88, 89, 155; environmental devastation, 32–33, 37, lack of schooling during, 62; persecution of Uyghurs during, 125; urban youth sent to countryside during, 36–37, 90; women identified with, 55–56

Dalai Lama, 33, 150
Dao (metaphysical category), 1
Daodejing (Laozi), 1, 235
Daofeng Inland Sea [*Daofeng neihai*] (Wang Chia-hsiang, 1997), 211–14, 280n52
Daoism, 6, 9, 22, 37, 139, 142, 240n15; creation stories, 110; ecological sustainability and, 39; feminine principle valorized by, 56; in *The King of Trees*, 40, 41; neo-Confucian syncretism and, 41, 194; as peripheral in Hanspace cosmology, 24, 47; perspectivism of, 41, 55; in *Soul Mountain*, 48; *wuwei* ("effortless action"), 40; in *The Man with the Compound Eyes*, 228.
"dark ecology," 70, 95, 99
Dark Ecology (Morton), 22, 227
dark humor, 102, 123–28
Darwin, Charles, 29, 31
Darwin, Leonard, 29
Datong shu [*One World/Book of the Great Community*] (Kang), 27
Davenport, Charles, 29
Davies, Henry Rodolph, 31

Dawut, Rahile, 116, 264n29
De, Prince, 260n65
decolonization, 3, 5, 195, 232, 235; of ecocriticism, 12, 17, 223; of minds and practices, 1, 220, 236; science and, 4; of subjectivity, 194, 195
"Deep in the Woods" ["Biye shenchu"] (Mandumai, 1985), 79, 257n29
Deep Love for the Cold Sea [*Lenghai qingshen*] (Syaman Rapongan, 1997), 219–23, 235
deforestation, 22, 37, 41, 42, 66, 157, 250n15, 251n28, 253n52; ecological reportage on, 44–45; in Taiwan, 191
Dekyi Drolma, 16, 147, *149*, 159, 178; "Grassland Feelings" ["Caoyuan guanhuai"], 180–83; "Losing Myself" ["Shiqu de wo"], 180; "Sheep Turd" [Yang fendan"], 179–80; "Straight and Bent" ["Zhi yu wan"], 179; "There is Running Water from Henan: To Jingdu" ["You yizhong huoshui laizi tianhe zhi nan—zhi Jingdu"], 178–79; "Young Brother Searched for the Missing Cow" ["Didi qu zhao zoudiao de nainiu"], 179
Deleuze, Gilles, 197, 266n59
Deng Xiaoping, 45, 79
Derrida, Jacques, 146, 235, 249n13
Descola, Philippe, 8–9
desertification, 44, 92, 93–94, 260n64; blamed on overgrazing, 71, 78; dune sand and, 85; "greening" efforts to combat, 8n7; Han agrarian logic and, 92
deserts, 8, 82, 83, 85–89, 129–30
Desert Wolf (Guo Xuebo), 82
deterritorialization, 13
dialogic, Bakhtinian, 209
Di Cosmo, Nicola, 73

Index   319

Dictionary of Xinjiang, A [*Xinjiang cidian*] (Shen Wei, 2005), 113–14, 128–32
Distant Sunflower Fields [*Yaoyuan de xiangrikui di*] (Li Juan, 2021), 133
Dong Zhongshu, 6
Doyle, Laura, 189
DPP [Democratic Progressive Party] (Taiwan), 192
Dream of Ding Village [*Dingzhuang meng*] (Yan Lianke), 121
Driscoll, Mark, 151
dualism, Western, 139
Dutch East India Company, 211
Dzungaria, 100, map *101*

Earth Charter (2000), 203
East Asian–Australasian Flyway, 8
Eastern Han dynasty, 19
Ecoambiguity: Environmental Crises and East Asian Literatures (Thornber), 14, 250n18, 258n44, 282n80
ecocriticism, 8, 9, 14, 16, 155, 167, 239n2; Anglo/European concepts and, 14; anti-agrarian, 82–83, 85–89; decolonization of, 12, 17, 223; diversification of, 2; rhetorical logic of Beijing western, 139; in Taiwan, 189
ecofeminism, 22, 78, 79; in Dekyi Drolma's poetry, 180; in fiction of Guo Xuebo, 87; in Hulmanbek's *Eternal Lamb*, 107–16
ecoliterature, 2, 79, 195, 232; ecological reportage, 43–46; by ethnic minority or Indigenous writers, 233; geopolitics and, 2; in Inner Mongolia, 12; inter-Asian regional knowledge in, 14–17; Kazakh, 12; Mongolian, 12, 69, 249n13;

post-Mao, 39, 277n16; Taiwanese, 12, 196, 208, 249n13; Tibetan, 12, 147; in Xinjiang, 102, 116
ecological civilization (*shengtai wenming*), 4, 25, 90, 93, 94, 102, 193; philosophical ideals of, 6; Belt and Road Initiative (BRI) and, 5–8; Sinocentric discourse of, 13; naturalizes extraction from peripheries to serve the core, 23; Chinese exceptionalism and, 25
ecological migration (*shengtai yimin*), 5
ecopoetry, Tibetan, 173–85; Wa, 59–60, 63–64; Yi (Nuosu Yi), 64–68
ecosystems: desert, 85–87, 89; diverse cosmologies of, 69; freshwater, 7; grassland (steppe), 70, 71, 89, 90; limestone, 8; marsh, 211; mountain (plateau), 74, 105, 163, 188; ocean (coastal), 8, 12, 217; urban, 131
ecotourism, 185, 203
Ellis, Havelock, 28
Elvin, Mark, 21, 22
Embodied Memories, Embedded Healing (Liu and Huang, eds., 2021), 232
Empty Mountain [*Kongshan*] (Alai, 2009), 148, 154–58, 272n23; *Celestial Fire* [*Tianhuo*] (second volume), 155; *Scattered in the Wind* [*Suifeng piaosan*] (first volume), 154–57
"Empty Valley Orchid" ["Konggu lan"] (Zhang Chang, 1979), 250n22
"enemy-cursing" rituals, of Yi people, 67
Engels, Friedrich, 31
English language, 15
Enwer, Mutellip, 124
Epic of Gesar (ca. 12th century CE), 160
Epic of Gesar, The [*Gesa'er Wang*] (Alai, 2009), 148

Eternal Albatross [*Yongyuan de xinweng*] (Liu Ka-shiang, 2008), 204, 279n38
Eternal Lamb [*Yongsheng yang*] (Hulmanbek, 2003), 100, 107–16, 200, 236; documentary film adaptation (Gao Feng, 2010), 262n15; "Grandmother Mud" ["Zumu ni"], 109, 114; "Memories of Baitag Bogd Mountain," 109, 262–63n18
Ethnicities Literature (journal), 127
eugenics, 15, 20, 26–27, 94, 173; in nineteenth-century America, 76, 92; in post-Mao China, 30; in *Wolf Totem*, 90
"Eugenics and Its Founders" (Zhou Jianren, 1920), 28–29
"Eugenics Movement Around the World in the Last Twenty Years, The" (Pan, 1925), 29–30
"Eugenics Problem in China, The" (Pan, 1924), 29
Evenki people, 211, 213
Evolution and Ethics (Huxley, 1898), 26
exceptionalism, American, 5
exceptionalism, Chinese, 5, 15, 24, 25–33
Exposition of Benevolence (Tan), 27
extinction, 4, 8, 14, 81; post-extinction world, 16, 82, 99; Sixth Mass Extinction, 211, 226, 228
Eyes of the Sea, The [*Dahai zhiyan*] (Syaman Rapongan, 2018), 223
Eyes of the Sky, The [*Tiankong de yanjing*] (Syaman Rapongan, 2007), 220, 223

"Face the Great Northwest, Develop a New Type of 'Western'" (Zhong Dianfei, conference keynote address, 1984), 34

"Failure, The" ["Shibaizhe"] (Amantay, 2016), 265n40
Fan, Victor, 232
Fanjingshan Nature Reserve (Guizhou Province), 55
Fei Xiaotong, 29
"Festival for the Pigs" ["Chosqilargha Bayram"] (Hoshur, 1999), 126–28, 171
Field of Life and Death [*Shengsi chang*] (Xiao Hong, 1934), 268n79
Fire Mother of the Grasslands [*Caoyuan huomu*] (Hulmanbek, 2006), 107–8
Fiskesjö, Magnus, 233–34, 235–36, 264n28, 286n5
Five Dynasties, 19
Flight Ways (Van Dooren), 80
Fly Eyes [*Yingyan*] (Qiu Huadong, 1998), 249n12
foraging, 4, 21, 71, 205, 211, 233
forests, 23, 49; encounter with primeval forest, 38, 51, 52, 249n12; management of, 23, 245n67; rain forests in Yunnan, 39–40, 44
"Forms of Time and the Chronotope of the Novel" (Bakhtin, 1937), 142
"Four-Eared Wolf and the Hunter, The" ["Si'er lang yu lieren"] (Mandumai, 1997), 79–80, 257n29
"Four Generations of Wa Women" ["Wazu sidai nüren"] (Burao Yilu, 1995), 59, 60–62
Fragments of Aspiration, The [*Qyal qyindilar*] (Qizihan), 104
Fragrance of Happiness, The [*Baqitting ysi*] (Qizihan), 104
Freeman, Mini Aodla, 282n77

Galton, Francis, 30
Gao Feng, 262n15

Index 321

Gao Xingjian, 15, 38, 46, 47, 121, 251n30; Cultural Revolution experience of, 47; Daoist rationalism of, 53; Hegelian dialectic and, 53, 54; as "root-seeking" author, 47, 57; *Wild Man* [*Yeren*] (1985), 48. See also *Soul Mountain* [*Lingshan*]
Gazetteer of Southern Yue (*Nanyue zhi*), 197
GCRP (Grassland Culture Research Project), 72, 73–74
gender stereotypes, 78
Genghis Khan, 71–72, 90, 97
genocide, 33, 153, 173, 264n28
geontopower, 16, 74, 99
geopolitics, 2, 26; logic of coloniality and, 3; in Sinophone world, 10; of Taiwan, 190
Ge Zhaoguang, 26, 57, 232
Ghosh, Amitav, 224–25
Glissant, Édouard, 1, 3, 8, 235
globalization, imperial and Sino-, 16, 147
Global South, 4, 13, 189
Gobi Desert, 12, 100, 136
Goodbody, Axel, 171, 266n59
"Grassland Feelings" ["Caoyuan guanhuai"] (Dekyi Drolma), 180–83
Grassland Literary Culture Series, 4
"grassland logic," 69, 92, 93
Great Derangement, The (Ghosh), 224–25
Greater East Asia Co-Prosperity Sphere, 193, 277n11
Great Leap Forward, 32–33, 85
Great Pacific Garbage Patch (Trash Vortex), 226, 230
green governance, 4, 5, 134, 160, 161, 186, 233
"Green Leaves of Hope" ["Xiwang de lüye"] (Zhang Chang, 1980), 44, 251n28
groundwater pumping, 7

Guangxi Zhuang Autonomous Region, map 2
Guattari, Félix, 197, 266n59
Guizhou Province, 55
Guo, Wei, 6
Guo Peng, 257n29
Guo Xuebo, 14, 16, *84*, 210, 251n28, 253n56; anti-agrarian ecocriticism of, 82–83, 85–89; "dark ecology" and, 70; desert in early stories of, 83, 85–89; in fiction of Guo Xuebo, 86; identification as an ecowriter, 257n34; *Moŋgoliya* [*Menggu liya*] (2014), 94–99, 103, 160, 161, 236, 261n68–69; *Sand Burial* [*Shazang*] (1996), 87–89; "The Sand Fox" ["Shahu"] (1985), 83, 85–86; *Sand Rites* [*Da Mohun*] (1996), 86–87; search for shamanic culture and, 86–87, 96, 97, 260n64, 260n66; *Wolf Totem* film critiqued by, 90, *91*
Gyal, Huatse, 160, 185

Hakka people/language, 9, 189, 217, 276n1
Hall, David, 50–51
Han Chinese, 2, 16; analogist ontology and, 9; assimilation into culture of, 72; Beijing westerns by, 34–57; invention of "Han" ethnic category, 9; male anxiety about "masculine" Inner Asians, 78; Maoist activism and, 32; migration to Xinjiang, 106; opium used to destroy Tibetan chieftain system, 149–50; scientific rationalism and, 93; seen as "universal" and "advanced," 36; shift in views of Mongols, 71–72; Taiwan dominated by, 190, 193; writers in Xinjiang, 102–3

322 *Index*

Han dynasty, 6, 35, 43, 145; Eastern Han, 19; Han–Xiongnu War, 267n66; Western Han, 22
Hanlon, Don, 130, 131
Han Shaogong, 57
Hanshu, 250n15
Hanspace cosmology, 17, 33, 129, 250n18; defined, 245n74; geographical determinism in, 87; Hegelian dialectic synthesized by, 46–57; homogenized nation-state ideal of, 219; patriarchy and, 56; sexual exoticism, 59; "South Seas Dreamscape" as alternative to, 190; syncretism of, 194; Tibetan writers' responses to, 173–74; violent relations comprising, 145; "the west" (*xibu*) and, 35, 36. *See also* core/center–periphery metaphysics
Han Yu, 79
Haraway, Donna, 127, 145, 266n58
Haslund-Christensen, Henning, 96–97, 210
Hau'ofa Epeli, 8, 12, 223, 230
heart-and-mind, philosophy of (*xinxue*), 26, 53, 134, 140
Heaven (*tian*), 23, 245n69
Hegel, Georg Wilhelm Friedrich, 214
Hegelian synthesis, reverse, 53–54
He Huaren, woodblock prints of birds by, 202, *202*, 279n32
Heise, Ursula, 13
He-lien-mo-mo the Humpback Whale [*Zuotoujing Helianmomo*] (Liu Ka-shiang, 1993), 204, 279n38
"Heroic Little Sisters of the Grassland" ["Caoyuan yingxiong xiao jiemei"] (1964), 76, *77*
Heshang [*River Elegy*] (PRC television series), 214

"He zhong" ["Racial Mixing"] (Tang, 1898), 27
Hill of Stray Dogs [*Yegou zhi qiu*] (Liu Ka-shiang, 2007), 204–6, 279n38
historical materialism, 39
Hogan, Linda, 8
Hoklo (Hokkien) people/language, 189, 191, 217, 276n1
Horse, Wolf, Home [*Junma, Canglang, Guxiang*] (Mandumai, 2015), 75–76
"Horse that Belongs to Me, The" ["Shuyu wo de ma"] (Li Juan), 136
Hoshur, Memtimin, 16, 102, 103, 123–28; "Festival for the Pigs" ["Chosqilargha Bayram"] (1999), 126–28, 171; "Idiot" (1989), 124; "Mustache Dispute" ["Burut Majrasi"] (1991), 124–25; *The Sand-Covered City* [*Qum Basqan Sheher*] (2003), 123; *This Is Not a Dream*, 123
"Houseful of Birds, A" (Qizihan), 105–6
Huang Chun-ming, 217
Huang, Hsinya, 8, 218, 223
Huang, Peter I-ming, 8, 14, 217, 218–19
Huang Tsung-Huei, 205
Hu Huanyong, 35
Hui, Yuk, 3, 207, 232
Hui people, 14, 82, 100, 149. *See also* Mao Mei, Zhang Chengzhi
Hu Line (Heihe–Tengchong Line) ecotone, 35, *36*, 37, 248n4
Hulmanbek, Yerkesh, 16, 100, 102, 107–8, *108*, 128, 129; *Eternal Lamb* [*Yongsheng yang*] (2003), 100, 107–16, 200, 236; *Fire Mother of the Grasslands* [*Caoyuan huomu*] (2006), 107–8; "Painless" ["Wutong"] (2005), 114, 120, 121, 123; *Selected Poems from Kazakhstan* [*Hasakesitan shixuan*] (2019), 108

Humes, Bruce, 96, 132
hunter-gatherers, 20, 21, 22, 155
Hunter's Stories [*Angshiliq Hukayalri*] (Qizihan, 2009), 15, 103–7
Huxley, Thomas, 26, 56

Ice Age, 22
"Idiot" (Hoshur, 1989), 124; "idiots" in Indigenous anti-epics, 96–97, 124, 150–53, 155–56
IISNC (International Institute for the Study of Nomadic Civilizations), 72
"Illusion of a Day, The" ["Nyin gcig gi cho 'phrul"] (Takbum Gyel, 1990), 66, 111, 162–65
imperialism and colonialism, 3, 13, 16, 25, 146, 192; as act of geographical violence, 147; Newtonian physics and, 4, 230, 285n106; serialized anti-imperialist novels, 151; "void" as ethical-material concept, 233
indigeneity, 4, 12, 70, 226; abstraction of, 95; ecological knowledge linked to, 11; reterritorialization of trans-indigeneity, 12, 17, 223
Indigenous cosmologies, 3, 13; agency attributed to the nonhuman, 75; human relation to technology and, 4; legal rights and, 11
indigenous–environmentalist alliance, 69, 95, 254n1
Indigenous futurism, 227, 228
Indigenous peoples/Indigenes, 3, 11, 12; in Bolivia, 95; in Brazil, 95; Indigenous scholars, 8; Chinese terms for, 10; in North America, 214–215; *See also* Austronesian Indigenes (Taiwan); knowledge, indigenous; *minzu*; people, Amis; Bai; Bunun; Evenki; Hui; Inuit; Kazakh; Kyrgyz; Macatao; Miao; Mongol; Paiwan; Pingpu; Qiang; Sirayan; Tao; Tibetan; Tujia; Uyghur; Wa; Yao; Yi
industrialization, 158, 208
Inner Mongolia Autonomous Region (IMAR), 12, 14, 75, 89, 103; climatic conditions in, 70–71; coal mining in, 94–98; desertification in, 93–94; Grassland Culture Research Project (GCRP) in, 72–74; Horchin Sandy Lands, 82, 83, 85; institutional precursors of, 260n65; Kubuqi Desert, 8; literacy rates in, 76, 236; literature set in, 69–99; map, 2
Inner Mongolia Art Theater, 76
inter-imperiality, 2, 4, 189, 232
Inter-Imperiality (Doyle), 189
"interlanguage," 217
"In the Mountains" (Wang Wei), 50
Inuit people, 282n77
invasives, invisible, 7
In Xinjiang [*Zai Xinjiang*] (Liu Liangcheng, 2012), 140
Islam and Muslims, 12, 106, 107, 110, 136, 261n9, 262n13; "Bismillah" prayer, 263n22. *See also* Hui people; Kazakhs; Uyghurs
Istanbul, 12–13
"It's a Magical Land" ["Zheshi yipian shenqi de tudi"] (Liang Xiaosheng, 1982), 250n21
Izgil, Tahir Hamut, 265n33

Jabb, Lama, 152
Jameson, Fredric, 227
Jangbu (Dorje Tsering Chenaktsang), 16, 147, 149, 159, 178; *Ani Lachem* (film, 2005), 165; *Kokonor* [*Lake Qinghai*]

(film, 2008), 165, 185–86, 276n71; "Odd Boots" (1998), 165–68; *Tantric Yogi* (film, 2005), 165; "Three Animal Stories" (2001), 168–71; *Voices of the Stone* (film, 2018), *162*, 165; *Yartsa Rinpoche* (film, 2014), 165
Japanese empire, 190, 193, 210, 277n11
Jetñil-Kijiner, Kathy, 229
Jiang Rong, 16, 57, 70, 89, 99
Jia Pingwa, 37
Jones, Andrew, 27
Ju Kalsang (Ju Kelzang), 15, 147, *149*, 174; "The Call of the Black Tent," 175; "Night Ecology," 174; "On Water" ["Shui jilu"] series, 175–78
Junggar Basin (Dzungarian Basin), 100
Jurchens, 19, 21
Justice, Daniel Heath, 214–15

Kafka, Franz, 121, 127, 128, 266n59
Kailash (Meru, Sumeru, Ri-rab), Mount, 178, 186, *187*, 188, 275n59
Kangxi emperor, 244n60
Kang Youwei, 27
Kant, Immanuel, 53, 227
Karakoram Highway, 102, *135*
Kashgar, city of, 12–13, 102, *117*, *120*
Kazakh Hunting Cultures [*Qazaqting sayashiliq madenyeti*] (Qizihan, 2014), 104
Kazakh language, 15. See also Qizihan, Nurila.
Kazakhs, 2, 4, 16, 100, 103, 135–36, 236; creation stories, 110–11; hunting eagles of, 104–5; knowledge of Altay grasslands (Xinjiang), 102, 103–16; See also Amantay, Aydos; Hulmanbek, Yerkesh; Qizihan, Nurila
Kazakhstan, 107, 111, 133

Key Works in Grassland Literature Project, 75
Kham (region of Greater Tibet), 148; map, *149*
King of Chess, The [*Qiwang*] (Ah Cheng, 1984), 40
King of Children, The [*Haiziwang*] (Ah Cheng, 1985), 40
King of Trees, The [*Shuwang*] (Ah Cheng, 1985), 36, 38, 44; abstracted representations in, 46; critical readings of, 250n18; *Soul Mountain* compared with, 47; triumph of neo-Confucian civilization in, 39–43
Kinkley, Jeffrey, 47, 57, 251n30
kinship studies, 8
KMT [Kuomintang] (Nationalist Party), 190–91, 214; facilities set up on Orchid Island, 217–18; "Great China" (Da Zhongguo) discourse, 193; "moving southward" (*nanxiang*) policy, 192, 211; settler-colonial practices of, 191. See also Taiwan (Republic of China)
Knotty Xiao (fictional character), 40–42
knowledge, indigenous, 32, 71, 78, 89; coopted by scientific rationality, 92; Kazakh knowledge of Altay grasslands (Xinjiang), 102, 103–16; of Tao people, 218; of Uyghur people, 130
Kokonor [*Lake Qinghai*] (Jangbu, film, 2008), 165, 185–86, 276n71
Koreans, 21, 82
Kuang Laowu, deleted Weibo post of (2020), *187*, 188
Kubin, Wolfgang, 93
Kubuqi Desert (Inner Mongolia), 8
Kyoto Protocol (1997), 203
Kyrgyz pastoralists, 100, 102, 265n32

Index 325

Land of Little Rain, The [*Kuyu zhidi*] (Wu Ming-yi, 2019), 224
language, as biometric marker, 31
"Language of Bauhinia Flower" ["Zijing hua wuyu"] (Burao Yilu, 2018), 59
Laozi, 1, 203, 235, 277n16
"Last Hunter, The" ["Zuihou de lieren"] (Topas Tamapima, 1987), 215–17, 219, 282n80
"last Indian" laments, 120, 213, 259n49
Last Quarter of the Moon [*E'erguna he you'an*] (Chi Zijian, 2005), 211
"lazy," non-farmers stigmatized as, 20, 21, 78, 185, 212, 216, 244n60
Lee, Haiyan, 257n45, 259n49
Lee Teng-hui, 192, 277n9
Lee Yuan-tseh, 192, 277n9
legalism, 9, 21
Legend of the Lone Ranger, The (film, 1981), 35
Letters from Lodgings (Liu Ka-shiang), 197
Liang Shuming, 53–54
Liberate Nature by Writing [*Yi shuxie jiefang ziran*] (Wu Ming-yi, 2004), 197
Life Among the Qallunaat (Freeman), 282n77
Light, Nathan, 124
Light of the Northern Star, The [*Soltustik uyek jarqili*] (Qizihan), 104
Li Juan, 16, 37, 103, *134*, 199; *Altay Corner* [*Aletai de jiaoluo*] (2010), 133; *Distant Sunflower Fields* [*Yaoyuan de xiangrikui di*] (2021), 133; ecocriticism on literature of, 139; family background, 133; "The Horse that Belongs to Me" ["Shuyu wo de ma"], 136; Hulmanbek as influence on, 137; idea of "labor" and, 134; "The Man Who Watches Me Make Noodles" ["Kanzhe wo lamian de nanren"], 134; "Motorcycling through the Wilderness of Spring" ["Motuoche chuanguo chuntian de huangye"], 138–39; *My Altay* [*Wode Aletai*] (2010), 133, 137; *Nine Chapters on Snow* [*Jiu pian xue*] (2003), 133; "Our Tailor Shop" ["Womende caifeng dian"], 134; "Snowshoe Hare Merely Twenty Centimeters from Springtime, A" ["Li chuntian zhiyou ershi gongfen de xuetu"], 137–38; "urban-rural integration" policies in writing of, 135; *The Way of Sheep Trilogy* [*Yangdao: Sanbuqu*] (2012), 133; *Winter Pasture* [*Dong muchang*] (2012), 133
Lin Biao, 89
Linda Hogan and Contemporary Taiwanese Writers (Huang), 14
Li Shizhen, 197
"Little Grass" (Chinese folk song, 1985), 179–80
"Little Green Mountain Series" (Liu Ka-shiang, 1995), 200, 203–4; "Brown Hawk-Owl," 201–3, *202*; "Discovering the Pond," 200–201
Litzinger, Ralph, 34, 57, 253n57
Liu, Lydia, 28, 29
Liu Cixin, 231–32, 254n2
Liu Ka-shiang [Liu Kexiang], 16–17, 195, 196–208, 277n16; *Bean Mouse Goes Home* [*Doushu huijia*] (2011), 204, 279n38; *Eternal Albatross* (2008), 204, 279n38; *He-lien-mo-mo the Humpback Whale* [*Zuotoujing Helianmomo*] (1993), 204, 279n38; *Hill of Stray Dogs* [*Yegou zhi qiu*]

(2007), 204–6, 279n38; *Letters from Lodgings*, 197; "Little Green Mountain Series" (1995), 200–204, 202; *Pinuocha, the Plover* [*fengniao pinuocha*] (1991), 204, 279n38; as pioneer of ecological consciousness, 196, 278n19; protests on behalf of animals and environment, 205, 280n42; "Sandpiper" ["Binyu"] (1982), 198–99; *Tiger Land Cats* [*Hudi mao*] (2016), 204, 206, 279n38; urban ecology tours led by, 207; *Views of a Flying Squirrel* [*Xiao wushu de kanfa*] (1988), 197
Liu Liangcheng, 37, 103, 119, 134, 139, 199; *Loose Earth* [*Xutu*] (2006), 140; *One Man's Village* [*Yigeren de cunzhuang*] (1998), 140, 142; Shawan County villages as home region of, 145, 269–70n87; "village as chronotope" notion of, 140–46, 180; "village philosopher" persona of, 133; *Zaokong* (2009), 140, *In Xinjiang* [*Zai Xinjiang*] (2012), 140
Liu Shi, 257n29
Liu Wenhui, 149
Liu Zaifu, 39
Liu Zhirong, 139
Liu Zongyuan, 48, 50, 79
Li Zehou, 39, 54
Loose Earth [*Xutu*] (Liu Liangcheng, 2006), 140
Lord Jim (Conrad), 151
"Losing Myself" ["Shiqu de wo"] (Dekyi Drolma), 180
Louie, Kam, 55, 56
"Love, Marriage, and the Future of our Race" (Zhou Jianren, 1922), 29
Lovers and Prostitutes [*Qingren yu jinü*] (Topas Tamapima, 1992), 215

Lu Shuyuan, 257n42
Lu Xun (Zhou Shuren), 28, 29, 71–72, 124, 169, 209, 274n49; "A Madman's Diary" ["Kuangren riji"] (1918), 124, 169, 173; "New Year's Sacrifice" ["Zhufu"] (1923), 28; "Technique for Creating Humans" ["Zaoren shu"] (1905), 28

Ma Bo, 254n2
Macatao Indigenes (Taiwan), 281n65
"Madman's Diary, A" ["Kuangren riji"] (Lu Xun, 1918), 124, 169, 173
magical realism, 47, 226, 230
Manchukuo, 96, 260n65
Manchus, 82
Mandarin Chinese language, 15, 253n61; Indigenous literature in, 83, 103, 147, 211, 217, 283n82; Taiwanese literature in, 189; translations into, 15, 70, 75, 103
Mandumai, 15, 16, 70, 83, 89, 164–65; anthropocosmic resonance between humans and animals in fiction of, 79; concessions to gender stereotypes, 78; "Deep in the Woods" ["Biye shenchu"] (1985), 79, 257n29; "The Four-Eared Wolf and the Hunter" ["Si'er lang yu (stet) lieren(stet)] (1997), 79–80, 257n29; *Horse, Wolf, Home* [*Junma, Canglang, Guxiang*] (2015), 76; "Old White-Hair" ["Lao Cangtou"] (1987), 80–81, 82; "Source of Fortune" ["Ruizhao zhiyuan"] (1981), 76, 78
Manifest Destiny, 5
"Man's Determination Conquers Nature" slogan [*ren ding sheng tian*], 32, 155

"Man Who Understands Donkeys, A" ["Tong lüxing de ren"] (Liu Liangcheng), 145–46

"Man Who Watches Me Make Noodles, The" ["Kanzhe wo lamian de nanren"] (Li Juan), 134

Man Without a Mailbox, The [*Meiyou Xinxiang de nanren*] (Syaman Rapongan, 2022), 223

Man with the Compound Eyes, The [*Fuyan ren*] (Wu Ming-yi, 2011), 193, 224, 225–27, 236, 277n16

Maoism, 31, 32–33, 39; collectivization under, 104, 106; critiqued in *zhiqing* literature, 38; deforestation project of, 250n15; environmental destruction and, 37, 44; ideology of mastery over nature, 37, 155; in *The King of Trees*, 40; "mass line," 46; "war against nature" of, 43, 106, 154, 155, 262n10; "will to power" of, 39, 41, 105

Mao Mei, 14

Mao Zedong, 20, 27, 30, 47, 272n20; "Long Life Palace," 157, 158; "Man's Determination Conquers Nature" slogan and, 32; Mao worship as new religion, 158; on resources in territory of minority nationalities, 31, 34; on "struggle against heaven," 37

Marx, Karl, 153

Marxism, 9, 40, 58, 72; Hegelian-Marxist historiography, 153; nationalities in Marxist theory, 31; on "primitive communism" ("primitive society"), 31, 58; subjectivity and, 39

Marxism and the National Colonial Question (Stalin, 1913), 31

masculinity, 78, 146

May Fourth movement, 27, 29, 38

Ma Yuan, 57

medicine, traditional Chinese, 8, 25, 89

Memory of Waves [*Hailang de jiyi*] (Syaman Rapongan, 2002), 223

Men and Gods in Mongolia (Haslund-Christensen, 1935), 96

Mencius (*Mengzi*), 22, 23, 39

Mencius and Mencian philosophy, 6, 23, 27, 256n29; agrarian metaphors in, 39, 41; Farmer of Song story, 41; four sprouts of virtue (*siduan*), 42; "love with distinctions" principle, 18, 243n46; on resource management, 22–23

Mendel, Gregor, 30

"Mengdong River" ["Mengdong he"] (Burao Yilu, 2016), 63

Merchant, Carolyn, 78

Mergen, 95

"Metropolis and Mental Life, The" (Simmel, 1905), 119, 120

Miao people, 47

Middle East, 7

Midnight's Children (Rushdie, 1981), 217

Mignolo, Walter, 1, 3

Miller, Ian, 245n67

Millward, James, 108

Ming dynasty, 20, 23, 149, 193

Minnan hua, 9, 191

minzu (nationality/ethnicity), 10, 12, 31, 32, 71, 241–42n32

minzu tuanjie (unification of national minorities), 12–13

misogyny, 55, 61, 87

modernity, 3, 8, 134–35, 183, 249n12; dichotomies of, 49; human–nature relation and, 140; industrial, 159; technomodernity, 226, 228; Western influences and, 9

Mohism, 18, 41

328 *Index*

Møller, Olsen, Astrid, 269n86
Mongolia (Outer Mongolia), 14, 71, 72, 74, 133
Mongolian language, 15, 70, 89
Mongolian Plateau, 73, 74
Mongols, 2, 14, 21, 71–74, 244n60; Andai Dance, 253n56; as agriculturalists, 21, 71; cosmology of, 79; gender stereotypes in representation of, 78, 93; literacy, 76, 236; rulers of Yuan dynasty, 19; views of sand, 85–86; "wolflike" genes of, 4, 93–94. See also Guo Xuebo; Inner Mongolia Autonomous Region; Mandumai
Mongoliya [*Menggu liya*] (Guo Xuebo, 2014), 94–99, 103, 160, 161, 236, 261nn68–69
"Moon Mountain" ["Yueliang shan"] (Burao Yilu, 2002), 59
Moore, Jason, 212
Moran, Thomas, 49, 53, 270n97
Morgan, Lewis Henry, 31
Mori Ushinosuke, 210, 211
Morton, Timothy, 21–22, 37, 69, 227; on agrilogistics, 83, 257n42
Mother's Songs [*Ana jiri*] (Qizihan), 104
"Motorcycling through the Wilderness of Spring" ["Motuoche chuanguo chuntian de huangye"] (Li Juan), 138–39
Mountain Patterns: The Survival of Nuosu Culture in China (Bamo Qubumo, 2000), 64
Mullaney, Thomas, 31
Muslims. See Islam and Muslims
"Mustache Dispute" ["Burut Majrasi"] (Hoshur, 1991), 124–25
My Altay [*Wode Aletai*] (Li Juan, 2010), 133, 137

Myanmar (Burma), 14
My Neighbor Totoro (Japanese anime film, 1998), 200, 279n30
My Tibetan Childhood (Naktsang Nulo, 2007), 33

Naktsang Nuden Lobsang [Naktsang Nulo] (*nags tshang nus ldan blo bzang*), 33
nationalism, Chinese, 9, 93, 94
nationalism, Taiwanese, 193, 194
national minorities, 10, 13
nation-states, 4, 5, 10, 26
Native Americans, 92, 124, 130
natural history, 27
naturalism, ontology of, 4, 9, 99, 195
natural selection, 26, 30, 32
nature, 46, 139; abstraction of, 70, 95; alienation from, 146; anthropomorphization of, 227; benevolent view of, 6; conceptualized as separate from humans, 83; conquest of, 154; dualistic bifurcation with culture, 85; indeterminacy of, 229; Mao's war against nature, 32; mastery over, 37, 41; "naturecultures" of Haraway, 127; primeval feminine Nature, 49; temporal conception of, 9
nature reserves, 47, 48
nature writing (*ziran xiezuo*), 189, 195–208
neo-Confucianism, 15, 16, 37, 43, 102, 250n18; in Beijing westerns, 38, 69; bifurcated self in, 54, 121; hierarchical complementarities and, 235; scientific rationalism and, 48, 142, 206; urban–rural dichotomy and, 139–40
neoliberalism, 2, 11, 79, 188
New Culture movement, 27

New Film Age (journal), 35
"New Year's Sacrifice" [*Zhufu*] (Lu Xun, 1923), 28, 173
Ngawa [Aba] Tibetan and Qiang Autonomous Prefecture (Sichuan), 48, 148; chieftain system in, 148, 153, 271n1; ethnic diversity of, 149; map, *149*; Tibetan uprisings in (1956), 154
"Night Ecology" (Ju Kalsang), 174
Nine Chapters on Snow [*Jiu pian xue*] (Li Juan, 2003), 133
Ningxia Hui Autonomous Region, map 2
nomadic peoples, 4, 17, 135; as barrier to expansion of civilization, 71; gender inequity and, 163; sense of time, 111; Tibetan black tent, 174–75, *175*. *See also* pastoralism
nongcun (countryside), 140, 269n81
North America, 76, 213, 214, 249n13
Northern Song dynasty, 24
"Notes on the Pekingese" (Takbum Gyel, 2009), 171–73
nuclear-waste disposal, 191
Nurbergen, 263n27
Nyangweso, Mary, 284n100

object relations theory, 115–16, 123
"Ocean in Us, The" (Hau'ofa Epeli, 1998), 223
oceans, 8, 12, 17, 213–14, 230, 284n94; Great Pacific Garbage Patch, 225; Kuroshio Current, 193, 217, 223; ocean-colonizing mindset, 214; Pacific islands as "empty of life" in, 223, 229; Taiwanese southward-oriented ocean imagination, 12, 192, 213; Tao relation to, 218–23; Tibetan plateau formed by, 176, 178; trans-Indigenous connections and, 2, 12, 14, 17, 223–24

"Odd Boots" (Jangbu, 1998), 165–68
"Old White-Hair" ["Lao Cangtou"] (Mandumai, 1987), 80–81, 82
One Man's Village [*Yigeren de cunzhuang*] (Liu Liangcheng, 1998), 140, 142, 269–70n87, 270n97; "A Man Who Understands Donkeys" ("Tong lüxing de ren"), 145–46; "The Things I Change" ("Wo gaibian de shiwu"), 141–42; "What I Stopped" ("Wo dangzhule shenme"), 142–43
On Lamatasinsin and Dahu Ali [*Guanyu Lamadaxianxian yu Lahe Alei*] (Wang Chia-Hsiang, 1995), 208n52, 209–11
On the Ten Major Relationships (Mao Zedong), 34
ontologies, 8–10, 12, 13, 49, 99, 143, 229
"On Water" ["Shui jilu"] series (Ju Kalsang), 175–78
Opium Wars, 148
Orchid Island (Lanyu, Pongso no Tao), 215, 217, *219*; KMT facilities set up on, 217–18; nuclear waste–disposal facility on, 191, 220; Tao culture on, 218
organic selectivity, 144, 270n93
Orientalism, 13, 81, 93
"Origin of Patterns, The" (Bamo Qubumo), 64–66
Other Chinas (Litzinger), 34, 253n57
"Our Sacred Land, Their Rubbish Dump" (Woeser, blog), 186
"Our Sea of Islands" (Hau'ofa Epeli, 1994), 223
"Our Tailor Shop" ["Womende caifeng dian"] (Li Juan), 134
Overview of Eugenics, An (Pan, 2012), 30
ovoo (cairn, Mn. *oboo*, Ch. *aobao*), Mongolian, 90, *91*, 96

"Painless" ["Wutong"] (Hulmanbek, 2005), 114–116, 120, 121, 123
Paiwan people, 283n89
Pakistan, China's border with, 102, 135
Pan Guangdan, 29–30
Pan Naimu, 30
pastoralism, 233; in Inner Mongolia, 70–72, 74, 87; in Tibet, 161, 162, 185; in Xinjiang, 100, 103. *See also* nomadic peoples
patriarchy, 22, 24, 56, 57; colonial power relations and, 109, 168, 194; Wa people and, 60
Payne, Christopher, 209–211
"Peach Blossom Spring" ["Taohuayuan ji"] (Tao Qian), 89
Pearson, Karl, 29
Pedersen, Morton, 78, 99
People's Liberation Army (PLA), 154
personhood, 9, 39
perspectivism, 9, 13, 55, 111, 241n27
Philosophy of World History (Hegel, 1837), 214
phrenology, 29
Pingpu people (plains Indigenes of Taiwan), 190, 281n65
Pinuocha, the Plover [*fengniao pinuocha*] (Liu Ka-shiang, 1991), 204, 279n38
Plato, 28
Pledge to the Sacred Tree: Songs from the Heart of a Wa Woman [*Shenshu de yueding: Wazu nüren xinzhong de ge*] (Burao Yilu, 2010), 59
pluriverse, 3
poetics of relation, 8
Poetics of Relation (Glissant), 1, 3
"Polar/Arctic Silk Road," 8
political correctness, Chinese communist, 75, 76, 81, 88; Aku Tonpa stories and, 152, 271n12; class background and, 156; gender types and, 78; Xinjiang "migrant" literature and, 132
pollution, 8, 44, 115, 118, 181, 191
posthumanism, 29, 74, 75, 82, 88
postmodernism, 9, 227
poststructuralism, 194, 235
Povinelli, Elizabeth, 74, 88–89
Powell, Miles, 130, 214
Prayer for Nature [*Ziran daogaozhe*] (Wang Chia-Hsiang, 1992), 209, 280n52
"primitive" 18, 47, 49, 57, 76, 234; "primitive communism" ("primitive society"), 31, 58
Private Life [*Siren shenghuo*] (Chen Ran, 1995), 119
Process and Reality: An Essay in Cosmology (Whitehead), 54, 142
productivity, 8, 23
Ptackova, Jarmila, 161
"Pygmy Tribe, The" ["Zhuru zu"] (Topas Tamapima), 215

qi (psychophysical energy, vital energy, breath), 19, 20, 139, 272n18
Qiang people, 47, 149, 273n31
Qin dynasty, 22, 43; pre-Qin, 4, *18*, 19, 26
Qing (Manchu) dynasty, 20, 72, 83, 96; expansion into Xinjiang, Tibet, and Mongolia, 100, 148; Han migration to Inner Mongolia during, 70–71; late Qing science fiction, 227, 228; reforestation during, 23; semicolonization of China by European powers during, 148; Taiwan and, 190
Qinghai Nationalities Press, 33
Qinghai Plateau, 25

Qinghai Province, 12, 33, *149*, 159, 161; Golok Prefecture, 174; Malho grasslands, 160; Malho Mongolian Autonomous County, 165, 178. *See also* Amdo

Qiu Huadong, 249n12

Qizihan, Ahman, 104

Qizihan, Nurila, 16, 102, 103, 104, 108; *The Fragments of Aspiration (Qyal qyindilar)*, 104; *The Fragrance of Happiness (Baqitting ysi)*, 104; "A Houseful of Birds," 105–6; *Hunter's Stories [Angshiliq Hukayalri]* (2009), 15, 103–7; *Kazakh Hunting Cultures [Qazaqting sayashiliq madenyeti]* (2014), 104; *The Light of the Northern Star (Soltustik uyek jarqili)*, 104; *Mother's Songs (Ana jiri)*, 104; *The Sound of Awil (Awil awenderi)*, 104; "We Have Surpassed the Bears," 106–7

Question Concerning Technology in China, The (Yuk Hui, 2016), 232

racism, 10, 20, 26, 31, 147, 194, 257n45; assimilationist, 19; environmental, 14, 79, 81, 191, 282n80; in European concept of civilization, 25; inter-imperiality and, 194; internalized, 183; pan-Asian, 71–72; "radioactive racism," 229; speciesism compared to, 266n52. *See also* Social Darwinism

realism, literary, 28, 29

realpolitik, 2, 4, 78, 192

Red Poppies (Alai, 2003). See *As the Dust Settles [Chenai luoding]*

reforestation (afforestation), 23, 83

relationality, 5, 8, 9, 13, 53, 110, 143, 229, 236

ren (love of kinship), 24, 28, 47

Renzhuo (journal), 178

Republic (Plato), 28

resource extraction, 8, 16, 23, 74, 94, 98, 147, 161, 182, 185

rites (*li*), 18, 24, 47

River Elegy [Heshang] (TV drama, 1980s), 93

Robin, Françoise, 174, 182

"root-seeking" literary aesthetics (*xungen wenxue*), 38, 40, 46, 57, 193

Routes in the Dream [Shuimian de hangxian] (Wu Ming-yi, 2007), 224

Rushdie, Salman, 117, 217

Sabit, Anar, 253n61

Sacred Routes of Uyghur History, The (Thum), 117

Said, Edward W., 147

Sakamoto, Hiroko, 27, 30

Sakuliu Pavavaljung, 283n89

Salimjan, Guldana, 103, 263n22

Sand Burial [Shazang] (Guo Xuebo, 1996), 87–89, 106

Sand-Covered City, The [Qum Basqan Sheher] (Hoshur, 2003), 123

"Sand Fox, The" ["Shahu"] (Guo Xuebo, 1985), 83, 85–86

"Sandpiper" ["Binyu"] (Liu Ka-shiang, 1982), 198–99

Sand Rites [Da Mohun] (Guo Xuebo, 1996), 86–87

Sanft, Charles, 43

sanjiao heyi syncretism, 41

Śāntarakṣita, 81

Santos-Granero, Fernando, 10

Scarfe, Adam C., 143

science, 5, 39, 46; fetishization of, 274n49; modernization and, 132; Newtonian physics, 4, 230, 285n106;

positivism, 99; scientific rationalism, 48, 70, 93, 195, 206
Science and the Modern World (Whitehead), 51, 143–44
science fiction, 28, 151, 231, 254n2
Science Fiction World (journal), 148
scientism, 26, 233
Scott, James, 124
Secret History of the Mongols, The (thirteenth-century epic), 97
Selected Poems from Kazakhstan [*Hasakesitan shixuan*] (Hulmanbek, 2019), 108
self-orientalism, 81
self/other dichotomy, 53, 54, 141
settler-colonial policies: in American and Chinese exceptionalism, 5, 35; "last Indian" laments and, 259n49; mappings of Pacific Island states and, 223; in Taiwan, 190, 191; in Tibetan regions, 188; in Xinjiang, 102, 103, 146. See also imperialism and colonialism
sexology, 28
shamanism, 4, 12, 13, 110; Andai Dance (Mongol ritual), 253n56; Bön and, 153, 272n18; *Daodejing* of Laozi and, 235; Daoist cosmology and, 228; eternity of the animistic world, 256n17; in Guo Xuebo's fiction, 86–87, 96, 260n64; in Mandumai's fiction, 79; as "ontology of transition," 99; as peripheral in Hanspace cosmology, 24; prohibited under socialism, 86–87; radical nonattachment to life, 75; seen as scientifically irrational, 75. See also animism
Shang dynasty, 17, 26
Shanxi Province, 39

Shapiro, Judith, 32
Sha Qing, 44
"Sheep Turd" ["Yang fendan"] (Dekyi Drolma), 179–80
Shen Congwen, 37, 57
Shennongjia National Nature Reserve, 48
shenshizhuyi ("mythorealism"), 121
Shen Wei, 16, 102, 113–14, 128–32, 146. See also *Dictionary of Xinjiang, A* [*Xinjiang cidian*]
Sherburne, Donald, 53
Shihezi, city of, 100
Shiji (*Records of the Grand Historian*), 19, 250n15
Shinjilt, 35
Shu Jinyu, 144
Sichuan Province, 48, 49, 157, 273n31. See also Ngawa [Aba] Tibetan and Qiang Autonomous Prefecture
Silent Grassland, The (Takbum Gyel), 162
Silk Road, 108, 267n66
Simmel, Georg, 119, 120
Singer, Peter, 266n52
Sinicization/Sinification, cultural, 11, 19
Sino-globalization, 16, 147
Sirayan Indigenes (Taiwan), 21, 211, 212–13, 281n65
Slingerland, Edward, 23
Slovic, Scott, 189, 276n2
"Snowshoe Hare Merely Twenty Centimeters from Springtime, A" ["Li chuntian zhiyou ershi gongfen de xuetu"] (Li Juan), 137–38
Social Darwinism, 4, 31, 130, 143, 155
socialist realism, 32, 38, 118
Song, Lili, 260n64
Song dynasty: Northern Song, 24; Southern Song, 19, 23

"Song of Liangzhou, A" ["Liangzhou ci"] (Wang Han), 132, 267nn66–67
Soqluman, Neqou, 14
Soul Mountain [*Lingshan*] (Gao Xingjian, 1989), 38, 46–57, 194, 235, 265n40; construction of identity with and through Others, 53, 54; narrative tension between "I" and "You" chapters, 49, 51–52, 56–57; Rapongan's *Deep Love* compared to, 235; Taiwanese nature writing compared to, 195; Tursun's *The Backstreets* compared to, 121, 122; Wa headhunting referenced in, 59
Sound of Awil, The [*Awil awenderi*] (Qizihan), 104
"Source of Fortune" ["Ruizhao zhiyuan"] (Mandumai, 1981), 76, 78
South Asia, 7
South China Sea, 4, 284n94
Southeast Asia, 4, 25, 193, 236; competition over markets in, 190; "moving southward" (*nanxiang*) policy of Taiwan and, 192; Sinophone literatures of, 284n94
Southern Song dynasty, 19, 23
South Seas, 12, 17
"South Seas Dreamscape," 190
Southwest China, 2, 14, 25; literature set in, 34–68
Soviet Union, 104
Spacious Steppe [*cheleger tala zazhi*] (journal), 75
speciesism, 18, 126, 127, 128, 168, 173, 266n52, 266n59
splittism/secessionism (*minzu fenlie*), 10
Spring Breeze [*Chunfeng*] (journal), 192
"Spring Water" (Aku Wuwu, 2015), 67–68
Stalin, Joseph, 31
"Statutes on Fields" (*tianlü*), 43

Stenger, Isabelle, 9
steppe, 89
sterilizations, 27, 30
Sterk, Darryl, 227, 282n80
Stoddard, Helen, 159, 165
Stolen Bicycle, The [*Danche shiqie ji*] (Wu Ming-yi, 2015), 211, 217, 224, 231, 234–35
"Straight and Bent" ["Zhi yu wan"] (Dekyi Drolma), 179
substance philosophy, Aristotelian, 8, 51, 53
Sui dynasty, 83
"Sunset Cicadas" ["Xiyang chan"] (Topas Tamapima), 215
Sun Zhongshan (Sun Yat-sen), 9, 72
Syaman Rapongan, 8, 17, 217–24, *219*; *Black Wings* [*Heise de chibang*] (1999), 223; *Deep Love for the Cold Sea* (1997), 219–23, 235; *The Eyes of the Sea* [*Dahai zhiyan*] (2018), 223; *The Eyes of the Sky* [*Tiankong de yanjing*] (2007), 220, 223; *The Man Without a Mailbox* [*Meiyou Xinxiang de nanren*] (2022), 223; *Memory of Waves* [*Hailang de jiyi*] (2002), 223

Taiwan (Republic of China), 2, 10; *bensheng ren* ("native Taiwanese"), 191, 196; different island imaginations of, *190*; Dutch colonizers of Formosa, 21, 212, 213; February 28 (1947) massacre, 196; Global South and, 4, 189; Han or Hua identity and, 10; history of, 190–91, 211; Indigenous writers in, 12; literary languages in, 189; literature set in, 189–230; officially recognized Indigenous Peoples in, 276n1; *waisheng ren* (Mainlanders),

191, 196; as multinational, 10, 13; *yuanzhu min* ("native inhabitants"), 10. *See also* KMT [Kuomintang]
Taiwan Trilogy film series [*Taiwan sanbuqu*] (Wei Te-sheng), 211
Takbum Gyel, 15, 16, 111, 147, *149*; "The Illusion of a Day" ["Nyin gcig gi cho 'phrul"] (1990), 66, 111, 162–65; "Notes on the Pekingese" (2009), 171–73; *The Silent Grassland*, 162
Taklamakan Desert, 100
Tales of the Moon Colony [*Yueqiu zhimindi xiaoshuo*] (Huangjiang diaosou, 1904), 151
Tang Caichang, 27
Tang dynasty, 79, 132, 174
Tang Junyi, 54
Tan Sitong, 27
Tantric Yogi (Jangbu, film, 2005), 165
Tao of Butterflies, The [*Die dao*] (Wu Ming-yi, 2003), 224
Tao people, 2, 17, 191, 217, 236; knowledge of the ocean, 218–23; protests against nuclear waste, 191, 220. *See also* Orchid Island (Lanyu, Pongso no Tao); Syaman Rapongan
Tao Qian, 89
Tarim Basin, 100, map *101*
Tashkent, 12–13
"Technique for Creating Humans" ["Zaoren shu"] (Lu Xun, 1905), 28
technology, 4, 5, 157, 188; biomimetic, 28; fetishization of, 274n49; technomodernity, 226–28
"There is Running Water from Henan: To Jingdu" ["You yizhong huoshui laizi tianhe zhi nan—zhi Jingdu"] (Dekyi Drolma), 178–79
"Things I Change, The" ["Wo gaibian de shiwu"] (Liu Liangcheng), 141–42

Thinking with Whitehead (Stenger), 9
"This Is a Story" (Armstrong), 214–15
This Is Not a Dream (Hoshur), 123
Thornber, Karen, 14, 49, 250n18, 257n44, 282n80
"Three Animal Stories" (Jangbu, 2001), 168; "He who Died in a Trap" (Gzeb nang nas shi ba'i), 170–71; "The Lamb" (Lu gu), 168–69, 173; "The Pheasant and the Chicken" (De pho dang khyim bya), 169–70
Three-Body Problem, The (Liu Cixin, 2016), 231–32, 254n2
Thum, Rian, 117, 265n32
Thurston, Timothy, 272n23
Tiananmen Square protests (1989), 89
tianren heyi (harmony between humanity and nature), 6
Tianshan Mountains, 100, map *101*, 130
tianxia ("all under Heaven"), 3, 15, 232; agrarian civilizational empire naturalized, 17–25; as alternative to modern nation-state, 26; eugenics and, 26; metamorphosis as imaginary utopia, 57; as racially infused idea, 25; revival of, 42
Tianxia System, The (Zhao, 2005), 26
Tianyan lun [*Evolution and Ethics*] (Yan, 1893), 27
Tibetan Empire, collapse of, 148
Tibetan language, 15, 33, 148, 155; Tibetophone literature, 155–189.
Tibetan Plateau, 2, 12, 14, 103, 160; archeologists on, 15; cultural and ecological genocide on, 173; environmental devastation on, 147; "Grassland Culture" and, 74; literature set on, 147–88; natural history of tectonic plates and, 178

Index 335

Tibetans, 47, 236; Amdo-speaking, 33, 148; gender inequity in nomadic life, 163; Gyalrong (Jiarong), 4, 148, 149, 153, 154, 159; Kham-speaking, 148; nomad's black tent, 174–75, *175*; poets, 64; police surveillance of cultural heritage event, *172*; political self-immolation by, 260n67. *See also* Alai; Dekyi Drolma; Jangbu; Ju Kalsang; Kuang Laowu; Takbum Gyel; Tsering Döndrup; Woeser

Tibet Autonomous Region, 154, *167*, *172*; map, 2, *149*

Tierney, Robert, 210

Tiger Land Cats [*Hudi mao*] (Liu Ka-shiang, 2016), 204, 206, 279n38

time: annihilation of space by, 153; in Buddhist cosmology, 178; human agency and, 141; illusory nature of time as Buddhist tenet, 164; Indigenous peoples' reckoning of, 218; nomadic peoples and, 111; space-time and time-space, 142, 143, 269n86; technologically mediated compression of time and space, 228

Todd, Zoe, 8

Todorov, Tzvetan, 227

"Tong zhong shuo" ["Thesis on Mixing the Races"] (Tang, 1898), 27

"Topas Tamapima" (Topas Tamapima, 1981), 215

Topas Tamapima, 17; "The Last Hunter" ["Zuihou de lieren"] (1987), 215–17, 219; *Lovers and Prostitutes* [*Qingren yu jinü*] (1992), 215; "The Pygmy Tribe" ["Zhuru zu"], 215; "Sunset Cicadas" ["Xiyang chan"], 215; "Topas Tamapima" (1981), 215

totemism, 9, 13

"Toward Race Preservation" (Huxley), 26

trans-indigeneity, 12, 14, 17, 223, 224–30

trickster figures: in North American indigenous writing, 214–15; in Tibetan literature, 16, 124, 147, 155, 157, 272n23

Trocki, Carl, 151

Tsagaan Uvgun (Lord of Nature and Bodhisattva of Longevity), 81

Tsai, Shu-fen, 213–14

Tsai Ing-wen, 190

Tsering Döndrup, 15, 147, *149*, 159, 165, 178

Tujia people, 14, 47. *See also* Chen Danling

Turpan Basin, 129–30, 132

Tursun, Perhat, 15, 16, 102, 103, 129; arrest and imprisonment of, 264n31, 265n33; *The Art of Suicide* (1999), 117; *The Backstreets* [*Chong Sheher*] (2013), 15, 116–23, 264n31, 265n41; compared to Salman Rushdie, 117

Ulanhu, 76

United States, 26, 193; "angry Black woman" stereotype in, 62; Western Apache humor, 124; "Indianizing" conversationists, 76, 214; "last Indian" laments, 130, 213, 259n49; nuclear tests in Marshall Islands, 229–30; settler colonialism of American West, 35; Taiwan ties to, 191

universality, 1, 3, *18*, 23, 36, 145, 207, 232, 270n97; *tianxia* and, 18, 25; Western, 3, *18*

urban ecologies, 102, 116–28, 131, 196, 200–206, *207*

urbanization, 102, 134, 140, 160, 258n42

Ürümchi, city of, 12–13, 102, 108, 117, 133, 135; "fog" of industrial pollution in, 118; as Han-dominated city, 122–23
Ü-Tsang (region of Greater Tibet), 148; map, *149*
Uyghur language, 15, 117, 264n31, 270n97
Uyghurs, 2, 4, 16, 100, 102, 131, 236, 253n61; cultural heritage destroyed by Chinese regime, 116, 130, 264n28; joking as challenge on the margins, 124; urban ecologies in Uyghur fiction, 116–28. *See also* Xinjiang Uyghur Autonomous Region; Hoshur, Memtimin; Izgil, Tahir Hamut; Tursun, Perhat; Yasin, Nurmuhemmet

Van Dooren, Thom, 80
Vanishing America (Powell), 130
Views of a Flying Squirrel [*Xiao wushu de kanfa*] (Liu Ka-shiang, 1988), 197
viruses, incidental spread of, 7
Voices of the Stone (Jangbu, film, 2018), *162*, 165

Wa (Va) people, 15, 37, 57; classified as "southern barbarians," 252n52; drum ritual of, 60, 253n56; Han exoticization of, 59–60, 62, 63; headhunting practice, 58, 59, 235–36; region inhabited by, 57–58, *58*; Si Gang Lih cave and Wa origin myth, 60, *61*, 63, 233–34; warfare unknown before colonial intervention, 286n5. *See also* Burao Yiling; Burao Yilu; Southwest China
Waltz, Kenneth, 232
Wang, Ban, 27
Wang, David Der-wei, 227
Wang Chen-ho, 217

Wang Chia-Hsiang, 208–13; *Civilizational Wilderness* [*Wenming huangye*] (1990), 208–9, 280n52; *Daofeng Inland Sea* [*Daofeng neihai*] (1997), 211–14, 280n52; *On Lamatasinsin and Dahu Ali* [*Guanyu Lamadaxianxian yu Lahe Alei*] (1995), 208n52, 209–11; *Prayer for Nature* [*Ziran daogaozhe*] (1992), 209, 280n52
Wang Fuzhi, 20, 78
Wang Han, 132
Wang Wei, 50, 174
Wang Yangming, 53
Wang Zhaojun (Cao Yu, 1978), 78
Warring States period, 17, 32
"wasteland," 21, 32, 64, 86, 154, 157, 160
"Water Lines" (Bamo Qubumo), 66, 67
Way of Sheep Trilogy, The [*Yangdao: Sanbuqu*] (Li Juan, 2012), 133
Way of the Ocean, 12, 223
"We Have Surpassed the Bears" (Qizihan), 106–7
Wei Qingqi, 9
Wei Te-sheng, 211
Weller, Robert, 24–25
"west, the" (*xibu*), 35, 36, 248n5
Western Films (journal), 35
Western Han dynasty, 22
Western Literature [*Xibu wenxue*] (journal), 128
"What I Stopped" ["Wo dangzhule shenme"] (Liu Liangcheng), 142
"What Must Be Said Before Giving Birth" (Zhou Jianren, 1922), 29
Whitehead, Alfred North, 9, 51, 53, 54, 142; *The Concept of Nature*, 51; *Process and Reality: An Essay in Cosmology*, 54, 142; *Science and the Modern World*, 51, 143–44

Why Indigenous Literatures Matter (Justice), 214
"Why Look at Animals?" (Berger, 1980), 270n98
Wild Man [*Yeren*] (Gao Xingjian, 1985), 48
"Wild Pigeon, The" (Yasin, 2004), 274n43
Williams, Dee Mack, 85, 263n25, 276n70
Winter Pasture [*Dong muchang*] (Li Juan, 2012), 133
Woeser (Tsering Woeser), 186, 188
Wolf Totem (Jiang Rong, 2004), 70, 76, 103, 131, 257n44; adaptation to film (2015), 90, *91*, *94*; criticized for Orientalist, eugenicist and racist views, 90, *91*, 93, 257n45, 259n49; ecological imperialism and eugenics in, 89–90, 92–94; Qizihan's *Hunter's Stories* compared with, 106
Wolong Nature Reserve, 48
women: agrarian patriarchy and, 22; Hanspace core-periphery and, 25; ecological Mother and female Nature, 78–79, 109–110; misogynist violence against, 55–56; nomadic patriarchy and, 163, 179; religion rationalizing misogyny against, 61
Woodcutter, Wake Up! [*Famuzhe, xinglai!*] (Xu Gang, 1986), 38, 44–46
Wu, Jin-Yung, 191
Wu Jingming, 249n11, 250n21
Wu Lan, 75–76
Wu Ming-yi, 17, 196, 197–98, 203, 208; *The Book of Lost Butterflies* [*Midie zhi*] (2000), 224; *The Land of Little Rain* [*Kuyu zhidi*] (2019), 224; *Liberate Nature by Writing* [*Yi shuxie jiefang ziran*] (2004), 197; *The Man with the Compound Eyes* [*Fuyan ren*] (2011), 193, 224, 225–27, 236, 277n16; *Routes in the Dream* [*Shuimian de hangxian*] (2007), 224; *The Stolen Bicycle* [*Danche shiqie ji*] (2015), 211, 217, 224, 231, 234–35; *The Tao of Butterflies* [*Die dao*] (2003), 224; trans-indigeneity and, 224–30

Xi'an Film Studios, 34
xiangcun (spiritual notion of village), 140, 269n81
Xiao Hong, 37, 79, 133, 268n79
Xia/yi dichotomy, 17, *18*, 20
Xie Jin, 35
Xi Jinping, 7, 95
Xinjiang Literature (journal), 35
Xinjiang Nationalities Literature (journal), 107
Xinjiang Uyghur Autonomous Region (XUAR), 2, 74; Chinese spatial reengineering projects in, 116–17, *117*; demographic composition of, 100, 132, 261n1; environmental damage in, 22; eugenics-oriented policies in, 30; genocide as state policy in, 264n28; Han settlers in, 122, 133–40, 265n41; Han writers' engagement with difference, 128–32; *karez* (subterranean aqueducts), 130, 131; Kazakh writers' human-animal relations and folklore, 103–116; literature set in, 100–146; Maoist collectivization in, 104, 106; map, 2, *101*; "migrant" literature, 132; Qing expansion into, 148; "reeducation" camps in, 201n2, 264n31; urban ecologies in Uyghur fiction, 116–28.

See also Altai Mountains; Altay; Altishahr; Dzungaria; Junggar Basin; Kazakhs; Tianshan Mountains; Uyghurs
Xinjiang Writers Association, 128
Xiongnu nomads, 35, 267n66
Xu Gang, 38, 44–46
Xu Zhaoshou, 139

Yan Fu, 26, 27
Yang Changzhen, 193, 277n11
Yan Lianke, 121
Yan Xuetong, 26
Yao people, 57, 252n52, 253n57
Yartsa Rinpoche (Jangbu, film, 2014), 165
Yasin, Nurmuhemmet, 274n43
Yeh, Emily, 154, 168
Yellen, Jeremy, 277n11
Yellow River, 24, 92
Ye Qianji, 5
Yi language, 15
Yi Nai, 27
yin–yang complementarity, 20, 24, 40, 193
Yi people, 47, 56–57, 249n15; animism of, 42; as "barbarians," 26, 252n52; *Book of Origins* [*Hnewo teyy*] (Nuosu Yi epic), 68, 254n68; *Meige* epic, 66; Nuosu, 4, 15, 37, 64–68; rituals of, 67; writers/poets, 2, 64–68. See also Southwest China; Aku Wuwu; Bamo Qubumo

"Young Brother Searched for the Missing Cow" ["Didi qu zhao zoudiao de nainiu"] (Dekyi Drolma), 179
Yuan dynasty, 19, 148, 271n1
Yue, Gang, 38, 153, 250n18
Yunnan Province, 39, 57

Zaokong (Liu Liangcheng, 2009), 140
Zeng Fanren, 9
Zhang Binglin, 31
Zhang Chang, 15, 37, 44, 250n22
Zhang Chengzhi, 14, 254n2
Zhang Huan, 186
Zhang, Ling, 24, 71
Zhao Liang, 95
Zhao Shuli, 37
Zhao Tingyang, 26
zhiqing ("educated youth") literature, 37, 38, 109, 249n11
Zhong Dianfei, 34–35
Zhou Enlai, 76
Zhou Jianren, 28–29
Zhou kings, 17, 22, 26, 243n51, 244n65
Zhou Libo, 37
Zhou Zuoren, 28
Zhuang, Pei, 6
Zhuangzi, 6, 9, 203, 241n27, 277n16
Zhuangzi, 39, 41, 48
zhutixing ("subjectentity"), 54–55
Zhu Xi, 48
Zuozhuan, 19
Zuo Zongtang, 23

GPSR Authorized Representative: Easy Access System Europe, Mustamäe tee
50, 10621 Tallinn, Estonia, gpsr.requests@easproject.com

www.ingramcontent.com/pod-product-compliance
Lightning Source LLC
Chambersburg PA
CBHW032334300426
44109CB00041B/803